Painted by Sir Joshua Reynolds.   Engraved by Will.ᵐ Doughty.

Samuel Johnson, LL.D.

London Published as the Act directs June 24ᵗʰ 1791 by John James Engraves Great Portland Street, Marylebone.

'Samuel Johnson, LL.D.', mezzotint by William Doughty, 1779, after the painting by Sir Joshua Reynolds.

Studies in Modern History

General Editor: **J. C. D. Clark**, Joyce and Elizabeth Hall Distinguished Professor of British History, University of Kansas

Titles include:

Jonathan Clark and Howard Erskine-Hill (*editors*)
SAMUEL JOHNSON IN HISTORICAL CONTEXT

Richard R. Follett
EVANGELICALISM, PENAL THEORY AND THE POLITICS OF CRIMINAL LAW REFORM IN ENGLAND, 1808–30

Andrew Godley
JEWISH IMMIGRANT ENTREPRENEURSHIP IN NEW YORK AND LONDON 1880–1914

Philip Hicks
NEOCLASSICAL HISTORY AND ENGLISH CULTURE
From Clarendon to Hume

Mark Keay
WILLIAM WORDSWORTH'S GOLDEN AGE THEORIES DURING THE INDUSTRIAL REVOLUTION IN ENGLAND, 1750–1850

Kim Lawes
PATERNALISM AND POLITICS
The Revival of Paternalism in Early Nineteenth-Century Britain

Marisa Linton
THE POLITICS OF VIRTUE IN ENLIGHTENMENT FRANCE

Marjorie Morgan
NATIONAL IDENTITIES AND TRAVEL IN VICTORIAN BRITAIN

James Muldoon
EMPIRE AND ORDER
The Concept of Empire, 800–1800

Lisa Steffen
TREASON AND NATIONAL IDENTITY
Defining a British State, 1608–1820

Lynne Taylor
BETWEEN RESISTANCE AND COLLABORATION
Popular Protest in Northern France, 1940–45

Studies in Modern History
Series Standing Order ISBN 0–333–79328–5
(*outside North America only*)

You can receive future titles in this series as they are published by placing a standing order. Please contact your bookseller or, in case of difficulty, write to us at the address below with your name and address, the title of the series and the ISBN quoted above.

Customer Services Department, Macmillan Distribution Ltd, Houndmills, Basingstoke, Hampshire RG21 6XS, England

Samuel Johnson in Historical Context

Edited by

Jonathan Clark

and

Howard Erskine-Hill

Editorial matter and selection © J.C.D. Clark and Howard Erskine-Hill 2002
Chapters 1–3 and 5–11 © Palgrave Publishers Ltd 2002
Chapter 4 and Conclusion © J.C.D. Clark 2002

First published 2002 by
PALGRAVE
Houndmills, Basingstoke, Hampshire RG21 6XS and
175 Fifth Avenue, New York, N. Y. 10010
Companies and representatives throughout the world

PALGRAVE is the new global academic imprint of
St. Martin's Press LLC Scholarly and Reference Division and
Palgrave Publishers Ltd (formerly Macmillan Press Ltd).

ISBN 0–333–80447–3

This book is printed on paper suitable for recycling and
made from fully managed and sustained forest sources.

A catalogue record for this book is available
from the British Library.

Library of Congress Cataloging-in-Publication Data
Samuel Johnson in historical context / edited by Jonathan Clark
and Howard Erskine-Hill.
        p. cm. — (Studies in modern history)
    Includes bibliographical references and index.
    ISBN 0–333–80447–3 (cloth)
    1. Johnson, Samuel, 1709–1784—Criticism and interpretation.
    2. Literature and history—Great Britain—History—18th century.
    3. Great Britain—Civilization—18th century. I. Clark, J. C. D.
    II. Erskine-Hill, Howard. III. Studies in modern history (Palgrave
    (Firm))
    PR3534 .S28 2001
    828'.609—dc21
                                                    2001046008

10 9 8 7 6 5 4 3 2 1
11 10 09 08 07 06 05 04 03 02

Printed and bound in Great Britain by
Antony Rowe Ltd, Chippenham, Wiltshire

Contents

v

List of Plates

Frontispiece and cover: 'Samuel Johnson, LL.D.', mezzotint by William Doughty, 1779, after the painting by Sir Joshua Reynolds (Ashmolean Museum)

1. William Kent, *The St. Clement Danes Altarpiece*, 1721 (destroyed 1940) (private collection)
2. William Hogarth, *The St. Clement Danes Altarpiece*, 1725, engraving (private collection)
3. Jakob Frey, *Queen Maria Clementina*, c. 1725, engraving (Drambuie Collection)
4. Oxford University Matriculation Register 1714–40, Oxford University Archives SP12: the oaths required on matriculation (Bodleian Library)
5. Oxford University Matriculation Register 1714–40: Samuel Johnson's signature (Bodleian Library)
6. Oxford University Graduation Register 1736–63, Oxford University Archives SP46: the oaths required on graduation (Bodleian Library)

Notes on Contributors

Jeremy Black MBE is Professor of History at the University of Exeter and was formerly Professor at the University of Durham. Editor of *Archives*, he is the author of several works including *Modern British History*; *A New History of England*; *War and the World 1450–2000*; *Pitt the Elder*; *Eighteenth-Century Europe*; *Maps and History*; and *Maps and Politics*.

Jonathan Clark's *Samuel Johnson* was published in 1994. His other works include *English Society 1660–1832* (1985, 2000), *The Language of Liberty 1660–1832* (1994); and an edition of Edmund Burke's *Reflections on the Revolution in France* (2001).

Eveline Cruickshanks wrote much of the volumes of the History of Parliament from 1660 to 1754. She has specialised on the Tories and Jacobitism, as well as parliamentary history. Her latest publications are (ed.), *The Stuart Courts* (Sutton Publishing, 2000) and *The Glorious Revolution* (Macmillan, 2000). She is a Fellow of the Institute of Historical Research.

Matthew M. Davis is a Senior Editor at the Core Knowledge Foundation. He has a PhD in English from the University of Virginia, where he wrote a dissertation on Johnson's literary criticism.

Howard Erskine-Hill is Professor of Literary History in the Faculty of English, University of Cambridge. His works include *The Social Milieu of Alexander Pope* (1975); *The Augustan Idea in English Literature* (1983); *Poetry and the Realm of Politics: Shakespeare to Dryden* (1996); *Poetry of Opposition and Revolution: Dryden to Wordsworth* (1996); and (ed.), *Alexander Pope: selected letters* (2000).

Thomas Kaminski is the author of *The Early Career of Samuel Johnson*. He is currently editing Johnson's Debates in Parliament for the *Yale Edition of the Works of Samuel Johnson*.

Niall MacKenzie took a BA in History from Washington and Lee University, has worked as a journalist in Canada and the United States, and is currently a PhD candidate in English at the University of Cambridge. His research deals with representations of women in Jacobite culture.

David Money is Senior Lecturer in English at the University of Sunderland, and Extraordinary Fellow in Classics at Wolfson College, Cambridge. His *The*

English Horace: Anthony Alsop and The Tradition of British Latin Verse (1998) was published by The British Academy.

Paul Monod is Professor of History at Middlebury College in Vermont. He has published *Jacobitism and the English People, 1688–1788* (1989), winner of the John Ben Snow Prize of the North American Conference on British Studies, and *The Power of Kings: Monarchy and Religion in Europe, 1589–1715* (1999), which was runner-up for the Association of American Publishers Professional/Scholarly Publishing Award in History. At present, he is working on a study of the survival of magic in eighteenth-century England.

Eirwen E.C. Nicholson read History and History of Art at Cambridge and has taught at the Universities of Edinburgh and St. Andrews. Her work to date has been in political graphics of the 1640–1840 period and their historiography, on which a volume of critical essays is forthcoming; and Jacobite material culture and its presentation. She is currently working on the iconography of the Duke of Monmouth over the period 1660–*c.* 1860.

Murray G.H. Pittock is Professor of Literature at the University of Strathclyde and Head of the Glasgow-Strathclyde School of Scottish Studies. He is the author of a number of studies on Jacobitism and on the broader aspects of national identity, including *Poetry and Jacobite Politics in Eighteenth-Century Britain and Ireland* (1994); *The Myth of the Jacobite Clans* (1995, 1999); *Celtic Identity and the British Image* (1999); and *Scottish Nationality* (2001).

Richard Sharp is Senior Research Fellow and Garden Master at Worcester College, Oxford. He is an ecclesiastical historian and the author of several articles on aspects of the old High Church and Nonjuring traditions. His *catalogue-raisonné, The Engraved Record of the Jacobite Movement,* was published in 1996.

Preface

Samuel Johnson is an inescapably dominant figure. Despite changes in public taste, and despite the flux of fashion in literary and historical scholarship, Johnson remains a massive and powerful presence, perhaps the most commanding of the 'commanding heights' of eighteenth-century English letters. Yet this peak is still contested ground in recent scholarship. What were Johnson's aims in literature, in literary criticism and in shaping the English language itself? What were his political and religious allegiances, and how did they shape his career and his writing?

This volume had its origins in a controversy which developed when an older picture of a Lockeian, Whig or politically detached Johnson was challenged. It brings together work by literary scholars and historians which illuminates a quite different Johnson: often alienated from his society, deeply engaged in political and religious causes, torn between rival alternatives, and developing as his world changed around him.

Samuel Johnson in Historical Context raises broad issues of both substance and scholarly method: what was at stake in the public arena in Johnson's lifetime? How did he respond to its pressures and challenges? How can literary scholars and historians cooperate to establish an authentic reading of his works? In a book that combines overviews with detailed and novel studies, the editors have assembled research which confirms that Johnson is a figure who indeed allows us to interpret his age.

Some of the material incorporated into chapter 4 was originally published in *The Age of Johnson*, 8 (1997), pp. 15–70 and *ELH*, 64 (1997), pp. 1029–67; it is reprinted here, where necessary, by permission.

Abbreviations

Add MSS	Additional Manuscripts
AJ	*The Age of Johnson*
BL	British Library
Boswell, *Life*	James Boswell, *Life of Johnson*, ed. George Birkbeck Hill and L.F. Powell (6 vols., Oxford, 1934–50)
Clark, *Samuel Johnson*	J.C.D. Clark, *Samuel Johnson: Literature, Religion and English Cultural Politics from the Restoration to Romanticism* (Cambridge, 1994)
CLRO	Corporation of London Record Office
Cruickshanks, *Political Untouchables*	Eveline Cruickshanks, *Political Untouchables: The Tories and the '45* (London, 1979)
DNB	*Dictionary of National Biography* (1st edn.)
ELH	*English Literary History*
Hawkins, *Life*	Sir John Hawkins, *The Life of Samuel Johnson, LL.D.* (2nd edn., London, 1787)
Hearne, *Collections*	C.E. Doble et al. (eds.), *Remarks and Collections of Thomas Hearne* (11 vols., Oxford, 1885–1918)
Henning, *HC*	Basil Duke Henning (ed.), *The History of Parliament: The House of Commons, 1660–1690* (3 vols., London, 1983)
HJ	*The Historical Journal*
HLQ	*Huntington Library Quarterly*
HMC	Historical Manuscripts Commission
Johnson, *Letters*	Bruce Redford (ed.), *The Letters of Samuel Johnson* (5 vols., Princeton, 1992–4)
Johnson, *Lives of the Poets*	Samuel Johnson, *Lives of the English Poets*, ed. George Birkbeck Hill (3 vols., Oxford, 1905)
Namier and Brooke, *HC*	Sir Lewis Namier and John Brooke (eds.), *The History of Parliament: The House of Commons, 1760–1790* (3 vols., London, 1964)
Parl Hist	William Cobbett (ed.), *The Parliamentary History of England, from the Earliest Period to the Year 1803* (36 vols., London, 1806–20)
PMLA	*Proceedings of the Modern Language Association*
PRO	Public Record Office

RASP	Royal Archives, Stuart Papers
Reade, *Johnsonian Gleanings*	Aleyn Lyell Reade, *Johnsonian Gleanings* (11 vols., privately printed, 1909–52)
Sedgwick, *HC*	Romney Sedgwick (ed.), *The History of Parliament: The House of Commons 1715–1754* (2 vols., London, 1970)
SP	State Papers
TRHS	*Transactions of the Royal Historical Society*
WRO	Westminster Record Office
Yale Edition	W.J. Bate et al. (eds.), *The Yale Edition of the Works of Samuel Johnson* (New Haven and London, 1958–)

Introduction

Howard Erskine-Hill

Passionate controversy may activate and extend an academic field. So it has recently done in the case of Samuel Johnson and the culture of mid-eighteenth-century Britain. For some years uncommitted readers looked on, fascinated and appalled by turns, as a new battle of the books was fought in which, like the battle Swift made famous, matters of fact were the more intensely disputed because they involved issues of wide cultural and methodological significance.[1] As in Swift's *Battle of the Books* this *querelle* was paradoxical. Traditionalists contended for a modern Johnson, pragmatic, progressive, enlightened in a sense of the term acceptable to the late twentieth century. Radical historicists, on the other hand, saw themselves as recognising an older and stranger Johnson, reacting to situations and problems not only alien to our own society, but which even modern historical scholarship on the eighteenth century has often diminished and occluded. In salient instances the eighteenth-century world was not our world. The eighteenth-century world was dominated by dynastic conflict; indeed dynasticism was the most obvious lever of political change. In that world, also, ecclesiastical commitment was central to the political realm; religion was not then a 'thing indifferent', a personal matter like a particular taste in music. Public office rested on oaths which drew dynasticism and religion together, backed by the force of law. Eighteenth-century society thus tried to make itself coherent and stable, its governors relying on religion and law to ensure political obedience. So much may be said in simple summary, and it should not need to be said also that for a modern scholar to characterise the nature of such a society, and those who defended or resisted it, is not the same thing as to hold a brief for it, or to vindicate those different people who composed it.

Such a formula for society, however, becomes dangerously coercive when confronted by fundamental religious disagreement, or when a segment of the political realm fails to abide by the laws of that realm as in the case of the invited invasion of the Prince of Orange, in 1688, and its aftermath. The regime of William and Mary had no right in terms of the ancient constitu-

1

tion, and that constitution, of King, Lords and Commons, had not consented to change itself.[2] There then opened up a cruel and tragic dilemma in which the obedient subject and loyal churchman could not be faithful to both sides of his twofold creed. The public world was then riven not just between party and party but even in its dominant ideology.[3] In this situation governments could not but be the more precarious, and turn to the imposition of further oaths to bind their supporters to them more strongly, and force their enemies into the open more decisively. It was in this situation that Samuel Johnson was born in 1709 and, public writer as he came to be, it was in this riven public realm that he lived until, in the years of his friendship with Boswell, the logic of conflict gradually relaxed and it became possible to speak more freely – even to make jokes about Jacobitism.

To read Johnson as a serious figure surviving in a society of the kind just described is the achievement of the new scholarship on Johnson. If the Johnson thus revealed seems more strange than many might expect, there can be little doubt that this Johnson, different from and independent of late twentieth-century assumptions, is a more challenging figure than the semi-modernised Johnson previously proposed. Further, the *querelle* has prompted not only a series of restatements of the *status quo ante*,[4] but, more interesting, a series of new essays which see Johnson in a new light, or from a different angle. The present volume, save for its Introduction and Conclusion, includes only one essay by a contributor who was a party to the Johnsonian *querelle*. The remaining contributions are by scholars non-combatant in the earlier disputes, but who in one way or another were prompted, or fortified, in their thinking by the Johnsonian debate.

We may start by recalling what was until recently the most forgotten aspect of Johnson's culture. It was not purely English but Anglo-Latin. This does not just mean that Johnson was learned in Latin and Greek antiquity, nor even that he was intimate with the Latin literature of the Renaissance, though in each case he was, something which the recent works of Robert DeMaria Jr. have kept in mind. He was himself a good Latin poet, and those who follow the somewhat sparse outline of his English verse with its lack of any poetic peak between *The Vanity of Human Wishes* (1749) and the poem to Levet (1783) may see that it is Johnson's Latin verse which raises his low profile during a period of about thirty years: first his hexameter poem 'Know Thyself' on the completion of his *Dictionary*, second the three Hebridean poems of 1773 which look very like his expression of the goal of his personal and public pilgrimage. In 1995 Barry Baldwin published his edition of the Latin poems of Johnson; three years later David Money's *The English Horace: Anthony Alsop and the Tradition of British Latin Verse* appeared, with some corrections and additions to Baldwin, and a notable section on Johnson. The example of Alsop reminds us that Latin verse circulated in manuscript seemed often a safer vehicle for Jacobite sentiment than English verse published in print. Money's detection of delicate Jacobite allusion in the Hebridean ode 'Ponti profundis . . .' is convincing at the level of a careful sub-text in a powerful philosophical and religious poem.[5] In the present volume Money valuably expands his discussion of Johnson's Latin verse in the context of other British writers of that time *qui Latine scripserunt*. This currency, he shows, was not then debased and neglected. The modern reader needs to take it into account. To do so means by no means only reading Johnson's Latin poetry; it means reading his English verse with sensitivity to the Latin roots of his words and their relation to his more overt classical allusion and imitation. In a markedly helpful essay, 'Some Alien Qualities of Samuel Johnson's Art', Thomas Kaminski demonstrates how the modern reader may resensitise himself to this aspect of Johnson's writing, whether in verse or prose.

Johnson's Hebridean poems raise the paradoxical question of his relation with Scotland. This is here addressed by Murray Pittock in his account of that 'long and trying journey by an ageing man to a country he was supposed universally to despise and detest, which he ended up dignifying'. Johnson may have detested Presbyterian Scotland, but he did not despise its Episcopalian tradition, nor its Latinity, attempting to buy while in Aberdeen a copy of Arthur Johnston's *Deliciae Poetarum Scotorum* (1637). Developing a series of highly perceptive hypotheses advanced by Pat Rogers, Pittock sees that for Johnson Scotland was less backward than self-betrayed and decayed. The dominant myth of history was then less one of inexorable progress than of a pattern of rise and fall. The northern kingdom was, like the Ireland of Swift, less the occasion for hostility or the object of pity than a monitory example for England.

Johnson's reverence for the episcopal hierarchy is, by his own *Dictionary* definition, part of his Tory vision. Other identifiably Tory sentiments are explored here. Jeremy Black relates Johnson's view on foreign war and colonialism to a Tory notion of foreign policy, while Eveline Cruickshanks expertly studies the careers of two great political magnates, Lord Gower and Lord Chesterfield, from whom many Tories and many Jacobites expected so much. Each sought to assist Johnson in some measure, Gower in the late 1730s at Pope's request, Chesterfield in the 1750s; neither with success. Johnson's condemnation of them stemmed no doubt from his disappointment at their ineffective patronage when he needed a patron, but of course their political careers were also displayed before his eyes. Each of them gained great power, but at a cost, especially in the case of Gower. Johnson had more cordial relations with a nobleman of very little power, the fifth Earl of Orrery; their exchanges of letters in 1751–2 were greatly appreciated on Orrery's part. Whether Johnson was aware that Orrery was among those lords who had, in 1743, invited the French to support a new attempt to restore the Stuarts we are never likely to know. Certainly the Jacobite leadership abroad hoped to see all three noblemen on their proposed Council of Regency.[6]

An historian's approach to Johnson can, with great value, work on an intimate and local scale: it can be micro-history. Along these lines Eirwen Nicholson here discusses the St. Clement Danes altarpiece by William Kent, which probably incorporated, and was certainly widely interpreted as incorporating, a representation of Maria Clementina, Queen to King James III. The particular response of William Hogarth opens up some large issues concerning the politics of eighteenth-century painting, and shows that the 'hour of notoriety' of Samuel Johnson's church would have confronted its congregation with a reminder and a challenge. In a similar mode Richard Sharp explores other features of the London locality that was Johnson's immediate home for the greater part of his life: the streets and lanes, churches and burial grounds, meeting rooms and taverns, printers and publishers, preachers and lecturers. Commentators on Johnson who rightly emphasise his extensive intellectual view may also recognise the influence of a particular locality that is regularly experienced over a long period.

On a larger scale Paul Monod here displays Johnson's other significant environment in the essay 'A Voyage out of Staffordshire', probably the best study we have ever had of Johnson's native region, its characteristic religious and political orientations, its rich array of significant figures, and its variations between latent rebellion and defiant ritual. Monod's widely researched discussion not only fills a space only partly populated by Boswell, Hawkins and later biographers, but in doing so affords the reader a new perspective on Johnson's life as a whole.

Author of *Jacobitism and the English People* (1989), Monod in his new essay squarely addresses the subject of Jacobitism. The pervasiveness of varieties of Jacobitism in the opposition politics of the eighteenth century is, however, arguably the outward sign of something deeper: the oath-bound religious society, already touched on above, in which there were Jurors and Abjurors, Nonjurors and Nonabjurors, not to mention the many, some significant Jacobites, who took oaths with private reservations, or swore them evasively, swore them the better to serve the cause the oaths were designed to exclude, or who, finally, managed in pragmatic ways to avoid having the oaths tendered to them. It does not follow that, if there were relatively few Nonjurors of whom record survives, the issue of the oaths was relatively marginal. The Jurors are, in terms of political culture, as important as the Nonjurors. Without remembering the importance of the oaths we shall find it hard to understand eighteenth-century society. In this connection Jonathan Clark's extended discussion of Johnson and the oaths gives us the fullest and most balanced treatment of this vital Johnsonian subject for which we could hope. Meticulous in its attention even to the physical character of surviving records, scrupulous in its weighing of evidence where evidence seems at first sight to point in different directions, this essay constitutes a major biographical overview, based on original research and on a new synthesis, of Johnson in the religious and political world of his time. Treatment and conclusion here accord with a close account of Johnson's society. The lack of such a close picture, one may hazard, originally occasioned so much bafflement[7] when issues of Jacobitism and Nonjuring were raised in recent debate.

The essays of Monod and Clark have profound consequences for how we should read Johnson and others of his contemporaries not confident and happy with what the establishment of the day liked to refer to as 'the present happy establishment'. Especially before 1760, but even after the accession of George III and the fading of Jacobitism as a significant political force, an open deployment of the conflicting arguments could hardly be published in Britain. Only briefly, during 1745–6, in areas controlled by the armed forces of Prince Charles Edward, could a Jacobite publish a free Jacobite work in Britain, as William Hamilton of Bangour did his *Ode on Gladsmuir* after the Battle of Prestonpans. Generally those with an inclination towards Jacobitism could intimate their view either in significantly moderated and generalised language, or in cryptic expression, or coded analogy.[8] There was in itself nothing new in this practice, which had been developed by the Catholic, Nonjuring, Dryden and others after the Revolution of 1688. It has not, however, been thought to extend much beyond the death of Pope. Such expression continued, however. Dryden had developed an analogy between Plantagenet history and Stuart history, Richard II and James II; what Johnson remembered in the tale of the Poor Parson in *The Fables* he developed, in a running contest with Warburton, in the politically marginal form of notes to *Richard II* in his Edition of Shakespeare (1765). This topic is here well developed in an admirable essay by Matthew M. Davis. New analogies, but of similar tragic import, were developed from eighteenth-century history. That between the 'Swedish Charles' of *The Vanity of Human Wishes* and Scottish Charles, nicely poised between admiration and reproof, was proposed as long ago as 1984 to a sceptical reception.[9] Here too new work has emerged, presenting new evidence for the eighteenth-century analogy, in two notable essays by Niall MacKenzie. The more recent of these, 'A Jacobite Undertone in "While Ladies Interpose"?' is included here.[10]

The Jacobite phenomenon in high politics, society and literature seems far from being exhausted as an academic subject, and is likely to go on changing our perspectives on the eighteenth century for a long period. New academic needs have become clear, and among them the thorough reassessment of Hawkins's biography, partly by a critical edition of his text, a work on which Gay and Skip Brack have been long engaged but which was too extensive to be included in a volume of this kind. New avenues have also been opened for younger scholars and, as the reviews of the Johnsonian *querelle* and its immediate aftermath roll out, useful evaluations emerge, and unanticipated viewpoints become apparent. The exchange about Johnson has left its mark, and it is a positive one. The clash of arms is over, but the present book is still protagonist against an older view. It does not aim at being a synthesis. The eighteenth century of Jonathan Clark and that of Paul Langford still confront one another.[11] The broad-bottom interpretation of the long eighteenth century is yet to come.

Notes

1. The origin of this *querelle* appears to have been my essay 'The Political Character of Samuel Johnson', in Isobel Grundy (ed.), *Samuel Johnson: New Critical Essays* (London, 1984). I was in debt to the new historiography, and especially Jonathan Clark's 'A General Theory of Party, Opposition and Government, 1688–1832', *HJ*, 23 (1980). 'The Political Character' lit a slow fuse which led to a disproportionate explosion in Donald Greene's new Introduction to the revised edition of *The Politics of Samuel Johnson* (1990). I replied to this briefly in my article, 'Johnson the Jacobite?' in *AJ*, 7 (1996) and, responding to lengthy further rejoinder in the same journal, in a second short article, 'A Kind of Liking for Jacobitism' (*AJ*, 8, 1997). Meanwhile Jonathan Clark, aware of the importance of Johnson in the picture of the eighteenth century which the new historiography was revealing, prepared in new work to join the debate, work which grew at length to be his book, *Samuel Johnson: Literature, Religion and English Cultural Politics from the Restoration to Romanticism* (Cambridge, 1994). This extended, in a literary direction, Clark's now famous *English Society, 1688–1832* (1985), now revised and enlarged in a second edition as *English Society 1660–1832* (2000). (Other essays relevant to the debate, by each author, are not listed in this concise footnote, but are cited in the works mentioned above.) In 1995 Paul Korshin, editor of *The Age of Johnson*, called a conference in the University of Pennsylvania, Philadelphia, on all the matters of dispute which had arisen since 1980. Some papers renewed the battle; some old combatants attempted new lines of research relevant to the old dispute, as did several more recent scholars. The conference was judged a success to the extent that the papers were in revised form accepted for publication in a special number of *English Literary History*, 64 (1997), *Jacobitism and Eighteenth-Century English Literature*. This volume is currently being reviewed at the time of writing (November 2000). Viewed in a larger perspective, these titles and dates are the signs of a confluence between a new historiography and a restless and responsive literary criticism. The traditionalists, for their part, appeared in shock: defensive, acrimonious and, with a few exceptions, unable to grasp the issues at stake. What should at least emerge from these exchanges, acceptable to both sides, is an enhanced appreciation of religion as central to the politics and literature of the time.
2. See 'A Kind of *Liking* for Jacobitism', *AJ*, 8 (1997), pp. 4–5. Robert Chambers's Vinerian Lectures seem to support this interpretation of Parliament, though I am not of course claiming that they do so because of the influence of Johnson, which could not be proved.
3. In my essay, 'The Political Character of Samuel Johnson: *The Lives of the Poets* and A Further Report on *The Vanity of Human Wishes*', in Eveline Cruickshanks and Jeremy Black (eds.), *The Jacobite Challenge* (1988) I draw attention to the tragic nature of the events of 1688–89, in Johnson's narratives, particularly in the Life of Granville.
4. For example, J.A. Downie's article 'Johnson's Politics', *AJ*, 11 (2000), pp. 81–104. Downie follows some of the false steps of his predecessors. He quotes the General Preface to the Index to the *Gentleman's Magazine* without acknowledging that we

do not know what part of this Preface Johnson wrote, and what part he did not (though he gives a finding reference to a one-sided discussion by Howard Weinbrot in his footnote (pp. 19, 103)). Again, Downie follows erroneous earlier debate in arguing that Johnson's statement about the oaths in Boswell 'I know not whether I could take them . . .' can mean anything other than that he had not taken them. It would also be a most bizarre hypothesis to claim that Johnson might have been able to take the oaths under George II, but not under George III. If there is anything in this it ought to be the other way round. It should be noted that Boswell is dealing with oaths 'with respect to the House of Stuart'. There was of course never any difficulty for the Anglican Johnson in taking the Oath of Supremacy or subscribing to the Thirty-nine Articles, and the recent debate about Johnson and Nonjuring has never been about that. Of course it may be argued, on this and a thousand other matters, that Boswell is not trustworthy. That is a quite different point. One is inclined to trust Boswell here because on the question of Johnson's Jacobite inclination he is supported by Hawkins, Mrs. Thrale and the Pension Letter, Charles Churchill, and other sources. (These points refer to Downie, pp. 91–2.)

5. Robert DeMaria Jr., *Johnson's Dictionary and the Language of Learning* (Oxford, 1986); *The Life of Johnson: A Critical Biography* (Oxford, 1993), where he speaks of 'a unified late Latin European cultural heritage' (p. xi). Barry Baldwin (ed.), *The Latin and Greek Poems of Samuel Johnson* (London, 1995); David Money, *The English Horace: Anthony Alsop and the Tradition of British Latin Verse* (Oxford; for the British Academy, 1998), pp. 218–23.

6. For Orrery, see Eveline Cruickshanks, *Political Untouchables: The Tories and the '45* (London, 1979), pp. 38–9 quoting the French *Archives étrangères*. Orrery corresponds with James III in the Stuart Papers, writing of the 'zeal I owe You, and which nothing but death can ever putt a Stop to' (177/181, 20 February 1735) and James for his part writes: 'I know you have inherited your Father's zeale for my Cause, you will I am sure do all you can to forward it . . .' (209/6, 28 August 1738). For the part the continental Jacobites hoped Gower and Chesterfield would play in the new restoration attempt, see *Political Untouchables*, pp. 44–7.

7. Unfamiliarity with the subject of the oaths was apparent in many quarters during the Johnsonian exchanges and is still to be noticed in Robert Folkenflik's review in *AJ* 11 of the *ELH* volume *Jacobitism and Eighteenth-Century English Literature*. The conflict over the oaths after 1689, and the recent academic dispute about Johnson as Nonjuror, turn entirely on the question of *de jure* right in the exiled House of Stuart. The Tudor Oath of Supremacy has nothing to do with this question. That oath was indeed terrible to conscientious Roman Catholics, but Johnson as a Protestant would find no terrors in it. Of course Johnson took this oath. The dispute has never been about this. That Weinbrot should have found that he did is nothing to the purpose.

8. The question becomes clear if we consider what could not be said at home but could be said abroad. Cryptic or coded expression is an attempt to bridge the gap between the two. I explain these points in 'Johnson the Jacobite?' (*AJ*, 7, pp. 9–11).

9. In 'Twofold Vision in Eighteenth-Century Writing', however, I demonstrate that the grounds for recognising this allusion are the same as those for other allusions that have been routinely accepted in twentieth-century criticism of eighteenth-century poetry (*Jacobitism and Eighteenth-Century English Literature*, pp. 916–18). The emergence of material additional to what was proposed by me now seems to put the allusion to Scottish Charles beyond doubt.

10. See Niall MacKenzie, '"A Great Affinity in Many Things": Further Evidence for the Jacobite Gloss on "Swedish Charles"', *AJ*, 12 (forthcoming, 2001).

11. See Paul Langford, *A Polite and Commercial People: England, 1727–1783* (Oxford, 1989). A rich and frequently judicious study, its bias appears in its more conventional judgements, its omissions and its Bibliography (particularly patchy on literature and the arts).

Part I
The Local Setting

1

A Voyage out of Staffordshire; or, Samuel Johnson's Jacobite Journey

Paul Monod

Jacobite Johnson

What sort of Jacobite was Samuel Johnson? Surely, he did not resemble his own satirical depiction in *The Idler* of the 'vehement and noisy' Tom Tempest, who was 'of opinion, that if the exiled family had continued to reign, there would have neither been worms in our ships nor caterpillars on our trees'.[1] Was he then more like the quiet scholar-poet Elijah Fenton, a fellow native of Staffordshire, whose life Johnson affectionately chronicled? He wrote of how Fenton, 'with many other wise and virtuous men, who at that time of discord and debate consulted conscience, whether well or ill informed, more than interest . . . doubted the legality of the government', and became a Nonjuror.[2] Did the great lexicographer do likewise? Or should we accept Boswell's critical assertion that, in later years at least, Johnson liked to give 'an affectation of more Jacobitism than he really had'? Boswell noted that 'at earlier periods he was wont often to exercise both his pleasantry and ingenuity in talking Jacobitism'.[3] Were his loud declarations of Jacobite sympathy then no more than a conversational strategy?

The depths of Johnson's Jacobitism are not easy to fathom. Although many of his close friends (James Boswell, Sir John Hawkins, Hester Thrale, Hannah More) attested to his Jacobite inclinations, their comments were based on verbal statements made mostly after 1760, when the Stuart cause had ceased to be politically serious. Johnson's writings sometimes pointed towards Jacobite sympathies, quite strongly in a few early cases (like the 1739 pamphlet *Marmor Norfolciense*); but none provides a straightforward exposition of his views. How can the complexities – and at times, the contradictions – in Johnson's attitude to Jacobitism best be explained?[4]

The problem is compounded by his public image, which became inseparable from his work. While the lives of most poets are unedifying histories of constant adaptation and petty compromise, Samuel Johnson's life was not like this, or so his admirers proclaimed. They depicted him as an exemplary moral character. Boswell did not invent this image; it originated with

Johnson's earliest hagiographers. 'Not contented with surpassing other Men in Genius,' gushed a biographical notice published in 1762, 'he makes it his Study to surpass them in Virtue, and all that Humanity and that sincere Attachment to Religion, which shine through his Writings, are equally conspicuous in his Life.'[5] That life seemed to contain few major conflicts, no sudden shifts. Johnson himself liked to advertise his adherence to unchanging ideals. 'I retain the same principles,' he announced to Boswell regarding his pension from George III.[6]

The image of virtuous consistency has plagued attempts to make sense of Johnson's politics. Donald Greene's treatment of the subject rightly emphasised the nuances in his views, but tended to conflate them with liberal broad-mindedness and principled non-partisanship.[7] Recently, Howard Erskine-Hill and J.C.D. Clark have placed Johnson in a different context, by stressing his hidden Tory and Jacobite sentiments. Erskine-Hill has referred to Johnson's 'serious Jacobite inclination' before 1749; thereafter, 'he could still write and talk like a sometime-Jacobite sympathizer'.[8] Clark has argued that Johnson was both a Jacobite and Nonjuror, although he remained 'a political realist' whose views 'evolved' after 1745.[9] The interpretive possibilities of such revisionism are exciting, so long as they are not used to sustain a new paradigm of Johnsonian consistency.

This essay will not propose that Johnson was a hypocrite or dissembler – merely that he was a complicated political being, full of tensions, twists and occasional turnings. To quote Clark, he 'did not display a simple, unchanging political identity'.[10] His life and work reflected a conscious effort to avoid a potential collision between rational self-interest and principle – in particular, Jacobite principle. I will explore this theme by trying to determine where his views came from, and how they altered. My purpose is to reconstruct the Jacobite political background of his youth and early adulthood in the West Midlands; to examine his personal experiences of Jacobitism before 1745; and to consider how his life and writings intersected with Jacobitism, especially that of his native region, between 1745 and 1760.

The main point that will emerge from this study is that Johnson's Jacobitism was a variegated and changing intellectual trait, which rose and fell in intensity. It was not simply a fixed or inherited 'prejudice'. In this regard, he was hardly unique among literary figures. The same can be said of John Dryden's Jacobitism, or that of Anne Finch, Alexander Pope, Richard Savage, Elijah Fenton, Jane Barker, Mary Delarivier Manley, Lord Lansdowne, William King, John Byrom, John Shebbeare or even the adolescent Edward Gibbon. The Jacobite disposition was never as uniform or simplistic as its enemies made it out to be. Its characteristics were diverse; they might encompass passivity and aggression, strict hierarchalism and wild populism, a desire for conformity and an impulse towards radical opposition. In the mind of a commercial writer like Johnson, such attitudes created a constant tension, but they could also inspire a subtle, allusive approach to the relationship between politics and art.

Locality and identity

Samuel Johnson was born into what was fast becoming a bastion of Jacobitism. During his childhood, the West Midlands gained a deserved reputation for pronounced disaffection to the ruling monarch. Jacobite allegiance in the area, however, often had less to do with restoring the Stuarts than with preserving local community. West Midlands Jacobitism developed into an important ideological underpinning to a potentially threatened social hierarchy. It bolstered political dependency, religious unity and economic paternalism against both external and internal pressures, providing a touchstone of stability in an area that was undergoing the first disruptive stages of industrial upheaval.[11]

West Midlands Jacobitism drew its strength from a pervasive localism. This does not mean that the region was cut off from wider developments. Localism should not be equated with backwardness or indifference to national issues. It was a dynamic aspect of social identity, a way of defining oneself within the nation and of engaging oneself with the world at large.[12] In the West Midlands, localism rested on several interlocking factors: geographical isolation from London and other major ports; a comparatively high degree of economic and cultural self-sufficiency; and an enduring resistance to centralised administrative control.

The civil wars of the 1640s had forged West Midlands localism. Disorder, whatever direction it might come from, was associated with 'outsiders' who had infiltrated the community. The famous stories of Lichfield's determined opposition to a Parliamentary army, or Birmingham's equally dogged resistance to a royalist one, testify to local resentment at invasion by external forces. Localism also generated neutrality, which was particularly widespread among the Staffordshire gentry. Neutralist groups calling themselves Clubmen even staged uprisings against the presence of troops in the West Midlands.[13]

When the victorious Parliament imposed puritan moral reform on the region, it sparked into life a festive royalist culture based on resistance to central government. At Wolverhampton, for example, a maypole was set up to celebrate the dismissal of the Rump Parliament. A scandalised puritan vicar reported from Staffordshire in 1655 that 'there are annually still observed and kept the wakes on the Sabboth dayes . . . Great part of the wake-weekes is spent in promiscuous danceing, maurice-danceing, tipleing, gameing, quarrelling, wantonness.' The Restoration of Charles II, which promised an end to moral reform from the centre, was warmly greeted throughout the West Midlands with bell-ringings, public rejoicings and loyal addresses from the gentry. Such rituals appeared to unify the community and to strengthen local identity, while enhancing the dominance of traditional elites.[14]

The Restoration brought in its wake an important social transformation which further bound together the dominant classes in the West Midlands. With the expulsion of Dissenters from the Church, the long-standing identification of puritan religious values with industry in the region began to wane. Anglican entrepreneurs such as Humphrey Jennens of Birmingham or George Jesson of West Bromwich became prominent in the metal-working trades, while some Dissenting manufacturers, like the Quaker ironmaster Ambrose Crowley of Stourbridge, rejoined the Church of England.[15] By allowing marital alliances to take shape between gentry and manufacturing families, this gradual religious shift would provide a firm economic basis for the spread of royalism, Toryism and Jacobitism. Johnson himself was related to the Jessons and Crowleys through his mother's family, the Fords. In the 1680s, moreover, his great-uncle Henry Ford was estate agent for a West Bromwich ironmaster, Brome Whorwood.[16]

The Exclusion Crisis of 1679–82, however, saw the sudden re-emergence of the feared 'Other' in the West Midlands, in the form of the Whig party. In most of the region, the Whigs were a vocal minority, relying upon religious Dissenters in larger towns like Coventry, as well as on scattered puritan landed families. The majority of landowners and people of the middling sort stuck with the crown and became Tories, although it was noted in 1682 that '[v]ery many of the gentry of Staffordshire in the late war found the advantage of neutrality, and they are much inclined to it at this time'. Localism remained a potent force, and the Parliamentary candidacies of 'strangers', whether Whigs or Tories, were always resented.[17]

The Glorious Revolution of 1688 did not at first disturb the localism of the West Midlands. If William and Mary were not enthusiastically embraced, nor were they rejected. Most people in the region probably would have agreed with Johnson's later judgement that the Revolution was 'necessary', although not laudable.[18] Few local gentlemen refused to take oaths to the new regime. Within the diocese of Lichfield, only two clergymen of any prominence became Nonjurors: Thomas Wagstaffe, chancellor of Lichfield, who ended up a Nonjuring bishop and Jacobite propagandist; and the learned John Kettlewell, vicar of Coleshill in Warwickshire.[19] To be sure, on the fringes of the West Midlands lived a couple of influential Nonjuring peers: the Earl of Chesterfield, who was the grandfather of Johnson's rejected patron, and the Earl of Huntingdon, whose main residence was at Ashby-de-la-Zouche, Leicestershire, where Michael Johnson kept a bookstall. Although both men plotted to restore James II, the Jacobite military conspiracies of the 1690s attracted very little support in the West Midlands. The ironmaster Thomas Brome Whorwood was sent a commission from King James to raise a secret regiment in the area, but he does not seem to have filled it.[20] Jacobite military conspiracies depended mostly on Roman Catholics, who lacked numbers or political clout in the West Midlands.

The aftermath of the Revolution, however, set in motion a shift among the local gentry, away from indifference or neutralism, towards fervent Toryism and, eventually, Jacobitism. Increasing Whig influence on national policy seemed to signal war, higher taxes, favours for religious Dissenters, and subtle humiliations for the Church of England – in short, a full-scale assault on localism. By 1700, some Tories were beginning to remember the king they had helped to exile, and to believe that peace, social order and the security of the Church could be assured only through a Stuart restoration.[21] The leader of these Jacobite Tories in the West Midlands was Sir John Pakington, MP for Worcestershire. He and his supporters did not want James II back, but they regarded James Francis Stuart as lawful heir to the throne. The Whigs feared that the lack of a direct Protestant line of succession 'may bring more to be of Sir John Packington's mind'.[22] Apparently, it did. A satirical poem of 1703 identified Pakington as the head of a powerful 'Worcester Cabal' of Jacobites. The satirist dared them to show their true sentiments instead of hiding them: 'Come on, Young *James's* Friends, now is the Time, come on; / Receive just Honours, and surround the Throne.' Among the Pretender's friends, according to the poem, were two successive deans of Lichfield. One of them, Jonathan Kimberley, called 'honest' (i.e. a Jacobite) by the Nonjuror Thomas Hearne, was a Pembroke College graduate who held office in the diocese throughout Samuel Johnson's childhood.[23]

During this frenetic period, a number of Tory clubs and convivial societies were formed throughout England, providing a safe venue for the expression of Jacobite sentiments. The private club was a small-scale 'imagined community', an exclusive society that could enforce its own rules of order and identity in defiance of outside forces. One of them was the 'Ancient Corporation of Cheadle', founded in 1699 in north-east Staffordshire. It consisted of local tradesmen, landowners and clergymen, among them members of the Adderley family, who were acquaintances of Johnson's father Michael. The Jacobite bias of the club is shown by the absence in its records of any reference to the ruling monarch, in contrast to real corporate minute books, and by constant mentions of the 'honesty' and 'loyalty' of the membership. Women attended some meetings of the Cheadle corporation, and in 1710 Ann Hollins was chosen as 'Stadtholder', in mockery of the late King William.[24]

In the same year, West Midlands Jacobitism widened from a 'Cabal' into an active popular movement, as a result of the trial of Dr. Henry Sacheverell. This notorious clergyman held curacies at Aston near Birmingham and at Cannock in Staffordshire, the second being a living in the gift of the dean and chapter of Lichfield. Sacheverell preached an allegedly seditious sermon at Lichfield in 1700. Two years later, he made a national reputation by writing a best-selling pamphlet in defence of Sir John Pakington. He followed up this success by delivering inflammatory Assize sermons on the subject of 'the Church in danger' at Oxford, Leicester and Derby. The Derby sermon was distributed through a bookseller in Lichfield – presumably, Michael Johnson. Sacheverell was already a Tory celebrity by the time he delivered his explosive harangue, *The Perils of False Brethren*, on 5 November 1709 in St. Paul's Cathedral.[25]

Quasi-Jacobite remarks made in his London and Derby sermons led to the impeachment of the fulminant preacher by the House of Commons. Sacheverell was convicted, but was sentenced merely to a three-year suspension from preaching. The lucky Doctor was then appointed to a rectory in Selattyn, Shropshire, and made a triumphant summer 'progress' from Oxford through Warwick, Coventry, Birmingham, Stafford, Newcastle-under-Lyme, Shrewsbury and other towns, ending up at Worcester. At Lichfield on 16 June he was greeted by the entire corporation in full regalia, including the city sheriff, Michael Johnson, whose wife had delivered a son, Samuel, only nine months before. It is possible that Michael carried his son with him on this occasion, which may account for the confusing story retold later by Boswell, in which Samuel is wrongly described as a three-year old.[26]

The endless corporate processions and parades of mounted gentry that welcomed Sacheverell to the West Midlands give us insight into the localist mentality. Like the political clubs, they served to delineate a ritual space of apparent social harmony and religious unity. This was also the purpose of many traditional ceremonies, like the annual 'riding' by the Lichfield corporation around the boundaries of the city. Within the well-ordered domain of ritual, gentlemen could mix with shopkeepers, and women could take active, if rarely serious, political roles. Outside its carefully policed precincts, however, lurked enemies – Whigs, Dissenters, foreign kings – who were always threatening to disrupt the Tory parade. The dichotomy between an idealised internal order and a menacing external world suffused the social values in which Samuel Johnson was raised, and it left an impact on his later thinking.

Many in the West Midlands must have hoped that the overwhelmingly Tory Parliament elected in the wake of Sacheverell's 'progress' would extend the space of High Church ritual throughout the whole realm, driving undesirable outsiders into oblivion. They were sorely disappointed. In the end, Queen Anne thwarted them and ensured the succession of the House of Hanover in August 1714.[27] Not everyone accepted this outcome. One week before George I was crowned, Henry Sacheverell delivered a furious Tory sermon at Sutton Coldfield, only nine miles from Lichfield. Michael Johnson may have travelled there to hear the Doctor speak; he could have stayed with his brother-in-law Nathaniel Ford, a clothier who became warden of the corporation in 1709. Sacheverell was later obliged to deny in a public letter that his sermon had anything to do with the violent anti-Hanoverian riots that followed on coronation day at Birmingham, Nuneaton, Shrewsbury, Worcester and Hereford. The riots had ominous Jacobite undertones. 'Wee will pull down this King and Sett up a King of our own,' cried one rioter at Birmingham, while others shouted 'Damn King George, Sacheverell for ever.'[28]

In the summer of 1715, the West Midlands witnessed what amounted to a local insurrection, taking the form of religious riots. These disturbances were probably connected with the hastily formulated Tory plan for an armed uprising in favour of the Stuart claimant. Dissenting meeting-houses throughout Worcestershire, Warwickshire, Shropshire and Staffordshire were destroyed by mobs of metalworkers, small tradesmen and artisans. The meeting-house attacks were encouraged, if not fomented, by local gentlemen and manufacturers.[29] Their Jacobite implications were obvious. The crowd of bucklemakers that tore down the meeting house at Wolverhampton, for example, forced a local Whig to kneel down and say, 'God bless King James and down with the Roundheads.'[30]

At Lichfield, the meeting-house was burned down on the night of 17–18 July. The only account of the event is a brief mention in a Whig newspaper. The Assize records do not indicate that anybody was arrested or presented for the riot. The town had its own sessions court, so it would have been easy for magistrates to suppress any prosecutions. None the less, a worried city magistracy assembled on 20 August to send a loyal address to King George. Michael Johnson, one of twenty-one Brethren of the corporation, was absent from the meeting.[31]

The mock-corporation of Cheadle also held urgent gatherings in the first year of King George's reign. It admitted as members several prominent 'persons of Loyalty & sound principles', including Charles Bagot, an alumnus of Lichfield school, and Ralph Sneyd of Keele, MP for the county in Queen Anne's last Parliament. Sneyd was arrested in July 1715, for taking part in the meeting-house riot at Newcastle-under-Lyme. An extraordinary meeting of the mock-corporation took place on 6 October, the week of the planned Jacobite uprising, but we do not know what was decided at it.[32] In any case, none of the Cheadle club members rode north to join the rebels in what quickly became a doomed enterprise. The defeat of the '15 rebellion ended the most aggressive phase of Jacobite activity in the West Midlands, but it did not end Jacobite sentiment there, which in the previous two decades had staked out a cultural territory that could not easily be conquered.

Samuel Johnson must have remembered some of the Jacobite uproar of his childhood. He was too young perhaps to recall the burning of the meeting-houses, but he would have been aware of the Parliamentary by-election in 1718, when William Sneyd campaigned for a seat at Lichfield with the assistance of a mob wearing paper in their hats cut into white roses, the Pretender's symbol.[33] He would certainly have known about the attempted prosecution for seditious acts of Theophilus Levett, the town clerk of Lichfield. Two weeks after the 1718 by-election, the parish clerk of St. Michael's Church deposed that at services, Levett had 'clapt his hand upon the Deponts. Mouth' when he was about to say 'Amen' to the final 'God save the King', which made the congregation laugh. Three years later, Levett was accused by Anne Murrall, wife of a local maltster, of wearing white roses on the Pretender's birthday and standing when King George was prayed for in church. A 'poor servant girl' further testified that she had seen him drinking healths to King James at a Lichfield inn, 'with other Gentlemen who were recconed the Jacobites of the Town'. Levett was defended, however, in a certificate sent to the crown by eighteen justices, gentlemen and magistrates, including Ralph and William Sneyd, Sir Walter Wagstaffe Bagot and the junior bailiff of Lichfield, Michael Johnson. A petition in Levett's favour signed by no fewer than 185 local worthies, among them Michael Johnson, was sent to the king soon after. All Levett's accusers eventually retracted their statements, blaming everything on the machinations of three malevolent Whig lawyers. The servant girl claimed that one of these gentlemen had promised to marry her, which had induced the love-struck young woman to give false testimony.[34]

At this distance, it is difficult to know what to make of the case against Theophilus Levett. Without doubt, it was politically motivated and malicious, but does this mean that it was false? The most believable story was that of the parish clerk, which seems too funny to have been invented out of spite. The clerk never denied that it had happened, only that Levett was the man responsible, which makes his initial complaint hard to understand. The case clearly reveals the local Tory community rallying around one of their own, against the attacks of outsiders who were so unscrupulous as to take advantage of poor servant girls. The petitions to the king were two-edged ploys, since George was hardly likely to suppress the proceedings and could only lose face for not doing so. As for Michael Johnson, he clearly sided with Levett, although he had recently been prosecuted by the town clerk for illegally practising the trade of tanner. Apparently, his party loyalty superseded personal interest. After Michael's death, Levett showed his gratitude by helping Samuel to obtain a short-lived post as a private tutor, and by advancing a mortgage on the Johnson family home in Lichfield.[35]

While the young Johnson was well acquainted with the Levetts, he was hardly likely to have known about the 'Ancient Corporation of Cheadle', although his life would later be connected with the lives of several of its members. John, Baron Gower, leader of the Staffordshire Tories, was chosen as mock-mayor of Cheadle in 1720–1; eighteen years later, he tried to obtain a position for Johnson as master of Appleby School. The mock-mayor in 1718, Brooke Boothby of Ashbourne, Derbyshire, had a longer association with the Johnson family. Several letters survive from his father, Sir William Boothby, to Michael Johnson, who stocked the baronet's voluminous library. Sir William later gave financial support to a Nonjuring clergyman. His son

Brooke Boothby was suspected of anti-Hanoverian sentiments, and was provoked into a fight by some soldiers on King George's accession day in 1716. A third member of the Cheadle corporation whose life intersected with Johnson's was John Beresford, a Nonjuror and lawyer residing at Ashbourne. Beresford was Brooke Boothby's brother-in-law, and one of the trustees of the Port Charity, a bequest made in 1719 by Catherine Port of Ilam to support the 'Orthodox Clergymen of the Church of England', that is, the Nonjuring clergy. In later years, Johnson preferred the rugged beauties of Ilam to all other estates in Staffordshire, and was on friendly terms with the Ports. We do not know if he was aware of their extraordinary charity.[36]

Young Samuel may well have heard something about a fourth, less well-born member of the Cheadle corporation: John Dearle, curate of Baswick-with-Walton and master of the grammar school at Stafford, who was presented at the Assizes in 1721 for circulating a hand-written copy of one of the Pretender's declarations. Dearle did not deny it, but solicited the help of William Leveson Gower, the county MP and a fellow Cheadle corporation member, in pleading that he had copied the paper simply out of curiosity. This rather unconvincing excuse was accepted by a local jury, and his indictment was found *ignoramus*.[37] In the Jacobite schoolmaster John Dearle, we can catch a glimpse of what Samuel Johnson might have been if he had been born a few years earlier and had stayed in Staffordshire.

The declaration that Dearle handed about was drawn up in preparation for another insurrectionary attempt, the Atterbury Plot of 1722. Young Johnson could only have heard rumours about it. Yet if by some chance he had been able to read in later life the list of Jacobite sympathisers given to James III at Rome in 1721, he might have been fascinated by the presence on it of so many local names that were of personal significance to him: those of his relative, George Jesson of West Bromwich; of Lord Gower, Ralph Sneyd, Brooke Boothby and 'Colonel' John Beresford; of the antiquarian William Inge, a 'gentleman of great eminence in Staffordshire', whose learning Johnson greatly admired; of Charles Jennens, Nonjuror and trustee of Appleby School; of the Lichfield School alumnus Charles Bagot, and his nephew Walter Wagstaffe Bagot, MP for Staffordshire; of Corbet Kynaston, whose kinsman and heir Andrew Corbet was Samuel's friend at school and university; and of Johnson's hated employer, Sir Wolstan Dixie, patron of Market Bosworth School.[38] The 1721 list is more reliable than any other compendium of Stuart supporters, not least because it includes a host of otherwise obscure country gentlemen. It reveals just how surrounded by Jacobitism young Samuel Johnson was.

Staffordshire, the document adds, was '[n]oted for perpetuated loyalty' to the Stuarts. The brightness of that loyalty was dimmed by the collapse of the Atterbury Plot, and the subsequent abandonment of hope for a swift restoration. It was further diminished by the death of Sir John Pakington in 1727, and the closing of the Cheadle corporation in 1729. Yet it was not extinguished. After all, the motivation for Jacobitism in the West Midlands had never been solely to preserve ideals of legitimism or bring about the return of the exiled king. It had always been sustained by the desire to keep out those elements of post-Revolutionary society that seemed, in Johnson's words, 'the negation of all principle': Whiggery, Dissent, atheism, rebellion. In this regard, the West Midlands Jacobites had not failed at all. Yet as the next sections will show, they did not succeed forever in warding off all external threats, and their embracing rituals could not keep the area's best-known literary son in their midst.

A writer in the making

To understand why Johnson did not become a Staffordshire Jacobite in the 'Tom Tempest' mould, we have to examine his direct contact with various forms of attachment to the Stuarts during his childhood and early career. Jacobite sentiments were certainly not all alike, and Johnson was exposed to a full range of them. They seem to have placed him in a difficult situation. While they deeply affected his early life, they gave him little professional security and may have added to his feelings of resentment about personal dependency. Lacking birth or fortune, he was obliged to seek out patronage; but as the Tory gentry gave meagre recognition to his talents, he was obliged to turn for support to local Whigs. In the end, he decided to separate himself from West Midlands society altogether, travel to London and seek fame as a national literary figure.

Given its complexity, we may assume that Johnson's Jacobitism was not simply inherited from his father. That idea was first advanced by Sir John Hawkins, who asserted of Michael Johnson that, 'though a very honest and sensible man, he, like many others inhabiting the county of Stafford, was a Jacobite'. Nothing in Michael's behaviour seriously contradicts this. Of course, as a local official, he took oaths to the ruling monarchs; but so did Pakington, Sacheverell and Atterbury. One of Michael's apprentices, Simon Martin, declined to take the oaths in 1727, as a magistrate in the notoriously Jacobite corporation of Leicester; but even he succumbed a year later, on his election as mayor.[39] For many Jacobites, such compromises were unfortunate necessities of political life. Still, it is unlikely that Michael's son Samuel adhered to the Stuarts through filial piety. 'Of parental authority, indeed,' Hester Piozzi later wrote of him, 'few people thought with a lower degree of estimation.' Samuel's relationship with Michael was fraught with emotional ambivalence, typified by his indignant refusal to attend his father's bookstall at Uttoxeter market. We may wonder how favourably young Samuel viewed Michael's 'time-serving' politics. Late in life, he pronounced before Boswell a harsh judgement on his father's taking the oaths of office: '*That*, Sir, he was to settle with himself.'[40]

Samuel apparently had other Jacobite mentors in his early years. In her memoirs of Lichfield, the poetess Anna Seward insisted that Michael

Johnson was 'very loyal' to the ruling house, but that John Hunter, master of the Lichfield school, was a Jacobite, and that Samuel 'imbibed his master's absurd zeal for the forfeit rights of the house of Stuart'. It may be allowed that Seward knew more about Hunter, who was her grandfather, than she did about Michael Johnson. Samuel Johnson remembered his old master with affection, in part because he 'whipt me very well. Without that, Sir, I should have done nothing.' Whether it was because they tended to be arch-traditionalists, or because they felt such keen competition from Dissenting academies, Anglican schoolmasters often inclined towards Jacobitism – John Dearle provides another local example. Johnson may have learned from John Hunter to associate the Latin culture, semi-clerical status and moral rigour of schoolmastering with an idealistic attachment to the exiled monarch.[41]

Another possible early influence on Johnson's Jacobitism was the physician Sir John Floyer, who is best known for recommending that the ailing toddler Samuel be sent to London to be touched for scrofula by Queen Anne. Sir John was closely connected with Johnson's family. Michael Johnson published his principal work, *The Touchstone of Medecines*, in 1687, and arranged for the London printing of two other books by him, in 1696 and 1719. Floyer had doctored Charles II, and was knighted by James II. With the help of his brother-in-law, Lord Dartmouth, and the Oxford antiquarian Elias Ashmole, he had tried to remodel the Lichfield corporation on a Tory basis in 1684–6. Sir John held no offices after the Glorious Revolution, which makes it likely that he was a Nonjuror. He apparently passed on his principles to his son, who was named to the French foreign ministry as a Jacobite sympathiser as late as 1743.[42] Floyer's combination of rational innovation – he was the inventor of the pulse watch – with belief in supernatural healing may have made a lasting impression on Johnson. Through Sir John Floyer, young Samuel may first have encountered a more scholarly brand of Jacobitism, one that rested as much on broad intellectual commitments as on local politics.

Not all Johnson's early mentors were Jacobites. Through his cousin, the bibulous parson Cornelius Ford, he encountered a very different kind of politics, one based on self-interested discretion. Ford was a likeable pedant who seems to have made little noise about his party allegiances. Educated at St. John's, Cambridge, a bastion of Nonjurors, Ford was a friend of the Nonjuring poet Elijah Fenton; but he received his benefice from the fourth Earl of Chesterfield, who was a Whig. Among Ford's drinking companions was 'Orator' John Henley, who wrote a newspaper, *The Hyp-Doctor*, in favour of Walpole's government. To be sure, Henley underwent a bizarre conversion to strident Jacobitism during the '45 rebellion, but this took place long after his friend Cornelius Ford was dead. An oblique reference to Ford's political beliefs is found in a eulogy published in the *Hyp-Doctor*, where it is stated that he 'was remarkable for defending the Honour and Cause of the Clergy against the Cavils of some Free-thinking Associates'. This passage hints that

Ford was a Tory, but it is hardly conclusive.[43] Whatever his views, Johnson was fond of his wayward cousin Cornelius, who offered him an agreeable glimpse of a learned sphere beyond Lichfield, where politics was secondary to career-making.

Cousin Ford's political reticence may have been influenced by his wife's close family relationship with a notorious Jacobite politician. Judith Ford, *née* Crowley, came from one of the most important families of industrialists in England. Her nephew John Crowley was heir to a vast fortune based on ironworks in Stourbridge and Durham. In spite of his lucrative contracts for supplying iron castings to the Navy, Crowley was a Tory and Jacobite, who had been imprisoned in 1715. A leading importer of Swedish iron, John Crowley offered £20,000 to a Jacobite agent in 1716 to fund a Stuart restoration attempt backed by the celebrated Charles XII of Sweden. The plan was soon discovered, however, and led to a Parliamentary prohibition on trade with Sweden, a direct blow at the Tory ironmasters.[44] Crowley's behaviour suggests that Jacobitism was not simply an affair of backwoods squires and small-town magistrates: it also attracted some of those industrialists whom Johnson so admired in later life. Crowley's role in the Swedish plot also helps to explain Johnson's long-lasting interest in 'Swedish Charles', whose 'pompous woes' are evoked in *The Vanity of Human Wishes*, and about whose life he planned to write a play in 1742.[45]

Cousin Ford's example pointed Johnson towards a scholarly career. He was further encouraged in that direction by his friend Andrew Corbet, whose kinsman Corbet Kynaston, MP for Shropshire, headed the West Midlands Jacobites after Sir John Pakington's death.[46] At Pembroke College in 1728–9, Johnson found himself in a haven of intellectual Toryism, Jacobitism and High Churchmanship, presided over by that 'fine Jacobite fellow', Dr. Matthew Panting. The Welsh squire John Philipps had been at the same college a few years before, and his experiences there had set him on a path from Whiggery towards ardent Jacobitism. It is worth noting, however, that Johnson was apparently not among those disaffected collegians who, like the Staffordshire poet William Shenstone, 'drank their favourite toasts on their knees'.[47] He was poor, serious-minded and circumspect. He had no wish to broadcast his beliefs. If he left the university, as J.C.D. Clark argues, not just on account of poverty, but because he could not take the oath of allegiance, he was careful never to make this reason public. Admittedly, such reticence was not unknown – one discreet Lancashire gentleman, for example, kept his Nonjuring principles out of public view for decades, until forced to decline an appointment as county sheriff in 1761![48]

Johnson's father died soon after his son's return from Oxford. Perhaps as an angry reaction to Michael's death, Samuel increasingly turned for support towards a very different sort of father-figure: Gilbert Walmesley, registrar of the ecclesiastical court of Lichfield. 'He was a Whig,' Johnson recalled, 'with all the virulence and malevolence of his party; yet difference of opinion did not keep us apart. I honoured him, and he endured me.'[49] Walmesley was indeed a Whig, and a constant enemy to what he called 'the Jacobite faction' in Lichfield, presumably including Michael Johnson. In 1710, he was even persuaded to stand for election to Parliament, in a vain protest against Lichfield's Sacheverellite high tide.[50] Yet Walmesley did not just 'endure' young Samuel; he willingly promoted him. It is not likely that he would have done the same for a young man whom he suspected of being a Nonjuror. It must be assumed that if Johnson considered himself to be one, he never spoke to Walmesley of it.

Between 1731 and 1739, Johnson tried hard to enlist patronage from both political camps, in order to further his career as a schoolmaster. To get himself a place at Market Bosworth School, controlled by the insufferable Sir Wolstan Dixie, he must have used Tory friends – presumably Andrew Corbet, whose sister married Dixie's brother. In his last unsuccessful endeavour at schoolmastering in 1739, he was recommended by the Tory leader Lord Gower to Appleby school. The governors of this august institution were rigid Tories and Jacobites to a man. They included Godfrey Clarke, whose father had a call for the return of the Stuarts carved on his tombstone; Charles Jennens, the pious Nonjuror and librettist of Handel's *Messiah*; and Sir Francis Burdett, who according to a family tradition (patently false, but not unbelievable) met Bonnie Prince Charlie in a boat on the River Trent in 1745![51] It is improbable that these men would have asked Johnson to take oaths to the ruling monarch. On the other hand, the private school that he opened with Walmesley's assistance at Edial in 1736 contained a boisterous contingent of young Whigs: not only the Garrick brothers, but also Lawrence Offley, whose family were mainstays of Whiggery in Staffordshire.[52] Without doubt, Johnson was pushed to this shift by economic necessity; but he was surely not such a strong party man, or such an unbending Nonjuror, as to reject the patronage of a Whig.

His marriage in 1735 to Elizabeth 'Tetty' Porter, widow of a Birmingham mercer, was a 'love match', without a discernible political basis. The views of Mrs. Johnson remain somewhat mysterious, but it may be significant that, in spite of considerable criticism of her character, nobody ever pilloried her for Jacobitism. That she was a High Churchwoman may be inferred from their marriage in St. Werburgh's church in Derby; but it cannot be assumed from this that she shared all of her husband's opinions.[53] She supported the Edial experiment, and if she did not exactly point him in the direction of writing, at least she did not discourage him from it.

Johnson's first published work, a translation of the Jesuit Father Lobo's *Voyage into Abyssinia*, appeared just before his marriage. Although efforts have been made to argue otherwise, it is hard to see that this treatise reflected much on English politics. To be sure, the preface Johnson prepared for it was critical of Catholicism (a common stance among Tories, who wanted to distance themselves from 'Popery', whatever their views of a

'Popish' king); and by toning down the Jesuit author's attacks on the Ethiopian Church, he implied a parallel with another 'true' national Church, that of England. Beyond this, however, the only small clue to the politics of the translator is the dedication to an obscure Tory gentleman, John Warren, a relative of the book's editor.[54] Johnson's *Voyage into Abyssinia*, therefore, is the work of a staunch Anglican, although not in any overt way that of a Jacobite. We may wonder none the less whether its translator was already thinking of remote Ethiopia as a metaphor for Staffordshire, the 'Happy Valley' free of moral challenges, from which Prince Rasselas would later escape.

A Voyage into Abyssinia set a pattern in Johnson's work. From now on, all his writing was a kind of translation – from everyday language, with its local accents and narrow frames of reference, into a confident, stately and scholarly version of English literary prose, the national language that he was to enshrine in his *Dictionary*. The elevated voice that Johnson adopted was a means of overcoming provincialism, and with it, the differences of opinion that fuelled party conflicts. It was not a style that lent itself to argument; rather, it rested on magisterial pronouncements that seemed to contain universal truths, although they often disguised highly partisan barbs. It sought to erase the sense of 'Otherness', to bring every reader within its rhetorical space; but it was inclusive only on Johnson's own moral and cultural terms. Writing therefore entailed, not an abandonment of partisan language, but its reshaping into a seemingly impartial discourse.

This studied approach informed the literary project that he proposed in November 1734 in a letter to Edward Cave, editor of the *Gentleman's Magazine*. The proposal contains a telling reference to his own past. Johnson offered to write poetry and critical remarks for the magazine, including 'loose pieces, like Floyers, worth preserving'. The 'loose piece' in question was a letter recently published in the magazine on the salubrious effects of cold baths, written by Sir John Floyer, who had died ten months before. Floyer, of course, represented a fragment of Johnson's Staffordshire youth; but he was also an early link with high culture, and his views were 'worth preserving' because they addressed issues of general concern. Johnson went on to assure Cave that his own articles would avoid 'low Jests, awkward Buffoonery, or the dull Scurrilities of either Party'. He argued that this would be more acceptable to the London public, and by implication, more profitable.[55] The national language to which Johnson now dedicated himself was the language of commercial London, not that of Lichfield or Oxford or even Birmingham.

In an intellectual as well as a physical sense, Johnson was already on 'the road to St. John's Gate'.[56] His journey from Lichfield to London in 1737, accompanied by the Whig David Garrick and 'with twopence halfpenny in my pocket', was the culmination of years of disorientation in his career, his connections and perhaps his character. It meant a break, decisive although never final, with the localism of Staffordshire and the Jacobite politics that had surrounded him. So as to 'be better recommended to the Publick', he was ready to move from an idealised local society into the threatening world outside, to become a national writer, and to begin rewriting himself.

In his first literary efforts, however, Johnson did not entirely renounce the past. He tried hard, but not always successfully, to raise the localist (and Jacobite) dichotomy between inner virtue and outer wickedness to a more scholarly level of moral discourse. His 1738 poem *London*, for example, is a patriotic satire on civic decay, peppered with anti-Hanoverian references. The cure for urban corruption and luxury is withdrawal from public life, and a return to provincial simplicity.[57] Yet the poet's point of view is manifestly erudite, Latinate, urbane. By constantly referring to classical models, especially Juvenal, Johnson blunted the political bite of his own verses. Similarly, his 1739 pamphlet, *Marmor Norfolciense*, included a bitter Jacobite depiction of the horse of Hanover draining life out of the British lion. This provocative passage, however, was more striking in its Latin original than in its English translation, and it was immersed in a laboured attack on the follies of antiquarianism. The pamphlet concluded, not with a call to resistance, but with a pious entreaty to 'all sects, factions, and distinctions of men among us, to lay aside for a time their party-feuds and petty animosities, and . . . teach posterity to sacrifice every private interest to the advantage of their country'.[58]

In these early works, Johnson appears torn between 'low' politics and 'high' moralism. Did life in London add to his confusion? The capital was an intellectual melting-pot, not the marketplace of politeness that he had envisaged in his letter to Cave. In London, where 'now a Rabble Rages, now a Fire', a Jacobite newspaper like *Fog's Weekly Journal* could quote John Locke with approval, and the writings of the republican James Harrington could be enlisted in support of the Pretender's cause.[59] Political hybridism and mutation were common, especially among those who espoused the broad-based 'Country' or patriot opposition. Christine Gerrard has argued that Johnson was deeply influenced by the 'Country' rhetoric of his friend Richard Savage, who was himself a reformed Jacobite.[60] At the *Gentleman's Magazine*, moreover, Johnson worked alongside William Guthrie, a Scot whose Jacobite sympathies did not prevent him from writing pamphlets for the Pelham ministry![61] While he did not go as far as Guthrie did in twisting his principles, Johnson understood from him and others that success in the London literary world demanded political flexibility rather than high-minded detachment. Johnson was not purely self-serving, but he had no desire to imitate John Byrom of Manchester, a principled Nonjuror who lived for periods in London, but kept out of the limelight and remained a provincial writer.

Johnson's most prolonged effort at political self-revision was the play *Irene*, which he carried with him from Lichfield. If it had been produced in

1737, amidst the fears of theatrical subversiveness that engendered the Licensing Act, *Irene* might well have been suppressed by the government as a rank piece of Jacobite propaganda. It was partly derived from a seventeenth-century history by Edward Knolles, best known for translating Jean Bodin's monarchist classic, *Six Books of the Commonwealth*. Knolles's *Generall Historie of the Turkes* had also been used in the 1674 drama *The Siege of Constantinople* by Henry Neville Payne, who later became famous as a Jacobite conspirator. In Payne's play, which Johnson evidently knew, the last Byzantine Emperor and his brother Thomazo resemble Charles II and James, Duke of York. Irene appears as Thomazo's lady-love; she is kidnapped by his political enemies, who try to make her the Sultan Mahomet's concubine. She escapes, and all ends well, if rather ludicrously, as Irene and Thomazo are given a kingdom by the magnanimous Turkish conqueror.[62] The potential for a Jacobite reworking of Payne's material, with William III or George I as a less benevolent Sultan, was obvious.

In some respects, Johnson's *Irene* came close to such a reworking. It deals with a Christian conspiracy against Mahomet, who is described as an exemplar of 'arbitrary Pow'r' (an evil heartily condemned by Jacobites, who associated it with the illegal rule of 'Dutch William' and the Hanoverians). An audience in 1737 would not have had to be reminded of how the late George I had been mocked by Jacobites for ruling like a despotic Turk, for keeping two Turkish servants, or for locking up his wife.[63] Irene, whose virtue is undone by the Sultan's promises of worldly dominion, might have been seen as Britannia herself, beset by doubts and assailed by the lusts of a wicked ruler. Her friend Aspasia, 'seiz'd in Sophia's Temple', exemplifies religious virtue and could be interpreted as a personification of the Church of England. The noblemen who bewail 'expiring Greece' sound like Tory politicians lamenting the corruption of the times. The grand vizier who secretly plots with the Greeks resembles a Whig minister conspiring with the Jacobites, a role played in real life by a succession of conniving politicians. The only missing element was an actual Pretender. Any reference to one would have made the play too treasonable to produce.[64]

In spite of that absence, *Irene* would have been strong stuff in 1737 – but luckily for Johnson, audiences did not see it then, or for many years thereafter. Moreover, when he finally found a producer in 1749, his play was not presented unvarnished. He had constantly reworked the manuscript over the intervening decade, submitting it to the criticism of his Whig mentor Gilbert Walmesley. The final version restricted political commentary (which was central in Johnson's early notes and drafts) to a few lines, avoided parallels with the present, and omitted any direct reference to Payne's play. Johnson's friend Garrick, who staged the play, tacked on an epilogue by the unimpeachable Whig politician Sir William Yonge. This was in keeping with the loyalist stance of the theatre in the aftermath of the '45 rebellion. To be sure, George II did not attend the opening night, probably as a comment on the playwright's suspected politics; but nobody else seems to have recognised in *Irene* anything other than an edifying and rather boring Christian drama.[65]

Irene illustrates the careful strategies by which Johnson offered his work, and himself, to the public. By the late 1740s, he had begun to formulate his self-image as a metropolitan sage who could address men and women of all parties in a Latinate language of Christian virtue. Glimpses of his own politics were occasionally caught from behind the imposing façade of impartiality; but they could easily be mixed with quite different political strains, as *Irene* was with Yonge's epilogue. Whether Jacobitism was integral to the great man's virtue or merely a rhetorical pose came to depend on the perspective of his audience, and on what they thought they knew about him. In any case, he had left young Sam Johnson, the scion of Jacobite Staffordshire, far behind him.

Fame and exile

For two decades, he did not come back to Staffordshire, to his youthful self, or to the Jacobitism of 'Tom Tempest'. What accounts for this long absence? As reports published in the *Gentleman's Magazine* show, he was kept well-informed about the explosive political events that disturbed the West Midlands through the 1740s and early 1750s. He was certainly aware of how the closely guarded boundaries of Jacobite Staffordshire were being challenged once again. He may even have perceived how the social order of the West Midlands was bending under the strain. This change was not unlike the personal journey Johnson himself had made twenty years before.

By the mid-1740s, after thirty years of opposition, the Tory party was on the verge of disintegration. In the West Midlands, it had been deeply wounded by the defection of the Leveson Gower family to the government. As late as 1743, a Jacobite agent at Lichfield Races had confidently reported that Lord Gower was one of the leaders of a county 'unanimement attachée au Roy legitime'. Gower's 'apostasy' over the next three years was therefore deeply resented, and it led Johnson to want to make 'a Gower' synonymous with 'a Renegade' in his *Dictionary* (a cautious printer removed the reference).[66]

What saved the West Midlands Tories from despair, while at the same time damning them to perpetual opposition, was the unexpected rebellion in Scotland. Although their support for this audacious attempt was negligible, it left a permanent mark on them. Those who backed the government with enthusiasm would soon be considered Whigs. Those who acquiesced in defensive measures, or who watched fearfully from the sidelines, might later claim that they had no alternative. Godfrey Bagnal Clarke, son of an Appleby School trustee, explained to Boswell twenty years later that the Tories did not join the rebellion 'because [they were] not [organised in] clans; so could not have a thousand men, but go out themselves and lose all'. He added that instead they '[g]ave money; thus cleared up'.[67] Johnson had nothing to clear up; even at this critical juncture, he remained totally aloof from any personal involvement with the Hanoverian regime.

'It was a noble attempt,' Johnson declared at Derby, thirty years later. The rebels marched through northeast Staffordshire on their way to Ashbourne, giving the slip to the Duke of Cumberland's advance guard, stationed at Lichfield. Yet only three Staffordshire men joined the rebels, while the Lichfield corporation and cathedral chapter sent a loyal address to George II.[68] Nevertheless, the enthusiasm of the county's population for the ruling monarch was muted at best. Writing shortly after the rebels had retreated from the county, a local Whig deplored what he saw as 'the natural Courage of the Nation lost', when 'such a naked Rabble cou'd march into the body of this Island unopposed and not every Man of em cut off by the People of the Counties through which they marched'.[69]

After the rebellion, in fact, Jacobitism again became a rallying point for Tories in the West Midlands, a means of demarcating their remaining political territory from the Whigs. In June 1746, Johnson's mentor Gilbert Walmesley wrote to Lord Chief Justice Parker from Lichfield, opining that a judicial visit to the town might serve

> not totally to Extinguish that Spirit of Jacobitism, which so much prevails amongst us; yet surely, such Limits & Boundarys ought to be set to it, as that the Kings friends may not be injur'd & oppres'd by the faction; & for want of a proper Encouragemt & protection, withdraw their affection to the present Establishment, & go over to them.[70]

How Walmesley had been 'injur'd & oppres'd' by the Lichfield Jacobites is unclear, but their counterparts in Shrewsbury had recently celebrated the Pretender's birthday by decorating maypoles with white roses and parading around the town with flags proclaiming Prince Charles.[71] Burton-upon-Trent was the scene of further shocking incidents. In July 1747 at the White Hart Inn, a sergeant-major of dragoons was beaten mercilessly by a dozen local men, including the vicar. As the soldier escaped, they cried out after him, 'Down with the Rump and Dam all Hannoverians Prince Charles for ever.' Three months later, in a more festive spirit, a bull was baited at Burton, 'dressed with orange colour'd Ribbons [for William of Orange], & the Dogs in Plaids'.[72]

The Whigs had provoked such outrages by a full-scale assault on the surviving strongholds of the High Church party in the elections of 1747. Lichfield's two Tory members were unseated by Whigs, one of them a son of the hated Lord Gower. At the Lichfield Races in August, supporters of the defeated candidates took their revenge by staging a Jacobite demonstration, replete with plaid costumes and seditious toasts. The Whig Duke of Bedford was whipped around the racetrack by an angry dancing master. On 23 September, a congress was held at Lichfield in order to establish a separate Tory race meeting. Sir Thomas Gresley, Sir Charles Sedley and 150 of 'the Burton Mobb' (the same label attached to the 1718 election rioters) entered the town 'most of 'em in Plaid Wastcoats, Plaid Ribbons round their Hatts, and some with white Cocades'. Sir Lister Holte of Aston, whose father had been Sacheverell's early patron, entered with 'the Birmingham people, most of them in the same dress'. They sported white roses made of ribbon, with plaid knee-bands or saddle-cloths. Treasonable healths were drunk by men '[d]own of their knees in the open Street', voices rose in Jacobite songs like 'The Highland Laddie', and an unfortunate military pensioner was assaulted for blessing King George. The jubilant crowd then called at Lord Uxbridge's house, where they 'warm'd themselves with his lordship's old beer'.[73]

The government called for the prosecution of 27 rioters from the August race meeting, including the dancing master, who bore the felicitous name of Christopher Sole. Those accused were almost all tradesmen, artisans and labourers; none was described as a gentleman. Ten of the rioters were natives of Lichfield, while the rest were mostly from Burton and Sutton Coldfield. Johnson would have recognised among these malefactors the name of Paul Lowe, schoolmaster at Sutton Coldfield for forty years, who had educated his cousin Samuel Ford. He would also have known Thomas Mallett, the sixteen-year-old son of the Lichfield sheriff, Jonathan Mallett, and of his wife Anne Deakin, a former servant to Michael Johnson. A third rioter was apprenticed to William Gill, a magistrate of Lichfield and relation to one of Michael Johnson's closest friends. As the *Gentleman's Magazine* reported, Sole and thirteen other rioters were eventually convicted at Assizes.[74]

The 'Banging-Bout' at Lichfield, like so many Jacobite riots before it, was a declaration of territorial dominance and social solidarity in the face of an incursion by hostile outsiders. Yet it differed from previous disturbances in important ways. First, the 'strangers', headed by the Leveson Gowers, were now firmly ensconced in the community, and could be contained only by drastic Tory separatism. Second, the Lichfield disorders of 1747 involved more respectable individuals of the middling sort than did the 1715 riots. This was in part an indication of the growing commercial prosperity of the town. The races themselves, like similar sporting events in provincial centres throughout England, have been cited by Peter Borsay as evidence of an 'urban renaissance', based on the leisure activities of the increasingly affluent gentry and middling classes.[75] Jacobite sentiment was affected by this infusion of commercial culture. Its rebellious gestures became less violent and more theatrical, less physical and more consciously representational. This was the third important characteristic of the Lichfield disturbances: they did not amount to partisan warfare. The burning of the meeting-house in 1715 was an aggressive cleansing of the town from the taint of Dissent; the wearing of Scottish plaid at the Races in 1747 was an individualistic and

symbolic assertion of Tory ideals. It established only the semblance of territorial control.

Just as Johnson had espoused a commercial writing style that translated
partisanship into a less dissonant moral rhetoric, so too the commercial
culture of Lichfield's 'urban renaissance' translated factional violence into a
less dangerous politics of symbolic expression. The presence of the 'Other'
was morally condemned, but reluctantly accepted as inevitable. This did not
mean that Jacobitism was bound to come to an end, in Johnson's mind or
in the place of his birth; but its disruptive impact was diminished, and its
effectiveness in cementing social order was reduced. No matter how intimi-
dating the 'Burton Mobb' had seemed in their plaids, they were not a real
army, and neither they nor their gentry leaders could keep the Leveson
Gowers from extending their interest in Lichfield.

Not every Jacobite town conformed to this model. Walsall, a manufacturing centre in southwest Staffordshire, presented a contrasting case.
Economic fluctuations and exploitation in the metal-working trades had
preserved at Walsall all the aggressiveness of popular Jacobitism. The town's
Whig magistracy was known contemptuously as 'the Rump' to the bucklemakers who lived in the suburb of Hill Top. After 1740, Walsall witnessed
gang battles between mobs of striking metal-workers, seeking a rise in wages,
and local tradesmen, led by the mayor. Religious Dissent was a particular
source of animosity to the bucklemakers. In 1743, the Hill Top mob attacked
the houses of Methodists and manhandled John Wesley himself. Eight years
later, a Presbyterian chapel under construction in Hill Top was destroyed in
the middle of the night, to the accompaniment of Jacobite songs. The most
serious of all, the Walsall riots, took place on Restoration day in 1750, when
the bucklemakers set up an effigy of George II, which they insulted, shot at,
hanged on a gibbet and finally burned. The Hill Top mob roamed the streets
for the next two months, singing Jacobite ditties and staying away from
their workshops. Soldiers were moved into the area, but the disorders spread
to Birmingham and Wednesbury. On 19 July, the *Gentleman's Magazine*
reported 'a great insurrection in *Birmingham*', the beheading of more effigies
in Walsall, and clashes with rioters that had led to the deaths of several
dragoons.[76]

The Walsall bucklemakers were not respectable rebels. They had not experienced an 'urban renaissance' or the mediations of commercial culture.
Their collective violence looked back to the localism of the past, while it
also foreshadowed the class conflicts of the future.[77] Clearly, Jacobite politics
no longer defined a harmonious ritual space in the West Midlands; its social
terrain had fragmented. If the temperature of party conflict had lowered
among the middling sort, it had mounted to a boiling point among the
metalworkers, setting men against masters.

Johnson was enough of an old-fashioned paternalist to have sympathised
with the plight of the bucklemakers. He believed, according to Mrs. Thrale,

that '[s]everity towards the poor was . . . an undoubted and constant attendant or consequence upon whiggism'. By contrast, he might have pointed to the benevolent (albeit coercive) code of working relations that operated in the ironworks of his Crowley relatives.[78] That he would have approved of an 'insurrection' among industrial labourers seems unlikely, although the Walsall rioters were in fact egged on by local Tory gentlemen.[79] What such men of property wanted to see emerge from the 'insurrection', however, was not better wages, but a Jacobite revival.

It was to advance this purpose further that an extraordinary meeting took place on James III's birthday, 10 June, 1750, at Hamstall Ridware, five miles north of Lichfield. The government got wind of the occasion by intercepting a letter about it from the Reverend John Taylor of Colton (not to be confused with Johnson's close friend John Taylor of Ashbourne). The names of a dozen of the seventy gentlemen who attended were found out, and Johnson would have recognised almost every one of them. They included the landowners Sir Edward Littleton of Teddesley Hall (brother-in-law of John Floyer junior), Egerton Bagot, William Meredith of Henbury in Cheshire, Clement Kinnersley of Loxley and 'Mr. Snede of holle bush'; also Robert Milward of Uttoxeter, representing an ironworking fortune; and 'Mr. Frogard Atty at Lichfield', possibly Gilbert Froggatt, a relative of Michael Johnson's apprentice Simon Martin. John Beresford was there, along with a 'Mr. Hollings of Leeke', who was a relative of the Boothbys. 'Mr. Robenson of Ridware' must have been one of the sons of James Robinson, bailiff of Lichfield and friend of the Johnsons.[80]

Finally, there was Reverend John Taylor himself. The *Gentleman's Magazine* closely followed the obscure clergyman's trial at Stafford Assizes for writing a seditious libel (that is, his letter announcing the 10 June 'jubilee'). Taylor was sentenced to two years' imprisonment and a £300 fine, but did not lose his benefice. In 1757, he was named as an executor and trustee in the will of Johnson's kinsman, John Dunn, grandfather of the Collier sisters, whose struggle to regain their inheritance the Doctor later championed.[81]

Samuel Johnson would have felt quite at home if he had attended the Hamstall Ridware Jacobite meeting. It was full of respectable middling men like himself, with many of whom he was already acquainted. He was not there, of course. By 1750, he was no longer contributing much to the *Gentleman's Magazine* either. He probably did not write the poem, sympathetic to the executed rebel leaders, that appeared in the April 1747 issue; and he surely had nothing to do with the magazine's publication three years later of the words and music to 'The Highland Laddie'.[82] Instead, he was busy writing essays for the *Rambler*, in which party politics did not greatly figure, and planning out the *Dictionary*. Moreover, as far as is known, he did not set foot in Lichfield from 1740 until 1760. The closest he came to the West Midlands was through occasional letters to John Levett or to his stepdaughter Lucy Porter, as well as through more regular correspondence (the bulk of it now lost) with his close friends from Ashbourne, Derbyshire: John Taylor, Hill Boothby and William Fitzherbert.

Johnson's ties with Ashbourne, however, bear some consideration. They reveal that, while the influence of political conflict may have been receding from his writings, it continued to permeate his personal relationships. The clergyman Richard Graves, in his novel *The Spiritual Quixote*, described Ashbourne as deeply divided by party, 'since the late march of the Rebels through that place'. The novel's chief characters are met there by 'a Jacobite Barber', who proudly shows them the bedchambers where Bonnie Prince Charlie and the rebel leaders spent the night. The hilly town also sheltered a little nest of Nonjurors.[83]

Johnson's friends in Ashbourne represented both political sides. His former schoolmate John Taylor was a Whig clergyman and strong anti-Jacobite – an avatar, perhaps, of the Whig father-figure, Gilbert Walmesley. The pious Hill Boothby, on the other hand, was the daughter of Brooke Boothby, and niece of the Nonjuring lawyer John Beresford. Jacobitism was as rooted in her background as it was in Johnson's. Graves included Hill Boothby in his *Spiritual Quixote* as 'Miss Sainthill'. He hinted at her political opinions in an episode where she gets the better of a military officer, Colonel Rappee, by making fun of his cowardice in fleeing the Highland broadswords at the battle of Prestonpans. Hill Boothby was apparently no admirer of King George's army. By his own account, Johnson wrote to her more than to any other woman, and he considered marrying her after 'Tetty's' death. How 'my sweet angel', as he called her, might have influenced him as his wife is a moot point; she died in 1756 before he had made any proposal of marriage.[84]

Hill Boothby lived at Tissington Hall, in the household of William Fitzherbert, who had married her best friend. Johnson, who often encountered him on trips to London, said of Fitzherbert that 'I never knew a man who was so generally acceptable'. He was certainly acceptable to the Nonjurors. They made him a trustee of the Port Charity, and after he committed suicide in 1772, a Nonjuring Bishop eulogised him as 'a friend indeed'. Although he was elected to Parliament in 1761 as a government supporter, and became an ally of John Wilkes, Fitzherbert was also a member of a mysterious Tory club whose existence Richard Graves, chaplain at Tissington, was anxious to conceal as late as 1799.[85]

Through Hill Boothby and William Fitzherbert, Johnson could have kept up private contacts with the Tory-Jacobite culture that had helped to shape his youth. John Taylor, on the other hand, would have reminded him of why that culture could not be a prominent part of his public persona. We do not know exactly how he responded to such tensions; but he seems to have felt a deep emotional ambivalence towards his native region, and to have forced himself into alienation from it. Johnson stayed away from Ashbourne, as he did from Lichfield. In later conversations, he would sometimes even distance himself from his Ashbourne connections by personal criticisms. He told Mrs. Thrale that Hill Boothby 'pushed her piety to bigotry, her devotion to enthusiasm', and assured Boswell that William Fitzherbert could not be a real friend to anyone.[86] Such apparently cruel remarks were typical of his deliberately 'impartial' approach to anything that touched on his past feelings, both personal and political.

There is no surviving evidence that anybody in Ashbourne kept him apprised of local political events. In fact, there is no evidence that Johnson even knew what was happening in his own London neighbourhood in September 1750, when Charles Edward Stuart suddenly arrived there. The Prince, carrying an order for 26,000 muskets, was headed for the Lichfield Races, where he hoped to raise a rebellion. He lodged in the Strand, a few hundred yards from Johnson's home in Gough Square, and took Anglican communion at St. Mary-le-Strand. As it was a secret visit, it is not likely that Johnson encountered him. If he had, he might have been as disillusioned as was the Oxford Jacobite William King, who found the Prince to be poorly educated and 'illiberal'. Charles was soon persuaded not to go to Staffordshire by a hastily assembled committee of Tory peers, headed by the Earl of Westmorland; and he slipped back into exile.[87]

The convoluted plot for a Jacobite rising dragged on until the arrest and execution of the Jacobite agent Dr. Archibald Cameron, in June 1753. Shortly after, according to Boswell, William Hogarth was discussing Cameron's trial at the house of Samuel Richardson, when he noticed a man in the room whom he did not recognise, and who was apparently having convulsions. The man suddenly burst into an eloquent harangue against George II. Hogarth later learned that he was Samuel Johnson.[88] If this story is true, it indicates that Johnson was at least emotionally caught up in the last important conspiracy to restore the Stuarts. Perhaps he realised how, for a few days in 1750, Charles Edward's life had paralleled his.

Jacobitism was now in its death throes, but Johnson still would not go back to Staffordshire. We do not know what he thought of the Lichfield by-election of November 1753, the last great demonstration of its kind, when young Sir Thomas Gresley rode into town with 700 supporters wearing Tory blue and Jacobite white ribbons. We do not have any idea of what his reaction was to his friend John Levett's announcement during the general election of 1754, that he 'was very well affected to the Government' and would support a Whig candidate. Levett had used the conveyancing of property (perhaps including the house mortgaged to him by Johnson) to create burgage votes in the town, which he now carried over from the Tories to the Whigs.[89] His change of heart was common. With the prospect of a restoration gone and Prince Charles a hopeless drunk, the Stuart cause was everywhere collapsing. Over the next few years, war against France would turn Tories into patriots, and undermine what was left of local attachment to the exiled house. In 1756, when a French invasion in favour of the Pretender was feared, it was noted by a Staffordshire Whig matron that 'most of our gentlemen of noat in this county have been stirring, except Sir Walter Bagot, Sir Edward Littleton, and Sir John Astley; they lye still'. A second invasion scare three years later caused no further rumours of disaffection in the county.[90] The language of national unity had finally triumphed over localism.

By the late 1750s, moreover, Jacobitism no longer worked to preserve social order in the West Midlands. A breakdown of paternalism contributed to violent and widespread riots against high grain prices in 1756–7. The crowds blamed their plight on landowners like the Earl of Uxbridge, who had shown themselves to be more concerned with increasing profits than with maintaining local harmony. Uxbridge's attempts to breed rabbits and deny common rights on Cannock Chase led to mob attacks on his warrens. The Earl had given tacit support to the Lichfield Jacobite demonstrations of 1747, but ten years later he was himself satirised by country folk in their own variants on popular Jacobite songs. His plebeian enemies had some assistance from his neighbour Sir Edward Littleton, an incorrigible Jacobite, fanatical fox-hunter and sometime poacher. Littleton was one of the last of his breed. While Tory paternalism did not expire in the 1750s, it gave up a lot of ground to the advance of less bridled forms of exploitation.[91]

Jacobite Staffordshire was changing; but at precisely this moment, the newly famous 'Dictionary Johnson' was beginning to assert that he had not changed, and never would. Surprisingly, his connections with what was left of the dwindling band of Stuart supporters suddenly became more open in the late 1750s. He had letters franked by the inveterate Jacobite Sir John Philipps. In the *Literary Magazine* and the *Idler*, he attacked the popular war against France, a position he shared with Tory-Jacobite diehards like John Shebbeare. He was at Oxford in the summer of 1759 for the installation of the Earl of Westmorland as Chancellor of the University, and 'clapped my hands till they are sore' at a speech by the Jacobite spokesman William King. (Curiously, Westmorland's code-name at the Stuart court in 1758–59 was 'Johnson'.)[92] No longer afraid to associate himself with a cause that was daily losing its treasonable sting, he was on his way towards becoming the harmless, cantankerous 'Jacobite Johnson', as Hannah More would later call him. He could now shed some of his ambivalence, and revel in Jacobitism as a moral principle, which made one 'neither an Atheist nor a Deist'.[93] He could accept a pension from a Hanoverian king without fear of blemishing his reputation for political righteousness. He could even go back to Staffordshire, as he did in 1760, after his mother's death.

By then, he had published *Rasselas*. Written to pay off his ailing mother's debts, it can be read as Johnson's attempt to reconcile himself to his own past.[94] The Prince of Abyssinia's voyage into the moral maelstrom of Cairo reflects two historical episodes that have been significant to this discussion. First, it has similarities to Charles Edward Stuart's visit to London in 1750. Like Rasselas, Charles was a young prince searching for knowledge, who found that it did not increase his happiness. The adventures of the Stuart prince, in fact, had already been recounted in a number of fantasy novels, one of which gave him the African nickname 'Young Juba'. *Rasselas* may owe something to these works, as it may to the *Persian Tales* that had often inspired opposition political satires. (One version of the *Persian Tales*, in fact, had been translated by William King.)[95] Whatever its provenance, the chastening finale of Johnson's fable could not have given much solace to the remaining Jacobites. Rasselas obtains a kingdom only in his own imagination, and even then, 'he could never fix the limits of his dominion, and was always adding to the number of his subjects'.[96] His only certain gain is a hope of eternal life.

The character of the Prince of Abyssinia, however, seems nearer to that of the young Johnson than to Charles Edward Stuart; and his voyage more closely resembles Johnson's own flight from Staffordshire. Rasselas's sense of moral engagement is first aroused by a dream that may remind us of young Samuel's own early writings. Rasselas imagines 'an orphan virgin robbed of her little portion by a treacherous lover, and crying after him for restitution and redress'.[97] Is this an echo of *Irene*? Is the 'orphan virgin' Britannia, her 'treacherous lover' a Hanoverian king – images that had been commonplace in the Jacobite poetry of Johnson's youth? The whole scene is an illusion, of course; but it produces a drastic effect. Like Johnson, Rasselas flees from 'the valley of happiness' (the vale of Trent?) because he thinks his aspiration to know truth can only be fulfilled in the great city. Guided by Imlac, a teacher-poet who bears some resemblance to Gilbert Walmesley, he rejects the confines of localism and tries to embrace the world outside. Alas, everything there also proves illusory, except for the existence of God and the immortality of the soul. In the end, Cairo (like London) does not make the Prince any wiser than his own dreams could have done. He and his friends resolve to return to Abyssinia. Their journey home, to an idealised society that may already have changed, will continue forever. 'Nothing is concluded', no questions are resolved. In *Rasselas*, Johnson described his own moral exodus and its disappointment. Now he could go back to Staffordshire.

The journey home

Johnson's Jacobitism was a complex emotional as well as intellectual trait, that grew out of his background, education and career. He could neither proclaim it nor renounce it. His tangled responses to it influenced his whole rhetorical approach. In dangerous times, he dealt with it by literary strategies and subterfuges, reserving his bolder verbal declarations for safer days. Not everyone forgave him these shifts. In 1773, the Scottish Nonjuror William Forbes cited a remark allegedly made by Johnson on his recent visit to Edinburgh. ' "Well, well," said the bluff Dr. – "George the 1st was a robber,

George the 2d a fool, and George the 3d is an idiot." ' Far from being pleased by this statement, Forbes was disgusted that it had been made by 'a pensioner at £500 [*sic*] a year'.[98] For him, as for Boswell, Johnson's Jacobitism contained something 'affected'. I have tried to show that this 'affectation' was not a mere pose, and that it did not emerge suddenly in 1760. It was the result of a long and tortuous process of self-fashioning, which turned a budding Staffordshire Jacobite into a failed scholar, a failed teacher, a commercial hack and, finally, a moral sage.

Throughout his several careers, as J.C.D. Clark has argued, Johnson's views were oriented towards certain positions: Anglo-Latin humanism, Toryism, High Churchmanship. This does not mean that he simply expressed a 'party line', because within each of these positions there existed many variations and divergences. I have suggested here that Johnson's life and writings were shaped, not so much by commitment to a cause, as through an often painful series of encounters between upbringing and moral education on the one hand, personal ambition and constraining cultural forces on the other. He longed at times to regain an idealised stability, a comfortable 'home' both within himself and in some 'Happy Valley'. This desire was hampered, however, by the intrusions of a rampantly commercialised, morally ambiguous 'outside', both frightening and desirable, to which he was strongly attracted but could not fully surrender himself.

Johnson was never quite the Jacobite he wanted in later life to appear to be. He was too wise to be 'Tom Tempest', too ambitious to be Elijah Fenton. Instead, he settled for integrating parts of both of them into the bluff moral persona which he displayed before rapturous audiences after 1760. His confident self-image, however, could never entirely overcome an awareness of his own shortcomings, or memories of past compromises, which frequently left him uneasy. This brings us back to the much maligned James Boswell, who made the Doctor's uneasiness about the past a central theme of his *Life*. Without denigrating the virtue of the great man, Boswell dropped hints that his friend's oracular manner disguised deep uncertainties, whose roots lay only partly buried. The subtlety of these hints about Johnson's troubled character was a mark of Boswell's own literary genius, and it is our own fault if, in our haste to condemn him or praise his mentor, we fail to notice them.

Notes

1. *The Idler*, no. 10 (17 June 1758) in Samuel Johnson, *The Idler and the Adventurer*, ed. W.J. Bate, John M. Bullitt and L.F. Powell, *Yale Edition* 2 (New Haven and London, 1963), pp. 34–5.
2. Johnson, *Lives of the Poets*, II, p. 257.
3. Boswell, *Life*, I, pp. 429–30. For the adequacy of Boswell's work as biography, see the articles collected in John A. Vance (ed.), *Boswell's Life of Johnson: New Questions, New Answers* (Athens, Ga., 1985).

4. The problem is well defined, although not fully answered, in John Cannon, *Samuel Johnson and the Politics of Hanoverian England* (Oxford, 1994), ch. 2.

5. William Rider, 'Mr. Johnson', in O.M. Brack and Robert E. Kelley (eds.), *The Early Biographies of Samuel Johnson* (Iowa City, 1974), p. 3.

6. Boswell, *Life*, I, p. 429.

7. Donald Greene, *The Politics of Samuel Johnson* (New Haven, Conn., 1960; Athens, Ga., 1990).

8. Howard Erskine-Hill, 'A Kind of *Liking* for Jacobitism', *AJ*, 8 (1997), pp. 3–13 at 4.

9. Clark, *Samuel Johnson*, pp. 176, 198.

10. Clark, *Samuel Johnson*, p. 7.

11. I have argued that Jacobitism played a similar role in parts of southern England: see Paul Monod, 'Dangerous Merchandise: Smuggling, Jacobitism and Commercial Culture in South-East England, 1690–1760', *Journal of British Studies*, 30 (1991), pp. 150–82.

12. For criticisms of localism, see Ann Hughes, *The Causes of the English Civil War* (London, 1991), pp. 19–27; David Harris Sacks, *The Widening Gate: Bristol and the Atlantic Economy, 1450–1700* (Berkeley, 1991), pp. 4–11. For a discussion focused on Staffordshire, see Joan R. Kent, 'The Centre and the Localities: State Formation and Parish Government in England, circa 1640–1740', *HJ*, 38 (1995), pp. 363–404, and, for a later period, John Money, *Experience and Identity: Birmingham and the West Midlands, 1760–1800* (Manchester, 1977).

13. John Morrill, *The Revolt of the Provinces: Conservatives and Radicals in the English Civil War, 1630–1650* (London, 1980), pp. 112–14; Anthony Fletcher, 'The Coming of War', in John Morrill (ed.), *Reactions to the English Civil War* (London, 1983), p. 37; Ronald Hutton, 'The Royalist War Effort', ibid., pp. 61–2; Ann Hughes, *Politics, Society and Civil War in Warwickshire, 1620–1660* (Cambridge, 1987), pp. 9, 114–68.

14. D.A. Johnson and D.G. Vaisey (eds.), *Staffordshire and the Great Rebellion* (Stoke-on-Trent, 1964), pp. 38–9, 81; Maurice Ashley, *The Greatness of Oliver Cromwell* (New York, 1957, 1963), p. 270; Christopher Hill, *Society and Puritanism in Pre-Revolutionary England* (New York, 1964, 1969), p. 180; but see Hughes, *Politics, Society and Civil War*, p. 337.

15. For Anglicans in the iron industry, see W.H.B. Court, *The Rise of the Midland Industries, 1600–1838* (London, 1938), p. 112; Oliver Fairclough, *The Grand Old Mansion: The Holtes and their Successors at Aston Hall* (Birmingham, 1984), pp. 19, 39; M.W. Flinn, *Men of Iron: The Crowleys in the Early Iron Industry* (Edinburgh, 1962), p. 224. For economic changes in the industry, see Marie B. Rowlands, *Masters and Men in the West Midlands Metal Trades before the Industrial Revolution* (Manchester, 1975).

16. Reade, *Johnsonian Gleanings*, III, pp. 63–4, 151–2, 178–9, IV, pp. 43–4; Court, *Rise of the Midland Industries*, p. 112.

17. Henning, *HC*, I, p. 382.

18. Boswell, *Life*, I, p. 430.

19. The most important lay Nonjuror was Sir Edward Mainwaring of Whitmore in Staffordshire, a former MP. For Nonjuring clergy, see J.H. Overton, *The Nonjurors: Their Lives, Principles, and Writings* (London, 1902), pp. 467–96.

20. HMC *Hastings* (2 vols., London, 1930), II, pp. 226–7, 238; Paul Hopkins, 'Aspects of Jacobite Conspiracy in England in the Reign of William III', doctoral thesis, Cambridge University, 1981, pp. 369–70, 478–9; Bodleian Library, Carte MSS 181,

ff. 501–2; Carte MSS 209, f. 182b. Decades later, Samuel Johnson related a story about the 9th Earl of Huntingdon's alleged Jacobitism, which suggests he kept in contact with the family: see Hester Lynch Piozzi, *Thraliana: The Diary of Mrs. Hester Lynch Thrale*, ed. Katherine Balderston (2 vols., Oxford, 1951), I, pp. 141–2. I owe this reference to Professor J.C.D. Clark.

21. See Paul Monod, 'Jacobitism and Country Principles in the Reign of William III', *HJ*, 30 (1987), pp. 289–310.

22. G.P.R. James (ed.), *Letters Illustrative of the Reign of William III. From 1696 to 1708. Addressed to the Earl of Shrewsbury, by James Vernon, Esq. Secretary of State* (3 vols., London, 1841), III, p. 121.

23. William Walsh, 'The Golden Age Restor'd' (January 1703), in Frank Ellis (ed.), *Poems on Affairs of State: Augustan Satirical Verse, 1660–1714, vol. VI: 1697–1704* (New Haven, Conn. and London, 1970), pp. 487–505, esp. lines 20, 71–2; Hearne, *Collections*, VII, p. 104.

24. T. Pape, 'The Ancient Corporation of Cheadle', in *North Staffordshire Field Club Transactions*, (1929–30), pp. 52–88, esp. pp. 69–76; Reade, *Johnsonian Gleanings*, III, p. 11. A certain Thomas Johnson was 'mayor' of the Cheadle mock corporation in 1713, but whether or not he was related to the Johnsons of Lichfield is unknown.

25. Geoffrey Holmes, *The Trial of Dr. Sacheverell* (London, 1973), pp. 9–11, 17–19, 48–60.

26. Ibid., pp. 239–48; [Abel Boyer], *The History of the Reign of Queen Anne, Digested into Annals* (11 vols., London, 1703–13), IX, pp. 202–9; Boswell, *Life*, I, p. 39.

27. Daniel Szechi, *Jacobitism and Tory Politics, 1710–1714* (Edinburgh, 1987); Edward Gregg, *Queen Anne* (London, 1984), ch. 14.

28. Holmes, *Trial of Sacheverell*, p. 265; Reade, *Johnsonian Gleanings*, III, pp. 105–6; Bodleian Library, Rawlinson MSS B 376, fs. 59–60; *An Account of the Riots, Tumults, and other Treasonable Practices; since His Majesty's Accession to the Throne* (London, 1715); PRO, SP 35/74/4.

29. The riots and their context are discussed in Sir Charles Petrie, 'The Jacobite Activities in South and West England in the Summer of 1715', *TRHS*, 4th series, 18 (1935), pp. 85–106; Nicholas Rogers, 'Riot and Popular Jacobitism in Early Hanoverian England', in Eveline Cruickshanks (ed.), *Ideology and Conspiracy: Aspects of Jacobitism, 1689–1759* (Edinburgh, 1982), pp. 70–88; Paul Monod, *Jacobitism and the English People, 1688–1788* (Cambridge, 1989), pp. 185–93; Kathleen Wilson, *The Sense of the People: Politics, Culture and Imperialism in England, 1715–1785* (Cambridge, 1995), pp. 101–17.

30. PRO, Assizes 4/18, p. 231.

31. *Flying Post*, July 19, 1715; PRO, Assi. 4/18, *passim*; James L. Clifford, *Young Samuel Johnson* (London, 1955), p. 38.

32. Pape, 'Ancient Corporation of Cheadle', p. 77; Reade, *Johnsonian Gleanings*, III, p. 134; J.H.Y. Briggs, 'The Burning of the Meeting House, July 1715: Dissent and Faction in Late Stuart Newcastle', *North Staffordshire Journal of Field Studies*, 14 (1974), pp. 70–3; PRO, Assi. 4/18, pp. 235, 240.

33. Josiah C. Wedgwood, *Staffordshire Parliamentary History from the Earliest Times to the Present Day* (2 vols., London, 1920, 1922), II, p. 215, note 2.

34. PRO, SP 35/12/21, 35/27/48, 35/28/1, f. 1, 35/28/12, f. 25, 25/28/68, f. 117, 35/30/17, f. 39, 35/48/27.

35. Reade, *Johnsonian Gleanings*, III, pp. 89–91; Clifford, *Young Samuel Johnson*, p. 149; Johnson, *Letters*, I, pp. 23, 37–40.

36. Pape, 'Ancient Corporation of Cheadle', pp. 79–81; Reade, *Johnsonian Gleanings*, VI, pp. 96–114, 173–4; A.L. Reade, 'Early Career of Dr. Johnson's Father', *Times Literary Supplement*, (17 June 1949), p. 404; Clifford, *Young Samuel Johnson*, pp. 64–5; Phil Mottram, 'Ilam and the Glorious Revolution', unpublished manuscript kindly sent to me by the author, p. 20, citing BL Add MSS 6692, p. 189 (Port Charity); Henry Broxap, *The Later Non-Jurors* (Cambridge, 1924), p. 233; Mary Alden Hopkins, *Dr. Johnson's Lichfield* (New York, 1952), pp. 34–8, 185 (Ilam). I am grateful to Phil Mottram for providing me with information about Sir William's Nonjuring connections and the 1716 disturbance in Ashbourne.
37. PRO, SP 35/25/53–4, /68; Assi. 2/7, Stafford Qua. 7 G. I.
38. RASP 65/16. The list is printed in Paul Fritz, *The English Ministers and Jacobitism between the Rebellions of 1715 and 1745* (Toronto, 1975), pp. 147–55, and partially in Sedgwick, *HC*, I, pp. 109–13. For Inge, see Johnson, *Lives of the Poets*, III, pp. 323–4; Reade, *Johnsonian Gleanings*, V, pp. 71–2.
39. Hawkins, *Life*, p. 3; Reade, *Johnsonian Gleanings*, I, p. 18 (Simon Martin); R.W. Greaves, *The Corporation of Leicester 1689–1836* (Leicester, 1939, 1970), pp. 91–5.
40. Hesther Lynch Piozzi, 'Anecdotes of the late Samuel Johnson, LL.D., during the Last Twenty Years of his Life', in George Birkbeck Hill (ed.), *Johnsonian Miscellanies* (2 vols., London, 1897), I, p. 162; Clifford, *Young Samuel Johnson*, pp. 20–1, 130; Boswell, *Life*, II, p. 322.
41. Walter Scott (ed.), *The Poetical Works of Anna Seward* (3 vols., Edinburgh, 1810), I, p. lxx; Boswell, *Life*, I, pp. 44–6, 526; for Jacobite schoolmasters, see Craig Rose, ' "Seminarys of Faction and Rebellion": Jacobites, Whigs and the London Charity Schools, 1716–1724', *HJ*, 34 (1991), pp. 831–56, and Monod, *Jacobitism and the English People*, p. 307.
42. *DNB*, under Floyer, Sir John; Reade, *Johnsonian Gleanings*, III, pp. 10, 19, 61, 66, 115, VI, p. 50; Henning, *HC*, I, pp. 385–6; Sedgwick, *HC*, II, p. 40; RASP 248/151.
43. Reade, *Johnsonian Gleanings*, IX, pp. 1–15; Graham Midgley, *The Life of Orator Henley* (Oxford, 1973), pp. 216–28, 234–45.
44. Flinn, *Men of Iron*, pp. 67–9; HMC *Calendar of the Stuart Papers belonging to His Majesty the King, preserved at Windsor Castle* (7 vols., London, 1902–23), II, p. 59, III, p. 160; Fritz, *English Ministers and Jacobitism*, pp. 14–18.
45. Reade, *Johnsonian Gleanings*, III, pp. 151–2; Samuel Johnson, 'The Vanity of Human Wishes', in *Poems*, ed. E.L. McAdam, Jr., with George Milne, *Yale Edition* VI (New Haven and London, 1964), pp. 101–2, lines 191–222; Johnson, *Letters*, I, p. 28: Johnson to John Taylor, 10 August 1742. See Howard Erskine-Hill, *Poetry of Opposition and Revolution: Dryden to Wordsworth* (Oxford, 1996), pp. 149–64, for parallels between Charles XII and Charles Edward Stuart, which are denied in Howard D. Weinbrot, 'Johnson, Jacobitism and Swedish Charles: "The Vanity of Human Wishes" and Scholarly Method', *ELH*, 64 (1997), pp. 945–82.
46. Sedgwick, *HC*, II, p. 194; Reade, *Johnsonian Gleanings*, V, pp. 119–23.
47. Sedgwick, *HC*, II, pp. 344–5; Richard Graves, *Recollections of Some Particulars in the Life of William Shenstone, Esq.* (London, 1787), p. 16.
48. Richard Parkinson, ed., *The Private Journals and Literary Remains of John Byrom*, II, part 2, Chetham Society Publications 44 (1857), pp. 624–9.
49. Johnson, *Lives of the Poets*, II, p. 21; also, Clifford, *Young Samuel Johnson*, pp. 92–7.
50. W.A. Speck, *Tory and Whig: The Struggle in the Constituencies, 1701–1715* (London, 1970), p. 56.
51. The governors of the school are listed in Reade, *Johnsonian Gleanings*, VI, pp. 107–8. See also L. Eardley-Simpson, *Derby and the '45* (London, 1933), p. 30;

Ruth Smith, 'The Achievements of Charles Jennens (1700–1773)', *Music and Letters*, 70 (1989), pp. 161–90; M.W. Patterson, *Sir Francis Burdett and his Times (1770–1844)* (London, 1931), p. 4.

52. Clifford, *Young Samuel Johnson*, pp. 153–7; Sedgwick, *HC*, II, p. 304.
53. Her family tree is laid out in Reade, *Johnsonian Gleanings*, VI. Jacobite marriage patterns are discussed in Paul Monod, 'The Politics of Matrimony: Jacobitism and Marriage in Eighteenth-Century England', in Cruickshanks and Black (eds.), *The Jacobite Challenge*, pp. 24–41. For clerical politics in Derby, see Eardley-Simpson, *Derby and the '45*, p. 14.
54. Father Jerome Lobo, *A Voyage to Abyssinia*, trans. Samuel Johnson, ed. Joel A. Gold, *Yale Edition* XV (1985), p. 2. Warren was High Sheriff of his county in 1712, the Tory heyday. His brother-in-law Lewis Wogan appears on the 1721 Jacobite list, and his son William was a member of the Society of Sea Sergeants, a Welsh Jacobite club. Reade, *Johnsonian Gleanings*, V, pp. 107–8; Henning, *HC*, III, pp. 752–3; RASP 65/16; Francis Jones, 'The Society of Sea Serjeants', *Transactions of the Honourable Society of Cymmrodorion*, (1967), part 1, pp. 87–8, 90.
55. Johnson, *Letters*, I, p. 6.
56. The phrase is borrowed from Thomas Kaminski, *The Early Career of Samuel Johnson* (Oxford, 1987), ch. 1.
57. Samuel Johnson, 'London', in *Poems*, pp. 45–61, esp. lines 50 and 246–7; Erskine-Hill, *Poetry of Opposition*, pp. 119–26.
58. Samuel Johnson, *Marmor Norfolciense*, in *Political Writings*, ed. Donald J. Greene, *Yale Edition* X (1977), p. 51; Christine Gerrard, *The Patriot Opposition to Walpole: Politics, Poetry, and National Myth, 1725–1742* (Oxford, 1994), pp. 238–41. The horse attacking the lion appeared in a Jacobite medal of 1721; the image was later reversed in a print of the Old Pretender James III and his two sons. See Clark, *Samuel Johnson*, pp. 161–2.
59. *Fog's Weekly Journal*, no. 184, 13 May 1732; Monod, *Jacobitism and the English People*, pp. 84–5.
60. Gerrard, *Patriot Opposition to Walpole*, ch. 8; Kaminski, *Early Career*, ch. 5; Clarence Tracy (ed.), *The Poetical Works of Richard Savage* (Cambridge, 1962), pp. 15–26.
61. See Kaminski, *Early Career*, pp. 33–4; Clark, *Samuel Johnson*, pp. 141–2. In 1756, Guthrie was accused of making Jacobite pronouncements by Eugene Aram, a scholar and journalist who was later hanged for murder: PRO, SP 36/136, fs. 75–7.
62. [Henry Neville Payne], *The Siege of Constantinople: A Tragedy* (London, 1675). See also the introduction to Payne's *The Fatal Jealousie*, ed. Willard Thorp, Augustan Reprint Society 16 (Ann Arbor, Michigan, 1949), pp. 2–3.
63. See Monod, *Jacobitism and the English People*, pp. 57–9. The Duke of Wharton's 'Persian Letter', in which George I appears as an Oriental usurper, appeared in *Mist's Weekly Journal*, 24 August 1728.
64. Samuel Johnson, *Irene*, in *Poems*, ed. E.L. McAdam, Jr., with George Milne, *Yale Edition* III (1964), pp. 109–239; but see also the introduction in *The Poems of Samuel Johnson*, ed. David Nichol Smith and Edward L. McAdam (Oxford, 1941, 1974), pp. 267–78.
65. James L. Clifford, *Dictionary Johnson: Samuel Johnson's Middle Years* (New York, 1979), ch. 1; Erskine-Hill, *Poetry of Opposition*, p. 138. For Jacobitism on the London stage, see Paul Monod, 'Pierre's White Hat: Theatre, Jacobitism and Popular Protest in London, 1689–1769', in Eveline Cruickshanks (ed.), *By Force or By Default? The Revolution of 1688–89* (Edinburgh, 1989), pp. 159–89.
66. Linda Colley, *In Defiance of Oligarchy: The Tory Party 1714–60* (Cambridge, 1982), pp. 236–51; Cruickshanks, *Political Untouchables*, p. 120; William King, *Political*

and Literary Anecdotes of His Own Times (London, 1819), pp. 46–7; Boswell, *Life*, I, pp. 296, 544.

67. Frank Brady and Frederick A. Pottle (eds.), *Boswell on the Grand Tour: Italy, Corsica and France, 1765–1766* (New York, 1955), p. 67.

68. Boswell, *Life*, III, p. 162; S.A.H. Burne, 'The Staffordshire Campaign of 1745', *North Staffordshire Field Club Transactions*, (1925–6), pp. 50–76.

69. BL Add MSS 29,913, fs. 17–18. Some of the letters in this volume were published in 'The Forty-Five in Staffordshire', *North Staffordshire Field Club Transactions*, (1923–4), pp. 87–96.

70. BL Add MSS 29,913, f. 4.

71. PRO SP 36/113, f. 183.

72. PRO SP 36/103, ff. 190–2; Yale University Library, Lee Family Papers, Box 4A T-2: George Venables Vernon to Chief Justice Lee, Sudbury, 12 October 1747.

73. Wedgwood, *Parliamentary History of Staffordshire*, II, pp. 252–4; Chatsworth Manuscripts, 343.1 (at Chatsworth, Derbyshire; I am grateful to Eveline Cruickshanks for this reference); Ann J. Kettle, 'The Struggle for the Lichfield Interest, 1747–68', in M.W. Greenslade, ed., *Essays in Staffordshire History*, Staffordshire Record Society, 4th Series, 6 (1970), pp. 115–35, esp. pp. 116–19; Henning, *HC*, II, p. 494; 'Great Britain's Union; OR Litchfield Races Transpos'd', in Frederick George Stephens (ed.), *Catalogue of Political and Personal Satires Preserved in the Department of Prints and Drawings in the British Museum* (2 vols., London, 1870, reprinted 1978), I, pp. 653–5, no. 2864.

74. PRO SP 36/102, f. 80; Reade, *Johnsonian Gleanings*, III, pp. 44–5, 94, VI, pp. 188–204, VIII, pp. 63, 65; *Gentleman's Magazine*, 18 (1748), p. 378.

75. Peter Borsay, *The English Urban Renaissance: Culture and Society in the Provincial Town, 1660–1789* (Oxford, 1989), esp. ch. 7; Ann J. Kettle, 'Lichfield Races', *Transactions of the Lichfield and South Staffordshire Archaeological Society*, 6 (1964–5), pp. 39–44; Hopkins, *Dr. Johnson's Lichfield*, ch. 4. See also John Money, *Experience and Identity: Birmingham and the West Midlands, 1760–1800* (Montreal, 1977).

76. Monod, *Jacobitism and the English People*, pp. 205–7; Ernest James Homeshaw, *The Corporation of the Borough and Foreign of Walsall* (Walsall, 1960), pp. 91–4; PRO SP 44/81, pp. 189–90, 192–3, 197–9; SP 36/113, fs 88–101, 128–9, 137–43, 145, 194; SP 44/318, p. 52; PRO, Assi. 2/15, Staffs. Sum. 24 G. II, Assi. 4/20, Staffs. Summer 24 G. II, Assi. 5/71, part 2, fs 27–29; *Gentleman's Magazine*, 14 (1744), p. 107, 20 (1750), p. 331.

77. For ideas of community among industrial workers, see John Rule, *The Labouring Classes in Early Industrial England, 1750–1850* (London, 1986), ch. 6.

78. Piozzi, 'Anecdotes', p. 204; Flinn, *Men of Iron*, ch. 13.

79. PRO SP 36/113, f. 196; King's Bench 1/10, part 1, Hilary 24 G. II, Rex vs. James & others.

80. PRO SP 36/114, fs 83 (the list of names), 96, 98–100, 102–3; Court, *Rise of the Midland Industries*, pp. 127–8 (Milward); Reade, *Johnsonian Gleanings*, IV, pp. 117–23 (Martin), VII, p. 154 (Frogatt), IX, pp. 110–11 (Robinson). Three of the four Robinson boys became clergymen, and one was the grandfather of the 'sleeping children' whose touching monument can be seen in Lichfield Cathedral.

81. Reade, *Johnsonian Gleanings*, VI, p. 174, IX, pp. 26–7; *Gentleman's Magazine*, 20 (1750), p. 343, 21 (1751), p. 375. Richard Graves the novelist, whose family was known to Johnson since at least 1731, had a sister Mary who married a Reverend John Taylor, but he may have been another cleric of the same name: see N.J.L. Lyons, 'William Shenstone, Mary Graves and Mrs. Delany', *Notes and Queries*, 217, 19 (1972), pp. 379–80; Clarence Tracy, *A Portrait of Richard Graves* (Toronto and

Buffalo, 1987), pp. 12–13, 58–9; Joseph Foster, *Alumni Oxonienses: The Members of the University of Oxford, 1715–1886* (4 vols., Oxford, 1888), IV, p. 1394; John and J.A. Venn, *Alumni Cantabrigienses . . . Part 1: From the Earliest Times to 1751* (4 vols., Cambridge, 1922–7), IV, p. 207.

82. *Gentleman's Magazine*, 17 (1747), p. 194, and 20 (1750), p. 325. For the 1747 poem, see Boswell, *Life*, I, p. 180; Smith and McAdam, eds., *Poems of Johnson*, p. 449; Johnson, *Poems*, eds. McAdam and Milne, p. 390. A reply to this poem by a Scottish Jacobite is found in Henry Paton (ed.), *The Lyon in Mourning*, Publications of the Scottish Historical Society, 20–2 (3 vols., Edinburgh, 1895–6, reprinted 1975), I, pp. 239–40.

83. Richard Graves, *The Spiritual Quixote, or The Summer's Ramble of Mr. Geoffrey Wildgoose*, ed. Clarence Tracy (London, 1967), pp. 360–1. Graves's experiences at Ashbourne are detailed in Tracy, *Portrait of Richard Graves*, ch. 6.

84. Reade, *Johnsonian Gleanings*, VI, pp. 173–4; Graves, *Spiritual Quixote*, p. 374.

85. Namier and Brooke, *HC*, II, pp. 428–30; Boswell, *Life*, III, p. 148; Mottram, 'Ilam and the Glorious Revolution', p. 28, citing PRO C38/560 1758; Paton, ed., *Lyon in Mourning*, III, p. 262; Tracy, *Portrait of Richard Graves*, pp. 52–3. This Tory club may have been connected with the Uttoxeter Bowling Green Club, whose membership turned out *en masse* for the Jacobite 'jubilee' at Hamstall Ridware. John Beresford was a member of the Uttoxeter Club, as was William Fitzherbert's Catholic kinsman Richard Fitzherbert of Somersal Herbert: PRO, SP 36/114, f. 87; Reade, *Johnsonian Gleanings*, VI, p. 173.

86. Piozzi, 'Anecdotes', p. 257; Boswell, *Life*, III, p. 149.

87. Sir Charles Petrie, 'The Elibank Plot, 1752–3', *TRHS*, 4th Series, 14 (1931), pp. 175–96; RASP 310/116; Lord Mahon (ed.), *The Decline of the Last Stuarts. Extracts from the Despatches of British Envoys to the Secretary of State* (London, 1843), p. 76; King, *Political and Literary Anecdotes*, pp. 196–211.

88. Boswell, *Life*, II, pp. 145–7.

89. Wedgwood, *Parliamentary History of Staffordshire*, II, pp. 254–6; Kettle, 'Struggle for the Lichfield Interest', pp. 119–21. John Levett later reverted to Toryism and briefly served as MP for Lichfield in 1761: Namier and Brooke, *HC*, III, p. 39.

90. Maud Wyndham, *Chronicles of the Eighteenth Century* (2 vols., London, 1856), II, p. 161; Claude Nordmann, 'Choiseul and the Last Jacobite Attempt of 1759', in Cruickshanks (ed.), *Ideology and Conspiracy*, pp. 201–17.

91. Jeremy N. Caple, '1756–7', in Andrew Charlesworth (ed.), *Atlas of Rural Protest in Britain, 1548–1900* (Philadelphia, 1983), pp. 86–8; Douglas Hay, 'Poaching and the Game Laws on Cannock Chase', in Douglas Hay et al., *Albion's Fatal Tree: Crime and Society in Eighteenth-Century England* (New York, 1975), pp. 189–253, esp. pp. 224–5; M.W. Farr, 'Sir Edward Littleton's Fox-hunting Diary, 1774–89', in Greenslade (ed.), *Essays in Staffordshire History*, pp. 136–70.

92. Johnson, *Letters*, I, pp. 160, 186, 195; Sedgwick, *HC*, II, pp. 344–5; Clifford, *Dictionary Johnson*, pp. 171–4, 198–9; Clark, *Samuel Johnson*, p. 102; RASP, printed papers, box 6, no. 226. Philipps and his wife were supporters of the blind poetess Anna Williams, who lived with Johnson. George Osborne, author of the Jacobite magazine *The True Briton*, also looked to Philipps for assistance at this time: BL Add MSS 28,236, fs. 66, 70.

93. Boswell, *Life*, I, p. 431.

94. For the composition of *Rasselas*, see Clifford, *Dictionary Johnson*, ch. 13; on the 'metaphor of travel' in the story, see Thomas M. Curley, *Samuel Johnson and the Age of Travel* (Athens, Ga., 1976), ch. 5.

95. 'M. Michell', pseud., *Young Juba: or, the History of the Young Chevalier from His Birth, to His Escape from Scotland, after the Battle of Culloden* (London, 1748); Monod, *Jacobitism and the English People*, pp. 37–8; Samuel Johnson, *Rasselas and Other Tales*, ed. Gwin J. Kolb, *Yale Edition* XVI (1990), editor's introduction, p. xl.
96. Samuel Johnson, *The History of Rasselas, Prince of Abyssinia*, in Kolb, ed., *Rasselas and Other Tales*, p. 176.
97. Johnson, *Rasselas*, p. 18; Monod, *Jacobitism and the English People*, pp. 62–6.
98. Paton, ed., *Lyon in Mourning*, III, p. 292. Birkbeck Hill, in *Johnsonian Miscellanies*, II, pp. 466–7, doubts that the story is true.

2

The Religious and Political Character of the Parish of St. Clement Danes

Richard Sharp

Samuel Johnson was, wrote Boswell, 'a sincere and zealous Christian, of high-Church-of-England and monarchical principles, which he would not tamely suffer to be questioned'.[1] He was an attentive reader of theological works, conscientious in private devotion and devout when attending public worship. His various homes, including Gough Square (1746?–59), Inner Temple Lane (1760–65), Johnson's Court (1765–76) and Bolt Court (1776–84), were close to the parish churches of St. Bride's and St. Dunstan's in Fleet Street, and also to the Temple Church. Not much further away was St. Andrew's, Holborn, where Dr. Henry Sacheverell had been Rector from 1713 until his death in 1724, and where a tradition of High Church observance was sustained throughout the eighteenth century.[2] Yet Johnson frequented none of these churches. Instead, he preferred to walk further, to a church where, he said, 'he was best known'.[3]

The parish church of St. Clement Danes lies at the eastern end of the Strand, just outside the western limit of the City of London, formerly marked by Temple Bar. Its extensive parish was reduced in 1723, when a portion was lost to the 'new Church' of St. Mary-le-Strand, but St. Clement's in the mid-eighteenth century remained the focal point of a populous and socially mixed neighbourhood. To the south of the Strand, John Rocque's 1:2500 scale map of London (1746) shows wide streets: Essex Street, Arundel Street and Norfolk Street, running down to the Thames. To the west and north of the church lay Lyons Inn, New Inn and Clements Inn. In a northerly direction, east of Clement's Lane, a network of yards and courts led down to Butcher Row, the easterly continuation of the Back Side of St. Clement's Churchyard. To the east of the church the Strand continued towards Temple Bar, approximately 150 yards away. The parish burial ground lay some 200 yards to the north of the church, just south of Portugal Street.[4]

Today, St. Clement Danes stands on an island, surrounded by traffic. However, in the eighteenth century, it lay on the north side of the Strand, opposite Essex Street to the east and Arundel Street to the west. The churchyard, then still an open space though no longer in use, lay immediately west of the church. Engravings by John Kip (1706) and John Maurer (1753) show that this area was surrounded by shops, and Maurer's view also includes the Crown and Anchor Tavern, opposite the church on the south side of the Strand, at the corner of Arundel Street.[5] The church itself dated from 1682, when the present structure was put up under the direction of Sir Christopher Wren. In 1719 the west tower was heightened and ornamented to a design by James Gibbs, architect of St. Mary-le-Strand.[6] The churchyard was newly paved in 1721, and in the same year a thorough programme of internal refurbishment was completed. Apart from the construction of William Kent's altarpiece, which caused so much controversy four years later, much other work was done, and at the end of September 1721 it was widely reported that St. Clement Danes 'may now pass (especially in regard of its Architecture and Contrivance) for the neatest Parish-Church in England'.[7]

The right of presentation to the Rectory of St. Clement Danes was vested throughout the eighteenth century with the Cecils of Burghley House, Stamford, who held the title of Earl of Exeter. The family had a strong tradition of loyalty to the Stuart dynasty and to the Church of England. After the Revolution of 1688 the 5th earl, John Cecil (succeeded 1688, died 1700), was regarded as a Jacobite sympathiser.[8] He also became a Nonjuror, maintaining a Nonjuring chaplain, Robert Jenkin, Fellow of St. John's College, Cambridge and Chaplain to John Lake, Bishop of Chichester, whose dying Declaration he had witnessed in 1689.[9] Like Jenkin and Lake, the 5th Earl of Exeter had been educated at St. John's College, Cambridge, where he was admitted as a Fellow Commoner in 1667 under the Mastership of Dr. Peter Gunning, a Royalist High Churchman and later Bishop of Ely. St. John's, which became the greatest Nonjuring college in either university after 1690, was the Cecil family's College.[10] Two sons of the 5th earl, Charles and Edward Cecil, followed their father as Fellow Commoners there in 1696. William Cecil, son of John Cecil, the 6th earl (succeeded 1700, died 1721) was a Fellow Commoner in 1718, together with his brother, Brownlow Cecil, the 8th earl (succeeded 1722, died 1754). The latter's son, Brownlow Cecil, the 9th earl (succeeded 1754, died 1793) followed his father to the College in 1744 and was created DCL at Oxford during the great Tory celebration that accompanied the opening of the Radcliffe Camera in April 1749.[11]

Perhaps not surprisingly, therefore, St. Clement Danes in the late seventeenth and early eighteenth centuries came to be regarded as a centre of political – and theological – High Churchmanship.[12] In 1714 the Communion was celebrated weekly, an unusually frequent rate for the time, and in 1746 public prayers were still being read daily, both morning and evening: this custom was probably still observed in 1779.[13] More remarkable still was the elaborate symbolism of the decorations at the east end of the church, which survived until the nineteenth century:

The *sacrarium* is a semicircle . . . the altar-piece consists of four Corinthian pilasters, with entablature and urns, and festoons over the Creed and Lord's Prayer. The Commandments are under an arch, which supports five candlesticks. In the tympanum a pelican. This is the intercolumniation of four isolated pillars, whose entablature has Attic pedestals, and good statues of Moses and Aaron. The table is of porphyry, as are two steps for candlesticks on it; the frame is of wrought iron gilt, the rails the same, the pavement marble.[14]

Decoration of this kind indicated a distinctively High Church eucharistic theology.[15] The pelican, alluding to material feeding in the Eucharist, and the figures of Moses and Aaron, emblems of the association of magistracy and priesthood, occurred in other churches, but seldom together.[16] The use of stone in the altar table recalled pre-Reformation practice, as did use of candles on the altar – a rare survival.[17]

Of the clergy who served at St. Clement Danes during the eighteenth century several can be shown to have been High Churchmen of an extreme type. Thomas Lewis (1689–1749), Lecturer in *c*. 1720, was especially notable. A member of Corpus Christi College, Oxford, where Dr. Thomas Turner, President from 1687 to 1714, had 'created a College which earned the reputation of being the home of the most assertive high Tories in the University',[18] Lewis had earned notoriety as author of *The Scourge, in Vindication of the Church of England*, a High Church satirical weekly published from February to November 1717. This attacked latitudinarians, especially Benjamin Hoadly, Bishop of Bangor (nos. 18, 21, 24, 27, 34), and Dissenters, who were represented as a greater threat than Roman Catholics (nos. 8, 11, 17, 26, 31, 37, 39). A collected edition of *The Scourge* was reprinted in 1720, together with other works of a similar nature: *The Danger of the Church-Establishment of England, From the Insolence of Protestant Dissenters* and *The Anatomy of the Heretical Synod of Dissenters at Salters-Hall*. Yet there was also a positive aspect to Lewis's High Churchmanship. He took a keen interest in doctrine and in liturgy, and his *Historical Essay, upon the Consecration of Churches* (1719), argued in favour of ideals taken from the model of the primitive Church. In this work, Lewis's advanced eucharistic views are evident from references to 'the Altar' for 'the commemorative sacrifice', with a *prothesis*, to allow for the preparation of the bread and wine prior to their solemn offering in the eucharist, in line with practices advocated by the 'usager' Nonjurors.[19] During the beautification of St. Clement Danes in 1721, Lewis published *The Obligation of Christians to Beautify and Adorn their Churches*, which he dedicated to the Churchwardens and Vestry of the parish, commending them on 'the distinguishing Zeal you have lately shewn to improve the Beauty and the Ornament of your Church . . . nearest to the Primitive Standard of any I have seen'. Maintaining that reaction against the superstitious ritual of the Roman Catholic Church had been carried too far since the Reformation, Lewis argued in characteristic High Church style in favour of 'other Ornaments which are not essential, but yet give a solemn lustre to our Churches: Organs, Historical Painting, Guilding, Pulpit Cloth and Cushions, Hoods for the Officiating Clergy, Conveniencies for Kneeling, Bells, Clocks, Chimes and whatever seems orderly and innocent, and promotes the Decency of . . . Publick Worship' (p. 35). Earlier, he had noted that 'primitive' churches had often possessed stone altars (p. 15), altar rails (p. 16), special cloths and vessels for use in the Communion (p. 17) and vestments for the ministers.[20] Lewis also considered that canopies over the altar (pp. 17–18), organs (p. 18) and pictures of angels, saints and pious princes such as King Charles I (p. 22) would be a further adornment.[21]

Amongst other High Church clergy at St. Clement Danes was Dr. John Rogers (1679–1729), Lecturer from 1712 to 1726 and another member of Corpus Christi College, Oxford.[22] He was best known as the author of *A Discourse on the Visible and Invisible Church of Christ* (1719), a notable defence of the independent spiritual powers of the clergy against the Erastian opinions of Benjamin Hoadly, Bishop of Bangor. Another Lecturer during the 1720s and 1730s, John Peters, had the reputation of being a 'great disciple' of the anti-Newtonian theological writer John Hutchinson.[23] Thomas Blackwell, Rector from 1721 until his death in 1773, had particularly close links with the Earls of Exeter, both as a native of Stamford, the Cecil family borough, and as a graduate of St. John's College, Cambridge.[24]

George Berkeley, Rector from 1786 to 1795 and son of the great philosopher-bishop of Cloyne, was another noted High Churchman. In his early years, a sermon preached for the anniversary of the Martyrdom of King Charles I on 30 January 1758 (reprinted with his collected *Sermons* in 1799) had attracted critical attention for its high-flying tone. It included a notable encomium on the Royal Martyr, 'that *real* defender of the Faith into which he was *duly* baptized' who 'derived his power from God, not from an association of rebels' (pp. 150–1), and concluded with a warning against the 'various sects of Protestant Dissenters, who have . . . by their damnable schism, cut themselves off from Christ's mystical body the Church: and indeed, none can be truly loyal subjects who do not embrace the doctrines of obedience and non-resistance' (pp. 157–8). Berkeley was a long-standing friend of the noted High Churchman Dr. George Horne, President of Magdalen College, Oxford, Dean of Canterbury and bishop of Norwich from 1790 until his death in 1792. He also had close links with the Scottish Episcopal Church and assisted the American Samuel Seabury to secure episcopal consecration in Scotland in 1784. 'His principles were those of a Tory and a High Churchman, but he was a friend to universal Toleration,' the *Gentleman's Magazine* reported at the time of Berkeley's death. As Rector of St. Clement Danes, he had attempted to introduce 'chanting the Psalms and preaching *in Pontificalibus*', and in the sermon at George Horne's consecration he had asserted, 'in the strongest terms, the high episcopal claims of divine right [and] that the priesthood is endowed with exclusive powers and has continued in uninterrupted succession'.[25] This was, indeed, an accurate summary of what Berkeley had said.

Visiting preachers appeared frequently in the pulpit at St. Clement Danes and many of these reinforced the High Church tone of the parish. During the critical period from 1687 to 1790, for example, sermons were delivered by several High Church clergy who later became Nonjurors.[26] Dr. Ralph Taylor, later a Nonjuring bishop, preached on 16 October 1687 and Thomas Aston, chaplain to the High Tory Earl of Clarendon, preached on 29 July, 26 August and 30 September 1688. Abednego Seller, author of the important *History of Passive Obedience since the Reformation* (1689) and its *Continuation* (1690), preached on 3 March 1689 and William Osborne, chaplain to the Nonjuring Viscount Weymouth, on 14 July, 25 August and 5 September 1689. Eminent Tory High Churchmen who did not become Nonjurors also preached at St. Clement Danes, including the young Francis Atterbury (on 10 April 1692 and 15 July 1693); Luke Milbourne (frequently, between 1692 and 1712); Dr. Henry Sacheverell (20 February and 23 October 1715, and again in April 1718); Andrew Snape (between 1698 and 1709); Philip Stubbs (between 1703 and 1720); Joseph Trapp (between 1712 and 1734) and Charles Wheatly (20 June and 4 July 1714 and 27 June 1716).

Membership of the congregation revealed a similar complexion. John Byrom, a lay Nonjuror, attended Sunday worship at St. Clement Danes regularly during his visits to London in 1735 and 1736.[27] Thomas, second son of the Nonjuring printer, William Bowyer (1699–1777), was baptised there on 24 September 1730.[28] Archibald Campbell, a Scottish Nonjuring bishop who lived in the parish and died there in 1744, was familiar with its High Church liturgical practices.[29] Parish bequests included £200 given in 1690 by Lady Middleton, wife of the later Jacobite Secretary of State.[30] Other residents in the parish of St. Clement Danes included the Nonjuring clergyman Matthias Earbery, arrested in September 1732 for 'publishing several scandalous Seditious and Treasonable libels, intituled the Universal Spy, or the Royal Oak Journal';[31] William Shippen, the Tory-Jacobite MP (1673–1743), of Norfolk Street[32] and Anne Drelincourt, dowager Viscountess Primrose, 'doyenne of the English Jacobites' with whom Prince Charles Edward stayed in Essex Street during September 1750.[33]

The area around St. Clement Danes Church was also noted for an element of High Tory and Jacobite publishing activity, although it held no kind of monopoly. Indeed, the most significant publishers of this kind of material were in business elsewhere. The Nonjuror James Bettenham (*fl.* 1712–74), for example, was in St. John's Lane;[34] George Strahan (*fl.* 1699–1756) was at the Golden Ball in Cornhill,[35] and John Wilford (*fl.* 1722–32) was at the 3 Golden Fleurs de Luces in Little Britain, where he had succeeded the high-flying George Sawbridge.[36] Moreover, some of the publishing businesses in the parish of St. Clement Danes were in no sense affected by the traditions of the Church itself. Samuel Buck, who operated from 'The Green Cannister by the Crown and Anchor Tavern, opposite St. Clement's Church' from *c.* 1749 to 1769, was an apolitical designer of topographical prints, best remembered, with his brother Nathaniel, for a series of magnificent panoramic views of English towns. James Hutton (*fl.* 1735–95) at 'The Bible and Sun, next the Rose Tavern, without Temple Bar' was a Methodist convert who published numerous works of Dissenting piety, including many of the writings of the Moravian Count Zinzendorf and the journal of George Whitefield.[37] Charles Reak, in business 'facing Crown Court, Butcher's Row' *c.* 1770, was actively involved with political disaffection and religious heterodoxy: he published a Wilkite mezzotint, *The Sweets of Liberty*, and later emigrated to North America, where he published a portrait of James Honyman, minister at Newport, Rhode Island, by Samuel Okey after Gains, on 2 November 1774.[38]

Nevertheless, a good deal of printed material of a High Tory or even Jacobite nature was readily available in the vicinity of St. Clement Danes. Sometimes it was just part of the mixed stock of a large, general, business. Thus, although publications by Andrew Millar (*fl.* 1728–68), one of the principal undertakers of Johnson's *Dictionary* in 1755 at 'Buchanan's Head, over against St. Clement's Church' and later opposite Catherine Street in the Strand, included Consett's *Present State of the Church in Russia*, advertised in *Fog's Weekly Journal* on 21 December 1728; *The Life of James Fitz-James, Duke of Berwick* (1738) and Thomas Carte's *Collection of Original Letters and Papers* (1739), Millar also published works of a very different nature, including the heterodox *Free and Candid Disquisitions* (1749) by John Jones, Arian Vicar of Alconbury.[39] Similarly, Ralph Minors of St. Clement's Churchyard (*fl.* 1738–42) published works on both sides during the controversy between orthodox High Churchmen and the Arian William Whiston.[40]

However, some publishers around St. Clement Danes had a more exclusively partisan reputation. Thomas Gardner (*fl.* 1735–63), at 'Cowley's Head without Temple Bar, opposite St. Clement's Church in the Strand', was well known to Johnson and has been regarded as the most likely actual printer of *Marmor Norfolciense*.[41] Arrested and examined in 1743 for printing *Old England's Te Deum*, Gardner later advertised *Memoirs of the Lives and Families of the Lords Kilmarnock, Cromertie and Balmerino*, and *A Sketch of the Life and Character of Mr. Ratcliffe* in 1746, and a *Brief History of England*, by the Nonjuring clergyman John Lindsay in 1763.[42] John Brett, whose name appears on the imprint of *Marmor Norfolciense*, was in business at 'the Golden Ball, over against St. Clement's Churchyard' from *c.* 1737 to 1745, and was known as the publisher of a group of opposition pamphlets directed against Sir Robert Walpole's administration. He also published *Common Sense, or, The Englishman's Journal*, run by Charles Molloy, an Irish Roman Catholic and former editor of *Fog's Weekly*, to which William King, Jacobite Principal of St. Mary Hall, Oxford, was a regular contributor.[43] William Bizet, a successor of Brett's at the Golden Ball, acquired notoriety in 1750–51 as a Jacobite publisher. On 4 February 1750 he was examined for selling *A Chart, wherein are marked all the different Routes of P[rince Charles] Edward in Great Britain*,[44] and in 1751 he acted as sole publisher of a mezzotint portrait, by John Faber II after Allen Ramsay, of Alexander Murray, brother of the Jacobite plotter Lord Elibank and later adviser to Prince Charles Edward Stuart.[45] Anne Dodd (*fl.* 1719–58), located at the Peacock, without Temple Bar and after 1743 near Essex Street in the Strand, was consistent in support of the Tory interest and a major retailer of the leading Tory paper, the *London Evening Post*. In 1737 action was taken against her by the authorities for her part in circulating a pamphlet, *The Tryal of Robert Nixon, a Nonjuring Clergy-Man, for a High Crime and Misdemeanour*.[46] This was not the first time she had assisted in the distribution of controversial material of this kind. In 1720 she had published a pamphlet, *A Letter to the Author of Mr Leslie's Defence*, by the Nonjuror Matthias Earbery: this had been followed in 1723 by an account of the Jacobite conspirator Christopher Layer,[47] and in 1725 by *A Letter from a Parishioner of St. Clement Danes, to the Rt Revd Father in God Edmund, Lord Bishop of London, occasion'd by his Lordship's causing the Picture over the Altar to be taken down*.

Dodd also published prints, many of which were explicitly aimed at a High Tory market.[48] In the *London Evening Post* for 17–19 June 1735, for example, she advertised a mezzotint, by Thomas Gardner after de Groot, published by John Faber II, of Thomas Coster, Tory MP for Bristol, who had been returned in 1734 after a violent contest.[49] Shortly after Sir Robert Walpole's resignation in 1742 she published the threepenny satire *A New Screen for an Old One; or the Screen of Screens*, together with the topical reissue of an original Screen satire of 1721 relating to the South Sea scandal.[50] Another inexpensive image published by Dodd appealed to the deepest kind of Tory loyalty:

> *Price Four-pence, or Three Shillings per Dozen, A Fine Head of the blessed Martyr King Charles I, representing his Majesty in his Dying Agonies, curiously engrav'd on a Copper-Plate by Mr Vertue, with the Presentment of the Grand Jury of the County of Middlesex in 1723, against those who vilified the Memory of that Martyr'd King . . . N.B. The Reason of this Copper-Plate being now sold and so cheap, is, That such Gentlemen as have a Regard for Monarchy and an Abhorrence of Commonwealth and Calves-Head Clubs, should buy Quantities of them to send down to their Tenants in the Country, to hang up in their Homes, that the unparallel'd Villany, committed as on that Day, may never be forgot.*[51]

This image of the Royal Martyr would have found a close parallel with the nearby picture inside St. Clement Danes Church. The example shows, in a small way, how the orthodox loyalty of this High Church parish interacted with everyday life, and may suggest why Samuel Johnson's long walks to Church made sense, after all.

Notes

1. F.A. Pottle and C.H. Bennett (eds.), *Boswell's Journal of A Tour to the Hebrides with Samuel Johnson, LL.D.* (New York, 1936), p. 6.
2. For the survival of daily morning and evening prayers at St. Andrew's into the nineteenth century see J. Wickham Legg, *English Church Life from the Restoration to the Tractarian Movement* (London, 1914), p. 108. The rich interior decoration is described in J.P. Malcolm, *Londinium Redivivum* (4 vols., London, 1802–7), II, pp. 200–1.
3. Hawkins, *Life*, p. 452. On his first coming to London, in March 1737, Johnson lodged in Exeter Street, adjoining Catherine Street on the north side of the Strand, about a quarter of a mile from St. Clement Danes, but closer still to the parish church of St. Mary-le-Strand. In 1740 and 1741 Johnson lodged near the Strand for two further periods, both very brief, and then in Bow Street: again, closer to St. Mary-le-Strand: Boswell, *Life*, III, pp. 405 n. 6, 534–6.
4. For a detailed description of the eighteenth-century parish, see J. Diprose, *Some Account of the Parish of St. Clement Danes* (1868), pp. 284–90.
5. For the Crown and Anchor Tavern, which had a great meeting room, measuring 84 feet by 35 feet, see Diprose, *Some Account*, p. 53. During the first half of the eighteenth century this was home to the Academy of Ancient Music from *c*. 1710 and to a Jacobite association, the Oak Society: see Paul Monod, *Jacobitism and the English People 1688–1788* (Cambridge, 1989), pp. 87, 230–1, 290. The St. Clement Danes altarpiece (discussed in this volume by Dr. Nicholson) was kept here for some years following its removal from the Vestry Room in the later part of the century.
6. For Gibbs, a Roman Catholic, see T. Friedman, *James Gibbs* (New Haven, 1984).
7. *St. James's Evening Post*, 26–28 September 1721. Identical reports appeared in the *Post Boy*, the *Weekly Journal*, *Applebee's Weekly Journal*, and other papers.
8. HMC *Finch*, II, p. 309, III, p. 74; P. Burger, 'Spymaster to Louis XIV: a Study of the Papers of the Abbé Eusèbe Renaudot' in Eveline Cruickshanks (ed.), *Ideology and Conspiracy: Aspects of Jacobitism, 1689–1759* (Edinburgh, 1982), p. 125.
9. Jenkin eventually complied in 1712 and was elected Master of St. John's: he held this post until his death in 1727. For Bishop Lake's *Declaration* see J.C.D. Clark, *English Society 1660–1832* (Cambridge, 2000), p. 85.
10. For the Nonjuring tradition at St John's, see J.H. Overton, *The Nonjurors* (London, 1902), pp. 186–98.
11. J.A. Venn, *Alumni Cantabrigienses*, I, pp. 312–13.
12. For the High Church tradition in the Church of England during the eighteenth century, see F.C. Mather, 'Georgian Churchmanship Reconsidered: Some Variations in Anglican Public Worship 1714–1830', *Journal of Ecclesiastical History*, 36 (1985), pp. 255–82; J.R. Sharp, 'New Perspectives on the High Church Tradition: Historical background 1730–1780', in Geoffrey Rowell (ed.), *Tradition Renewed: The Oxford Movement Conference Papers* (London, 1986), pp. 4–23; and Clark, *English Society 1660–1832*, passim.
13. Wickham Legg, *English Church Life*, pp. 31, 91, 108.
14. Malcolm, *Londinium Redivivum*, III, p. 395.

15. For an important investigation of this subject, see P.M. Doll, 'After the Primitive Christians: The Eighteenth-Century Anglican Eucharist in its Architectural Setting', *Alcuin/GROW Joint Liturgical Studies*, 37 (Cambridge, 1997), esp. pp. 25–41.

16. One church where this happened was St. Giles' Cripplegate (see Malcolm, *Londinium Redivivum*, III, p. 281). This had been the Church of Edward Stephens (d. 1706), author of *The Liturgy of the Ancients Represented* (London, 1696), a notable attempt to revive a material understanding of the eucharist along the lines of the Anglican liturgies of 1549 and 1637: Stephens had also been an advocate of daily eucharistic celebration (see W. Jardine Grisbrooke, *Anglican Liturgies of the Seventeenth and Eighteenth Centuries*, Alcuin Club Collections 40 (1958), pp. 37–56, 201–20). Others were St. Magnus Martyr (Malcolm, *Londinium Redivivum*, IV, p. 32) and St. Giles in the Fields (ibid., III, p. 491). The pelican alone featured at St. Michael Cornhill (ibid., IV, p. 503); St. Vedast, Farringdon Within, where Nathaniel Marshall, editor of Cyprian and writer on ecclesiastical discipline, had been Rector from 1716 to 1731 (ibid., IV, p. 636); St. Mary Abchurch (ibid., II, p. 324) and All Hallows' Lombard Street (ibid., I, p. 54). Figures of Moses and Aaron alone were to be found at St. Margaret Lothbury (ibid., IV, p. 110); St. Mary, Whitechapel (ibid., IV, p. 447); St. Michael Cornhill (ibid., IV, p. 503); and All Hallows' Barking (ibid., I, p. 421).

17. The use of stone in altars during this period is surveyed by Wickham Legg, *English Church Life*, pp. 134–6. Marble occurred at All Hallows the Great, St. Antholin's Watling Street, St. Mary Woolnoth and St. Mary, Rotherhithe. Porphyry, as at St. Clement Danes, was used at St. Bartholomew, Broad Street (ibid., p. 141). For the use of candles: ibid., pp. 139–44. Other examples were to be found at All Hallows' Barking (Malcolm, II, p. 421) and St. Botolph, Aldersgate (ibid., p. 549).

18. G.V. Bennett, 'Against the Tide: Oxford under William III', in L.S. Sutherland and L.G. Mitchell (eds.), *The History of the University of Oxford*, V (Oxford, 1986), p. 43.

19. *Historical Essay*, p. 96. For the 'usages' controversy, and its bearing on the eucharistic theology of the later Nonjurors, see Grisbrooke, *Anglican Liturgies*, esp. pp. 71–135.

20. *The Obligation*, p. 19, following Exodus xxviii. 2, and the Ornaments Rubric in the Common Prayer book, as interpreted by Anthony Sparrow, *A Rationale upon the Book of Common Prayer*.

21. Many of Lewis's recommendations were effected at St. Clement Danes. Parishes with pictures of King Charles I included St. Olave, Hart Street (*Notes and Queries*, I. i. 184–5); St. Botolph Bishopgate (Malcolm, *Londinium Redivivum*, I, pp. 340–1: this was a version of the portrait used as the frontispiece to the *Eikon Basilike*); St. Paul's Covent Garden, in stained glass and painting, by Lely (*New View of London* (1708), pp. 219–20) and St. Andrew Undershaft, where Dr. William Berriman, a noted High Churchman, was Rector between 1722 and 1749 (Malcolm, I, p. 64).

22. Rogers proceeded BA in 1697, MA in 1700, BD in 1710 and DD in 1721, and was also a Fellow of Corpus until his marriage in 1717.

23. The opinion of the Scottish Nonjuring bishop, Archibald Campbell: Bodleian MS. Eng. Th. *c.* 33 f. 403–4. For a recent discussion of Hutchinson's significance, see Clark, *English Society 1660–1832*, pp. 259–61.

24. Blackwell proceeded BA in 1719 and MA in 1722 (Venn, *Alumni Cantabrigienses*, I, p. 162).

25. *Gentleman's Magazine*, 65 (1795), pp. 85–6, 92–4, 235, 436–7, 739.

26. *Register of Visiting Preachers* (Westminster Record Office, B. 1049).

27. Richard Parkinson (ed.), *The Private Journals and Literary Remains of John Byrom* (Chetham Society, Manchester, 1854–57), I, pp. 569, 572, 576, 579, 595; II, pp. 7, 20, 26.

28. John Nichols, *Literary Anecdotes of the Eighteenth Century* (9 vols., London, 1812), I, p. 457.

29. Campbell reported that, quite exceptionally, the eucharistic Elements were reserved at St. Clement Danes, presumably for sick-communions (Campbell to Thomas Brett, 3 February 1730: Bodleian MS. Eng. Th. *c.* 30 f. 495). For Campbell, best remembered for his work on *The Doctrines of a Middle State between Death and the Resurrection* (1721), see J.H. Overton, *The Nonjurors* (1902), pp. 402–4, 445–6; and Clark, *Samuel Johnson*, pp. 127, 133, 135, 142, 155.

30. J. Diprose, *Some Account of the Parish of St. Clement Danes* (London, 1868), p. 21.

31. PRO, SPD 44/82/93, 96.

32. Sedgwick, *HC*, II, pp. 422–3.

33. Frank McLynn, *Charles Edward Stuart: A Tragedy in many Acts* (London, 1988), pp. 396, 398–9.

34. H.R. Plomer, *A Dictionary of the Printers and Booksellers who were at work in England, Scotland and Ireland from 1668–1725* (London, 1922), pp. 33–4.

35. Plomer, *Dictionary . . . 1688–1725*, p. 282. Strahan, the principal publisher of works by the Nonjuring intellectual Charles Leslie, had continued the loyalist publishing business of the Hindmarsh dynasty, ibid., p. 156.

36. For Wilford, see Plomer, p. 314; for Sawbridge, see ibid., p. 263.

37. In 1738 Hutton also advertised one of the earliest engraved portraits of Whitefield, a mezzotint by John Faber jun., after Beard (*London Evening Post*, 21–24 January 1738). See also Plomer, *A Dictionary . . . 1726–75* (London, 1932), pp. 134–5.

38. J. Chaloner Smith, *British Mezzotinto Portraits* (4 vols., London, 1883), pp. 952–3.

39. For Millar see Plomer, *Dictionary . . . 1726–75*, pp. 171–3. See also Boswell, *Life*, I, p. 287, n. 3.

40. See Plomer, *A Dictionary . . . 1726–75*, p. 173; Clark, *Samuel Johnson*, p. 156.

41. Boswell, *Life*, II, pp. 344–5. Gardner's probable involvement with *Marmor Norfolciense* has been explored by A.D. Barker: 'The Printing and Publishing of Johnson's *Marmor Norfolciense* (1739) and *London* (1738 and 1739)', *The Library*, 6th ser., III, no. 4 (December 1981), pp. 287–304. See also Plomer, *Dictionary of . . . 1726–1775*, pp. 100–1. Gardner collaborated extensively with Edward Cave in the period 1738–41; he also printed works by authors who had been contemporaries of Johnson's at Pembroke College, Oxford: Tipping Silvester's *A Critical Dissertation on Titus III, 10–11, wherein Mr. Foster's Notion of Heresy is Consider'd and Confuted and the Power of the Church to censure Hereticks is vindicated* (1738); and John Fludyer's *A Correct and familiar Exposition on the Common-Prayer Book of the Church of England, collected from the Works of Bishop Sparrow, Bishop Andrewes, Bishop Beveridge, Bishop Pearson, Dr. Comber, Dr. Nichols, Dr. Bisse and other Divines* (1739). Silvester (1700–68) was a Fellow of Pembroke, where Fludyer (1712–73) had matriculated in November 1728, less than three weeks before Johnson. Johnson's later opinion of Fludyer was low (Boswell, *Life*, II, p. 444), but the *Exposition*, with its hostility towards 'Deistical, Arian and Socinian Notions concerning the Object of Worship' (*preface*) and detailed paraphrase and vindication of the Athanasian Creed (pp. 144–204) was calculated to appeal to an orthodox High Church market.

42. *London Evening Post*, 14–16 April 1763.
43. For John Brett see Plomer, *Dictionary . . . 1726–75*, p. 33, and Clark, *Samuel Johnson*, pp. 156–7. In 1739 *Common Sense* was presented at the Court of King's Bench as a seditious libel: Brett was prosecuted again in 1740 and 1745 (PRO, SPD 36/48/34–39, 36/50/270, 44/82/174, 182, 223). John Brett was possibly related to the Nonjuring bishop Thomas Brett (1667–1744) and may also have been related to Katherine Brett, bookseller of St. Clement Danes, who was prosecuted in January 1744 for selling William Shropshire's *Old England's Te Deum* (PRO SPD 44/82/194–6).
44. For the map see J.R. Sharp, *The Engraved Record of the Jacobite Movement* (Aldershot, 1996), no. 755. The account of Bizet's examination is at PRO SPD 36/116/21-v.
45. Chaloner Smith, *British Mezzotinto Portraits*, J. Faber II, no. 251; Sharp, *Engraved Record*, no. 538.
46. The warrant for Anne Dodd's arrest is at PRO SPD 44/82/136. The printer, Samuel Slow of Devereux Court, without Temple Bar and the bookseller John Torbuck, also of St. Clement Danes were taken up at the same time: see Clark, *Samuel Johnson*, p. 152 n. 52. For Dodd see Plomer, *Dictionary . . . 1726–75*, p. 75, T.J. Clayton, *The English Print 1688–1802* (New Haven, 1997), pp. 9–10, 112 and H.M. Atherton, *Political Prints in the Age of Hogarth* (1974), p. 13.
47. Advertised in the *Whitehall Evening Post*, 18–21 May 1723.
48. Not all Dodd's publications were like this: cf. her advertisement for an engraving by Vertue of the Hanoverian Prince Frederick (*Post Boy*, 27–30 June 1719).
49. The print is described in Chaloner Smith, *British Mezzotinto Portraits*, p. 333. For Coster, see Sedgwick, *HC*, I, p. 583.
50. *London Evening Post*, 16–18 March 1742.
51. *London Evening Post*, 13–15 February 1735.

3

The St. Clement Danes Altarpiece and the Iconography of post-Revolution England[1]

Eirwen E.C. Nicholson

> In England, religion does not avail itself of the assistance of paint-
> ing to inspire devotion; their churches at the most are adorned with
> an altarpiece, which nobody takes notice of.
>
> A. Rouquet, *The Present State of the Arts in England*
> (London, 1755)[2]

The characteristics which are likely to have informed Johnson's preference
for the church of St. Clement Danes are the subject of Richard Sharp's contribution to this volume. This essay offers the first full examination of that
church's earlier claim to public notice, the altarpiece controversy of 1726,
remembered now only from one of William Hogarth's early and uncele-
brated print satires. It is, indeed, Hogarth rather than Johnson who domi-
nates this essay, although the episode may further illuminate Johnson's own
gravitation to St. Clement Danes. What the 1726 controversy and Hogarth's
role in it suggest, it will be argued, is that during Johnson's formative years,
the dynastic issue informed the very act of seeing and thus the iconology –
the discussion of pictures – at precisely that time in which conventional art
history has located the emergence of new discourses whereby eighteenth-
century England would accommodate and develop the visual arts.[3]

In 1720/21, the church of St. Clement Danes in the Strand commissioned
an altarpiece (Plate 1) from William Kent, protégé of the third Earl of
Burlington. Full payment for the work is recorded in the Churchwardens'
Accounts of late August 1721[4] and the picture is described as 'just finish'd'
in the *Post Boy* of 26–28 September of the same year.

At what point it was installed is not clear, but it was not until August 1725
that its presence excited controversy. Readers of the London press were
informed that Kent's painting was

> a musical representation, variously explained, some finding in it St.
> Cecilia and her Harp, and some Princess Sobieski and her Son [that is,
> Queen Maria Clementina, wife of the exiled Stuart monarch, and Prince

Charles Edward Stuart, Prince of Wales], but the generality agreeing it was not a thing proper to be placed there; upon complaints to the Bishop of London [Edmund Gibson], at his last Visitation of the said Church, we hear his Lordship, in order to secure the solemnity of the place and worship, hath lately very prudently ordered the churchwardens to take it down.[5]

That the church was slow in complying with Gibson's order (as claimed by the *Daily Journal* of 27 August and 4 September and the *Post Boy* of 4 September) is borne out by the Churchwardens' Accounts.[6] These also confirm the chronology of the painting's deposition offered by the *Evening Post* of 7 September: 'the picture over the altar in St. Clement Danes was taken down, pursuant to the order of the Bishop of London' on 'Saturday last' (that is, 4 September or very shortly thereafter), recording as they do payment on 11 September of 10*s*.6*d*. 'to Mr. Sayer for Bays [i.e., baize] to fill up the Frame were [*sic*] the Alterpiece was taken out'.[7]

The picture was removed to the Vestry Room, where, according to the inventories, which survive to 1754, it remained until 1752 being then moved to 'the long Room'.[8] Far from being a dingy back-room, the Vestry Room would appear to have been a very comfortably appointed, semi-public meeting-place; the 1734 inventory records the painting's presence together with 'one Ovall Table – two Dozen of Rushin [in 1726 'Russia'] chaires a Great Hazitoon Chaire & Cushion to it a large Turkey Carpett . . . Two new Mahogany Presses to put the parish books & writings in a Looking Glass three wooden Standishes and Crimson Mantua Silk Curtaines for the Windows'.[9]

The picture's removal from the public gaze was not, however, sufficient to still the controversy. On 10 September a pamphlet was published, purporting to come from a parishioner of the church and congratulating the Bishop upon his prompt action.[10] Kent's painting is condemned as a 'ridiculous, superstitious Piece of Popish Foppery', a 'Vile and impertinent . . . Representation' and its removal hailed as acceptable 'to all true Protestants' and 'all honest Men'. The anonymous author defied anyone to deny that

the Picture of that Angel in white Garment and blue Mantle, which is there supposed to be beating time to the Music, is not directly a great Likeness of that Princess; this I insist on, and will stand or fall by my Assertion, provided they do not play any Tricks with the Picture, or alter it for Contradiction sake now it is down.[11]

Confident in his identification, he demanded to know 'To what End or Purpose was it put there, but to *affront* our *most gracious Sovereign*, by placing at our very *Altar*, the *known Resemblance* of a Person, who is the Wife of his *utter Enemy*, and *Pensioner* to the *Whore of Babylon*?' Its presence had rendered the Church a mecca for the idle and the curious ('a continual *hurly-burly of Loiterers*, from *all* Parts of the *Town* to see our popish *Raree Show'*) the motives of many of whom were suspect, and for whom attendance at divine service was potentially an occasion of both idolatry and treason:

> our Church has been throng'd with Spectators, to the great Hindrance of *Divine Worship*, and *Annoyance* of the Parishioners, when those Crouds of Irreverend Persons, which were ever *pouring* in, came not there to join in *Prayer* with the rest of the Congregation, but to worship their *popish Saint*, and hug themselves in the Conceit of being alone in the *Secret*.[12]

We lack a publication date for the print by William Hogarth (Plate 2), which is the only known graphic contribution to the controversy and which is at the centre of this essay. It does, however, contain a reference to the taking down of the painting, so that Hogarth's entry into the controversy cannot have pre-dated the first week of September.[13] As far as it is possible to tell from the poor photograph (Plate 1) which is our only visual record of the altarpiece (destroyed during the Blitz), Hogarth's print exaggerates Kent's draughtsmanship but does not deviate from the composition of the original in any significant respect. The supporting inscription is a model of disingenuous disinterestedness and veracity:

> This Print is exactly Engraiv'd after ye Celebrated Altar-Peice in St. Clement Church which has been taken down by Order of ye Lord Bishop of London {as tis thought} to prevent Disputs and Laying of wagers among ye Parrshioners about ye Artists meaning in it, for publick Satisfaction here is a particular Explanation of it humbly Offerd to be writ under ye *Original*, that it may be put up again by which means ye Parish'es 60 pounds which they wisely gave for it may not be Entirely lost 1st Tis not the Pretender's Wife and Children[14] as our weak brethren imagin 2ly Nor St. Cecilia as the Connoisseurs think but a Choir of Angells playing in Consort[.]

This inscription is in turn supported by a lettered key ostensibly breaking down the composition of the painting, but in many instances identifying alleged deficiencies in draughtsmanship (for example, 'F} the inside of his Leg, but whether right or Left is yet undiscover'd'). This print, with which – significantly, as this essay will suggest – Hogarth scholars have failed to engage, and the context in which it appeared, merit closer examination because they suggest that Hogarth's well-documented hostility towards Kent and the Burlington cultural nexus partook of a political dimension, which, it can be argued, also informed Hogarth's efforts to define and establish a contemporary English art, but to which both old and 'new' art histories, and Hogarth studies, have been insensitive.

Before considering the significance of Hogarth's participation in this episode, it is necessary to return to Kent's painting and the objections which it excited, and to consider the grounds for controversy which the commission offered. Previous accounts of the episode have registered the Jacobite credentials of the painting only to dismiss them. Ronald Paulson's verdict, for example, is that Kent was 'apparently so influenced by Italian art that he unthinkingly produced a subject at odds with Protestant tradition . . . and through sheer clumsiness stumbled into a likeness of the Pretender's wife'.[15] Conversely, J. Wickham Legg is sceptical on the grounds that the figure identified as Clementina was not that of St. Cecilia herself but that of an attendant angel, a subordinate placing in the composition which a 'true Jacobite' would have found 'disrespectful'.[16]

Other than the record of payment noted above, primary evidence for the commission itself is wanting. Circumstantial evidence, however, suggests that if contemporaries erred in fixing a Jacobite signification onto Kent's painting, their error was understandable. The first such evidence concerns the identification of 'the angel in the white garment . . . beating time to the music' with Clementina (from which the identification of secondary figures as her son, or sons, would follow). The poor quality of the photograph of the altarpiece militates against any conclusive comparison with portraits of Clementina, but at least one hint to this end had already appeared in the quasi-Jacobite press. May 1723 saw the publication in *The Loyal Observator Reviv'd* of a piece in the 'Instructions to a Painter' genre in which 'Dr Gaylard' addresses a painter who can only be Kent:

Mr Painter, As I am going to set up a new Printing-House, I would adorn my Gallery with several sorts of Pictures of a peculiar Fancy and Beauty . . . You have been in Italy, and there gained immortal Glory [a reference to Kent's having been awarded the Pope's prize for painting in 1713] . . . You have since given your soft Strokes of Art to the *Altar-Piece* of *St. Clement's* Church. There the sweet *Cecilia* displays, at one View, the finest Turn of Face and Mind. Who cannot but admire your Strength of Fancy, to take the Image from the warm Original, and transfer the beauteous Shades into an *English* Church.[17]

The phrase 'the warm Original' is suggestive; the reference to 'Cecilia' must be set against Wickham-Legg's grounds for dismissing the accusations of Jacobitism in the painting. It also suggests that the painting was known in London at this date, two years after its completion but two years before it attracted controversy.

The author of the *Letter from a Parishioner* was confident in his identification: 'When I say known Resemblance, I speak not only according to my own Knowledge, but appeal to all Mankind who have seen the Princess Sobieski or any Picture or Resemblance of her'.[18] 'A Parishioner' does not elaborate on the source of his 'own Knowledge', but representations of Clementina had been available in London from the period of her marriage to James Francis Edward Stuart in 1718 (indeed, the *Letter*, in one of several Hogarthian swipes at Kent's Italian training, asks whether the artist of the altarpiece was not also responsible for the importation of such prints or other representations).[19] The sixteen-year-old Princess's exotic Polish background and the dramatic circumstances of her marriage (*en route* to Italy she had been captured and imprisoned by the Emperor at the request of George I)[20] rendered her a figure of interest even to non-Jacobites; an interest which newspaper advertisements of the period 1719–20 show to have taken the conventional form of portrait prints.[21]

Prints sold openly would have avoided the risk of prosecution or harassment[22] by omitting any identifying inscription (unlike Plate 3) or by recourse to such oblique identifications as 'A Polish Lady' or 'a Polish Princess now residing at Rome', but the identity of the sitter would not have been in doubt. It is not unreasonable, then, to suggest that those who claimed to discover her in Kent's altarpiece based their identification on familiarity with such portrait engravings. Such engravings might, moreover, have been purchased only a few yards from the church itself. In the decades before 1760, the attention of the authorities was frequently excited by the availability of publications of a Nonjuring and Jacobite tenor from booksellers and publishers in the immediate vicinity of St. Clement Danes.[23] That such dealers would have been potential sources for, among other items, prints of Clementina is, again, a reasonable proposition.

The tenor of publishing in the vicinity is of a piece with what is known of St. Clement Danes itself. 'A Parishioner' might exclaim 'can any thing be more absurd than such a Picture in such a Place!?' but, as Richard Sharp demonstrates, St. Clement Danes was a church whose spiritual nexus was until well into the second half of the century High Church and Nonjuring, and whose political nexus was Tory and potentially crypto-Jacobite.[24] Nor was Kent's altarpiece the only work of art acquired by the church which it would have been possible to construe as a political statement; in the same year (1721) in which payment to Kent is recorded, the church acquired a fine portrait of Charles I as Martyr.[25] Among visiting preachers, Henry Sacheverell preached twice in 1715, the year in which his name was invoked in a series of anti-Hanoverian riots in several parts of the country, and again in 1718.[26]

The *Letter from a Parishioner* complains in general terms of Jacobite influence in the vestry (perhaps the clergyman and several parishioners reported in the press as having attempted to overturn Gibson's injunction against the painting),[27] and would appear to have one particular individual in mind when he exhorts Gibson to 'further enquire after the Person who employ'd'

Kent, 'Whether he be a Protestant? Or, If he call himself so, whether his Children were not sent Abroad to popish Seminaries for Education'.[28] The identities and motives of those who commissioned the altarpiece have yet to be established, not least the identity of the individual on whose Protestantism 'A Parishioner' casts doubt.[29] Rather more is known, however, of another figure associated with St. Clement Danes in *c.* 1720, Thomas Lewis. Ordained in 1713, Lewis (1689–1749?) was the author of *The Scourge, A Vindication of the Church of England* (1717), a short-lived periodical ('weekly excrement', in the words of one of its detractors)[30] distinguished by its 'violent and trenchant abuse of dissenters, broad churchmen and papists' for which he was presented to the grand jury at Westminster as 'a libeller and embroiler of the nation'.[31] Ordered to stand trial for sedition before the King's Bench, Lewis went into hiding, from which position he responded with *The Danger of the Church Establishment of England from the Insolence of the Protestant Dissenters* and subsequently (1719) *The Anatomy of the Heretical Synod of Dissenters at Salters-Hall*.[32] Lewis appears to have come to St. Clement Danes as a curate at some point in 1720, and it is to the churchwardens and vestry of the church that he dedicated *The Obligation of Christians to beautify and adorn their Churches . . . , from the Practice of the Primitive Church and from the Discipline of the Church of England Established by Law*, published in the year in which St. Clement Danes acquired both its Royal Martyr and its altarpiece. There is no evidence that it was Lewis who headed the attempt to overturn Gibson's decision, but it would be a gesture characteristic of a cleric who combined combativeness with a commitment to church furniture.

If the identity of those most closely connected with the commission is obscure, the chronology of the controversy also raises questions which the available evidence does not answer. With the exception of the *Loyal Observator* reference, Kent's painting does not appear to have excited notice until the summer of 1725. It would be reasonable to assume that the controversy and particularly its emphasis on visual encoding were informed by the climate of suspicion created by the discovery of the Atterbury Plot three years before. Yet this begs the question of the painting's uncontroversial presence (as it may be supposed) in the church at the very time of the Atterbury revelations, when the new altarpiece at St. Clement Danes might have offered those with an interest in exposing the tenacity of Stuart sympathies within the Established Church a timely *casus belli*. At the parish level, moreover, any who sought to implicate the incumbent and vestry might be expected to have taken more immediate advantage of this climate. Unless the *Post Boy* announcement was premature and the painting was *not* 'finish'd' in 1721, or else, contrary to what is implied by Gaylard, was not on public display above the altar before 1725,[33] the 'breaking' of the St. Clement Danes controversy can only be assumed to have its roots in internal, parish, politics as yet unrecovered.

Returning to the Jacobite credentials of Kent's painting, it is suggestive that while the polemic against the picture employed the conventional rhetoric of Protestant iconophobia, with 'A Parishioner' doubting whether 'ANY PICTURE CAN BE PROPER' in a Protestant church,[34] the untroubled career of another, virtually contemporary, altarpiece by Kent – that of the new church of St. George's, Hanover Square (1725)[35] – suggests that it was on political as opposed to doctrinal grounds that the St. Clement Danes image was found objectionable and dangerous.

The closest precedent for the St. Clement Danes controversy would appear to bear this out. Eleven years previously, in 1714, an altarpiece depicting the Last Supper commissioned by Dr. Richard Welton (Nonjuror, 1715)[36] for St. Mary's Whitechapel had provoked a flurry of journalistic activity concerning the allegedly deliberate and provocative resemblance of, first, the figure of Judas Iscariot to White Kennett, dean and later Bishop of Peterborough and odious to Jacobites and 'high-flyers' within the Church of England for his vocal support for the Revolution settlement in Church and State, and, anticipating the allegations against Kent's painting, the resemblance of a youthful disciple to James Francis Edward Stuart. Like the St. Clement Danes painting, that at Whitechapel drew 'multitudes' of the curious to the church on a daily basis and elicited, aside from several pamphlets and letters to the press, at least one print and counter-print in which its claims to the character of 'a dumb Libel' were contested. The Whig *Daily Courant* offered a ten guinea reward for information leading to the prosecution of the promoter of the design, and the attention which the painting received in 'the Publick Prints' forced the hand of the then Bishop of London, John Robinson. On 26 April it was ordered to be taken down 'since the said Picture, by SOME of the Figures there represented, will give an Occasion of Scandal and Offence, if continu'd there'. As at St. Clement Danes, this order was contested; more emphatically, indeed, than would be the case in 1725, with Welton taking the case (unsuccessfully) to the Court of Delegates.[37] Unsurprisingly, the episode features heavily in the *Letter from a Parishioner* as another instance whereby

the *Enemies* of our *Church* took . . . an *Opportunity* to *prophane* the *Church* . . . by making [God's] *Holy Altar* the Scene of their *Ribaldry*, to be approached with *Wantonness and Curiosity*, by the *Sons of Belial*,[38] who come there to *decypher* the *dumb Libel*, and sneer at the *pictur'd Lampoon*.[39]

In both cases the polemic turned on the propriety of religious images in Anglican churches. Thomas Lewis's dedication of his 1721 treatise on *The Obligation of Christians to Beautify and Adorn their Churches* to the church-wardens and vestry of St. Clement Danes has already been noted. In 1714, Welton published a sermon, *Church-Ornament without Idolatry Vindicated*, responses to which included *The Judgement of the Church of England, concerning Images and Pictures in Churches* and *Images an Abomination to the Lord: Or, Dr. Kenet's Reasons for pulling Down the Altarpiece at White-Chapel.*[40]

In this context, the absence of controversy with regard to Kent's altarpiece at St. George's Hanover Square is worth recalling, suggesting as it does that it was only when a conventional and residual Protestant iconophobia was joined with the insecurities of the *de facto* monarchy that contemporaries were drawn to iconology, or the discourse of images.[41] Relevant instances include the pamphlet and newspaper debates in which the Jacobite credentials of the engraved allegories which accompanied the *Oxford Almanacs* (dismissed by Shaftesbury in 1712 as 'Those famous academical anaglyphics, of annual edition – emblematic nostradamus's . . . renowned for prophecies in church and state')[42] for the years 1700, 1701, 1702, 1706, 1710, 1711, 1712, 1717, 1733 and 1755 were held up to scrutiny.[43] The suspicion of the potential for hidden meanings and 'hieroglyphick' correspondences in pictures to which the *Oxford Almanac* literature testifies was to be further excited by the role of verbal symbolisation in the evidence for the Atterbury Plot.[44]

At the heart of this discourse lay a set of conflicting assumptions concerning the rhetorical capacity of the pictorial image. On the one hand, the demands that the St. Clement Danes painting be removed from public display testify to a fear of the articulacy and appeal of the image.[45] At the same time, the politically grounded *ekphrases* of the 'Explanations' and 'unriddlings' of the *Oxford Almanac* pictures and the pamphlet exposés of the Whitechapel and St. Clement Danes altarpieces testify to anxiety that the 'true' messages of these pictures might in fact elude those contemporaries who were not 'in the secret'. These messages had therefore to be spelt out before they and the pictures which carried them (and, ideally, the contrivers of those images) could be repudiated.

These politically grounded *ekphrases* should therefore be seen as exercises in the control of the reception of these and related images. Hogarth's contribution to the St. Clement Danes controversy exemplifies this. The print's inscription refers to the 'disputes and laying of wagers among the parishioners about the artist's meaning'; Hogarth's sardonic suggestion that his 'Explanation' be inscribed under the altarpiece, allowing it to remain on display, can be seen as an attempt to render the painting impotent by closing it down, as it were, to one level of meaning.

One problem, of course, was that such exercises could be counterproductive, alerting the sympathetic to the possibility of a level of signification in an image which, whether it was intended by the authors of the image or existed only in the eye of the accuser, might otherwise have gone unseen. The other problem was (and is) that the very susceptibility of the pictorial image to *ekphrasis* could frustrate attempts to place political limits on its meaning. As the author of *The Oxford Almanack of 1712, Explain'd* acknowledged:

tho' I were infallibly certain that I hit right in explaining the Design and Meaning of the Contrivers [. . .] still, it were impossible to prove to others that I had at all hit their Meaning, in case Men of their Kidney had a mind to controvert it.[46]

It was this aspect of the pictorial which operated against attempts to retaliate by recourse to the law, notwithstanding the demands of Sir John Gonson, a pro-ministerial magistrate whom Hogarth was later to include in the third plate of *A Harlot's Progress*, that pictorial material be prosecuted as 'Dumb Scandal' or 'Scandal by Pictures or by Signs'.[47]

Hogarth's 'burlesque' of Kent's altarpiece can, then, be seen as a contribution to a political discourse of images which was at least twenty-five years old.[48] Like the altarpiece which it subverts, however, Hogarth's print has long been regarded as a minor work of limited interest. It is notably omitted from a 1987 study which professed the intention of reappraising Hogarth's prints of the 1720s as a related (and politically coherent) body of work.[49]

The St. Clement Danes satire was the second print published by Hogarth hostile to Kent and Burlington and the 'connoisseurship' with which they are associated.[50] It has been conventional to interpret Hogarth's attacks on Burlington and Kent in terms of a struggle for the limited patronage available to English artists in this period, and where the St. Clement Danes episode is mentioned, the print is explained as an act of retaliation on Hogarth's part for Kent's having wrested the commission of the decorative painting at Kensington Palace from Sir James Thornhill, with whose interest Hogarth closely identified, and which interest was suffering as a direct consequence of the efforts of Burlington on behalf of his protégé.[51]

A related orthodoxy has characterised the print as a satire which was justified by the weaknesses of the original painting. Thus F.G. Stephens in the British Museum *Catalogue of Personal and Political Satires* disparages Kent's composition as being 'in the debased mode of late Italian art'.[52] For Ronald Paulson a century later, the print confirms that Kent could be 'a ridiculously bad painter' with a poor grasp of anatomy.[53] Michael Wilson's 1984 biography of Kent takes the same line; Hogarth's print satirises what 'seems quite simply to have been a bad picture, revealing only too well just those deficiencies in Kent's technique' which his decorative painting to some extent hid.[54] The Jacobite dimension to the controversy is consistently marginalised.[55]

If, however, we reconsider Kent's altarpiece in the light of the circumstantial evidence offered above, and in the context of the character of St. Clement Danes' churchmanship, we may also reconsider Hogarth's engagement in the St. Clement Danes controversy, the political or ideological basis of Hogarth's aesthetic, and his repudiation of that of the Burlington circle. The past decade has seen some reassessment of the politics of Lord Burlington and of the implications of this for Burlington as architect and patron.[56] If the emergent picture of a figure sympathetic to a Stuart restoration is correct, then it is possible that Hogarth's antagonism – as manifested in his participation in the St. Clement Danes controversy – partook of a political dimension.

It was for many years conventional to present Hogarth as an apolitical figure whose critiques of contemporary society, while seldom wanting in political allusion, were, at least until the 1760s, non-partisan.[57] In recent years, however, as part of a larger historiographical shift within the discipline of art history, this approach to Hogarth has been revised.[58] The emphases and omissions of this retrospective politicisation continue, however, to obscure the religious and dynastic perspectives which can be shown to inform Hogarth's self-conscious chauvinism and his repudiation of the 'tyranny' of Continental models.[59]

Taking its cue from the historical orthodoxies of the day, both pre-Paulsonian and Paulsonian Hogarth scholarship marginalised Jacobitism as a political irrelevance and an intellectual anachronism.[60] At the same time, preoccupation with Hogarth as a critic of his society to a great extent distracted attention from the fact that Hogarth's critique of the Hanoverian present[61] offers no evidence of sympathy for the Stuart past[62] still less a restoration. His several paintings of the Hanoverian royal family aside, Hogarth's support for the *de facto* monarchy can be said to be implicit in the (variously) Latitudinarian, Dissenting and Deist theology, 'Shaftesburian philosophy and Whiggish politics' which have been identified as significant influences upon the artist's aesthetic.[63]

The extent to which Hogarth's aesthetic, as articulated in his published and unpublished writings, is informed by the selective xenophobia and violent 'no popery' of popular anti-Jacobitism has been insufficiently explored.[64] Hogarth's terms and metaphors of choice in his writings are, however, characteristic, consistent and significant.[65] The aesthetic to which he is opposed – that of the connoisseurs represented by Burlington and Kent – is repudiated in terms which recall the contemporary conceptualisation of Roman Catholicism. Recurrent tropes of sight and blindness – 'I have hope of succeeding a little with such as *dare think for themselves* and can *believe their own eyes*' (emphases added) (as opposed to those who 'imbibing false oppinions [*sic*], in favour of pictures and statues, and thus by losing sight of nature, ['these who take things upon trust': struck through] ... *blindly* descend, by such kind of prejudices, into the coal pit of conoiseiurship [*sic*]; where the cunning dealers in obscure works lie in wait')[66] – echo the phraseology of, to take just one example, Charles Leslie's *The Case Stated Between the Church of Rome and the Church of England* (1714), in which transubstantiation is repudiated as *deceptio visus* and (Anglican) reason is equated with clarity of sight. According to Leslie's Anglican protagonist, a man will ultimately 'Thank those who have raised him ... to *Seeing* with his own

Eyes, instead of being led by others *Implicitly* in the *Dark'*. 'The Bigot' in 'his *Blindness'*, however, is 'Persuaded there is less Danger of *Stumbling*, than if his *Eyes* were open . . . does not a Stick look *Crooked* in the *Water*? Why then should I trust my Eyes . . . ?'[67] Hogarth's association of connoisseurship with the *deceptio visus* of popery is explicit in his characterisation of connoisseurs as those who 'have been brought up to the *old religion* of pictures who love to deceive and delight in *antiquity* and the marvelous and *what they do not understand'* (emphases added).[68]

The terms 'bigot', 'biggoted' and 'bigotry' which recur in Leslie's *Case* against the Roman faith are favourites with Hogarth, occurring, significantly, in passages in which connoisseurship is associated with false religion or idolatry.[69] Thus he claims that ignorance of the serpentine line which accounts for 'elegance' in even the more imperfect artworks of antiquity has made their effects appear 'mysterious and [has] drawn mankind into a sort of religious esteem and even bigotry'. In a frequently quoted passage in his unfinished 'Autobiographical Notes', Hogarth contrasts his own 'notions of Painting' with 'those of Bigots who have taken theirs from books or upon trust' – usually interpreted as a thrust at Burlington and the Palladians, as, similarly, his reference to 'some biggoted Architect, or Builder, who holds the five orders as sacred as the Jews do their Pentateuch . . . and dare not strike a stroke without book'.[70]

The metaphors of sight, blindness and deceit recur in the letter of 7–9 June 1737 to the *St James Evening Post* signed 'Britophil' and attributed to Hogarth. Exhorting English patrons 'to see with their own Eyes', 'Britophil' vilifies 'Picture-Jobbers from abroad' who confuse the judgement and pervert the natural taste of Britons, and decries the debased taste for 'dead Christs, holy families Madonnas and other dismal dark objects'.[71] What is significant about the Britophil letter is that, like Hogarth's satires on Kent, it entails the defence of Sir James Thornhill. More particularly, it is a defence of Thornhill's decorative painting at Greenwich Hospital; that is to say, the allegories of the Glorious Revolution and Hanoverian Succession, painted between 1708 and 1727. Thornhill's commitment to the latter is suggested by his incorporation of an emphatic self-portrait in the company of George I and his family.[72] In Hogarth's defence of Thornhill's achievement, an 'English' aesthetic is implicitly associated with Protestantism (the rejection of Madonnas and dead Christs) and Protestantism with the settlements of 1688 and 1714. The settlements of 1688 and 1714 entail the repudiation of 'holy families' – and of representations of them.

In his *Apology for Painters* (1761) Hogarth characterised connoisseurs as those who 'bring over wonderful copies of bad originals adored for their names only'.[73] To those who believed – or found it convenient to believe – the warming-pan myth, James Francis Edward Stuart could be repudiated as a 'wonderfull [i.e. a suppositious] copy' of a 'bad original' – James II.[74] The phrase is also suggestive of the portrait engravings by means of which it was felt that *de jure* loyalties might be both perpetuated or inspired. Similarly, those 'adored for their names only' could mean both the Continental artists, including the Italian-trained Kent, preferred by the connoisseurs to the alleged detriment of English art, and the family to whom Hogarth would deny an hereditary claim. The word 'adored' is also suggestive; as in the polemic against the St. Clement Danes altarpiece, Jacobitism and idolatry are implicitly equated.[75]

The satire upon the St. Clement Danes altarpiece is of a piece with this interpretation of Hogarth's aesthetic. It has been claimed as a characteristic of Hogarth's method as a satirist that this entails the destruction (or at least the subversion) of the very iconographic models upon which the satire is based,

> removing any sense of the 'alluded-to' as an ideal . . . As a result of this aggressive scrutiny-by-transformation, certain aesthetic interpretations of the past . . . and certain of its themes, actions, and characters are exposed as *ideologically misleading, morally false, and inappropriate to Georgian London*

words which both Hogarth and 'A Parishioner' might have applied to the St. Clement Danes altarpiece.[76]

There is, then, a sense in which Hogarth's engagement in this episode and his 'war with the connoisseurs' was about more than a struggle for patronage. It was about the iconography appropriate to post-Revolution England. To make this claim is to recall the terms in which F.D. Klingender defended Hogarth's repudiation of the Baroque and his failure 'to beat the Italianizers at their own game' in his own essays in history painting: 'an art which expressed the final triumph of the counter-reformation and of absolutism could not but conflict with everything Hogarth, *the painter of eighteenth-century England*, stood for' (emphases added).[77] It is to acknowledge a political dimension to English philistinism in this period – a 'philistinism and liberty' thesis, as it were (Vicesimus Knox's 'We shall not easily find a Hampden in a connoisseur') – in which, his advocacy of an English school of painting notwithstanding, Hogarth partook.[78]

The marginalisation of Jacobitism in Paulsonian Hogarth scholarship ensured an inadequate contextualisation of the St. Clement Danes altarpiece episode. David Dabydeen's omission of this print from his attempted recovery of the political 'thematic unity of [Hogarth's] prints of the 1720s' is not the only evidence that post-Paulsonian scholarship has yet to accommodate the scholarly reclamation of Jacobitism[79] as 'part of the cultural totality' of England in this period in its assessment of the artist hailed by his contemporaries as the 'all-reflecting mirror of the age'.[80] For Sean Shesgreen, for example, Hogarth's rejection of the 'old religion of pictures' and his insistence on seeing with his own eyes are evidence of his promotion of 'Lockeian empiricism' in art, a promotion which was 'well-suited to the anti-authoritarian, individualistic spirit and utilitarian outlook of the middle classes with their secular, highly rational vision of things'.[81] But if the 'new art history' offers a Hogarth created in its own image, a liberal, secular and anti-monarchical figure engaged with the issues of class, gender and race,[82] the St. Clement Danes episode allows us not only to explore an episode of which Johnson will have been cognisant, but to reconsider another figure whose verbal and visual polemic was a significant and self-conscious contribution to the iconology as well as the iconography of Hanoverian England.

Notes

1. Preliminary versions of this essay were read in 1995 at the 3rd Burlington Conference, London, and the Royal Stuart Society symposium, 'London and Jacobitism', at the Courtauld Institute. I am indebted to the subsequent generosity of Richard Sharp who pursued my St. Clement Danes archival enquiries simultaneously with his own.
2. Facsimile reprint (London, 1970) introduction by R.W. Lightbown, p. 27. For Rouquet's relationship with Hogarth, see Ronald Paulson, *Hogarth: his Life, Art and Times* (hereafter Paulson, *HLAT*) (2 vols., London, 1971), II, pp. 203, 211.
3. For an illuminating study of Johnson's attitude to the visual arts and its historiography, see M.R. Brownell, *Samuel Johnson's Attitude to the Arts* (Oxford, 1989); for Johnson and Hogarth, see p. 83. For the unsettled nature of aesthetic discourse in the first half of the century, see p. 2; and Paul Monod, 'Painters and Party Politics in England, 1714–1760', *Eighteenth-century Studies*, 26 (1993), pp. 367–98.
4. WRO, B 15, St. Clement Danes Churchwardens' Accounts: payment 'Aug 29th To Mr. Wm. Kent in full for the Picture at the Alter put 2 rects 63*l*. 0*s*. 0*d*.', also 'Aug 5th To Mr. James Richards in pte for Carveing works done at the Alter He last year put 3 sevall rects 115*l*. 0*s*. 0*d*.' All WRO references supplied by Richard Sharp. Paulson, *HLAT*, I, p. 158, dates Kent's commission to 1725, without supporting evidence, an error repeated in his 1992 revision of *HLAT* (3 vols., Cambridge, 1992–3), I, p. 138.
5. *Postman* no. 8479, 24–26 August 1725. See also *Daily Journal* no. 1438, 25 August: 'Last Week the Bishop of London sent an Order to take down the Picture set up at the Altar of St. Clement's-Danes Church, by some supposed to be St Cecilia, by others the P—— Sobieski and her little Boy'; *Evening Post* no. 2510; *Post Boy*; *St James's Evening Post* no. 1606; *Flying Post* no. 5083; *Whitehall Evening Post*: all 24–26 August 1725. Also *London Journal* no. 318; *Weekly Journal* no. 18; *British Journal* no. 154; *Applebee's Original Weekly Journal*: all 28 August 1725.
6. *Daily Journal* no. 1440, 27 August 1725: 'We hear that a Clergyman, together with several of the Parishioners of St. Clement's Danes, are using Endeavours to get the Order . . . for taking down the Picture over the Altar of the Church superseded'; WRO B.15 Churchwardens' Accounts: payment of 13*s*. 6*d*. 'expences & wateridge to & from the Bishops of London abt the Alterpiece'; *Daily Journal* no. 1447, 4 September, 'We hear, that the Picture . . . is not to be taken down'.

7. The *Whitehall Evening Post* no. 1091 4–7 September says that it is 'down at last'; *St James's Evening Post* no. 1611 4–7 September that it was taken down on 4 September. See also *Applebee's Weekly Journal* and *Weekly Journal*, both of 11 September.

8. WRO B1055, St. Clement Danes Inventories; described April 1726, May 1727, May 1729, 1733, 1734, 1751 as 'A Picture taken out of the Chancell now in the vestry room'. This becomes, in 1752, 1753 and 1754, 'In the long Room a Picture of St Cecilia in a gilt frame'. For the continued presence of the painting into the later eighteenth century see the *Gentleman's Magazine* 59 (1789), p. 391 and J.P. Malcolm, *Londinium Redivivum* (London, 1807), III, p. 395n. J. Wickham-Legg, *English Church Life from the Restoration to the Tractarian Movement* (London, 1914), p. 131, records it 'hidden away on a back staircase' in 1907. It was photographed *c*. 1930 for T. Cox, 'William Kent as a Painter', *Artwork*, VII (1931), p. 28, repro-duced as Plate 1 here. The story that it was occasionally set up in the music room of the Crown and Anchor Tavern opposite (see Clark, *Samuel Johnson*, p. 138) on 'music evenings' is suggestive with reference to that tavern's identity as a meeting-place from *c*. 1726 of several societies with Tory/Jacobite connec-tions, most notably from *c*. 1740 the Oak Society (Paul Kléber Monod, *Jacobitism and the English People, 1688–1788* (Cambridge, 1993), p. 230). For the Academy of Vocal Music/Academy of Ancient Music, see Clark, *Samuel Johnson*, p. 154 and William Weber, *The Rise of Musical Classics in Eighteenth-Century England: A Study in Canon, Ritual and Ideology* (Oxford, 1992), pp. 56–73, esp. pp. 63, 67–8. That Hogarth should be listed among the 69 Academy subscribers entered for 1729 (and be thus potentially in a position to re-encounter Kent's painting) is worth noting. The Apollo Society, which had seceded from the Academy of Vocal Music in 1731, met at the Crown and Anchor until 1784; information from Jane Clark.

9. Some idea of the appearance in the eighteenth century of such rooms is given by the nineteenth-century photograph of the vestry of St. Lawrence Jewry repro-duced in Colin Amery, *Wren's London* (Bedfordshire: Lennard Publishing, 1988), p. 98.

10. *A LETTER from a Parishioner of St. Clement Danes, To the Right Reverend Father in God, EDMUND, Lord Bishop of London, Occasion'd by His Lordship's causing the Picture, over the Altar, to be taken down. With Some Observations on the Use and Abuse of Church Paintings in General, and of that Picture in Particular. Exodus Chap. xxxii. Ver. 20, 'And he took the Calf which they had made, and burnt it in the Fire, and ground it to Powder, and strawed it upon the Water, and made the Children of Israel drink of it'*. Printed and Sold by J. Roberts, in Warwick-Lane; A. Dod without Temple Bar; and E. Nutt, at the Royal Exchange 6d. 10 September 1725. [British Library 698.g.] Advertised *London Journal* no. 320 11 September; *Mist's Weekly Journal* no. 20, 11 September; *Flying-Post* no. 5091, 11–14, 14–16 and 16–18 September 1725. Mist's coverage is interesting; a letter from 'Clementinus' in the *Weekly Journal* of 11 September defending Gibson's part in the affair and referring to the parish as 'equally divided in their sentiments about the Picture' claims that Mist refused to publish a similar letter. Paulson, *Graphic Works*, I, p. 112, does not rule out the possibility of Hogarth's being the author of *A Letter from a Parishioner*; certainly both the sentiments and idiolect are Hogarthian.

11. *A Letter*, p. 3. This may be a reference to an earlier episode, that of the Whitechapel altarpiece (1714), when not only was a print produced in which the controversial features of the painting were modified, but the rector offered to have these features repainted in the original. See G.V. Bennett, *White Kennett*

1660–1728 Bishop of Peterborough: A Study in the Political and Ecclesiastical History of the Early Eighteenth Century (London, 1957), pp. 3, 130–2.

12. *A Letter*, pp. 3, 9.

13. The British Museum copy of the print bears the manuscript date 'Octobr 1725'; F.G. Stephens, *Catalogue of Prints and Drawings in the British Museum. Division I: Political and Personal Satires* (4 vols., London, 1870–83), II, no. 1764, pp. 620–3. Hogarth's print appears to have been the only source of information for the painting's appearance for those who had not been able to view it in person. The *Post Boy* of 26–28 September 1721 which announced the painting's completion adds 'We hear a Print of the Altar Piece will with convenient Speed be publish'd by Jos. Smith in Exeter Exchange', but no such print has yet been traced, which suggests that one was not in fact produced. Information from Richard Sharp.

14. If the painting was completed and installed at some point between September and December 1721, it would have been possible to identify one of the *putti* with Prince Charles Edward Stuart (born 31 December 1720 New Style). By the summer of 1725 such an identification might have been extended to include Prince Henry, Duke of York (born 6 March 1725), but this would require the identification of a figure appropriate to the then five-year-old Prince Charles.

15. Paulson, *HLAT*, I, p. 160; paraphrased by Mary Webster, *Hogarth* (London, 1979), pp. 11–12. See also Paulson, *Hogarth's Graphic Works* (2 vols., New Haven and London, 1965), I, p. 112; Paulson, *Hogarth* I, 139; Paulson, *Graphic Works* (3rd revised edn., London, 1989), p. 57.

16. *English Church Life*, pp. 131–2.

17. *The Loyal Observator Reviv'd; or, Gaylard's Journal*, no. 23, 11 May 1723. For Gaylard and the *Loyal Observator Reviv'd* see Monod, *Jacobitism*, pp. 29, 78, 119.

18. *A Letter*, p. 3.

19. *A Letter*, p. 7 'When your Lordship shall examine, Who is the Painter, and of what Principle? How long he had been from the Court of *Rome*, before he Painted that Picture? And, Whether he brought no Picture, or Resemblance of the Princess *Sobieski* over with him? You will not repent of what you have done.'

20. Monod, *Jacobitism*, p. 79; Noel Woolf, *The Medallic Record of the Jacobite Movement* (London, 1988), pp. 78–9.

21. *Post Boy*, 6–8 August 1719, 'Just publish'd / A curious Print of a Polish Princess, in a Polish Habit, now residing at Rome, finely ingraved after an original Painting sold by the Printsellers of London and Westminster', advertisement repeated in most issues until early October; also *London Journal*, 11 August 1719 and *Weekly Journal*, 15 August 1719; in these 'Lady' is substituted for 'Princess'; *Post Boy*, 18–20 February 1720, 'Lately imported / A very fine Print of a Polish Princess now residing at Rome, grav'd at Paris by Du Change, that grav'd the Luxemburg Gallery. Sold by the Printsellers of London and Westminster. Price 2s. 6d.', readvertised *Post Boy*, 3–5 May 1720, with other prints, 'All sold at the Golden Buck in Fleetstreet near St. Dunstan's Church'. These may refer to the portrait with the engraved inscription *A Polish Lady* (British Museum, Dept. of Prints and Drawings, 1850-2-23-1009).

22. For government interest in Jacobite and quasi-Jacobite graphics in this period, see Monod, *Jacobitism*, p. 78n; H.M. Atherton, *Political Prints in the Age of Hogarth: A Study in the Ideographic Representation of Politics* (Oxford, 1974), pp. 69–82. Richard Sharp, *The Engraved Record of the Jacobite Movement* (Aldershot, 1996), pp. 40–69 argues against such a simplification and for a more complex and surprisingly unproscriptive official response to the existence of such works.

23. Clark, *Samuel Johnson*, pp. 52n, 152n, 154–6, 157n, 180; Atherton, *Political Prints in the Age of Hogarth*, pp. 4, 10, 13n, 17. 'E. Nutt' and 'A. Dod' are cited in the publication line of *A Letter from a Parishioner*, together with J. Roberts of Warwick Lane, for whom see Atherton pp. 7 and (in connexion with A. Dodd and E. Nutt) 13n. The 'highflying' record of these publishers is not incompatible with the publication of the *Letter from a Parishioner*; commercial considerations aside, hostile *ekphrasis* of this kind was not necessarily unwelcome to the parties it sought to expose.

24. See also Clark, *Samuel Johnson*, pp. 52n, 71, 119n, 121–2n, 138–40, 154, 169n.

25. St. Clement Danes was not unique in this. *A New View of LONDON; Or, An Ample Account of that CITY* (2 vols., London, 1708) records (I, pp. 168–9) a large painting based on the *Eikon Basilike* frontispiece at St. Botolph, Bishopsgate, and, at St. Paul's, Covent Garden (II, p. 478) 'a spacious Picture of Char.I with Angels adorned with twisted Columns &c.'. See also T. Lewis, *The Obligation of Christians to Beautify & Adorn their Churches* (1721), p. 21 on the 'Churches of the First Christians': 'to the Saints and Martyrs were joyned the Pictures of Pious Kings and Princes, which Custom, I suppose, introduced King Charles the Martyr as a solemn Ornament to some of the Churches in this City' (for Lewis's association with St. Clement Danes, see below). For the Royal Martyr as providing Jacobites with one model in 'a repertory of graphic propaganda' see Monod, *Jacobitism*, p. 72. For a description of the ornamentation of St. Clement Danes as it stood in 1708 and the orthodox gold-on-black Commandments, Creed and Lord's Prayer which Kent's altarpiece may be supposed to have replaced, see *A New View of London*, I, pp. 202–6.

26. WRO, St. Clement Danes, B 1049 Register of Visiting Preachers. Interestingly in view of his involvement in an earlier altarpiece controversy (see below), White Kennett is recorded as having preached on 8 December 1723.

27. See note 3 above. The vestry is described in *A New View of London*, I, p. 206 as select. The patronage of the living is ascribed to the Earl of Exeter; for the 5th Earl and his implication in the 1696 Assassination Plot see Monod, *Jacobitism*, pp. 99, 142, 169.

28. 'When your Lordship shall examine unto these Particulars, I doubt not of the Inferences so wise a Man will draw from such convincing Circumstances'; *A Letter*, p. 7.

29. For Thomas Blackwell, Rector 1721–73 and John Rodgers, Lecturer 1712–26 see Sharp, 'The Parish of St. Clement Danes'. Blackwell's predecessor and so possibly associated with Kent's commission was Thomas Blomer, matriculated at Hart Hall, Oxford 1697; MA Trinity College, Cambridge 1704; DD (Comitiis Regiis) 1728; Vicar of Lavington, Lincs, 1723–.

30. *The Scourge Scourged, or a short Account of the Life of the Author of the Scourge* (London, 1717).

31. *DNB* under Lewis, Thomas (1689–?1749).

32. For a satirical engraving titled 'The Heretical Synod at Salters-Hall', see Stephens, *Catalogue*, II, BM 1262. I have not been able to establish whether this is one of the 'plates' referred to by the ESTC in the entry for the 1720 collected edition of *The Scourge*.

33. If it was in possession of the church before this but not displayed, this suggests that the resemblance to available prints of Clementina was not only sufficient to attract unwelcome attention at this time but an aspect of the painting of which those concerned in its commission and/or installation were fully aware.

34. *A Letter*, p. 10.
35. Michael I. Wilson, *William Kent (1685–1748) Architect, Designer, Painter, Gardener* (London, 1984) errs when he suggests (p. 61) that this must have been commissioned and installed before that of St. Clement Danes. Cf. Paulson, *HLAT*, I, p. 158. Another uncontroversial contemporary altarpiece was that of the Last Supper painted by and presented to the parish church of Melcombe Regis, Dorset, by their MP and Hogarth's father-in-law, Sir James Thornhill: *DNB*, under Thornhill, Sir James (1675–1734).
36. *DNB*, under Welton, Richard (?1671–1726).
37. Bennett, *White Kennett*, pp. 126–31, 251, offers a useful précis of this episode, which this author hopes to develop with reference to what may be the original painting.
38. Cf. Milton: 'The sons of Belial, flown with insolence and wine' *Paradise Lost*, I, 501–2.
39. *A Letter*, p. 10.
40. Anon, *The Judgement of the Church of England, concerning Images and Pictures in Churches* (2 May 1714); *Images an Abomination to the Lord: Or, Dr Kenet's Reasons for pulling Down the Altarpiece at White-Chapel* (3 May 1714); *The Case Concerning setting up Images or Painting of them in Churches, Writ by the Learned Dr. Thomas Barlow late Bishop of Lincoln, upon his suffering such images to be defaced in his Diocess; wherein it is Disapproved and Condemned by the Statutes and Ecclesiastical Laws of this Kingdom, and the Book of Homilies, &c. Published upon occasion of a Painting set up in White-chappel Church* (1714); 'Willoughby Willer', *A Letter to the Church-wardens of White-chaple, occasioned by a new altarpiece set up in their churchs with general remarks on the whole contents* (1714); see also Bodleian Library, Rawlinson MS B 376 f. 46.
41. Cf. Monod, *Jacobitism*, p. 72. In the one further instance cited by Wickham-Legg, *English Church Life*, p. 132, that of the petition of one Thomas Watson to the Bishop of London against the altarpiece (the Nativity flanked by portraits of Moses and Aaron) set up at St. James, Clerkenwell, the bishop refused to act. Watson printed his objections in the *Old Whig*, 30 October 1735 but this tactic appears to have failed to excite any heat against the painting. In this context it is worth noting that Hogarth himself produced an altarpiece depicting the Ascension and Resurrection for St. Mary Redcliffe, Bristol in 1755, for a fee of £525; see Joseph Burke (ed.), *William Hogarth, The Analysis of Beauty: With the rejected passages from the manuscript drafts and autobiographical notes* (Oxford, 1955), p. xvii; Paulson, *HLAT*, II, pp. 228–34.
42. *Second Characters or the Language of Forms by the . . . Author of Characteristics*, ed. Benjamin Rand (Cambridge, 1914), p. 92n.
43. [Benjamin Buckler], *A Proper Explanation of the Oxford Almanack for this present Year M.D.CC.LV* (London, [1755]); *The Oxford Almanack of 1712, Explain'd: or, the Emblems Of it, Unriddl'd. Together With some Prefatory Account of the Emblems of the Two preceding Years* (London, 1711). For the *Oxford Almanacs*, see Helen Petter, *The Oxford Almanacs* (Oxford, 1974), pp. 3–11, 13, 14, 41–4, 46, 47, 50, 59, 67, 68.
44. See Jonathan Swift, *Gulliver's Travels* (London, 1726), part III, chapter VI (Oxford World's Classics, 1985 edition, pp. 177–8); David Dabydeen, *Hogarth, Walpole and Commercial Britain* [hereafter Dabydeen, *HWCB*] (London, 1987), p. 13; Paul Langford, *Walpole and the Robinocracy* (Cambridge, 1986), p. 16.
45. For the Jacobite concept of 'Look, love and follow', see Monod, *Jacobitism*, pp. 70–3.

46. *The Oxford Almanack of 1712, Explain'd* (BL Sach 249/1), pp. 4, 5. Twenty-three pages of *ekphrasis* end with the *non sequitur* 'However, I am not concerned what you or any may judge of this performance'. For a relevant episode touching the Thornhill paintings at Greenwich, see Paulson, *HLAT*, I, p. 160.

47. *Sir John Gonson's Five Charges to Several Grand Juries* (3rd edn., London, 1737), p. 37, cited Dabydeen, *HWCB*, p. 113.

48. The history of published political *ekphrasis* in England might be traced back to the 'discovery' of the 'popish' 'Sussex Picture' in 1644, and the varying responses to the *Eikon Basilike* frontispiece. See Lois Potter, *Secret Rites and Secret Writing: Royalist Literature 1641–1660* (Cambridge, 1989), pp. xiv, 10, 45–8, 162, 176–82.

49. Dabydeen, *HWCB*; see also Sean Shesgreen, *Engravings by Hogarth* (New York, 1973).

50. The first being the general satire on *The Taste of the Town*, better known as *Masquerades and Operas*, BM 1742 (February 1723/4) in which Burlington House is characterised as 'Accademy of Arts' and on which Kent is raised above Michelangelo and Raphael. The conventional ascription to Hogarth of the 1731 print *Taste* (BM 1873), a riposte to Pope's 'Of Taste, an Epistle to the Rt. Hon. Richard, Earl of Burlington', Epistle IV of the *Moral Essays* is rejected by Paulson, *HLAT*, I, p. 541n and *Hogarth's Graphic Works* (3rd revised edn.), p. 35; its depiction of the gateway of Burlington House borrows from *Masquerades and Operas*. Of Hogarth's later works, there is a critical architectural reference in *Marriage à la Mode, I: The Marriage Contract* (*c.* 1743) and the satire on Kent's Horse Guards in the second plate of the *Election* series (1757). For Hogarth's 'war with the conniossurs' (*sic*), see Burke (ed.), *The Analysis of Beauty*, pp. xii–xv.

51. Paulson, *HLAT*, I, pp. 157–60; Paulson, *Graphic Works*, I, pp. 11, 105; Wilson, *William Kent*, pp. 60–1; William Gaunt, *The World of William Hogarth* (London, 1978), p. 23; Webster, *Hogarth*, pp. 11–12. For the relevant episode, see Geoffrey Beard, *Craftsmen and Interior Decoration in England 1660–1820* (London, 1981), pp. 126–7; H.M. Colvin (ed.), *The History of the King's Works*, V, 1660–1782 (1976). Subsequently (1733) Kent was credited by Vertue with having deprived Hogarth of the commission to paint the wedding portrait of the Princess Royal and a Hanoverian family conversation piece for which two oil sketches survive; 'its effect of carricatures wch he has hertofore toucht Mr. Kent. and diverted the Town. wch he is like to pay for, when he least thought of it. add to that there is some other causes relating to Sir James Thornhill . . .'; quoted Lawrence Gowing, *Hogarth* (London, 1971), p. 25.

52. Stephens, *Catalogue*, II, 623; *DNB*, XI, 24 (under William Kent) refers to 'the feeble composition and bad draughtsmanship which had already led Bishop Gibson to order its removal from the church'.

53. *Graphic Works*, p. 112; *HLAT*, I, p. 160; *Hogarth*, I, p. 139. Kent's deficiencies as interpreted by Hogarth might instructively be compared with Hogarth's own *Music Introduced to Apollo by Minerva* (1727), reproduced Paulson, *Graphic Works* (3rd edn.), p. 109a.

54. *William Kent*, pp. 60–1.

55. For example, Joseph Burke and Colin Caldwell, *Hogarth: the Complete Engravings* (London, 1968), p. 17, 'One of the objections being an alleged likeness . . .'

56. Jane Clark, 'The Mysterious Mr Buck: Patronage and Politics, 1688–1745', *Apollo*, CXXIX 327 (May 1989), pp. 317–22; idem, 'For Kings and Senates Fit', *The Georgian Group Journal*, (1989), pp. 55–63; Toby Barnard and Jane Clark (eds.), *Lord Burlington: Architecture, Art and Life* (London, 1994).

57. For example, Paulson, *HLAT*, I, p. 170; Atherton, *Political Prints*, pp. 47–50; Charles Press, 'The Georgian Political Print and Democratic Institutions', *Comparative Studies in Society and History*, 19 (1977), p. 220.

58. Dabydeen, *HWCB*, p. 11 and passim. It has, however, proved singularly enduring; see Anthony Strugnell, 'Diderot, Hogarth and the ideal model', *British Journal for Eighteenth-Century Studies*, 18 (1995), p. 137n. For the historiographical shift, see A.L. Rees and Frances Borzello (eds.), *The New Art History* (London, 1986).

59. Shesgreen, *Four Times of the Day*, p. 157; Shesgreen unconsciously employs the vocabulary of anti-Jacobitism. Ronald Paulson has recently come close to making this identification: in *Hogarth*, II, p. 362 he observes that while 'the great religious issue of Catholic versus Protestant indeed England versus France (the Pretender had lived in France since 1688) which underlay the problem of legitimacy and succession, played into Hogarth's hands . . . it was already at issue in the subject of art . . . and patronage. In *Marriage à la Mode* [Hogarth] made a great deal out of the patriarchal oppressiveness of baroque, Counterreformation Roman Catholic painting'; ibid., III, p. 371: 'Factionalism also linked for Hogarth the politics of government with the politics of art . . . His support of an Hanoverian regime dedicated to defending against French Catholic dominance on the Continent was parallel to his support for an indigenous, English drawing school against the idea of an academy on the French model.' See also Paulson, *Graphic Works* (3rd edn.), p. 4: 'Hogarth had learned from his literary models Dryden, Swift and Pope, never to represent art without invoking also religion and politics (and vice versa).'

60. F.D. Klingender, *Hogarth and English Caricature* (London, 1944) and cited as a seminal text of the 'new art history' (Charles Harrison, 'Taste and Tendency', in Rees and Borzello, *The New Art History*, p. 78) dismissed Jacobitism, p. vii, as 'an intermittent fever' of Grub Street and 'rural backwoodsmen' which could not distract 'the middle classes' from 'their proper business of economic enterprise'. The omission of 'Jacobitism' from the index to Paulson, *HLAT* (1971 edition) reflects its standing at this date; Paulson's 1992–3 revision of *HLAT*, *Hogarth*, improves on this but fails to engage with the counter-ideology and cultural politics of English Jacobitism as reconstructed by Monod. For the provenance of the Paulsonian view of eighteenth-century England, see Paulson, *Popular and Polite Art in the Age of Hogarth and Fielding* (Notre Dame, 1979), p. ix.

61. For example, Dabydeen, *HWCB*, pp. 50, 134, Appendix I, pp. 151–9; Shesgreen, *Four Times of the Day*, p. 149 writes that, 'temperamentally and ideologically', Hogarth's 'affinities are not with . . . static hierarchic values whether social or artistic'.

62. Shesgreen, *Four Times of the Day*, p. 120 ascribes a critical impulse to Hogarth's depiction of oak-leaf-wearing revellers in the 1736 painting *Night* (set on either 29 May or, as Shesgreen argues, 3 September) as participants in a nocturnal saturnalia in keeping with 'the Stuart monarch whose return promised to bring with it law and order but instead served only to introduce immorality and chaos'. On p. 122 Shesgreen refers to 'the turbulent world ushered in by Charles II' and p. 133, to 'the approaching bonfires kindled in honor of Charles II, patron and architect of England's moral climate since the Restoration'. Paulson, *Graphic Works*, I, p. 182 identifies Restoration Day as a Jacobite celebration; for oak leaves and Restoration Day see Monod, *Jacobitism*, pp. 182, 204, 209, 215.

63. Paulson, *Graphic Works*, p. 49. See also Paulson, *HLAT*, I, pp. 9–12, 253–4; II, pp. 203, 220, 443–4n; Clark, *Samuel Johnson*, p. 180. Marina Warner, *No Go the*

Bogeyman (London, 1998), p. 109 overlooks this nexus when she identifies the artist as 'an Anglican'.

64. For anti-Catholicism in Hogarth's work, see Shesgreen, *Four Times of the Day*, pp. 142, 145. For a recent accommodation of Hogarth's anti-popery and some acknowledgement of the dissenting and heterodox as opposed to orthodox Protestantism which informed it, see Paulson, 'Hogarth and the Distribution of Visual Images', in Brian Allen (ed.), *Studies in British Art 1: Towards a Modern Art World* (London and New Haven, 1995), p. 30 ('and so in a sense all he is doing is rooting out the residue of papist superstition in England whether it be in Old Master paintings or in the clergy'), and pp. 43–4.

65. Michael Kitson, 'Hogarth's *An Apology for Painters*', *Walpole Society*, XLI (1966–8), pp. 49, 52, 55. The ideolectic nature of Hogarth's writing will become apparent from a scrutiny of the MSS. transcribed by Burke, *Analysis* and Kitson; the 'Britophil' letter has been attributed to Hogarth on these grounds (Burke, p. xxiiin). For the methodological issues involved in selecting from Hogarth's finished and unfinished prose see Kitson, pp. 49–53, 70–1, 74–5; Burke, pp. xxix–xxxvii. As far as chronology is concerned we are dealing with statements articulated over a period of fewer than thirty years; eleven years fewer than the chronology of Hogarth's entire pictorial output, which has generally been approached as an *oeuvre*. I am grateful to Professor David Solkin for raising this issue.

66. Rejected fragment for *Analysis* ('Something of a first Intended Introduction', BM Add MS 27,992 ff. 6, 7) reproduced Burke, p. 190; cf. 'the blind veneration that generally is paid to antiquity' (*Analysis*, p. 91, Burke, p. 105) and 'double-ground connoisseur-spectacles' without which the qualities of works 'defaced and maimed by time' are impossible to distinguish (*Analysis*, p. 92; Burke, p. 106). Similarly ocular in emphasis is a passage, which can be taken as another stab at Kent, in which the training of English artists abroad is contrasted with his own, 'wholly obtain'd by Observation by which method be where I would with my Eyes open I could have been at my studys' (*Analysis*, Draft C f. 9; Burke, p. 185); 'evry unprejudiced Eye' (Autobiographical Notes f. 19; Burke, p. 215); 'Some have been so misled by their prejudice, as almost to see black for white' (*Analysis*, Draft C 3015 ff. 166b; Burke, p. 186).

67. *The Case Stated. . . . Wherein is Shewed, That the Doubt and Danger is in the Former, and the Certainty and Safety in the Latter Communion* (4th edn., London, 1714), pp. 97, 144–5, 207, 211. For other passages relevant to the issues at stake in the St. Clement Danes controversy, see pp. 57, 65, 109, 112–14, 133–6, 161–2, 207, 208. Leslie was, of course, one of St. Germain's most distinguished orthodox Anglican polemicists.

68. Fragment, Autobiographical Notes [BM Add MS 27,991 f. 11b]; Burke, *Analysis*, pp. 209, 210.

69. The extent to which Hogarth articulates his own aesthetic in terms of religious heterodoxy – 'I grew so profane as to admire Nature beyond the finest pictures and I confess sometimes objected to the devinity of even Raphael Urbin Corregio and Michael Angelo, for which I have been severely treated' (Autobiographical Notes f. 10; Burke, *Analysis of Beauty*, p. 209) – is worth noting. Paulson, 'Distribution of Visual Images', p. 33, acknowledges the 'vocabulary of specifically religious persecution' in this and the 'bigots'/'old religion' passages.

70. *Autobiographical Notes* (BL Egerton MS 3013, f. 65); Burke, p. 182.

71. For a graphic repudiation of such pictures, see Hogarth's ticket design *The Battle of the Pictures* (1744/45) reproduced in Paulson, *Graphic Works*, II, plate 175.

72. This detail is reproduced in Paulson, *Hogarth*, I, figures 23 and 24. For the impact of Thornhill's Greenwich paintings to the apprenticed Hogarth, see the *Autobiographical Notes*, p. xxxi (BM Add MS 27,991 f. 5). Thornhill's support for Walpole in the Excise Crisis (1733) is noted by Dabydeen, *HWCB*, p. 141.

73. Kitson, *Apology for Painters*, transcript p. XVIII lines 609–10. Earlier, in *The Analysis of Beauty* (p. 92; Burke, p. 106), he had written of 'some who still carry on a comfortable trade . . . in cooked-up copies, which they are very apt to putt off for originals . . . whoever dares be bold enough to detect such impositions finds himself immediately branded, and given out as one of low ideas, ignorant of the true sublime, envious, &c . . .'

74. The analogy between human and artistic legitimacy would be employed in a later issue of authenticity and attribution in which Johnson himself engaged. Brownell, *Samuel Johnson's Attitude to the Arts*, pp. 43–4 suggests that Johnson's reply to James Upton's *Critical Observations on Shakespeare* (1746), which had demanded of one play that it 'seek for its parent elsewhere. How otherwise do painters distinguish copies from originals?', was grounded in the elder Jonathan Richardson's 1719 *The Connoisseur: An Essay on the Art of Criticism as it Relates to Painting, Shewing how to Judge . . . III Whether it is an Original or a Copy*, Johnson writing 'Copies are easily known, but good imitations are not detected with equal certainty, and are, by the best judges, often mistaken' (Arthur Sherbo (ed.), *Johnson on Shakespeare*, Yale Edition, VII (New Haven, 1968), pp. 161–2).

75. Cf. Kitson, *Apology for Painters* transcript p. xv, line 570.

76. Shesgreen, *Four Times of the Day*, p. 151, emphases added. Cf. *A Letter from A Parishioner*, p. 21: even supposing that Kent's altarpiece 'were not the Pretender's Spouse, and, probably, some more of his Family, under the Form of Angels' it is 'the most . . . foreign [thing] I ever saw or heard of'. Cf. also Hogarth's argument for eschewing 'beaten subjects either from the Scriptures or from the old ridiculous stories of the Heathen gods as neither the Religion of the one or the other required promoting among Protestants as they formerly did in greece and more lately at Rome ['in the more bigoted times of nonsense in one and popery in the other' – [struck through]]' (loose page in Hogarth's autograph auctioned 1935: transcribed Burke, p. 195).

77. Klingender, p. v; cf. Gaunt, p. 24. R.D. Gwynn, *Huguenot Heritage: the History and Contribution of Huguenots in Britain* (London, 1985), writes, p. 100, of Thornhill's success in an 'alien' idiom.

78. Vicesimus Knox, quoted Paul Langford, *A Polite and Commercial People: England 1727–1783* (Oxford, 1989), p. 305. Langford comments: 'It seemed all too possible that the very spirit which accounted for a robust libertarian tradition prohibited cultural sophistication'. Cf. Hogarth, 'to enter into competition with [Continental] art is ridiculous; we are a commercial people, and can purchase their curiosities ready-made' (quoted Michael Foss, *The Age of Patronage: The Arts in Society 1660–1750* (London, 1971), p. 204). See also John Brewer, *The Pleasures of the Imagination: English Culture in the Eighteenth Century* (London, 1997), pp. 208, 219.

79. Or, indeed, Toryism. For a notable instance of the latter's marginalisation, see David Solkin, *Painting for Money: The Visual Arts and the Public Sphere in Eighteenth-Century England* (London and New Haven, 1993), especially pp. 99–100. The tacit

Whiggery of the 'new' historiography of eighteenth-century British art and its failure to accommodate a high church and Tory cultural discourse are conceded by John Brewer, 'Cultural Production, Consumption, and the Place of the artist in Eighteenth-Century England', in Allen (ed.), *Towards a Modern Art World*, pp. 7, 12–13.

80. Dabydeen, *HWCB*, pp. 11–12; Stephens, *Catalogue*, III, Part II (1877), BM 3278 (1754).
81. Shesgreen, *Engravings*, p. xiv.
82. For example, Shesgreen, *Four Times of the Day*, pp. 107, 150; for race see Dabydeen, *Hogarth's Blacks* (Kingston-on-Thames, 1985); for 'class' and the 'cash nexus' see Jack Lindsay, *Hogarth, his Art and his World* (London, 1977), p. 31; for a conceptualisation of Hogarth and his 'age' in terms of secularism and the 'failure' of the Established Church, see Dabydeen, *HWCB*, pp. 22, 31, 62, 105. For a recent instance of a 'usable Hogarth', see M.A.P. Godby, *'The Battle of the Pictures': An Historical Instance of Conflict Between Different Definitions of Art* (Cape Town, 1990).

Part II
The Public Realm

4
Religion and Political Identity: Samuel Johnson as a Nonjuror

J.C.D. Clark

The Johnsonian problem

In the privileged retrospect of literary scholarship, Samuel Johnson appears as the Colossus who bestrode his age: a literary critic himself, he seems to provide standards by which his age might be judged. This belief has strengthened the assumption that he stood aside from the conflicts of his day, an Olympian above personal commitment to any merely local and temporary cause. One effect of replacing him in his historical context is to deflate that assumption. In this new vision, Johnson's peculiar authority as a moral critic derives from an austere position of internal exile which was no less acute for being, from one perspective, self-imposed. It was not only 'the human condition' in general with which this moralist grappled, but a particular set of moral, religious and political dilemmas; the contribution of the historian is not only to bring Johnson down to earth, but to make him more real, more plausible as a troubled observer of his age. Yet the historical landscape in which he has landed looks significantly different than it recently did, for a number of political and religious traditions alternative to the mainstream Whig tradition have been recovered and given substance. In turn, they have profoundly modified our understanding of what that mainstream tradition was.

The most striking of these minor traditions was that of the Nonjurors. Among those who stood out against Williamite and Hanoverian rule, their protest was the most principled. Nonjurors were formerly overlooked not least because they were identified solely with a tiny minority, that dwindling body of clergy who were deprived of their benefices after 1689 for refusing to subscribe the relevant oaths and thereafter ministered to separated congregations, continuing to ordain priests and consecrate bishops in their own succession. This identification is not wrong, but it is far too narrow. Johnson indeed condemned churchmen who separated themselves in this way from the larger body of the Church, and defined 'Nonjuror' much more widely as 'One who conceiving James II. unjustly deposed, refuses to swear allegiance to those who have succeeded him.'[1] Even in 1755, Johnson used the present tense, 'refuses', rather than 'refused': the problem was not in the past.

Such people, potentially far more numerous than the deprived clergy, might continue to worship with the juring Church of England, as even men like the deprived bishops Robert Frampton and Thomas Ken did or advised others to do, not joining in the 'immoral prayers' for the current monarchs prescribed by the updated *Book of Common Prayer*, but debarred in civil life from many professions in which legal requirements to take the oaths were unavoidable. Even Thomas Brett, who was deprived of his livings for refusing to subscribe in 1715, remained in communion with the juring Church until persuaded otherwise by George Hickes.[2] Another Nonjuror, Samuel Hawes, argued against the practice of worshipping with the juring Church but implicitly conceded that it occurred, for 'Some good people grow uneasy out of fear that they should live like Heathens, and as without God in the world, if they should not repair to some place of public worship.' This willingness of even some among the early Nonjurors to worship with the juring Church was shared by later Nonjurors of the scholarship, piety or polemical force of Thomas Baker, William Law and Charles Leslie;[3] the evidence indicates that this was Johnson's position also.

It was not the Nonjurors alone who were preoccupied with oaths as definitions and guarantees of identity. Such ideas had long been widespread in English society, and remained near the centre of public debate. They were indeed appropriate to the moral and theological characteristics of its deeply-rooted and lasting patterns of discourse: allegiance rather than contract, writs rather than rights, casuistry rather than ideology were its keynotes.[4] Johnson's Oxford contemporary Thomas Alcock, who matriculated at Brasenose College in March 1727/8, published in 1754 a careful analysis of oaths, their nature and obligation, necessary since 'Oaths are now so much used in this Nation'.[5] This essay outlines the culture of oaths into which Johnson was born, and reviews the evidence which locates him at the beginning of his career within one of the social constituencies into which his world was divided. Johnson developed as the years passed: he had no monolithic, unchanging identity. Yet the nature and timing of that development can only be assessed if his starting point is grasped, and this demands a correct map of the choices open to men in early Hanoverian England.

A polity defined by oaths

The social importance of oaths as declarations and performative enactments of natural allegiance was at least as old as feudal ties. It took on added significance with the Reformation and its attendant oath of supremacy, recognising the sovereign as head of the Church in England and disavowing the Pope. By 1614, as one author argued,

The safety of the King himself . . . every man's estate in particular, and the state of the realm in general, doth depend upon the truth and sincerity of men's oaths . . . The law and civil policy of England, being chiefly founded upon religion and the fear of God, doth use the religious ceremony of an oath, not only in legal proceedings but in other transactions and affairs of most importance in the commonwealth; esteeming oaths not only as the best touchstone of trust in matters of controversy, but as the safest knot of civil society, and the firmest band to tie all men to the performance of their several duties.[6]

The nature of an oath, the force of its operation and the senses in which men might be released from it by a prior obligation continued to be matters of both careful enquiry and forceful polemic. Successive political problems in the seventeenth century touched the same raw nerve and increased the state's reliance on declarations of loyalty.

A succession of such texts was presented for public assent in the 1640s. This culminated in the 'Engagement Controversy', which developed from 1649 as the new English republic sought to ensure the allegiance of its supporters and identify its opponents by imposing an oath.[7] That conscience rather than coercion was the best basis of stable government was a lesson widely drawn after the civil wars, and the use of oaths increased rather than diminished after 1660.[8] The Corporation (1661) and Test (1673, 1678) Acts made subscription an even more central aspect of participation in public life, for they confined a wide range of offices to Anglicans. Oaths were therefore still defended by churchmen of all positions on the spectrum. Isaac Barrow (1630–77) argued against debasement of sacred obligations by 'bad language':

That justice should be administered between men, it is necessary that testimonies of fact be alleged; and that witnesses should apprehend themselves greatly obliged to discover the truth, according to their conscience, in dark and doubtful cases.

That men should uprightly discharge offices serviceable to publick good, it doth behove that they be firmly engaged to perform the trusts reposed in them.

That in affairs of very considerable importance, men should deal with one another with satisfaction of mind, and mutual confidence, they must receive competent assurances concerning the integrity, fidelity and constancy each of other.

That the safety of governors may be preserved, and the obedience due to them maintained secure from attempts to which they are liable, (by the treachery, levity, perverseness, timorousness, ambition, all such lusts and ill humours of men,) it is expedient that men should be tied with the strictest bands of allegiance.

An oath was still supposed to be such a band, 'common reason not being able to devise any engagement more obliging than it'.[9] Barrow did not complain that misuse had discredited such declarations.

John Tillotson (1630–94), later Archbishop of Canterbury, defended similar doctrine in 1681 against the Quakers' refusal to swear. Oaths were merely instances of a wider dependence on God, he argued. It was religion which was necessary for 'the support of humane society', and an oath was a religious act:

> Not, that an Oath is alwaies a certain and infallible decision of things according to truth and right; but, that this is the utmost credit that we can give to any thing, and the last resort of truth and confidence among men: After this we can go no farther; for if the Religion of an Oath will not oblige men to speak truth, nothing will.

The '*necessity* of Oaths' was

> so great, that humane Society can very hardly, if at all, subsist long without them. Government would many times be very insecure: And for the faithfull discharge of Offices of great trust, in which the welfare of the Publick is nearly concerned, it is not possible to find any security equall to that of an Oath; because the obligation of that reacheth to the most secret and hidden practices of men, and takes hold of them in many cases where the penalty of no humane law can have any awe or force upon them.[10]

These questions were not ignored in any mood of pragmatism after the Revolution of 1688: on the contrary, the Allegiance Controversy of the 1690s was one of the most closely contested of its time, as men already committed to a view of the obligation of oaths examined their consciences over the change in the succession.[11] The new oath of allegiance directly challenged the intelligentsia by requiring subscription before 1 August 1689 from 'any person or persons now being master, governor, head, or fellow of any college or hall, in either of the two universities, or of any other college, or master of any hospital or school, or professor of divinity, law, physick, or other science in either of the two universities, or in the city of *London*' (1 W & M, s. 1, c. 8, clause VIII) on pain of deprivation. The formidable oath of abjuration of James Francis Edward Stuart, imposed after James II's death on 6 September 1701 by the statute of 13 W III, c. 6, was a matter for heart-searching even among its advocates, in Scotland as well as England.[12] It asserted, unlike the watered-down oath of allegiance of 1689, that William was 'lawful and rightful' king. The royal assent was signified by commission, since William was too ill to attend Parliament and died on 8 March 1701/2. Nevertheless, subscription was required before 1 August 1702 of all civil and military officers, and 'all ecclesiastical persons, all members of colleges and halls in either university, that are or shall be of the foundation (being of the age of eighteen years) and all persons teaching pupils in either university', together with other listed categories including schoolmasters, Dissenting ministers and lawyers, on pain of deprivation.

After the accession of George I, new legislation, centrally the Act of 1 Geo. I, s. 2, c. 13, re-emphasised the degree to which the regime defended and defined itself with oaths. It was this Act which again imposed the oaths of allegiance and abjuration on 'all ecclesiastical persons, heads or governors, of what denomination soever, and all other members of colleges and halls in any university, that are or shall be of the foundation, or that do or shall enjoy any exhibition, (being of the age of eighteen years) and all persons teaching or reading to pupils in any university', and others, on pain of deprivation. It also offered the enormous sum of £100,000 for the Pretender, 'alive or dead'. This sweeping and draconian Act, perhaps an incitement to assassination, called forth a handbook to the legislation in force,[13] published in 1716 and reprinted in 1723 and 1744. Even into the 1730s, a strategic threat to the state, which materialised in the French invasion attempt of 1744, justified a defence of the oaths: 'as we have the Word of Truth for it, *That a Kingdom divided against itself cannot stand*; I pray God open our Eyes, and make us duly sensible of the Danger of our Divisions, especially at this critical Juncture, when such powerful enemies are combined against us.'[14]

In the face of these legal requirements to subscribe men might adopt one of a number of courses. Whigs simply took the oaths (with a good or bad conscience). Men of opposite principles might openly refuse to take them, and suffer the legal penalties which would follow. Those refusing the oath of allegiance of 1689 were termed 'Nonjurors'; those refusing the oath of abjuration of 1702 were further specified as 'Nonabjurors'; conventionally, both are covered by the term 'Nonjuror'. Such men paid a high price if discovered: not peaceful obscurity, but public odium, was their lot. Even in 1718, a Whig insisted that 'a *Non-Juror*, in Principle, is an *Assassin*', committed necessarily to conspiracies that threatened the lives of his fellow men. Nonjurors were 'a Band of Cut-Throats; who are Schismaticks in the Church, by destroying all Obligations both natural and religious, and can be made Friends to the State, on no other Condition, than by villainously spilling the Blood of the Prince who presides therein'.[15] Nonjurors could reply in similar terms.

Between public assent and public refusal lay a wide spectrum of possibilities. Some men might seek to pursue careers but avoid being confronted with the oaths by clever manoeuvre or collusion, although this was often difficult or impossible. Others might quietly avoid courses of life in which the oaths would be tendered to them, tacitly accepting their disabilities; both classes of men were Nonjurors. Others again might find honourable or dishonourable reasons for taking the oaths with mental reservations.[16] In January 1714/15 Thomas Hearne recorded a highly ingenious equivocation over the oath of allegiance: 'even those that name K[ing] George in this Oath may suppose K[ing] James (our true King) who goes by the name of ye Chevalier St. George, a name he hath assumed on purpose for the Sake of his Friends here, who may otherwise be pinched'.[17]

Most mental reservations exploited the more substantial distinction between *de jure* and *de facto* authority. The newly-phrased oath of allegiance to William and Mary had omitted the words 'rightful and lawful' hitherto present in that oath, and merely stated:

> I *A. B. do sincerely promise, and swear, that I will be faithful, and bear true Allegiance to their Majesties, King* William *and Queen* Mary, *So help me God.*

This reopened the whole question of *de facto* power, already explored in the 1650s. As a lawyer pointed out, the new oath was open to two different interpretations, depending on the meaning attached to the terms 'faithful' and 'true allegiance'. The oath might mean

> 1. That kind of Fidelity, and Obedience which Captives may promise to their Conquerors, or oppressed Subjects to Usurpers; and oblige them only to a quiet, and peaceable submission, while they are under their Power, and does not debar them from assisting their Lawful Sovereign in the Recovery of his Crown; or,
> 2. All that Fidelity and Allegiance, which was formerly sworn to the Kings of *England*, whereby their subjects were obliged to defend their Crown, and Dignity against all Persons whatsoever; not reserving any Branch of their Allegiance, as Due to any other.

On this distinction rested two different interpretations of the oath. The 'highest construction' was:

> I *A. B.* am sincerely resolv'd to adhere faithfully to King *William* and Queen *Mary*, to perform all the Duties of Allegiance, and Subjection unto them alone, and to defend their Crown and Dignity with my Life and Fortune to the uttermost of my power against all Persons whatsoever.

But 'the lowest construction' was:

> Whereas *W.* and *M.* are actually in possession of the Regal Power, so long, as they continue in the full possession of it, I do swear, that I will pay them that Obedience, and Submission, which may lawfully be paid to an Actual Sovereign, not engaging hereby to uphold them in the possession

of the Throne against the K[ing] *de Jure*, nor debarring my self from exert-
ing my sworn Allegiance to him upon any emergent opportunity for the
recovery of his Right.

This second construction did not exclude men's 'former obligations to
K[ing] J[ames]'. The author argued for the highest construction, notwithstanding the omission of the word 'rightful' from the new oath. He quoted
Bishop Sanderson (1587–1663): 'it is much safer to refuse the Oath propounded, when the Words according to the common, and obvious sense,
do seem to contain any thing unlawful in it self; than by a loose Interpretation so to mollifie them to our purpose, as that we may the more safely
take it.'[18]

Sanderson's remained the definitive account. He was one of the 'great
English church-men' with whom, according to Hawkins, Johnson was
'conversant'.[19] Even in 1829, the Bishop of Llandaff appealed to Sanderson
to justify Copleston's support for Catholic Emancipation, Sanderson having
written 'not only cases of conscience with the most rigorous strictness, but
a treatise *De juramento*, still held to be the best interpretation of the nature
of an oath extant'.[20] It was not anachronistic, then, that a Jacobite of 1750
should reassure a hypothetical sympathiser:

> Your first Question is, Whether the Oath or Covenant that was taken to
> *Oliver Cromwell* was binding upon such as solemnly took it? I answer, No.
> And the great Dr *Saunderson*, and all Casuists, and considerable Divines,
> are of my Opinion, that nothing can bind to Iniquity, and therefore the
> great Sin was in taking such Oaths, and not in breaking them.[21]

In 1650 Sanderson had also argued, in *The Case of the Engagement*, that
allegiance was 'intrinsical' and did not result from the oath of allegiance:
the mere absence of that oath did not absolve subjects from their allegiance
to their rightful sovereign, nor was allegiance conditional upon protection.

> Nevertheless, Sanderson admitted that a subject could submit to the force
> of a usurper and obey him in lawful things in order to preserve trade,
> government, and civil society, and out of gratitude for the protection pro-
> vided . . . Sanderson further professed that subjects might take an oath
> to an usurper, provided that it amounted to no more than a promise of
> fidelity that 'every good patriot oweth to the commonwealth whereof he
> is a member, in endeavouring faithfully . . . to maintain the safety of the
> nation'.

This *submission*, however, fell far short of *allegiance*,[22] and such a *de facto*
oath was much less than that with which Johnson would be faced by the
new oath of abjuration introduced in 1702.

Subscribing with mental reservations in this way continued to provoke violent reactions rather than a bland or ecumenical resignedness to the demands of circumstance. If private conscience were the Jacobites' excuse for acknowledging the right of the exiled dynasty, urged the turncoat Bolingbroke in 1749, how could the Jacobite

> be excused when he forswears the principles he retains, acknowledges the right he renounces, takes oaths with an intent to violate them, and calls God to witness to a premeditated lye? Some casuistry has been employed to excuse these men to themselves and to others. But such casuistry, and in truth every other, destroys, by distinctions and exceptions, all morality, and effaces the essential difference between right and wrong, good and evil. This the schoolmen in general have done on many occasions; the sons of LOYOLA in particular: and I wish with all my heart that nothing of the same kind could be objected to any other divines. Some political reasoning has been employed, as well as the casuistry here spoken of, and to the same purpose. It has been said, that the conduct of those who are enemies to the establishment, to which they submit and swear, is justified by the principles of the Revolution. But nothing can be more false and frivolous. By the principles of the Revolution, a subject may resist, no doubt, the prince who endeavours to ruin and enslave his people, and may push this resistance to the dethronement and exclusion of him and his race: but will it follow, that, because we may justly take arms against a prince whose right to govern we once acknowledged, and who by subsequent acts has forfeited that right, we may swear to a right we do not acknowledge, and resist a prince whose conduct has not forfeited the right we swore to, nor given any just dispensation from our oaths?[23]

The question of oaths related directly to denominational integrity. The Whig Richard Steele addressed the clergy of the Church of England:

> You have bound Your Selves by the strongest Engagements that Religion can lay upon Men, to support the Succession . . . You have tied down Your Souls by an Oath to maintain it as it is settled in the House of *Hanover*; nay, You have gone much further than is usual in Cases of this Nature, as You have *personally* abjured the Pretender to this Crown, and that expressly, without any Equivocations or mental Reservations whatsoever, that is, without any possible Escapes, by which the Subtelty of temporizing Casuists might hope to elude the force of these solemn Obligations.

What then would follow if the clergy broke such undertakings?

What a Triumph would it furnish to those evil Men among us who are Enemies to Your Sacred Order? What Occasion would it administer to Atheists and Unbelievers, to say that Christianity is nothing else but an outward Show and Pretence among the most knowing of its Professors? What could we afterwards object to Jesuits? what would be the Scandal brought upon our holy Church, which is at present the Glory and Bulwark of the Reformation? how would our present Clergy appear in the Eyes of their Posterity and even to the Successors of their own Order, under a Government introduced and established by a Conduct so directly opposite to all the Rules of Honour and Precepts of Christianity?[24]

Whigs claimed that they alone could be trusted. They argued that 'Popish' princes could not commit themselves by oath to safeguard the liberties of their subjects, being bound by the decision of the Council of Constance 'That Faith is not to be kept with Heretics': this had led to 'repeated Acts of Treachery . . . in all Ages . . . against the Protestants' and made it impossible ever to trust such Catholic princes. Jacobites who had sworn the oaths to the new regime (with mental reservations) would be equally untrustworthy to the Pretender: 'how can he depend even on the Oaths of such Men, who tho they believ'd King *James* could not forfeit his Right to their Allegiance, and knew he claim'd it to the last, could yet swear Allegiance to his Enemy?'[25] The author of these remarks failed to point out that the greater number of Whigs who had sworn allegiance to James II and now did the same to William or Anne, and abjured the Pretender, were equally untrustworthy to monarchs whom they supported for merely pragmatic reasons. In an age in which many were open to charges of hypocrisy, the Nonjurors were confident that they alone had placed their religious duty above their worldly advantage. Ironically, the Whig insistence on the Providential divine right of Hanoverian monarchs and on the continuing necessity of oaths of allegiance subtly modified Whig understandings of the nature of an oath itself: to them, it became only a promise to obey the monarch for the time being, as identified by Parliament.[26] Oaths did not, therefore, obviously strengthen the allegiance of Whigs. What they were intended to do was to identify men of principle whose understanding of oaths, and so of political allegiance, was very different.

Oxford University and the oaths

The principles of the University of Oxford under Charles II and James II were well remembered by opponents as well as friends.[27] Whigs were given to lamenting the disaffection of both universities. Richard Steele complained in 1714:

if the late Acts of Parliament mentioned in the following Treatise had been from Time to Time put in a fair and clear Light, and been carefully recommended to the Perusal of young Gentlemen in Colleges, with a Preference to all other Civil Institutions whatsoever; this Kingdom had not been in its present Condition, but the Constitution would have had, in every Member the Universities have sent into the World ever since the Revolution, an Advocate for our Rights and Liberties.[28]

Plainly, he thought, this had not been the case.

What oaths did undergraduates and dons take? Evidence now available is powerful that usage at Oxford University in the early eighteenth century conformed to the requirements of its own Laudian statutes of 1636. For the ceremony of matriculation, the Laudian statutes read:

> And all those of 16 years of age who come to be matriculated shall sub-scribe the Articles of Faith and Religion, and shall take their corporal oath to acknowledge the supremacy of the King, to be faithful to the Univer-sity, and to observe its statutes, privileges, and customs, according to the form hitherto in use.[29]

From 1636, Oxford University itself required of matriculants only the oath of supremacy among the state oaths, not an oath of allegiance. The oath of allegiance had been imposed on graduands in 1610 by parliamentary statute (7 Jac. I, c. 6), a requirement that the university at once incorporated into its graduation ceremony,[30] and that the Laudian statutes repeated in 1636 in their section on graduation.

Oxford's Laudian statutes were later supplemented in other ways by parliamentary statute. In 1689, 1 W. & M., s. 1, c. 8 imposed the oaths of allegiance and supremacy on Heads of Houses, Fellows and Professors (but not on matriculants). In 1702, 13 W. III, c. 6 contained a new oath of allegiance describing the monarch as 'lawful and rightful King', added an oath of abjuration of James III, and for the first time extended the require-ment that these be subscribed to 'all persons teaching pupils in either uni-versity', and all members of colleges 'that are or shall be of the foundation (being of the age of eighteen years)', that is, those supported by the endow-ment: in most colleges, scholars, exhibitioners and servitors.[31] In 1714, 1 Geo. I, s. 2, c. 13 restated these requirements. This, then, was the picture at matriculation.

At graduation, parliamentary legislation of 1610 had imposed the oath of allegiance; the Laudian University Statutes additionally provided that the candidates 'are severally to subscribe the Articles of Faith and Religion ... and also the three Articles contained in the thirty-sixth Canon ... of the book of Ecclesiastical Constitutions and Canons, passed in the Synod begun at London in the year of our Lord 1603'.[32] Those who then took college fellowships were required to take the oaths of allegiance and abjuration at that point also. All therefore subscribed the oath of supremacy both at matriculation and at graduation, but this was not a central point of controversy: Jacobites who were not Roman Catholics might easily take the oath of supremacy, since the 'Foreign Prince' whose authority was abjured in that oath was not named, and could be understood to refer to a Hanoverian. In 1716 Nicholas Carter acknowledged that Jacobites had indeed taken the oath of supremacy while maintaining allegiance to James Francis Edward Stuart, and condemned them for having done so on the grounds that they would thereby 'assist a *Papist* Pretender'.[33]

It has recently been claimed that the oath of *allegiance* was required of all Oxford undergraduates at matriculation, commoners and foundationers alike. If so, Johnson would have subscribed with his contemporaries, and there would be no room for an argument that he consistently maintained a principled objection to the dynasty on the throne. This is, however, an error, resting on a misinterpretation of evidence and a failure to uncover more decisive material. There is no documentary evidence (as there is for the adoption of the oath of allegiance on graduation in 1610) that the university ever adopted that oath for *all* candidates on matriculation. Oxford's practice conformed to parliamentary statute in requiring the oath of allegiance only of foundationers on matriculation, not of commoners like Johnson. Yet it is not as easy as it might appear to establish that this was indeed the procedure, and the testimony of three contemporaries appears at first sight to point in another direction. It needs to be scrutinised carefully if it is not to mislead us.

First Nicholas Amhurst, an undergraduate at St. John's College from 1716 to 1719. Amhurst (1697–1742) was a zealous, perhaps an obsessional, Whig. Even as an undergraduate, he had angled for the patronage of the great with a poetic compilation which elevated the usual Freethinking images of the day into an eulogy of the Brunswick succession, Hoadly and Stanhope.[34] Even while an undergraduate he satirised his university by impugning its loyalty to the new dynasty, fictitiously addressing the prior claimant:

> Your *Isis* Sons, a firm unshaken Train,
> Mourn your ill-fated Birth, and baffled Reign;
> Impatient of their Thraldom, they disown
> A foreign Lineage, and a plunder'd Throne;
> Nor Heav'n nor Earth, Laws Human or Divine,
> Shall disunite them from the STUART line.

This loyalty Oxonians expressed, he claimed, not by military valour but by sowing 'delusive Fears' and 'Suspicious Doubts' to 'sap the Credit of the Government':

> Thus would our *Oxford*, with officious Love,
> Her Vows unbroken, and Allegiance prove.

It was a charge of personal dishonesty as well as political error:

> Nor Fame nor Conscience shake a *Tory's* Mind,
> Nor plighted Oaths his fixt Resolves unbind.[35]

On 29 June 1719, within sight of a Fellowship, Amhurst was expelled (as he claimed, for political reasons; as others recorded, for personal immorality).

Moving to London, he took his revenge in a series of 52 papers entitled *Terrae-Filius*, published from 11 January to 12 July 1721. Amhurst complained that the first experience of many freshmen, arriving at their colleges, was 'perjury':

> If he comes elected from any publick school, as from *Westminster, Winchester*, or *Merchant-Taylor's*, to be admitted upon the foundation of any college, he swears to a great volume of [college] statutes, which he never read, and to observe a thousand customs, rights and privileges, which he knows nothing of, and with which, if he did, he could not perhaps honestly comply.[36]

Parliamentary statute required that a foundationer would, unlike a commoner, also have to take the oath of allegiance with the other oaths at the university ceremony of matriculation. Amhurst himself was a foundationer, for he had been educated at Merchant Taylors, and became a scholar of St. John's College, Oxford, on 16 June 1716.[37] His account of matriculation correctly recorded his own experience:

> Within fifteen days after his admission into any college, he is obliged to be *matriculated*, or admitted a member of the university; at which time he subscribes the *thirty-nine* articles of religion, though often without knowing what he is doing, being ordered to write his name in a book, without mentioning upon what account; for which he pays *ten shillings and six pence*.
>
> At the same time he takes the oaths of allegiance and supremacy, which he is praetaught to evade, or think null: some have thought themselves sufficiently absolved from them by kissing their *thumbs*, instead of the book; others, in the crowd, or by the favour of an *honest*[38] beadle, have not had the book given to them at all.
>
> He also swears to another volume of [university] statutes, which he knows no more of than of his private college-statutes, and which contradict one another in many instances, and demand unjust compli-

ances in many others; all which he swallows ignorantly, and in the dark, without any wicked design.

This was not the only absurdity:

> But I have not mention'd the most absurd thing in *matriculation* yet. The statute says, if the person to be *matriculated* is sixteen years of age, he must subscribe the *thirty nine* articles, and take the oaths of *allegiance* and *supremacy*, as also an oath of fidelity to the university: but, if the person is not *sixteen* years of age, and above *twelve*, then he is ONLY to subscribe the *thirty nine* articles.[39]

Yet this was not what the Laudian statute said: it did not require the oath of allegiance, merely the oath of supremacy. Amhurst had evidently not consulted its text, and had probably relied on his own recollection of the event. He failed to record that the great majority of his freshmen contemporaries, who were not foundationers like himself, did not take the oath of allegiance at matriculation; and because he was expelled from the university, Amhurst had no opportunity to discover his error at the ceremony of graduation.

Amhurst did, however, half-grasp one relevant fact: many men at Oxford had not taken the oath of allegiance. Amhurst merely interpreted this fact in the way most discreditable to them:

> It is hardly worth mentioning, amongst all these absurdities, that by this statute many persons avoid taking the oaths of allegiance and supremacy at all; for being, or pretending to be, under *sixteen* when they are *matriculated*, they are excused from it at that time; and I never heard that any body was ever call'd upon afterwards to take them, unless they take a degree; but how many are there who stay many years at OXFORD, without taking any degree?[40]

It is more likely that such persons were unwilling to perjure themselves on graduation than that they had done so by falsely claiming to be under age.

Later, Amhurst returned to the same theme, printing two anonymous letters in his issue of 15 March 1721. The first, from 'J. R.', complained that Oxford's practice was undermining the sacred force of oaths by making matriculants swear to obey statutes they had not seen and subscribe the Thirty-nine Articles, over the meaning of which even learned clergy might disagree. The second purported to be a letter from 'Philalethes', complaining of another abuse at matriculation:

> When I was *matriculated* I was about seventeen years of age, and consequently entitled to take all the oaths; accordingly I subscrib'd the thirty-

nine articles of religion, (*though, by the bye, I did not know that I had done it till near six months afterwards*) and the then V[ice] Ch[ancello]r Dr. B[aro]n,[41] coming out of the convocation house, I took the oaths of *supremacy*, and of observing the *statutes, privileges,* &c. of the university. After which the doctor sign'd my *matriculation* paper, testifying that I had also taken the oath of *allegiance*, though not one word of it, or his majesty King GEORGE, was then mention'd.

Amhurst apologised for the two insertions:

> I confess an *anonymous* letter is not a sufficient voucher of the truth of any fact, and therefore I do not urge the *last* of these letters as such; let every reader believe or disbelieve it, as he thinks fit. All that I can assure him is, that it is a *genuine* letter, and came to my hands just as I publish it. But the *first*, which consists of *argument* upon the *known practice* of the university, is not liable to the same objection.[42]

Importantly, Amhurst only endorsed the claim of 'J. R.' On reconsideration, Amhurst did not repeat what he had earlier claimed in *Terrae-Filius* no. 3 (linking the oaths of allegiance and supremacy) and was not willing again to maintain that it was the '*known practice*' of the university to give matriculation certificates recording the taking of the oath of allegiance to candidates who had not in fact taken that oath. Amhurst would presumably have so maintained had he been able credibly to do so, for it would have been a major point scored against disaffected Oxford: his caution here is telling evidence. As a Whig, the Vice-Chancellor Dr. Baron had no reason knowingly to have handed out such inaccurate certificates to disaffected undergraduates.

Matriculation certificates in fact made no mention of the oath of allegiance, and the evidence currently available does not establish that foundationers received different certificates from commoners. All the surviving examples take the same form, recording the requirements common to both classes of undergraduate. The earliest so far located dates from 1722, a slip of paper[43] printed with the formula:

> Oxoniae [blank] Anno Domini 1722
> QUO die comparuit coram me [blank] subscripsit Articulis Fidei, & Religionis; & juramentum suscepit de agnoscenda suprema Regiae Majestatis potestate; & de observandis Statutis, Privilegiis, & Consuetudinibus hujus Universitatis.

In one hand the first blank has been filled in with the date, 'Feb: 20mo' and the second blank with the name of the candidate, 'Eduardus Green e Coll: Aen: Nas: Arm: fil:'. The certificate is signed, in another hand, 'Rob: Shippen

Vice Can:'.[44] This formula was unaltered on all the surviving examples. Joshua Ellis, a near-contemporary of Samuel Johnson, from Johnson's own Pembroke College, was given an identical certificate (the year only being changed) in December 1727, just as the statutes required; it similarly recorded only his assent to the Thirty-nine Articles, the statutes of the University, and the oath of supremacy.[45] Moreover, the Vice-Chancellor concerned, John Mather, demonstrated his active Hanoverian sympathies: he was one of only seven heads of houses, and an embarrassingly modest number of county gentry, who during the rebellion signed the Association in defence of King George on 14 October 1745 (together with staunch Whigs like Henry Brooke and John Conybeare).[46] Why would a pro-Hanoverian Vice-Chancellor systematically have allowed disaffected undergraduates to matriculate by giving them deliberately falsified matriculation certificates? There is no evidence that he or any of his colleagues did so.

The possible confusion between the oath of supremacy, which all matriculants took, and the oath of allegiance, which only foundationers took on matriculation, allowed some Whigs to make capital by suggesting that all undergraduates took both. Where Amhurst later shied away from that claim, which would not bear public scrutiny, Thomas Tanner made it in his edition of Anthony à Wood's *Athenae Oxoniensis* (1721). It was this which provoked Thomas Hearne's accurate correction: Tanner

> hath altered all things so, & made him [Wood] talk in such a manner, as if Mr. Wood had been a downright Villain, & had not known what even the most ignorant Scholar knows. How comes it, otherwise, to pass that more than once Gentlemen, when they are matriculated, are represented to take the Oaths of Allegiance & Supremacy? Mr. Wood could not write so, since nobody knew better that the Oath of Supremacy only, & not the Oath of Allegiance, is then taken. Nor does the [Laudian] Statute require an Oath of Allegiance at that time. But this was added [by Tanner] to bring a slur upon the University, and out of a Trimming Design . . .[47]

Some Whigs did try to exploit this confusion between oaths and argue that, since all undergraduates had taken the oath of allegiance, an overt loyalty to the House of Hanover could be demanded of them. A junior Whig don, Richard Blacow, so argued before the Vice-Chancellor, Dr. John Purnell, Warden of New College, on 29 February 1747/8, Blacow urging the University to take disciplinary action against certain undergraduates who had, he claimed, uttered 'treasonable Words' during a riot on the birthday of Henry Benedict Stuart. Blacow was evidently unsuccessful, for Purnell was willing to punish the undergraduates only for their disorderly behaviour, not for their having broken any oath of allegiance. Purnell deliberately avoided the point, according to Blacow's account:

Upon asking the Vice-Chancellor, Whether such Treasonable Behaviour did not imply Perjury; he answered, *Mad young Fellows did not think about Perjury, and it would be hard to proceed against Boys in too severe a manner.* I answered, That, as the Wisdom of the University thought them of proper Capacities to take the Oaths, *four years ago*, they might be thought of proper Capacities *now* to be punish'd for the breach of those Oaths.

But Purnell refused to take legal depositions of evidence against the under-graduates; Blacow could advance his cause only by taking it to the highest authority, the Duke of Newcastle, a Secretary of State.[48] Evidently, the offending undergraduates were not proceeded against for a breach of the University statutes.

The same conflation of the oath of supremacy and the oath of allegiance was the tactic of a Whig partisan, Benjamin Kennicott, seeking to call in question the integrity of the notoriously Jacobite don William King:

Every person, at his *Matriculation*, if *sixteen* years of age, takes the Oaths of *Allegiance* and *Supremacy*; and every person, admitted either a *Clerk*, *Exhibitioner*, *Scholar*, *Fellow*, *Head* of any *College*, or, Sir, *Head* of any *Hall*, takes (or is requir'd by *Act of Parliament* to take) the Oath of *Abjuration*.

Kennicott then reprinted the text of the latter oath.[49] This was a fair point: King (Principal of St. Mary Hall)[50] and others like him would presumably have taken the oath of abjuration with mental reservations. But Kennicott, like Amhurst, was probably also making a genuine mistake over the other oath, since Kennicott as an undergraduate had been a foundationer, a scholar of Wadham College,[51] and like Amhurst would indeed have taken the oath of allegiance at matriculation. The whole weight of Kennicott's argument thereafter rested on the oath of abjuration required of founda-tioners: it is likely that he introduced his reference to matriculation without reflection, for he did not subsequently return to it. Kennicott's argument was addressed to the case of Blacow of Brasenose, who 'took the degree of *Master of Arts* in 1747. In consequence of an *Exhibition* (for which he was not indebted to any members of the University) he had taken the Oath of *Abjuration*; by which he had *bound his Soul* to discover all Treasons against his Sovereign, that should come to his knowledge'.[52] Blacow, argued Kenni-cott, was not an informer: he had done only what he was pre-engaged to do by his oath.

Although the oath of allegiance was not a requirement placed on all undergraduates at matriculation, testing oaths were certainly demanded of Oxonians at other stages of their careers, and another individual illustrates the difficulties created by these oaths for a scholar with a conscience. Thomas Hearne (1678–1735), later famous as an antiquarian and Nonjuror, took the oath of allegiance on graduation in 1699, and in 1700 had written a tract justifying his action to his patron, the Nonjuror Francis Cherry of Shottesbrooke.[53] After Cherry's death in 1713 the manuscript passed to the Bodleian, from which archive one of Hearne's enemies, John Bilstone, later published it. Hearne had elsewhere argued from a utilitarian calculation that because of James II's conduct 'the *Common GOOD of the NATION* requires either his Deposition, or, at least, that a Restraint should be put upon him some other way'; in the tract now published he produced arguments from medieval and ancient history, including a utilitarian interpretation of the binding force of an oath:

> The *Prime* End of an Oath is to be preferred to one which is *Inferior*. The *Prime* End of an Oath is *The Good of the Persons* concerned in it . . . *if the keeping of the Oath be really and truly inconsistent with the Welfare of a People, in subverting the Fundamental Laws which Support it; I do not see how such an Oath continues to Oblige.*[54]

Yet Hearne's views were changing. On 19 January 1714/15 he was pressed by his friends to stand, and was elected, as Archetypographus and Esquire Bedell of Civil Law, but evaded the oath of allegiance tendered to him:

> All the Objections, such as being a Papist, a Non-Juror, &c. were started against the Writer. But these would not sway in the Case, so as to turn him [Hearne] by. The Abjuration Oath he is always resolved to refuse. Nor did he take the Oath of Allegiance, reading only the first Part of it, so as to suppose K[ing] J[ames] wch he did by speaking in a very low Voice, tho' this was not regarded, to his great Surprize.

The entry in the Register of Convocation therefore recorded that Hearne

> was accordingly admitted to both Offices having first taken the Oaths of Supremacy & Allegiance, without saying to whom ye Allegiance Oath was taken, in wch he [George Cooper, the Registrar] did right, it being certain yt if he had said I swore to K. James (as I really did) he should be brought into a Scrape as well as myself.[55]

His views continued to evolve: he now realised that even this evasion was unacceptable. According to Bilstone,

> Soon after this Promotion he acquired better Reasons (to *Himself* at least) for Non-Compliance with the Oaths that were necessary for *keeping* it, than he had before for the *Acceptance* of it; and accordingly resigns that advantageous Post, which the University had so lately conferred on him, as inconsistent with his *Conscience*, or at least, his Manner of *Thinking*.[56]

In November 1715, Hearne resigned the post of Bedell to try to pre-empt a Whig manoeuvre to deprive him of his sub-librarianship. He would soon have resigned anyway, he recorded, rather than subscribe the oaths of allegiance and abjuration now required, by the statute of 1 Geo. I, s. 2, c. 13, to be taken by 23 January 1716:

> For indeed it was my full Resolution then, if the King [James] should not come in, not to act in either office, because I am fully resolved not to take the Oaths (i.e. as the Oath of Allegiance is clogg'd with the damnable Oath of Abjuration), come what will of it. Most people were surprized at this, especially considering that the Beadleship is worth ten times as much as the Office of Sublibrarian. But as I never was yet guided by Interest, so it fell out now, it being no other Principle than that of Honesty & Conscience & Regard for Learning that I went upon.[57]

By resigning, Hearne, aged 37, now gave the most convincing disavowal of the arguments for defeasible succession which, aged 22, he had set out in *A Vindication*. Hearne's career illustrates both the evolution of a scholar's thinking on the oaths, the greater challenge imposed by the oath of abjuration in 1715, and also a poor man placing conscience before worldly advantage. Subsequently, he may also have refused appointment to other offices which would have required the oaths: the Camden chair of history in 1720 and 1727, the posts of keeper of the archives in 1726, and Bodley's librarian in 1719 and 1729. Hearne was neither duplicitous, nor did he use pragmatic arguments to shrug off the significance of oaths. The reality was almost the reverse, for he explicitly condemned those who took the oaths with mental reservations:

> Notwithstanding the abominable Wickedness of the said Abjuration Oath, it is incredible wt Numbers of all Kinds run in to swear, abundance pretending that as 'tis a forced Oath, they may do it, especially since the Imposers have no right to advance such an Oath, & they think, therefore, yt all the Crime will fall upon them. But this reason will bring off any wickedness . . .[58]

Refusal of the oaths was not merely a procedural scruple, but declaratory of adherence to an extensive and interlocking set of religious and political beliefs. There is evidence that this was a widespread culture, for it persisted among undergraduates as well as their seniors. Johnson left Pembroke College in December 1729; the poet Richard Graves, who matriculated at the same College on 7 November 1732, recorded being drawn into a circle of gentleman commoners there who 'drank their favourite toasts on their knees',[59] an easily recognised Jacobite allusion. On 23 February 1747/8, as we have seen, a minor disturbance in the streets of Oxford took on more serious overtones when undergraduates shouted Jacobite slogans at a Whig don, Richard Blacow. As a result of Blacow's information, three undergraduates were arrested and taken to London for trial.

This persecution provoked the publication of a piece of coded writing which revealed the issues of principle still at stake: a reprint of Robert Sanderson's Oxford pamphlet of 1647. Its editor, writing in 1749, offered no application of his century-old text to the aftermath of the riot; but it was of the essence of a university, he argued, that it have 'a power of determining causes, wherein any of its members were concerned, without appeal to the ordinary Courts of justice . . . that the youth might not be called away from their studies by litigious suits'. Without specifying the present occasion, the anonymous author argued that 'they who design to subvert the laws and liberties of any nation, commonly begin with the privileges and immunities of the Universities'. Still without openly drawing the moral, he presented his modern readers with the Puritan attempt '*to subvert the Constitution of the Church and State of* England' in the 1640s, specifically the Ordinance of 1 May 1647 which threatened the deprivation of all in the University who had not taken the Solemn League and Covenant and the 'Negative Oath', an oath not to assist the King in the civil war.[60] Oxford's reasons for refusing these demands in 1647 were now reprinted in full. On 1 June 1647, two days before the arrival of the Commissioners, Convocation had produced a lengthy and defiant statement of principle against the Solemn League and Covenant; a disavowal of the 'Negative Oath' (it could not be taken without 'abjuring our *natural Allegiance*, and violating the *Oathes of Supremacy and Allegiance* by us formerly taken'), and a condemnation of the Directory of Public Worship.[61] These remarkable and courageous documents, for which many Oxford dons suffered swift retribution in the 1640s, were now reprinted with only the briefest of editorial introductions. The application was plain: the documents could be left to speak for themselves.

Whigs charged Tory dons with having perjured themselves in taking the oaths in order to hold their fellowships, but motives were open to challenge on the Whig side, too. Defending his role in the riot, Blacow later claimed that 'I thought myself doubly bound to take notice of the Treason: because I had taken the Oath of Abjuration, and had been invested by the University with the authority of an officer in that particular Street', that is, the minor disciplinary office of Master of the Streets.[62] Yet Blacow's role attracted a variety of criticism. As well as acting as '*Delator* and *Informer*', one critic charged him with manipulating his testimony at the behest of the Duke of Newcastle to secure the acquittal of one of the three undergraduates charged, who happened inconveniently to be the son of '*John Luxmore* of *Oakhampton*, a Person who had the absolute Power of returning Two Members of Parliament for that Borough, which he had constantly been engaged to do by the Ministerial Party'. Blacow was impelled by ambition, it was claimed, not by a sense of the inviolability of an oath.[63]

Even if Amhurst had been mistaken about the oaths in the early 1720s, had the University's practice changed by a later date? A variety of evidence suggests that it had not. Other matriculation certificates of later dates survive, identical to Edward Green's of 1722 and Joshua Ellis's of 1727: one for William Drake of Brasenose on 2 October 1739, signed by John Mather as Vice-Chancellor;[64] one for Thomas Holme of the same college on 5 June 1751, signed by Stephen Niblett, as the Vice-Chancellor's deputy.[65] Richard Heber's, dated 14 December 1790, took the same form and used the same words.[66] So did Henry Ellis's, dated 27 June 1796.[67] So too did Henry Hoper's, dated 26 November 1806.[68] If university practice had evolved over time to include the oath of allegiance at matriculation for all candidates, the wording of the certificate would presumably have been amended to record this; no such change was made over many decades.

Clear evidence that practice was unchanged was given by Edward Bentham (1707–76), who matriculated at Corpus in 1724 and became a tutor of Oriel in 1732. On the basis of long knowledge of both the University's statutes and practice, he warned an imagined undergraduate of dubious loyalties in 1748: 'Upon your Promotion to any *Degree*, you will be called upon to take the Oath of *Allegiance*; and if advanced to any Preferment, in or out of the University, any Office Military, Civil, or Ecclesiastical, you must necessarily take the Oath of *Abjuration*.' He added an explanatory footnote: 'All Heads, Fellows and Foundationers of Colleges or Halls, all Readers or Tutors in the University are required to take the Oath of *Abjuration*, under Penalty of forfeiting their Places, and Five hundred pounds, if exercising any Office.'[69] Bentham's argument to encourage his wavering pupil would have been stronger had he been able to remind his undergraduate that he had already taken the oath of allegiance on matriculation; but he could not do so. Had Bentham, improbably, been in error on this point, he could have corrected himself, and advanced the stronger argument, in a subsequent pamphlet on similar themes; again, he did not do so.[70] He, and his intended audience, were familiar with what the University's rites of passage required.

Although the evidence establishes that university practice did not vary without statutory authorisation, it has been suggested that one college did change, but in the opposite direction of accommodating those with scruples about the oaths. At Christ Church, a Student[71] who passed the necessary university examination for the BA or MA degree had also to obtain from the Dean and Chapter a 'grace', signifying their consent and approval, before he could formally take his degree in the university's ceremony of graduation. These graces came to be treated within Christ Church itself as equivalent to the corresponding degrees. The college's most recent historian has argued that some Students in the late seventeenth and early eighteenth centuries took advantage of this system, omitting to take their university degrees in order to avoid the oath of allegiance.[72] If so, no such option was available to Samuel Johnson at neighbouring Pembroke. Yet even this degree of latitude is doubtful: Students would have been obliged to take the oaths of allegiance and abjuration on admission to their studentships, like the Westminster Student William Murray (since he was then a Jacobite, he presumably subscribed with mental reservations);[73] having done so, it is likely that few would have been helped by a procedural evasion of the oaths on graduation. Oxford's formal requirements were difficult to evade: practice conformed to the statutes.

Two later controversies also suggest that the University's practice had not evolved to require the oath of allegiance on matriculation from commoners. The first occurred in the late 1750s when Oxford was imbroiled in legal controversy over whether it had, alone, the authority to alter its Laudian statutes of 1636, since these were a royal grant. In the point of substance at issue, Oxonians keeping their names on their colleges' books for many years merely in order to vote, it was argued that Statute III, section i 'seems clearly to prove, that *Matriculation alone* doth not give a Right to the Privileges of the University' without admission to and residence in 'some College or Hall'.[74] The participants in the controversy did not argue that the statutory requirements at matriculation were not strictly complied with; on the contrary, the defenders of the statutes prided themselves on the success with which their framers had taken care in 'securing the perpetual Observance of them'.[75] The second controversy arose in the early 1770s over the question of subscription to the Thirty-nine Articles at matriculation. None of the participants argued that the practice at that ceremony had evolved to include the imposition of the oath of allegiance also. Such a point would probably have been made by both the critics and the supporters of exacting oaths from matriculants had that been the current practice.[76] Evidently it was not.

Samuel Johnson at Oxford

The strongest evidence of all, which bears directly on Johnson's own conduct, comes from the archives of the University of Oxford. These records have always been held to establish that the procedure on matriculation had been laid down in the Laudian statutes of 1636, and remained unaltered: if over 16, the candidate was required to subscribe the Thirty-nine Articles, swear to obey the University statutes, and take the oath of supremacy.[77] This is confirmed by the subscription register on matriculation for the years 1714–40.[78] A folio volume, it contains, pasted on its first leaf, the relevant section from the printed University statutes, 'Titulus II. De Matricula Universitatis. s. 3. *De Tempore & conditionibus Matriculationis*' (see plate 4). This section set out the requirements to subscribe the Articles of Religion and the statutes of the University, and to take the oath of supremacy.[79] The oath of allegiance was not listed: it was imposed on foundationers only and by a subsequent Act of Parliament (1 Geo. I, s. 2, c. 13) rather than as a condition of admission in the Laudian statutes. On the following page was pasted a printed table of fees for different ranks of undergraduate. Before the next page was tipped in the printed text of the Articles of Religion, evidently removed from a Prayer Book. The following pages are filled with the signatures of undergraduates, beginning on 8 October 1714. Under the entry for 14 December 1729 appears the signature 'Samuel Johnson e Coll: Pembr: Gen: Fil:' (see plate 5). Johnson chose to describe himself as the son of a gentleman, so paying a fee of 10s 6d, rather than the son of a plebeian, who would pay only 6s 8d. We know, then, that Johnson subscribed the oath of supremacy; there is no evidence that he subscribed the oaths of allegiance or abjuration.

Had Johnson not left the university early, but gone on to graduate, he would have been confronted by different requirements. These, too, are reliably documented. The subscription register on graduation is missing for the years 1706–36, but the volume for 1736–63 survives,[80] and no legislation was passed to vary the practice between 1732 (when Johnson might have graduated) and 1736. It is a smaller volume than the matriculation register, and could easily have been held in the hand. Like the matriculation register, it opens with two printed pages giving the texts of the university and parliamentary requirements at that stage: '*The Oath of Allegiance*', '*The Oath of Supremacy*', and '*Three Articles in the 36th Canon*' (see plate 6).[81] Unlike the texts in the matriculation register, however, these pages were specially printed to fit the volume, and printed on vellum. The reason for the choice of a more durable, though more expensive, material is revealed by the soiled state of these two pages, especially the wide black mark in the gutter at their foot: candidates held the book open (often with their thumbs) at that page as they read aloud the texts of the oaths before writing their signatures on the blank pages which followed. After these vellum pages is inserted, once more, a printed copy of the Thirty-nine Articles. Candidates could not be unaware of the oaths that they were required to take.

That a reading aloud was called for on graduation is confirmed by a contemporary authority. In 1773 Charles Jenkinson, MP, anticipating a second attempt by Sir William Meredith, MP, to relax clerical subscription to the Thirty-nine Articles, took advice from Nathan Wetherell, Master of University College and friend of Samuel Johnson, on Oxford's current practice.[82] Wetherell's memorandum in reply revealed, *inter alia*, that a candidate at matriculation *said* nothing to signify his assent to the Articles: 'He writes his name only in a Book *to which the 39 Articles are prefixed.*' At graduation, however,

the case is much altered. Each Candidate is obliged by Statute within three days of his petitioning for his Degree to read the Articles. He then subscribes in Congregation in the presence of all the Magistrates, after which one of the Proctors announces to the several members present that he has subscribed, & then the Candidate declares in the strongest manner his assent to the truth of the Doctrine in the words of the 36th Canon.[83]

Again, this evidence establishes conformity to the requirements of the Laudian statutes. Title IX ('Of the Congregations of the Regent Masters'), section 6 ('Of the Oaths of the Persons Presented'), chapter 3 ('The Common Form of Binding every Presentee by oath, and of exacting from all persons the Oath of Royal Supremacy and Allegiance'), included the passage:

> Next, the senior of the presentees shall read aloud, with a clear voice, so as to be heard by all the rest, the oath of the royal supremacy, and shall kiss the book when tendered by the proctor, and after him all the rest who are presented on the same day; and lastly, while he distinctly leads with the oath of fealty and allegiance, all the others shall repeat it, word for word, and shall all, one after another, kiss the book in confirmation of the oath.[84]

Why did Johnson leave Oxford without graduating? A monocausal explanation, whether in terms of poverty or principle, is unpersuasive, but whatever the arguments over poverty, there is evidence that principle was necessarily involved at graduation. Poverty would have been a stronger sole reason for Johnson's departure had the length of time in residence for an Oxford BA degree been sixteen terms over four years, as was formally required; but Oxford made explicit and documented provision for shortening this course. Of this time, 'By an ordinary dispensation and liberal construction' only twelve terms (over three years) were actually required to be spent in residence by those who were willing to pay the small fee for obtaining a dispensation from Convocation.[85]

It is improbable (although possible) that Johnson's parents would have sent their son to Oxford without expecting to be able to support him there until graduation. Could Johnson have afforded to finance three years' residence on his family's resources?[86] Johnson's battels, while in residence, were about 8 shillings a week, a normal amount for a commoner (he was evidently not economising), plus a quarterly charge of 4s 7d.[87] This suggests an annual bill of approximately £21, depending on his time in residence, plus fees and incidental expenses. The expenses of wealthy undergraduates were much higher than those of poor commoners, but one estimate in 1760 was that 'a frugal young man' could 'live pretty well on the yearly sum of 20 gns'.[88]

Some evidence suggests that even less might have sufficed. Richard Newton, Principal of Hart Hall, in his careful draft regulations intended to secure for his society the grant of collegiate status, addressed the problem of the erratic presence of undergraduates and the need 'to Secure their strict

Residence in Term Time'. His view was that 'The only Objection against such a Residence is the Expense of it', and that non-residence would be cured by an adequate allowance. He proposed a scheme of scholarships of £10 per annum as 'Sufficient to Answer this Expence', arguing firmly against scholarships of higher value.[89] Poverty at least meant self-discipline. There was another recognised means of financing a degree: boys without sufficient financial resources might hold a servitorship, a sort of scholarship requiring in return certain menial duties. The Cambridge equivalent of a servitor was called a sizar. Even in 1775, almost half a century after Johnson, a Cambridge don could estimate: 'A sizar, as he has frequently great assistances in college, is under no necessity of costing his friends more than forty or fifty, never so much as sixty pounds a year.'[90] George Whitefield, who matriculated as a servitor at Johnson's own Pembroke College in 1732, claimed that he called on his family for only £24 over the course of the three years' BA course.[91] Johnson, then, might possibly have been able to finance three years at Oxford from his family's resources. He might also have held the office of servitor;[92] but a servitorship, being 'of the foundation', required the oaths of allegiance and abjuration.

We have no evidence whether Johnson foresaw or failed to foresee the problem of subscription before he matriculated. Even after his departure from Oxford, he left his valuable library, part of his father's stock, in the care of his friend John Taylor of Christ Church. Did Johnson hope to return? Was he caught in a moral dilemma between his commitment to the life of the mind and his inability to subscribe the additional oaths? Evidence on this part of his early life is too fragmentary to allow conclusive arguments about his motives: the evidence does, however, suggest that Johnson did not take the oaths of allegiance or abjuration in circumstances in which it would have been in his worldly interest to have done so. He also continued to believe, as Hawkins recorded, that he had been denied a proper place in life by 'his adverse fortunes' and that others occupied places to which he himself 'had a better title'.[93]

Johnson as a schoolmaster

Poverty as well as principle was no doubt involved in Johnson's decision to leave Oxford without graduating, though Johnson must have known that the lack of a degree would condemn him to worse poverty thereafter by barring him from many of the professions. Johnson went down from Oxford not to better his condition by entering a profession, but without any employment in prospect. His engagement with the life of scholarship was already plain, however, and like many of his contemporaries he expressed his commitment to a set of late-humanist cultural ideals by persistently and repeatedly seeking posts as a schoolmaster. Formally, to take such a post should have involved a newly appointed master in subscribing the oaths.

There were two occasions in his schoolmasterly career on which Johnson might have been formally required to swear on taking up such employment.[94] Did he in fact do so on these occasions?

The evidence strongly suggests that he did not. The system for requiring oaths from schoolmasters was often far from watertight, as can be established by the subscription books, surviving in diocesan archives, in which these acts were systematically recorded when they occurred. Contemporary practice as evidenced by the Diocese of Norwich's subscription books, the subject of a careful monograph, suggests that the oaths came to be tendered much less often to schoolmasters than to parish clergy: the lack of a formal ritual like induction to a living or to an Oxbridge fellowship led to schoolmasters often being left in peace, as those taking such posts must have known. Clergy greatly outnumber schoolteachers in the subscription books of the Dioceses of Lichfield and Lincoln also, and although the absolute numbers of men in either profession are not known the disparity is so great as to suggest a higher incidence of subscription among the clergy. Without a regular ceremony like university matriculation and graduation, the number of schoolmasters subscribing in the diocese of Norwich fluctuated widely, reaching peaks in the years 1662, 1677, 1686, 1706, 1716, 1723, 1735, 1740 and 1753, but in intervening years falling to low levels:[95] this suggests that subscription was most often demanded at moments of political tension rather than being regularly exacted at induction to a teaching post (the same peaks are observable in the figures of subscriptions by doctors). The Norwich evidence also shows that many schools known to have existed provided no subscribers in the registers:[96] large numbers of schoolmasters evidently escaped the attention of the authorities.

What was the experience of Samuel Johnson? In March 1732 he was appointed usher of Market Bosworth school, thirteen miles from Leicester, in the parish of Market Bosworth, of the Diocese of Lincoln. I formerly presumed that since Johnson's appointment meant that Sir Wolstan Dixie, the school's chief trustee and petty tyrant, ignored the requirement that the under-master have a BA degree, Dixie was unlikely to have been a careful observer of requirements to take state oaths. The evidence of the subscription books of the Diocese of Lincoln, however, establishes a much more interesting picture: the exact opposite was the case. The headmasters and ushers of Market Bosworth school all took the oaths during the time of Dixie's dominance; with one exception.[97] This uniform practice makes it more remarkable that the name of Samuel Johnson is absent from the relevant subscription books of the Archdeaconry of Leicester,[98] and also (even if this were not the relevant series) absent from the subscription books of the other Archdeaconries of the Diocese of Lincoln.[99] The presence of Dixie's other appointees makes it highly unlikely that Johnson or Dixie was merely unaware of the requirement to subscribe.

We know that Johnson communicated his extreme unhappiness about this period of his life to both Hawkins and Boswell, and Johnson is our main source for Dixie's overbearing character. Hawkins wrote that Dixie, 'in the pride of wealth, shewed no regard for learning or parts, nor respected any man for his mental endowments'.[100] Yet Dixie had appointed that well-known author on the classics, Anthony Blackwall,[101] and then the precocious Johnson himself: this was not a negligible record of enlightened patronage. Boswell recorded 'a disagreement' between Johnson and Dixie, ascribing it to Dixie's 'intolerable harshness', and dwelt on the boredom and frustration of teaching;[102] yet Johnson continued to pursue other teaching posts, and did so as late as 1739, when his career in London had, although tenuously, begun. Why did such a short spell of teaching produce such lasting revulsion in Johnson? Dixie's own identity suggests an answer. Although evidence for his politics is not abundant, it is telling: Dixie's name appeared in a list submitted to James Francis Edward Stuart in 1721, evidently a survey of those men expected to support a rising at the time of the Atterbury plot.[103] One explanation consistent with the evidence is that Dixie overbearingly demanded that Johnson subscribe the oaths, with mental reservations or disregarding their sacred force, that Johnson refused and was obliged to resign his post; but the evidence currently available is not sufficient to establish that this occurred. We know only that Johnson's name is not in the subscription books, and that there is no merely procedural reason to explain its absence.

Johnson held only one other teaching post: the school at Edial, two miles west of Lichfield, in the diocese of Lichfield. He began it in July 1735, and continued it, with some publicity, until the autumn of 1736. Since the school was Johnson's own, he is unlikely to have volunteered himself to take the oaths; his name is not present in the subscription books of the Diocese of Lichfield.[104] Since schoolmasters were legally required to renew their subscription on appointment to each post, Johnson would not have been released from the formal obligation to subscribe at Edial, even if he had subscribed at Market Bosworth (or at Oxford): the absence of his name from both the Leicester and the Lichfield subscription books is therefore doubly telling. We have no evidence on whether or not Johnson expected that the irregularity of the exaction of oaths from schoolmasters might have allowed him a loophole. This possibility, however, established by the relatively small number of schoolmaster subscriptions in the Lincoln and Lichfield registers, may have encouraged Johnson in 1739 when he applied for the headmastership of Appleby Grammar School near Lichfield, supported by a recommendation from the Jacobite Lord Gower, especially since 'The governors of this august institution were rigid Tories and Jacobites to a man'.[105] Yet even here Johnson was disqualified by his lack of a degree: formal requirements could not often be evaded, even among like-minded men.

In summary: documentary evidence indicates that Johnson did not sub-scribe the oath of allegiance or the oath of abjuration while an Oxford undergraduate, or while a schoolmaster at Edial; similar evidence strongly suggests, although it is not conclusive, that Johnson did not subscribe at Market Bosworth either.[106]

Johnson in London: the oaths and the Trained Bands

The dilemma in which Johnson's objection to the oaths placed him was one which faced other men of letters also: Johnson was among the last of the line, but he was not unique. Indeed, it can be shown that one and perhaps two of the most famous men of letters of the preceding generation had been in a similar position. John Dryden forfeited hopes of official patronage after 1688 for the same reason. In June 1692, while living in Gerrard Street, in St. Anne's parish, Soho, he was summoned before the justices to take the oath of allegiance, refused and was fined.[107] His identity was known. In 1698, he protested to the Duke of Ormonde, then abroad: 'We Jacobites have no more reason to thank you than we have our present King who has enriched Holland wth the wealth of England.'[108] The most Dryden could now hope for was to be left alone. 'If they will consider me as a Man, who have done my best to improve the Language, & Especially the Poetry, & will be content with my acquiescence under the present Government, & forbearing satire on it, that I can promise, because I can perform it: but I can neither take the Oaths, nor forsake my Religion.'[109] It was not enough to avert political hostility, however, Dryden 'not being capable of renounceing the Cause, for which I have so long Sufferd'.[110]

Alexander Pope's leading modern biographer has concluded that 'Pope was in essentials simply a Roman Catholic nonjuror', capable of 'secret hopes when an invasion loomed; and obviously affronted by the indis-criminate legalized oppression of his kind; yet – for whatever reasons, expe-dient or principled – stoutly opposed to the kind of agitation that might bring on social unrest and civil war'.[111] It is possible that he was the Mr. Pope who in 1715 'being duely summoned did not appear [before the justices] to take the said Oathes or . . . subscribe the Declaration' against transubstantiation required by law.[112] If Dryden and Pope both fell into the category of Nonjuror, it is more plausible that other men of letters may have done so too. Yet Dryden and Pope were both Roman Catholics: further evidence is required to make the case for any member of the Church of England. What, then, was the position in Johnson's London?

Those not known to the authorities as Roman Catholic recusants had a greater chance of escaping attention. Only occasionally were the oaths administered *en masse*, as on 8–10 April 1696 when the Commissioners of the Land Tax in each ward of the City of London compiled returns of those taking the oaths of allegiance and supremacy prescribed by the act of 1 W

& M, c. 8.[113] Normally, however, the oaths were tendered to men on taking up some office that required them, or to individuals of suspect loyalty who were called upon to declare themselves. In the City of London, such subscriptions were effected by signing (for the illiterate, with a mark) one of the Abjuration Rolls, lengthy vellum documents printed at the top with the texts of the oath of allegiance, the declaration against the Pope's deposing power, and the oath of abjuration (together with, in most cases, the declaration against transubstantiation). These voluminous columns of signatures constitute one more location where Johnson's signature might have appeared, had he subscribed; again, his name is absent.[114]

It may be that this was a fortuitous absence, but other evidence tells against this interpretation. There was, for example, Johnson's demeanour at the Ivy Lane club (1749–56) as reported by Hawkins.[115] There is also evidence from Johnson's hand of his sense of profound alienation from the regime. *The Rambler* no. 148 (17 August 1751), began:

> Politicians remark, that no oppression is so heavy or lasting as that which is inflicted by the perversion and exorbitance of legal authority. The robber may be seized, and the invader repelled, wherever they are found; they who pretend no right but that of force, may by force be punished or suppressed. But when plunder bears the name of impost, and murder is perpetrated by a judicial sentence, fortitude is intimidated, and wisdom confounded: resistance shrinks from an alliance with rebellion, and the villain remains secure in the robes of the magistrate.

Johnson did not apply his moral to a specific case. It was unnecessary and unwise to do so, under a government which into the early 1750s still brought Jacobite activists to the gallows.

Subscription was not merely an academic matter; allegiance, as tested by oaths, bore directly on men's public conduct in a number of spheres. One such was military service, and it created for successive ministries the problem of organising a reliable militia in a partly unreliable society. Charles Sackville, Earl of Middlesex, later 2nd Duke of Dorset, formerly a supporter of '*the best and most truly* PATRIOT PRINCE' Frederick, Prince of Wales, advocated a militia scheme in 1752 which anticipated George Townshend's abortive initiative of 1756 and William Pitt's scheme, implemented in 1757. The plan would, wrote Sackville,

> (it is hoped,) meet with no Opposition, from any but Those, who would wish to see the present FAMILY indefensible, and without an Army. – *Party* is, or ought to be, out of the Question; and all Men, except the *Jacobites*, should unite in obtaining a Power for the Nation, that will make it rise again in Grandeur and Respect, to the Height it was at in the Reign of Queen *Elizabeth*.

His qualification – 'ought to be' – was telling, for his plan acknowledged a difficulty: 'All disaffected Persons, who refuse the legal OATHS of *Supremacy* and *Abjuration*, should be obliged to pay, but not permitted to SERVE.'[116]

Johnson's reasons for avoiding service in the Trained Bands of the City of London therefore bear on the question of oaths. The Militia Act of 1662, 13 & 14 Car. II, c. 3, was the foundation document. It imposed the oath of allegiance on all officers and militiamen (clause XIX); it abolished England's ancient Trained Bands and replaced them with the reformed structures; but it left London's untouched (clause XXVII): the Lieutenants for the City of London 'may and shall continue to list and levy the trained bands and auxiliaries of the said city in manner as heretofore'. These Trained Bands survived, governed by their own customs, until reorganised by the Act of 34 Geo. III, c. 81 in 1794.[117] The Militia Act of 1757, 30 Geo. II, c. 25, clause LXV, again specifically confirmed the City's ancient privileges, and it was in the City's Trained Bands that Johnson was, according to Boswell, picked to serve. It follows that Johnson was not chosen after and under the terms of the 1757 Militia Act (as has been suggested, in mid- to late 1759), when Johnson (born in 1709) might more possibly have been deterred from serving by his age. Age and ill-health are, of course, not implausible explanations, but more may also have been involved, and it is important that Johnson's selection be dated as accurately as possible. It could have been at any time after he moved into his first house at 17 Gough Square (his tenancy of which lasted from some time after June 1746 until March 1759) and so, as a housekeeper, became liable to be chosen.[118] Johnson must have been aware from the late 1740s, while working on the *Dictionary*, that he might now be confronted with the moral dilemma which his selection for militia duty would have posed.

Where the militia established elsewhere by the legislation of the 1660s decayed,[119] London's Trained Bands continued on a regular basis into the 1740s and 1750s, financed by a regular levy known as the 'Trophy Tax', picked from regularly revised muster rolls, and exercised as regiments at the Artillery Ground on days of 'General March and Muster' appointed by the Lieutenancy of the City of London: all this preceded the Militia Act of 1757.[120] Lists of those picked to serve do not survive, but it may be possible to infer a time frame for Johnson's selection. Boswell recorded that Johnson's colonel was Benjamin Rackstrow. This attribution of rank was clearly an error. The colonelcy of one of the City's six regiments was a senior position, conferred as an honour only on men of high standing in public life: Rackstrow (proprietor of the 'Museum of Anatomy and Curiosities' at 197 Fleet Street) could never have aspired to it.[121] His career in the Orange Regiment can however be established: he was promoted Ensign on 16 January 1745/6, Lieutenant on 2 July 1747, Captain on 5 February 1752, Major on 17 May 1759 and Captain Lieutenant on 17 May 1763.[122] Even if Boswell meant 'Lieutenant Colonel', a later date for Johnson's service than the 1750s is ruled out by the fact that the Lieutenant Colonelcy of Rackstrow's Orange Regiment was held by Alexander Dalmahoy from 1 May 1763 to his demise in August 1778.[123]

Boswell probably meant that Rackstrow was Johnson's captain rather than his colonel: if so, the possible time frame is from 5 February 1752 to 17 May 1759. Within this period, the Lieutenancy ordered new muster rolls to be drawn up on 23 April 1752 (there follows a probably unimportant gap in the records between 9 August 1753 and 28 February 1754), 25 April 1754, 29 May 1755 and subsequently. Events began to move more rapidly when on 15 November 1755 the Lieutenancy received the government's instructions that the militia be put in readiness in response to the outbreak of hostilities with France. They accordingly 'Ordered that Charging Tickets be forthwith printed in the usual Form and Delivered to the several Persons charged in the Muster Rolls to bear Arms to hold themselves in readiness fit for immediate service.' Five days later, and on subsequent occasions, the Lieutenancy ordered exercise days for the regiments.[124]

Charging tickets were printed call-up papers, summoning named individuals to appear or send a substitute. Their text included the command:

> The Arms every Soldier is to appear with and with which you are charged are a Musket with a Bayonet to fix to the Muzzle thereof a Cartouch Box or Pouch a Belt of Buff Four Inches broad and a two Edged Sword.

This was evidently the equipment Boswell later discovered in Johnson's possession. An order of the Lieutenancy in 1739 had laid down that all persons so chosen must obtain these arms within one month notwithstanding their having purchased exemptions from serving in person.[125] The charging ticket also indicated the acceptable ages for militiamen: 'N.B. No Person in your Stead will be accepted by the proper Officer who shall be under the Age of Eighteen or above the Age of Fifty five.'[126] Johnson did not celebrate his fifty-fifth birthday until 1764.

It is likely that Johnson's name first appeared on the Muster Roll not later than April 1752, that a charging ticket was delivered to him in Gough Square by Captain Rackstrow, and that Johnson was not disqualified by age from the summons to serve in person that Rackstrow had embraced during the rebellion of 1745. It is possible that this unwelcome demand came in 1752 or 1754, but the likely date is mid-November 1755. Johnson did suffer ill health a month later, from mid-December 1755 until April 1756,[127] but his health had not hampered him in his travels the previous summer, and as late as October he had written optimistically that 'There is a kind of restoration to youth in the revival of old friendships.'[128] Sir Joshua Reynolds's first portrait of Johnson, painted in 1756, shows a robust, solidly built man in his forties, not a valetudinarian.[129]

Despite Johnson's many ailments, observers agreed in their descriptions: 'His stature was remarkably high, and his limbs exceedingly large' (Mrs Thrale); 'large, robust, I may say approaching to the gigantick' (Boswell). Johnson was evidently both preoccupied with his symptoms and vain about his physical strength and stamina. The most recent study of the subject suggests that reports of Johnson's 'blindness' are 'part of the mythology surrounding this disabled giant'; 'Johnson, though short-sighted in the right eye, and having limited peripheral vision in the left, was by no means "blind"', as his work on the *Dictionary* in the early 1750s establishes. John Wiltshire also casts doubt on the diagnosis of Johnson's 'strange gestures' as Tourette's syndrome and inclines to Sir Joshua Reynolds's opinion that 'it proceeded from a habit which he had indulged himself in, of accompanying his thoughts with certain untoward actions', rather than from a nervous disease. Johnson began to experience attacks of what he termed gout only in 1775; it was only as a result of serious illness in 1768 that, he wrote, 'I have never since cared much to walk'. Wiltshire traces the beginning of his bronchial complaint to December 1755, and this seems the sole disorder possibly relevant to his not serving in the Trained Bands.[130]

It is possible that Johnson's health may have been one reason for his not serving in person, just as his poverty may have been one reason for his leaving Oxford without a degree; what the earlier date of November 1755 for his call-up would suggest is that it would probably not have been the only factor, for this date, if accurate, would establish that Johnson's agonisings in the *Literary Magazine* no. 2 (15 May–15 June 1756) on the oath of allegiance required of militiamen[131] echoed his recent experience and dilemma. His principled refusal, if such it was, can only have been made more fraught by his poverty, for on 16 March 1756 he was arrested for debt.[132] His decision to hire a substitute rather than serve in person is open to the explanation that he sought at considerable expense to avoid the oath of allegiance that service in person would have entailed.

This phase of Johnson's literary career supplies some important evidence from his own pen, and relevant contextual documents. In 1756, he became acting editor of a new journal, *The Literary Magazine: or, Universal Review*.[133] It was not a success. Launched in May 1756, it ceased publication with no. 27 in July 1758. It won only one-seventh of the subscribers of the *Gentleman's Magazine*; 'Perhaps one reason may have been the unpopular political position taken by the new journal,' suggested James Clifford. The most overt feature of this position was scepticism about the ministry's conduct of the war then beginning, and after the fourth number Johnson ceased to write articles: 'The proprietors somehow eased him out of the post as general editor' in August or September 1756.[134]

Johnson's article 'Remarks on the Militia Bill' is, in its context, a document which reveals a deeper anti-ministerial commitment than criticism of the conduct of the war alone. It protested against any man who was not 'faithful to his king' (an interesting choice of words) being pressured into subscribing contrary to his conscience: rather than accepting a pragmatic flexibility on the oaths, Johnson tried implausibly to suggest a way of finding good recruits without subjecting them to the challenge to subscribe. The object of the Act was 'that men of disloyal principles should be forced to discover their tenets by refusing their test'. Johnson did not condemn any such men of 'disloyal principles' who refused the oaths, for either their principles or their refusal. His concern was chiefly that 'mean men', men in low social stations, would on the contrary be pressured by their superiors and so 'will be more afraid of man than God, and will take the oath taken and offered by their betters, without understanding, without examining, perhaps without hearing it'. Johnson did not class himself among the 'mean men': he did not suggest that he had himself been in any doubt as to the meaning of the oath of allegiance, or that he had ever himself subscribed, nor did he urge men in doubt to abandon their scruples. It was a serious matter, for 'The frequent imposition of oaths has almost ruined the morals of this unhappy nation': his article was a condemnation of taking the oaths under pressure or with mental reservations, a thing that he had not done.[135]

Yet some Jacobites did just that. As late as 1758, a Whig clergyman complained:

> I am sorry to have Occasion to pass this *severe Sentence* on any of my own Profession; but I am obliged to do so by the Importance of the Subject, especially as I am told it is a common Practice in some Counties for Clergymen of the *established Church* to live in open Profession of Adherence to that Pretender whom they have *solemnly* abjured![136]

Johnson offered no defence of such a practice. Nor was he alone in the political concerns which his 'Remarks on the Militia Bill' expressed. At an even later date, some of the riots of 1758 provoked across the country by the implementation of the 1757 Militia Act were interpreted by the ministry as having Jacobite undertones;[137] many counties refused to participate in the 1757 scheme and some (including Tory Oxfordshire and Johnson's Staffordshire) held out until the American war in the 1770s.[138]

Johnson continued to write controversial book reviews for the *Literary Magazine*,[139] and to find other like-minded contributors, including a precocious Oxford undergraduate, Robert Chambers.[140] No. 4 contained a favourable review by Johnson of Robert Keith's *A Large New Catalogue of the Bishops of the Several Sees within the Kingdom of Scotland down to the Year 1688*, published in Edinburgh by T. and W. Ruddiman, episcopalians and Jacobites. Johnson's review focused on just one episode in the book: he reprinted at length Bishop Alexander Ross's account of his dealings with William of Orange in 1688–9 which led to William's imposition of Presbyterianism on the Scots Church. Johnson concluded: '*Note*, This letter was written to the Honourable *Archibald Campbell*, bishop' – the Scots Nonjuring bishop (d. 1744), consecrated in 1711, whom Johnson had known in London. The book was, admitted Johnson with considerable understatement, 'perhaps not likely to find many readers';[141] it was, however, highly relevant to a Nonjuror.

A review in issue no. 14 (May 15–June 15, 1757), the authorship of which has not been established, helps to reveal the context in which Johnson's article on the militia and oaths had appeared twelve months before. The work for review was a pamphlet printing a collection of letters by England's most prominent Nonjuror, William Sancroft, Archbishop of Canterbury, deprived in February 1690 for refusing the oaths. The reviewer's attention was caught:

> of all the gratifications of curiosity there are not, I think, any which the mind dwells upon with such a melancholy delight, as the reverses of fortune, by which men of elevated stations are reduced to taste the bitter cup of affliction; and this the more especially if the downfal is the consequence of a steddy and inflexible virtue; curiosity begins then to be tinctured with friendship, and if we perceive that the shock is born with firmness of mind, we begin to glow with admiration and applause.[142]

Indeed, Sancroft had doubly distinguished himself in that respect, since in 1651, as a young Fellow of Emmanuel College Cambridge, he was 'ejected from his fellowship' for refusing to take the Engagement to the republic. The reviewer praised Sancroft's 'placid resignation to the will of heaven' after 1690: his 'character deserves the admiration of posterity, and shines out in his humble cot at *Fresingfield* in *Suffolk*, with a brilliancy, that eclipses the diadem on the brow of him [William III] who deprived him of his dignities'. The reviewer offered no criticism of Sancroft's conduct; on the contrary, he promised:

> As Dr. *Sancroft* has been variously represented by the *Tillotsonians* and the *Nonjurors*, we shall in our next (since the pamphlet before us has started the subject) enter into an examen of the writings on each side of the question; both parties shall join issue, and we will endeavour impartially and candidly to sum up the evidence, that we may enable our readers to give their verdict upon the life and conduct of so distinguished a prelate.[143]

This careful profession of impartiality fell far short of the simple condemnation of the Nonjurors which a Whig would have expected; in its praise of Sancroft's principle and integrity, it went more than half way towards its subject's position. Perhaps for that reason, the promised continuation of the article never appeared.

The review of Sancroft's *Letters* is not normally ascribed to Johnson.[144] Was he the author? One of his best known pieces, a review of Soame Jenyns's *A Free Inquiry into the Nature and Origins of Evil*, was begun in issue no. 13 (April 15–May 15 1757), continued in no. 14, and concluded in no. 15 (June 15–July 15, 1757). The last piece certainly by Johnson to be newly commissioned for the magazine was a reply to Jonas Hanway also in no. 14, part of an exchange in which the governors of the Foundling Hospital almost sued the magazine, and Johnson himself.[145] The proprietors of the *Literary Magazine* had had enough: 'Johnson was never asked to do another review, or, at least, nothing of his ever appeared in later numbers.'[146] On the criteria proposed by Greene,[147] it is possible that the review of Sancroft's *Letters* was by Johnson, but such a claim is not made here. If (as I suggest) it was by another hand – Arthur Murphy being a likely candidate – the pamphlet and the review would be evidence for the continued newsworthiness of the issue; for the political complexion of the *Literary Magazine*; and for the argument that the intellectual context in which Johnson's article on the oath of allegiance had occurred a year before was one that still included the intractable issues of principle raised by the Revolution of 1688. A similar context is established by the review in 1757 of 'Voltaire's *account of the late rebellion in* Scotland *in the history of the war of 1741*', a sympathetic account of Charles Edward Stuart which audaciously announced that 'Part of the inhabitants of *London* were secretly attached to his interests'.[148]

The fate of *The Literary Magazine* did not end Johnson's journalistic career. His own periodical *The Idler* (15 April 1758–5 April 1760) showed to far greater effect his command of the medium of the weekly essay. It was in issue no. 10 of that journal (17 June 1758) that Johnson produced his witty parody of 'credulity' in those 'political zealots', the Jacobite Tom Tempest and the Whig Jack Sneaker. Examined more closely, Johnson's caricatures prove to be far from an even-handed eulogy of moderation. Johnson gently parodied Tom Tempest's superstitious belief in a link between the natural and political worlds, ill consequences in the first being produced by violations in the second, but said nothing to challenge the basic Jacobite commitment to legal hereditary right. Johnson's account of Jack Sneaker was altogether more harsh, and offered as Jack's only ground for his Whig principle the 'warming pan' myth, the claim (in fact, untrue) that James Francis Edward Stuart was not the child born to James II on 10 June 1688. Jack Sneaker, moreover, 'does not think the present Oaths sufficiently binding, and wishes that some better security could be found for the succession of *Hanover*'.[149]

On 15 April 1773, according to Boswell, Johnson reviewed the question of allegiance, and said: 'To oblige people to take oaths as to the disputed right, is wrong. I know not whether I could take them: but I do not blame those who do.'[150] This passage has been interpreted in two ways: first, that Johnson had taken the oaths in the past, but did not know in 1773 whether he could take them again; or, second, that Johnson had never before taken the oaths, and even as late as 1773 did not know whether he could do so. The first interpretation is unsupported by any evidence that Johnson had previously taken the oaths (he might in 1773 simply have said that he had formerly been reluctantly pressured into swearing, had he indeed done so) or by any reason for the taking of these oaths becoming harder with the passage of years; on the contrary, we know that it often seemed easier, as acknowledgement of the Hanoverians' *de facto* title grew over time. The second interpretation is supported by evidence that Johnson was never in a position throughout his career in which the oaths were tendered to him, and by the evidence that Johnson (and others) increasingly acknowledged a *de facto* title in George III which might have made the prospect of an oath of allegiance to that monarch less unpalatable than it would have been to George II. The evidence, after testing scrutiny, emerges as extremely strong that Johnson never took the oaths of allegiance or abjuration, and on 15 April 1773 disclosed that he had not done so.

To sum up: the evidence currently available establishes beyond reasonable doubt that Samuel Johnson, while at Oxford, was faced with university practice which conformed to its statutes. The recent suggestion that the university's practice in this respect had changed is not substantiated. The evidence suggests that Johnson then and later never took the oaths of allegiance or abjuration; throughout his career he avoided situations which would have required them. Johnson, in the sense of the word defined in his own *Dictionary*, was a Nonjuror.

Johnson's ideological identity and the end of party

If the early Johnson is to be accurately identified as a political partisan rather than as a neutral and detached figure, it must first be demonstrated that the party alignments of Hanoverian England, until the 1750s, remained those of Whig and Tory rather than reconfiguring themselves around the vaguer themes of Court and Country. Since the publication of the relevant volumes of the *History of Parliament* in 1970, the survival of Whig and Tory has been securely established.[151] Second, it must be shown that this parliamentary alignment structured political discourse also. In this second area evidence must be handled with care, for in an England so bitterly polarised between Whig and Tory, men had motives both for declarations of party loyalty and also, at times, for claiming to be of no party. Many, of course, continued robustly to speak of Whig and Tory. In the 1730s and 1740s, however, some asserted that a non-party 'Country' opposition (in fact composed of mutually suspicious opposites, Tories and extreme Whigs) best embodied national ideals in their campaign against the corruption and mis-conduct of ministers.

This was not always persuasive. 'Court' and 'Country' could be merely synonyms or euphemisms for the more familiar terms, as a Whig pointed out in 1751:

> Patriotism and Country Interest are generally the Weapons with which the Agents and Emissaries of every Jacobite Candidate encounter every Man whose [Whig] Loyalty is unsuspected, and whose upright View it is, by getting a Seat in Parliament, to contribute his utmost to the Welfare of King and People indiscriminately. But should we examine a little into the Expressions of Court and Country Interest, we should not find that they imported contrary Meanings [to Whig and Tory], as some by the Use they have made of them have endeavoured to incul-cate. Country Interest in the Mind of a Tory or Jacobite is the Interest of the Pretender; and in that Sense indeed it is directly opposite to a Court Interest

– that is, the Whig interest of the House of Hanover.[152]

Other men, increasingly from the 1750s and with dramatic practical ana-logues from the 1760s, claimed that the extinction of the Jacobite challenge and the increasingly pragmatic nature of Westminster politics in the 1750s provided the basis for party reconciliation (usually on Whig terms). Whigs argued thus in order to persuade Tories to renounce the Stuart allegiance that was residual in some of them; Tories argued likewise in order to secure admission to office and emolument. For that reason, contemporary asser-tions that party conflict was dead cannot be simply taken as reportage; such statements embodied tactical political purposes.

Because of these tactical complexities, the evidence of contemporaries must be carefully scrutinised: claims that party conflict had ceased were not always what they appeared to be. Three examples from Johnson's Oxford University illustrate the way in which even academics far from the conflicts of Westminster were polarised by the issues contested there: this evidence is important not least because it has recently been misinterpreted to suggest that party conflict was indeed a thing of the past in Johnson's circle. First, Nicholas Amhurst once more, on Oxford. In the Preface to the collected edition of *Terrae-Filius* in 1726, Amhurst set out in general terms 'my charge of a *treasonable* spirit reigning in the university at that time', that is, the time of his residence as an undergraduate from 1716 to 1719. In 1726, he added:

> It must be confess'd, indeed, that this *seditious* spirit, and these *treason-able* practices have, of late years, so much *abated*, if not entirely *ceased*

there, that it induced his majesty, out of his royal goodness, to distinguish his subjects at *Oxford* with several valuable *donations*, and marks of
his affection

which the Oxonians acknowledged with two separate addresses of thanks.
This 'shews how far they have *alter'd* their sentiments, and how well
they *deserve* his majesty's farther encouragement'. To have said otherwise
would have been an indictment of royal policy, which Amhurst naturally
had to avoid; but he also thereby exploited the university's present professions of loyalty to contrast them ironically with their former disaffection,
and to claim a hostage for the future. Their 'being good subjects now does
not prove that they were so *nine* or *ten* years ago',[153] he argued, and left it
to his readers to speculate on Oxford's possible conduct nine or ten years
hence. Amhurst was far from being a simple reporter of a change of heart
in his alma mater.

Second, Richard Newton (1676–1753). In 1735 he was Principal of Hart
Hall, one of the university's ancient halls, and was campaigning for it to
achieve collegiate status by the grant of a royal charter. In this he found
bitter opposition from the notoriously Whig Fellows of Exeter College, and
from the ambitious Whig Dean of Christ Church. In view of his practical
goal, Newton wisely professed his neutrality: 'if the Government *Itself* be
not of any Party, that I am not can be no Mark of Disaffection in me to it.'
The Dean of Christ Church was less persuaded:

> Hath he ever declared his Respect to, and affection for, the *Present Gov-
> ernment?* Not that I ever heard. And yet he now steps forth, and boasts,
> as though he, good Man, merited more from the Government than any
> of his Brethren. I am far from charging him with *Jacobitism*, or any
> Measure of *Disaffection* to the State: But this I will say, That, as far as I
> ever saw, or have been told, he hath contented himself to lie by quiet;
> and hath never employed his Eloquence, either to support HIS MAJESTY'S
> Title, or to recommend His Administration. He himself tells us, 'Not being
> of any Party, I never pretend to be.' I forbear to comment on these words,
> which I leave to be considered by the Reader.[154]

Plainly, Conybeare insinuated just such a doubt of Newton's loyalty.

In his reply of 1735, Newton included Chapter XIII, 'Concerning Affection to the Government', in an attempt to clear himself from this insinua-
tion in the minds of 'the Great Men above'. Newton went through the usual
litany of professing support for the Revolution and the Hanoverian succession, pausing only to emphasise (what some would rightly interpret as an
anti-ministerial slip) that Parliament should be '*freely* chosen'. He boasted:
'I have not only taken the *Oaths* to the Government *Myself*, but have also

removed the *Scruples* which *Others* have had to do it.'[155] Newton's politics were not so clear, however. On 9 February 1737, in the parliamentary by-election for the University caused by the death of George Clarke, Newton voted for the Jacobite sympathiser William Bromley, Jr.[156] against the Whig Robert Trevor, a choice in which he concurred with the Jacobites William King of St. Mary Hall and Dr. Panting, Master of Johnson's Pembroke College. At Christ Church, Conybeare naturally voted for Trevor.[157] Hertford eventually obtained its royal charter on 8 September 1740, with Newton its first Principal, and with statutes based on his model of 1720. They provided for the text of the oath to be taken 'upon Admission . . . By every student and scholar', but this was merely a promise not to do '*any thing Injurious to this College*', and had no wider content. Nor was it even an oath to obey the statutes: since a student 'cannot have *Considered* them sufficiently . . . Young Men will often break them without *Adverting* that they do so. To them an *Oath* to observe the Statutes will be a Snare.'[158] This was not Whig orthodoxy.

Nor did the Principal of Hertford sign the Association in 1745. Ten years later, Newton republished Chapter XIII of his tract of 1735 as a separate pamphlet, complaining in the Introduction: '*The reader will here perceive, that the spirit which at present prevails, long since had a beginning; but is now nursed up into full maturity by the indefatigable industry of* a society of informers.'[159] The 'informers' against whom Newton, like Samuel Johnson, was so indignant were the Whig dons such as Richard Blacow, who thought it their duty in the late 1740s and early 1750s to broadcast to the world what they claimed were the University's Jacobite loyalties.[160]

Third, the Whig loyalist Henry Brooke, jurist and author of *A Letter to the Oxford Tories* (1750).[161] Brooke had held the Regius chair of civil law at Oxford since 1736, hardly a post to be given by the Crown to a person of suspected loyalty.[162] His Whig zeal was not in doubt; his aim in 1750 was to promote the disintegration of the rival party. Dating his anonymous pamphlet from the Middle Temple on 1 January 1750, Brooke professed, clearly for tactical reasons, to be ignorant of 'the genuine and fixed Import' of the word Tory:

I call you Tories, because such you call yourselves: But the real and essential Difference between a Church of England Academick *Tory* and a Church of England Academick *Whig* is, I confess, a Secret to my Understanding; both these having subscribed the same Articles of *Religious* Faith; Both having given to the same Government the same Solemn Security for their *Civil* Obedience: Surely then there can be no Absurdity in an Assertion that a Distinction made between Members of the same Communion, *sworn* Subjects to the same Prince, is a Distinction without a *Difference*, an Opposition in *Name* only, destitute of any Foundation in *Fact*.

But Brooke could only argue that Toryism was indistinguishable from Whiggism by disassociating Toryism from Jacobitism: 'I see you eager on all Occasions to disavow the Creed of *Jacobitism*.' As Brooke progressed in his argument, he disclosed his real purposes: not to advance evidence to prove the dissolution of the 'Tory' identity, but to neutralise the Tories by vilifying the dynastic allegiances of a part of their number. Of Jacobites he wrote: 'Men so absurd, so very impious place Themselves much below the Dignity of *Reason* and *Argument*.' Brooke's prime target was that '*Chimera, a Juring Jacobite*':

> He, who can, for his own Temporal Advantage, enter into Obligations *sacred* and *solemn*, as the Oaths of *Allegiance* and *Abjuration* are, and This done, dispute, clamour, drink, or riot for the Person whom He has abjured, then wipe his Mouth and say 'I have done no Wickedness,' must have a System of Morality peculiar to Himself, must be deaf to the Voice of *Persuasion*, must be left to the Lashes of a Fiend of his own creating, an *Evil Conscience*.

Was the world not right to draw inferences from the conduct of the Tories? If, Brooke urged inconsistently,

> on a fair Scrutiny into the Conduct of the Leaders of your Party, for more than thirty Years last past, it shall appear that no one *Minister*, no one *Measure* of Government has obtained your Approbation, or escaped your Displeasure, can you, in such Case, expect that the World should have such a Partiality for your Sentiments, as to pronounce that the Rulers of *Great Britain* are always *wrong*, and the Rulers of *Oxford* always *right*? And will not Those, to whom you are not thoroughly known, be rather led to conclude, from such a Continuance, from such an Obstinacy of Opposition, that your Dislike to *every* Publick Measure proceeds from a determined Aversion to '*the Powers that Be*?'

Plainly, observers would infer this, and Brooke's phrase 'to whom you are not thoroughly known' was irony. The pent-up resentment of an Oxford Whig over many decades now revealed itself: his opponents, he ranted, had manipulated fellowship and parliamentary elections, and heaped abuse on loyal Hanoverians. What Brooke intended as 'a Defence of *your* Party against the heavy Charge of *Jacobitism*' ended as a diatribe against the Tories for giving too many grounds for such a charge.[163]

Benjamin Kennicott, Whig Fellow of Whiggish Exeter College, pursued a similar tactic in his campaign against William King. He first acknowledged, reasonably enough, that '*The Old Interest*, in the County of *Oxford*, is a Political Interest, *long* supported there, partly by *Tories*, partly by *Jacobites*; but probably by a much greater number of the former than the latter, especially *since the late Rebellion.*' His tactical task was to split the Tories from the Jacobites by a definition, and leave the latter politically isolated. Hence, wrote Kennicott,

we must first settle the proper distinction between *a Tory* and *a Jacobite*. 1. A TORY then (I speak here of a *true, sober, thinking, systematic* TORY) is one, who wishes the true glory of *the Church of England*, in opposition to *Dissenter* on the one hand and *Papist* on the other; and who wishes the true glory of *British Liberty*, in opposition to *Licentiousness*, in being *free* to do every thing, and *Slavery* in being *permitted* to do nothing. 2. He has high notions of *Regal Authority*; but wisely distinguishes between *a King* and *a Tyrant*; and, tho' he believes it his duty, with *the most active Loyalty* to serve the *former*, he thinks himself not bound to *submit passively* to the *latter*, when he has brought the Religion and Liberty of his Country into extreme danger. 3. He is therefore an hearty friend to *the Revolution*; and consequently a sworn foe to the doctrine of *hereditary* Right, *absolute and indefeasible*. 4. He affirms, that *no claim of Right* properly belongs to the Descendants (even *admitting* Descendants) of *James the second:* but that the only rightful claim is *Lineal Descent*, limited by such *Conditions* as the wisdom of the Nation has fix'd, for the more effectual security of our sacred and civil Freedom. 5. He acknowledges this rightful claim in *His Majesty King* GEORGE *the Second*; to whom he readily swears Allegiance: and this the more readily, as he considers the present ROYAL FAMILY the most likely of all others, to perpetuate the Blessings of *Englishmen* and *Protestants*. 6. But tho' zealously loyal to *The* KING, he is perhaps dissatisfied with *the Administration*: he may think (and yet without proper foundation) that *the Ministry* frequently pursue such Measures, as tend to the detriment and disgrace of the Kingdom: and he may think himself the true *Friend* to *The* KING, for being an *Enemy* to the wrong Measures of *those*, who are, by their high Office, *The* KING's principal Servants. 7. But then – in order to preserve his Loyalty from suspicion – to perform his Oath of supporting His Majesty to the utmost of his power – and to give weight to his Censures of any Measure, that he apprehends to be wrong – he most zealously supports every Measure, that appears to be right: laying down this, as a fundamental Maxim, 'No one, but *The* KING's Enemy, can censure, oppose and distress ALL the Measures of *The* KING's Ministry.'

I must just remark here, by a necessary digression, that the preceding is the proper Character of *every honest* WHIG, as well as of *every honest* TORY; for I can *in these days*, perceive no real difference: excepting – that, as *the Tory* (in the Church) thinks more favourably of *the Papist*, than the *Whig* does; so *the Whig* (in the Church) thinks more favourably of *the Dissenter*, than *the Tory* does. But then, as every *Whig* is not a Dissenter, nor every *Tory* a Papist; so both *Whig and Tory* may be sincere *Members* of, and zealous *Friends* to, *The Church of England* . . .[164]

Kennicott went on to deduce from his definition consequences intended to drive a wedge into the Old Interest:

> From the preceding Character of *an honest* TORY we may soon infer that of a *weak* or a *wicked* JACOBITE. The *Tory* approves *the Revolution*; the *Jacobite* curses it. The Tory denies any rightful claim of the *British* Crown to the *Pretender James* and *his Descendants*; the *Jacobite* takes his very *name* from his Zeal for *that* Family. The *Tory* not only allows the rightful claim of *King* GEORGE, which the *Jacobite* denies; but he is resolute to *support* His Majesty, *to the utmost of his power*, for the security of *the Church of England* and *British Liberty:* whereas the *Jacobite* labours to introduce the Family of *James*, and with him the Sceptre from *France* and the Mitre from *Rome*, to enslave both our Bodies and our Souls.[165]

Kennicott's choice of themes was shrewd; but as his rationale went on, it clearly became more prescriptive than descriptive, and ended by confronting without resolving a major source of lasting differences between Whigs and Tories, religion. These differences survived into the 1750s in stark terms: another plausible strategy for each party was merely to seek the total elimination of the other. One pamphleteer set out such assumptions in 1753:

> I
>
> THAT there are two different PARTIES, who usually *oppose* each other with great zeal and violence in our parliamentary elections.
>
> II
>
> THAT one of these Parties is generally composed of secret *Papists, Jacobites, Nonjurors*, and such *bigotted Churchmen* as from a high conceit of their own *Infallibility* are mortal enemies to a TOLERATION in matters of religion; who are all commonly called TORIES.
>
> III
>
> THAT the other Party is generally composed of the more *moderate Churchmen*, and the main body of *protestant Dissenters* of all denominations, who are all true lovers of BRITISH LIBERTY and the present ROYAL FAMILY, and are commonly called WHIGS.[166]

Whigs and Tories were in the 1760s to find much more common ground, but not by the success of the ideological solvent Brooke and Kennicott tried to apply: it took the destruction of the parliamentary Tory party in the 1750s, the abandonment of hope by most of the Jacobite interest, and the accession of a monarch influenced by Bolingbrokean supra-party theories, to make the decisive change. Any who really believed in the growth of non-partisan behaviour were quickly undeceived by the university's partisanship in the bitterly contested Oxfordshire election of 1754. One Whig complained: 'Out of twenty Colleges, nineteen, beside the Halls, have behav'd with what they call *great Decency*, and stuck close to what may properly enough be term'd the *Old Interest* of OXFORD. Such is the force of Academical Bigotry, and the *Prejudice of Education!*'[167]

To sum up: Samuel Johnson's early life, until the 1750s, was spent in a public culture still heavily polarised between the parties of Whig and Tory. Occasional claims that parties no longer existed were tactics which sought to manipulate that polarised world of discourse. Johnson was a partisan, not a detached political sceptic in a society that had left political commitment behind.

The years of transition

A decade of particular difficulty in explaining Johnson is the 1750s, for during it his political opinions may, in some ways, have adapted to changing circumstances. An important but unreliable document is the Preface to the consolidated Index to the *Gentleman's Magazine*, published in 1753 and reportedly written by Johnson and another. Since we do not know the relative contributions of Johnson and his anonymous colleague, I judged that 'the evidence is inconclusive',[168] a view which, on reconsideration, I still hold, and based my argument on the more secure evidence of Johnson's *Dictionary* (1755). As we have seen, Johnson's writings in *The Literary Magazine* point in the same direction to the lexicon of political terms embedded in his two folio volumes of 1755.

That reconciliation was not easy is shown by the conflicts which broke out in the 1760s: plainly, the events of the previous decade had not been sufficient to heal old wounds. At court, after the young king's marriage, the University of Oxford's attempt to rebuild bridges was marred by its Chancellor's gaffe: 'Ld. Westmorland kneeled to Lady Sarah Lennox mistaking her for the queen, as she stood next to Her Majesty, being first bridesmaid. It was observed that there is a fatality on the Chancellors of Oxford, always to mistake their kings and queens. George Selwyn says the lady in waiting should have told him that [Lady Sarah Lennox] was the Pretender.'[169] (According to rumour, George III and Lady Sarah Lennox had been romantically linked.) Oxford's Chancellor was the Earl of Westmorland, the last champion of the university's Tory-Jacobite interest, at whose installation in 1759 Johnson wrote: 'I have clapped my hands till they are sore' at the Jacobite Dr. King's speech.[170]

Now that the ascendancy at court of Pelham and Newcastle was over, one Whig argued in 1764 that the conversions from Toryism of the preceding reign had always been insincere:

No body, I dare say, ever thought; and no friend to his country could ever think, of proscribing men for a *name*; or of barring the conversion of the rankest tory that ever existed. I am sure the practice has been the contrary. Witness the list of honours, and offices, in the last reign; witness how many, who had been called tories, not to say even real Jacobites, were well rewarded for coming into court, where their descendants now flourish, with the additional comfort, of daring to avow, and act, upon the same principles of prerogative, and arbitrary power, which their ancestors were paid for pretending to renounce.[171]

The initial effect of the eirenic policy of the young George III was not to produce a mood of tranquil reconciliation, but to heighten tensions as winners and losers at court eyed each other with jealous watchfulness.

Politics therefore moved into a new phase, but continued to echo the old conflicts. The most famous journalistic critic of the new regime, adopting the name Junius, was preoccupied with claiming that a strange alliance stood behind George III. In 1769, he addressed that monarch: 'It is not then from the alienated affections of Ireland or America, that you can reasonably look for assistance; still less from the people of England, who are actually contending for their rights, and in this great question, are parties against you. You are not, however, destitute of every appearance of support: You have all the Jacobites, Non-jurors, Roman Catholics, and Tories of this country, and all Scotland without exception.'[172] Lord Mansfield was equally reproached with his youthful allegiance: 'Lord Ravensworth produced the most satisfactory Evidence of his having frequently drank [*sic*] the Pretender's health upon his knees',[173] an inconvenient recollection of the Privy Council's inquiry of February 1753 into the education of the Prince of Wales.[174]

In 1759 and in the 1760s, there is evidence suggesting in Johnson a sophisticated understanding of the legal points at issue, notably the law relating to the succession. In 1736 was published, posthumously, the two folio volumes of a work by the great lawyer Sir Matthew Hale (1609–76) under the title *Historia Placitorum Coronae: The History of the Pleas of the Crown;*[175] Samuel Johnson owned a copy.[176] Hale had been occupied in the 1650s and 1660s on this work, which included the central issues of allegiance and treason. He had argued that the common law held the existence of '*a sacred Bond between the King and his Kingdom, that cannot be dissolved without the free and mutual Consent of both in Parliament*'; Hale had acknowledged some *de facto* authority, but maintained that

If the Right Heir of the Crown be in the actual Exercise of the Sovereignty, suppose in one Part of the Kingdom, and an Usurper be in the actual Exercise of the Sovereignty in another; yet the Law judgeth him in Possession of the Crown, that hath the True Right; and the other is in Truth not so much as a King *de Facto*; but a Disturber only, and therefore not a King within this Act

(the 1495 Treason Act): a *de facto* sovereign was no longer even that if the rightful claimant appeared in the realm and asserted his title. Moreover, according to Hale, 'That Lawful Prince that hath the Prior Obligation of Allegiance from his Subjects, cannot lose that Interest without his own Consent, by his Subject's resigning himself to the Succession of another.' In his *The History and Analysis of the Common Law*, Hale had argued that 'possibly no determinate Time' would prove 'implied consent' or 'tacite Acceptance', valid though these were, and observed that, in the case of 'Usurpation by a Subject', 'several Ages and Descents do not purge the Unlawfulness of such an Usurpation'.[177]

In the 1736 first printing of *Pleas of the Crown*,[178] however, the text was altered by the editor[179] to make Hale appear to support *de facto* authority, a meaning opposite to his own.[180] Johnson was in Oxford for the installation of the Jacobite Earl of Westmorland as Chancellor of the University on 5 July 1759, socialising with the civil lawyer Robert Vansittart and perhaps also with the rising common lawyer Robert Chambers.[181] This may be relevant to the content of no. 65 of *The Idler*, of 14 July 1759, which was devoted to 'posthumous compositions'. Johnson included Hale's:

> Some works, indeed, have escaped total destruction, but yet have had reason to lament the fate of orphans exposed to the frauds of unfaithful guardians. How *Hale* would have borne the mutilations which his *Pleas of the Crown* have suffered from the editor, they who know his character will easily conceive.

How did Johnson know that Hale's text had been falsified? It is likely that he drew on a Nonjuror source. George Harbin, in *The Hereditary Right of the Crown of England Asserted* (London, 1713), had used Hale's then unpublished manuscript and printed substantial passages from it, including those quoted above,[182] in order to support the legal doctrine of indefeasible natural allegiance expressed in *Calvin's Case* (1608) and to refute *de facto* interpretations of monarchy.[183] It was a classic text, with which a legally informed Nonjuror might have been familiar.[184]

Johnson's insight into Sir Matthew Hale came before his better-known involvement, in 1766–70, in helping Robert Chambers compose his course of Vinerian law lectures, and so cannot have been a by-product of Johnson's Vinerian researches. Nevertheless, these lectures disclose an interpretation of English law which was far from Whig orthodoxy. Because we know so little about the contribution of the two men, it is not possible to use Chambers's text as reliable evidence for Johnson's loyalties alone. Little new evidence has yet emerged since the first publication of the lectures in 1986 about the carefully private processes of their composition or the strategic purposes of Chambers in writing as he did; yet whatever the balance of authorial contributions,[185] the content of the lectures is far from securely Hanoverian, indeed highly ambiguous on the major points at issue. Where Blackstone's *Commentaries* reflected a further phase of the accommodation of early eighteenth-century Tory-Jacobite Oxford with the Hanoverian regime in and after the middle of the century,[186] Chambers's lectures were actually more ambiguous than Blackstone's on the fundamental questions of politics.

Chambers's Vinerian course gave a decidedly un-Whiggish account of allegiance. Since 'by far the greatest part' of the common law 'still retains the spirit of the feudal system', it followed that the king's 'power over his subjects is conceived as more than political . . . For this reason allegiance is always by the law termed natural.' It was a natural status, not a functional response to the command of the king; 'allegiance being considered as a duty produced by causes with which the subject did not co-operate, and from which as he did not incur it by his own choice, he cannot by his own choice set himself free'. It was exactly the theory of indefeasible allegiance which had caused such divided loyalties in and after 1688. Chambers even reminded his audience of the statute of 25 Edw. III, c. 2, by which 'it is declared "that the law is and ever has been that the *king's children* wherever born ought to inherit" '.[187]

Chambers acknowledged that the personal tie of '*Liege homage* or allegiance', evolved in feudal law and restated after 1603 by Sir Edward Coke, was somewhat modified by the new oath of allegiance introduced after 1688 by the Act of 1 W & M, c. 8: 'As this oath was enacted by an assembly busy in re-establishing an unsettled government and therefore desirous to avoid all obstacles of scrupulosity; and by men who in political opinions differed very widely from each other, and agreed only in excluding the absent monarch, it is conceived in very general terms which the law is left to interpret.' This fell far short of a glowing account of the Glorious Revolution and discarded the Whig theory of abdication in favour of a frank admission of James II's deposition, though a reluctant deposition. It was immediately followed by a remark susceptible of an anti-Revolution interpretation: 'While allegiance was considered as being the consequence of birth it is no wonder that our monarchs made great distinction between aliens and native subjects and were unwilling to grant property to those of whose obedience they did not think themselves secure.' Alas, 'The idea of natural allegiance has long been wearing away with other consequences of the feudal system . . .'[188]

The *Lectures* candidly defined one key term: 'The Parliament used in the popular sense as comprising only the House of Lords and Commons is not strictly in the *legal* sense a Parliament. It may be termed a political body of which the king is the political soul, for unanimated by regal authority they have neither voice nor motion':[189] by implication, the 'Convention Parliament' of 1689 which declared William and Mary sovereigns was no parliament. Chambers was also ambiguous about Hanoverian kingship and the changes which the institution of monarchy was experiencing:

> coronation in ancient times procured to the king the homage of his nobles, with a public acknowledgement of his right, gave notoriety to his accession and conferred sacredness on his person. What are its effects at present it is not so easy to determine. It is perhaps now to the nation, the regular and legal notification of their sovereign. It is provided by the statute of the 11 Hen. 7, *c.* 1, that the king, reigning by whatever title, may so far legitimate the actions of those who carry his commission, that though he should be afterwards deposed, no man can be punished for having acted under him.[190]

This was consistent with the law of treason, which defended *de facto* as well as *de jure* monarchs:

> For though it be evident that *he* may be a king *de facto* who is no king *de jure*, that he may be in present possession of the royal authority by force of arms or otherwise who has no just title to the power which he exercises; yet since by the same right whatever it be by which he executes the laws for the protection of the people, he must be supposed to execute them likewise in vindication of himself, the peace of the world requires that those who accept the advantages of his protection should submit to the penalties of disobedience.[191]

This was a highly unflattering account of *de facto* titles, yet the argument that civil order required acceptance of *de facto* monarchs was close to Johnson's position after the early 1760s.

Despite this, the lectures offered little comfort to those who might have difficulties about their religious duty. An oath was 'a direct appeal to the Supreme Being, by whom perjury will undoubtedly be avenged'.[192] The one hopeful point was the claim that the problem was now receding. After explaining the penalties for treason under the Acts of 13 W III, c. 3, 6 Anne c, 17 and 17 Geo. I, c. 19, Chambers added that 'the laws against popery being made in the animosity of contest and in dread of danger are now almost forgotten, and that the Protestant succession gathering daily strength all danger of committing treason by opposing it is now at an end'.[193] To postpone such a gathering of strength to the late 1760s hardly suggested a strong confidence in the security of the first two Hanoverian monarchs; and Chambers's odd phrasing, suggesting that his audience might indeed have been in some danger of falling into treason, hardly credited them with an overwhelming zeal for the House of Hanover.

The process of accommodation to the dynasty in the 1750s and 1760s was not an easy one; Chambers, Blackstone and Johnson all illustrate aspects of it. Johnson's growing links with the monarchy of George III might be evidence against Johnson's early Jacobitism only if the structures of English politics in his lifetime remained constant: we now know they did not. Johnson indeed made critical remarks about many sovereigns, from Charles II to George III. But his critical remarks were couched in very different terms from monarch to monarch, and his opinions of individuals did not determine his opinions of the validity of their titles. Johnson was quite capable of making candidly critical remarks about Charles II and James II while remaining profoundly uneasy at the events of 1688–9. In no way has it been suggested that Johnson looked back on Stuart monarchy before 1688 as 'the good old days': he was a realist, keenly aware of the limitations of governance at all times. Far from James II's being 'the Jacobite darling', his Protestant sympathisers were often highly critical of his conduct and religion, and regarded him even more than his brother as having made the very worst of the opportunities with which they had been presented in 1660. None of these judgements involved Johnson's endorsing a right in the people to depose James II. Similarly, Nonjurors had for certain purposes made common cause with juring churchmen, even under the first two Georges but far more often after 1760;[194] it does not establish that Johnson was not a Nonjuror that he should have defended Church and State against the threats which the establishment faced in the late 1760s and 1770s.

Johnson's reputation

Johnson's early political identity was well known in the later part of his life, as an exchange in the House of Commons in 1771 shows. An opposition MP, Thomas Townshend,[195] angered by Johnson's pro-ministerial pamphlet on the Falkland Islands crisis, alleged that Johnson, 'a Jacobite by principle, has been encouraged, fostered, pensioned, because he was a Jacobite'. Alexander Wedderburn, the new Solicitor-General, a Scot who had first entered Parliament in 1761 on Lord Bute's interest and had first proposed Johnson's pension to Bute, was forced to defend the author and, by implication, Wedderburn himself:

> From the course of my pursuits I have not seen the man four times in my life. This, however, I know, – that he was not pensioned because he was a Jacobite, nor on account of his political principles; that he was not pensioned from any such illiberal motive. The only motive for granting that pension was Dr. Johnson's distinction in the literary world, and the prospect of approaching distress. The person [Wedderburn] who solicited it for him was totally unacquainted with any other circumstance. He

[Wedderburn] knew that he [Johnson] was a man of letters by his great work, the Dictionary of the English language. The minister [Bute] to whom the application was made, and the man who made the application, never enquired into his political character. The pension was applied for solely upon the ground I have stated. Let it never be said in this House, nor in any other, that the royal bounty is to be so restrained. If he had been a papist, and at the same time a great mathematician, a great poet, and distinguished for literary merit in various ways, it would have been becoming to extend that bounty to him.[196]

On a superficial reading, this might be interpreted as Wedderburn's rejection of Johnson's Jacobitism. A parliamentarian or a political historian would appreciate, on the contrary, that Wedderburn had markedly failed to deny that Johnson subscribed to such views; he had argued instead that Johnson's views had not been formally noticed, and that whatever they were, even if they were extreme and abhorrent, his pension was justified by his literary merits alone. This omission was an implicit admission. The claim of ignorance was also, of course, at once seen to be implausible, as Thomas Townshend pointed out in his reply: 'I desire not to be understood as wishing for literary rewards to be confined to party. How the learned gentleman could be acquainted with Dr. Johnson's literary merits, and not be aware at the same time of his political conduct, is to me surprising.'[197]

This perception of Johnson's early career was widespread, and it is important evidence for its essential accuracy that it was never contradicted by Johnson himself or by his close associates. Even a sympathiser like James Boswell moved with the times more than Johnson did. On 29 February 1776, Boswell recorded:

I had read this week his *Marmor Norfolciense*,[198] republished by some envious enemy[199] with intention to hurt him. I had pleasure in perusing it as a piece of composition; but, my *Antihanoverian* warmth being much abated, I had not so high a relish of it as I should have had formerly; and it appeared to me not to have so much force of genius as his later productions.[200]

The pamphlet was not forgotten, and this characterisation of Johnson continued after his death.

New evidence bearing on Johnson's reputation in the latter part of his life continues to accumulate. *The European Magazine* of May 1785 wrote of Johnson: 'He was a furious Jacobite, while one hope for the Stuart line remained; and his politics, always leaning towards despotism, were inimical to liberty, and the natural rights of man.' *The India Gazette: or, Calcutta Public Advertiser* of 21 May 1787 similarly wrote: 'As a *Tory* he was always notorious; but we are indebted to his friends for the discovery of his being a convert from the Jacobite faction, or rather a Jacobite retaining his principles, but transferring his allegiance from the unfortunate *Stuarts* to royal munificence and congenial devotion.'[201] There is no evidence that these were misconceptions or attempts at defamation, however unfriendly; the second comment indeed drew an insightful distinction which was not far from what can now be established.

In 1789, one author cited the case of Johnson to justify the unwelcome republication of two anonymous tracts by Bishop Warburton:

> Some Editor less timid or less delicate than the R[ight] R[everend] Editor of Warburton's Works,[202] has lately republished the Marmor Norfolciense of Johnson,[203] though it had lost probably much of it's original Value in the Mind of the Author, though it is pronounced a dull Work by his Biographer, and though it was once thought even by the most impartial Readers, seditious in it's Tendency. I know not whether Johnson left any Directions with his Executors about the M[armor] N[orfolciense] nor whether Bp. Warburton laid any Injunctions upon his R[ight] R[everend] Friend concerning the two Books now republished . . . I should add, that the M[armor] N[orfolciense] had been 'republished before' in 1775, during the Life of Johnson, by some Person, who approved as little of his Jacobite Politics, as I do of the Sentiments contained in the 'anonymous Letters'[204] which were written by some Warburtonian to 'Jortin' and to 'Leland'.[205]

One critic of the sermon of Dr. Richard Price on 4 November 1789, which also inspired Burke's *Reflections on the Revolution in France*, was moved to vindicate George III's conduct. Had the king's libertarian inclinations not been repeatedly shown?

> Has the making the judges independent? Has the granting the most complete toleration to this *very man* [Price] and his sectaries? Has the diminution of the ancient and just prerogatives and power of the crown, with the adoption of every scheme of advantage and improvement for the benefit of his majesty's subjects, and the patronage and encouragement of the arts and sciences, particularly LITERATURE *without excepting even Jacobite Johnson*, or *presbyterian P[rice]*. Have these it is asked with multitudes of others, been no proofs of the king's former good conduct in public life?[206]

Remarkably, neither Johnson nor his immediate circle ever protested, in conversation or in print, that such characterisations were inaccurate. At best, his friends sought to play down his political commitments, to palliate them, or to redescribe them as ineffective Romantic proclivities. None of these retrospective reinterpretations is justified. The evidence suggests that Johnson's position was partly adapting to changing circumstances, not that he had been a lifelong Hanoverian. His reputation after 1760 correctly recalled his commitment against the dynasty under the first two Georges.

It was clear enough, then, what had been Johnson's politics. Accounting for the principled origin of them was much more difficult, since he clearly did not idealise or romanticise the Stuarts. It took inside information to identify Johnson, as did Thomas Tyers in 1784, as 'one of the few non-jurors that were left'.[207] Yet this was also implicitly the view of Johnson's first major biographer, the Whig Sir John Hawkins. Johnson, he recorded, heaped 'bigoted censure' on senior churchmen appointed since 1714, like Wake, Gibson, Sherlock, Butler, Herring, Pearce and especially Hoadly; 'in competition with whom he would set Hickes, Brett, Leslie, and others of the nonjurors, whose names are scarcely now remembered'. Hawkins described Johnson as 'a high-churchman', but one who resented any clergyman beneath the rank of bishop as 'little better than an usurper', filling an office which Johnson had missed by 'his adverse fortunes', but 'to which [he] himself had a better title'.

With the offer of a pension in 1763, Johnson 'found himself in a predicament similar to that of Dr. [William] Sherlock, who, at the Revolution, was a non-juror to king William, but, after deliberating on his refusal as a case of conscience, took the side that made for his interest, but against his reputation' (Hawkins might have made clearer that Sherlock took the oaths to retain his offices; Johnson's pension did not require them). Hawkins related Johnson's practice of praying for the dead to a controversy of about 1715 among the Nonjuring clergy, 'of whom, and also of their writings, Johnson was ever used to speak with great respect'. Johnson 'seems to have taken part with Dr. Brett' in favour of the restoration of prayers for the dead, as sanctioned by the first Prayer Book of Edward VI. This controversy nevertheless 'was, as Johnson once told me, the ruin of the nonjuring cause'. He had some reason to know this, recorded Hawkins, since 'Johnson in his early years associated with this sect of nonjurors, and from them, probably, imbibed many of his religious and political principles'. Johnson, in Hawkins's eyes, was a man of principle: 'his religious and political principles he retained and cherished'.

Johnson's politics were clear to Hawkins: 'That he was a tory, he not only never hesitated to confess, but, by his frequent invectives against the whigs, was forward to proclaim.' He did not endorse Filmer, or hold the view that 'the resistance of tyranny and oppression is, in all cases, unlawful'. Consequently he 'condemned the conduct of James the second during his short reign' and, suggested Hawkins, had Johnson been a subject of that monarch he would have 'resisted any invasion of his right or unwarrantable exertion of power' with the same spirit as the Fellows of Magdalen or the Seven Bishops in the 1680s.[208] Hawkins did not note that five of the seven became Nonjurors, but candidly recorded that Johnson 'almost asserted in terms, that the succession to the crown had been illegally interrupted'. Boswell, in a passage in his journals suppressed in his *Life*, recorded that Johnson *had* called George III an usurper.[209]

Hawkins's Whig preferences have long been known, but it can be shown in addition that he had some grasp of the issues at stake as well as an eirenic purpose. In 1780, Hawkins added a footnote to his charge to a grand jury:

> Touching the Origin of civil Government, there are two Opinions sever-ally maintained by the Writers on that Subject; the one termed *patriar-chal*, which supposes the Right of Dominion to be founded on the express Donation of God, the other called the *popular* Scheme, which supposes the same Right to be the Gift, or to arise from the Consent, of the People. Of the former, Sir *Robert Filmer*, *Hobbes of Malmesbury*, and a few others; of the latter, Mr. *Locke*, and if I remember right, Bishop *Hoadley*, are the Abettors.

Hawkins recommended a 'middle Hypothesis', namely that 'the Rights, the Powers, and Privileges of Dominion are from God, but the Choice of the Person who shall exercise them is the Right of the People'.[210] To associate the Stuart dynastic alternative with untypical extremists like Filmer and Hobbes was a familiar Whig tactic; it was less common to dismiss Locke and Hoadly in similar terms, but Hawkins's middle option was one which commended itself to more and more Englishmen as the century went on. The evidence suggests, however, that it never fully persuaded Johnson: his growing acceptance of George III's *de facto* authority never issued in a renun-ciation of *de jure* right.

Johnson's world continued to change, even after George III's accession. Oaths did not so much lose their prominence as English public discourse developed in the eighteenth century, as change their application. The area of major contention shifted from the issue of allegiance to one or other dynasty, to the matter of subscription to the Creeds and Articles of the Church. Where controversy in Johnson's youth centred on the binding force of political oaths, the debate moved on with the slow acceptance of the House of Hanover. Yet although the debate changed its ground, its terms altered less. What did it mean to subscribe the Thirty-nine Articles? What mental reservations might reconcile doubtful consciences with the literal meanings of the text?[211] The controversy of 1773 about whether Oxford undergraduates should be required to subscribe the Thirty-nine Articles naturally caught Johnson's attention. Although in one way merely a tech-nical matter of the forms of an Oxford University ceremony, it raised the widest questions of the public role of religion. It caught the attention of the young Jeremy Bentham too, and his unpublished writings on the question laid the groundwork for his sustained crusade to extirpate orthodox religion in the years 1809–23.[212] At Johnson's death this controversy was really just about to begin.[213] This last was a debate which he had never entered: he had had no doubt that subscription to the Thirty-nine Articles should be required of Oxford undergraduates.[214] It was oaths bearing on politics, not on orthodox religion, that challenged Johnson to define his public identity in an area in which, for such profound reasons, he often sought to evade definition.

Notes

1. Samuel Johnson, *A Dictionary of the English Language* (2 vols., London, 1755).
2. J.H. Overton, *The Nonjurors* (London, 1902), pp. 66, 72, 140.
3. Overton, *Nonjurors*, pp. 136, 191, 281, 331.
4. For a full survey, see David Martin Jones, *Conscience and Allegiance in Seventeenth Century England: The Political Significance of Oaths and Engagements* (Rochester, NY, 1999), which also shows the role of oaths within the developing meanings of 'conscience', and John Spurr, 'Perjury, Profanity and Politics', *The Seventeenth Century*, 8 (1993), pp. 29–50. Jones criticises a number of historians, including myself, for using the anachronistic term 'ideology' of the early eighteenth century (p. 231). I accept the point: we are here examining not ideology, but law and religion.
5. Thomas Alcock, *The Nature and Obligation of Oaths. An Assize Sermon Preached in the Cathedral-Church of St Peter, Exon, on Wednesday, Aug. 7, 1754* (Oxford, 1755), p. 1. Alcock sought a reduction in the use of oaths.
6. *The Case of Concealment or mentall reservation* (1614), Ellesmere MSS, quoted by Christopher Hill, 'From Oaths to Interest', in *Society and Puritanism in Pre-Revolutionary England* (London, 1964), pp. 382–419, at 382. Hill argued for a transition from the first to the second as a parallel to a putative transition to a 'capitalist society', by implication with 'the new Hobbist society' of the mid-seventeenth century or the 'weary realism' which followed the Glorious Revolution, and described the Nonjurors as the 'final *reductio ad absurdum* of the traditional position' (pp. 414–15, 418). Others have contended similarly for a transition from a culture of oaths to one of propertied self-interest in the eighteenth century. It will be argued here that the culture of political oaths was powerful at least to the 1750s, and, for Johnson, throughout his life.
7. Quentin Skinner, 'Conquest and Consent: Thomas Hobbes and the Engagement Controversy', in G.E. Aylmer (ed.), *The Interregnum: The Quest for Settlement 1649–1660* (London, 1972); Jones, *Conscience and Allegiance*, ch. 3. The controversies of the 1640s were to be deliberately recalled in Oxford, with a new reference, in 1749: see below, n. 60.
8. Jones, *Conscience and Allegiance*, ch. 4.
9. 'Against rash and vain Swearing', sermon XV, in John Tillotson (ed.), *The Works Of the Learned Isaac Barrow, DD. Late Master of Trinity-College in Cambridge* (3 vols., London, 1722), I, pp. 152–3; first published in the first edition of Tillotson's collection (1683–9).
10. John Tillotson, *The Lawfulness, and Obligation of Oaths. A Sermon Preach'd at the Assises Held at Kingston upon Thames, July 21. 1681* (London, 1681), pp. 1–2, 4, 6.
11. Mark Goldie, 'The Revolution of 1689 and the Structure of Political Argument', *Bulletin of Research in the Humanities* 83 (1980), pp. 473–564, provides an exhaus-

tive bibliographical guide to this exchange. See also Jones, *Conscience and Allegiance*, pp. 201–27.

12. For example, *The Case of the Abjuration Oath Endeavoured to be Cleared, To the Satisfaction of those who are Required to take it* (London, 1702); [Robert Wodrow], *The Oath of Abjuration Considered, both As to the Lawfulness and Expediency of it's being taken by the Ministers of the Church of Scotland, In a Letter to a Friend* (Edinburgh, 1712).

13. *A Summary of the Penal Laws relating to Nonjurors, Papists, Popish Recusants and Nonconformists. And of the late Statutes concerning the Succession, Riots, and Imprisonment of Suspected Persons. Collected and put into such a Method, that the Reader may at one View satisfie his Enquiry. The Offences and Penalties being ranged opposite to each other. To which are added, Several adjudged Cases, and Notes upon the most material Points: Wherein are contained all the Oaths, Submissions, Declarations, Confessions of Faith and Affirmations, Required by the Government, since the first Year of Queen Elizabeth, to this present Year 1716. With an Historical Introduction, giving an Account of the Behaviour and Practices of the Roman Catholicks and Dissenters, which gave rise to these Laws* (London, 1716).

14. *The Case of the Oaths of Allegiance and Abjuration Briefly Stated* (London, 1737), p. 17.

15. *Observations on the Conspiracies of the Non-Jurors; And their Spiriting up Assassins and Murtherers* (London, 1718), pp. 4, 6.

16. For a review of such arguments see L.M. Hawkins, *Allegiance in Church and State: The Problem of the Nonjurors in the English Revolution* (London, 1928), pp. 108–11. For contemporary reflections on these problems see Howard Erskine-Hill, 'Alexander Pope: The Political Poet in His Time', *Eighteenth-Century Studies*, 15 (1981–2), pp. 123–48, at 143, and idem, 'Pope and Civil Conflict', in Eiichi Hara, Hiroshi Ozawa and Peter Robinson (eds.), *Enlightened Groves: Essays in Honour of Professor Zenzo Suzuki* (Tokyo, 1996), pp. 90–114, at 102.

17. Hearne, *Collections*, V, p. 18. (I owe this point to Richard Sharp.)

18. *A Discourse concerning the Signification of Allegiance, as it is to be understood in the new Oath of Allegiance* (n.p., n.d. [?1689]), pp. 1–2, 26. The author quoted Robert Sanderson's classic text *De Juramenti promisorii obligatione praelectiones septem. Habitae in Schola Theologica Oxon . . .* (London, 1647; reprinted 1661, 1670, 1676, 1683, 1686, 1710, 1719), Prael. 2, s. 9, 'Juramentum non nimis laxe interpretandum'. This work was translated as *De Juramento. Seven lectures concerning the obligation of promissory Oathes. Read publickly at the Divinity School at Oxford. Translated into English by His late Majesties speciall Command, and afterwards revised and approved under His Majesties own hand* (London, 1655; reprinted 1716). In 1678 the London printer Richard Marriott reissued *Bishop Sanderson's Judgement Concerning Submission to Usurpers* together with another Sanderson tract, *Reasons of the Present Judgement of the University of Oxford Concerning the Solemn League and Covenant* (1647). For the second, see n. 60 below. An abridgement was also available: *A Discourse Concerning the Nature and Obligation of Oaths. Wherein all the cases which have any Relation to Oaths enjoyned by governments, are Briefly Considered* (London: J. Roberts, 1716), as was a full collection: *A Preservative against Schism and Rebellion, in the most Trying Times . . . In a course of lectures read in the Divinity School at Oxford, in the time of the great rebellion. By Robert Sanderson . . . To which is added, the judgement of the University of Oxford, concerning the Solemn League and Covenant . . . Translated by Mr. Lewis* (3 vols., London: Charles Rivington, 1722). Sanderson was also reprinted in Dublin in 1755. He

continued to be invoked in political controversy after 1688, e.g. *A Friendly Conference concerning the new oath of allegiance, wherein the objections against taking the oaths are impartially examined, and the reasons of obedience confirm'd, from the writings of . . . Bishop Sanderson* (London, 1689); *A Friendly Debate between Dr. Kingsman . . . and Gratianus Trimmer . . . With some Considerations on Bishop Sanderson . . . about Monarchy, Oaths, etc.* (London, 1689).

19. Hawkins, *Life*, p. 543.

20. William James Copleston, *Memoir of Edward Copleston, D.D. Bishop of Llandaff* (London, 1851), p. 130.

21. *A Letter from a Gentleman in Town to His Friend in the Country, Recommending the Necessity of Frugality* (London, 1750), pp. 14–15. The purpose of frugality was to make funds available for remission to the exiled claimant.

22. Jones, *Conscience and Allegiance*, pp. 211–12. Jurors who swore to the *de facto* William III thinking 'that they had discovered a lesser construction of allegiance in Sanderson were mistaken, for not only was this view alien to Sanderson, it also could not properly be described as allegiance': ibid., pp. 215, 218.

23. *The Idea of a Patriot King* (1749), in David Mallet (ed.), *The Works of the late Right Honorable Henry St. John, Lord Viscount Bolingbroke* (5 vols., London, 1754), III, pp. 33–125, at 94–5.

24. Richard Steele, *The Crisis: or, a Discourse Representing, From the most Authentic Records, The just Causes of the late Happy Revolution* (London, 1714), pp. ii–iii.

25. [John, Viscount Barrington], *A Dissuasive from Jacobitism: Shewing in general What the Nation is to expect from a Popish King; and in particular, from the Pretender* (2nd edn., London, 1713), pp. 5–6, 17, 26.

26. Jones, *Conscience and Allegiance*, pp. 236–7.

27. E.g. *University Loyalty: or, the Genuine Explanation of the Principles and Practices of the English Clergy, as Established and Directed by the Decree of the University of Oxford, past in their Convocation 21 July 1683. and Republish'd at the Trying of Dr H. Sacheverell for High Crimes and Misdemeanours* (London, 1710).

28. Steele, *The Crisis*, p. ii.

29. G.R.M. Ward (trans.), *Oxford University Statutes. Volume I. Containing the Caroline Code, or Laudian Statutes, Promulgated AD 1636* (2 vols., London, 1845), I, p. 10.

30. Bodleian Librar̈y, Oxford University Archives, SP/E/6. I am grateful to Simon Bailey, Keeper of the Archives, for advice on this source. See also Nicholas Tyacke (ed.), *The History of the University of Oxford. Volume IV: Seventeenth-Century Oxford* (Oxford, 1997), pp. 187–8.

31. Samuel Johnson was never 'of the foundation'.

32. Ward (trans.), *Oxford University Statutes*, I, pp. 106–7; Clark, *Samuel Johnson*, p. 96. Ward undertook the translation in an effort to promote University reform (I, pp. iii–v): he would presumably have recorded that practice had changed in ways not prescribed by the statutes, if he could have done so.

33. Nicholas Carter, *The Obligation of an Oath; and particularly of the Oaths of Allegiance, Supremacy, and Abjuration* (London, 1716), pp. 18–19; cited in *AJ*, 8 (1997), p. 95.

34. [Nicholas Amhurst], *The Protestant Session, a Poem. Addressed to the Right Honourable Earl Stanhope. By a Member of the Constitution-Club at Oxford* (London, 1719).

35. [Nicholas Amhurst], *An Epistle from a Student at Oxford, to the Chevalier. Occasioned by His Removal over the Alps, And the Discovery of the Swedish Conspiracy* (London, 1717), pp. 4–5, 7.

36. [Amhurst], Terrae-Filius no. 3 (21 January 1721), in *Terrae-Filius* (London, 1726), pp. 11–12.

37. *DNB*, under 'Amhurst'.

38. 'Honest' was a recognised synonym for 'Jacobite'.

39. [Amhurst], *Terrae-Filius*, pp. 13, 15.

40. [Amhurst], *Terrae-Filius*, p. 15.

41. John Baron, a Whig, was Vice Chancellor in 1715–18.

42. [Amhurst], Terrae-Filius no. 17, 15 March 1721, in *Terrae-Filius*, pp. 86–93.

43. Brasenose College Archives, MPP 90 A1. I am grateful to the Archivist of Brasenose, Mrs. Elizabeth Boardman, for guidance on the college's collections, and to other college archivists for their efforts to locate copies of the matriculation certificate.

44. This was Robert Shippen (1677–1745), matriculated at Merton 1693, fellow of Brasenose 1699, Principal of Brasenose 1710–45. He was evidently a kinsman of the Jacobite MP William Shippen. Although a professed High Churchman, Robert Shippen subscribed the oaths, and was accused of triumphalism in succeeding the deprived Nonjuror Richard Welton in the living of St. Mary's, Whitechapel. He contended that it was better that he should take the living 'than that It should fall Into the Hands of Whiggs': *The Spiritual Intruder Unmask'd* (London, 1716), pp. 19, 36, 101.

45. Clark, *Samuel Johnson*, p. 94. This was printed in George Birkbeck Hill (ed.), *Johnsonian Miscellanies* (2 vols., Oxford, 1892), II, p. 85, with the note that it was 'pasted in at the end of a copy of *Parecbolae sive Excerpta e corpore Statutorum Universitatis Oxoniensis*. It was shown me by Mr. Viner Ellis, a descendant of Johnson's contemporary at Pembroke to whom it had been given.' The original volume does not survive in the Bodleian or (I am advised by the librarian) at Pembroke College.

46. *An Authentick Copy of the Association entred into by Part of the Nobility, Gentlemen and Clergy of Oxford, at the Time of the late Unnatural Rebellion in the Year 1745, together with the Names of all the Persons who Subscribed thereto* (broadsheet, n.p., n.d.). College affiliations are not given in the list, but can be established from other sources. Of the heads of 21 colleges, only the following signed: John Conybeare (Christ Church); John Mather (Corpus); James Edgcumbe (Exeter); Thomas Pardo (Jesus); Euseby Isham (Lincoln); Joseph Smith (Queen's); George Huddesford (Trinity). Edward Butler, Whig President of Magdalen College, was probably prevented from doing so by terminal illness. In addition, the Principals of St. Mary Hall, Alban Hall, St. Mary Magdalen Hall and New Inn Hall did not sign.

47. Hearne, *Collections*, 22 November 1721: VII, pp. 300–1.

48. Richard Blacow, *A Letter to William King, LL.D. Principal of St. Mary Hall in Oxford. Containing a particular Account of the Treasonable Riot at Oxford, in Feb. 1747* (2nd edn., London, 1755), pp. 14–24, at 17.

49. [Benjamin Kennicott], *A Letter to Doctor King, Occasion'd by his late Apology; And, in particular, By such parts of it as are meant to defame Mr. Kennicott, Fellow of Exeter College. By a Friend to Mr. Kennicott, And lately A Member of the University of Oxford* (London, 1755), pp. 25–6.

50. William King (1685–1763), matriculated Balliol College 9 July 1701; graduated BCL 12 July 1709; Principal of St. Mary Hall 1719 – d.

51. [Kennicott], *Letter to Doctor King*, p. 16.

52. [Kennicott], *Letter to Doctor King*, pp. 44–5.

53. Hearne's case illustrates how men might become Nonjurors after having once taken the oaths, by developing principled objections which prevented them from subscribing again. This may apply to Elijah Fenton (1683–1730), who graduated BA at Jesus College, Cambridge, in 1704, but was described as a Nonjuror in Johnson's *Lives of the Poets*.

54. [Thomas Hearne], *A Vindication Of those who take the Oath of Allegiance, To His Present Majestie from the Perjurie, Injustice, and Disloyaltie, Charged upon them by Such as are against it . . . In a Letter to a Non-Juror* ([London], 1731), pp. 1, 24. The editor, John Bilstone, is identified by mss. notes in the Bodleian's copy, Mus Bibl II 101.

55. Hearne, *Collections*, V, pp. 17–18, 45–6, 139.

56. [John Bilstone], 'To the Reader', in [Hearne], *A Vindication*, p. xv.

57. Hearne, *Collections*, V, p. 137. On 24 January 1715/16, after the last day allowed by 1 Geo. I, s. 2, c. 13, he wrote to Bodley's Librarian declining to act as sublibrarian in an attempt to avoid the penalties to which he would have been liable had that post come within the scope of the Act (he was unsure that it did so): ibid., pp. 164–5, 284.

58. Hearne, *Collections*, 3 October 1723, VIII, pp. 121–2.

59. [Richard Graves], *Recollection of Some Particulars In the Life of the late William Shenstone, Esq.* (London, 1788), p. 16.

60. [Robert Sanderson, H. Hammond, G. Morley, G. Sheldon and R. Zouch], *Reasons of the Present Judgement of the University of Oxford, concerning The Solemn League and Covenant. The Negative Oath. The Ordinances concerning Discipline and Worship. Approved by generall Consent in a full Convocation, 1. Jun. 1647. And Presented to Consideration* (London, 1749), pp. i–v. For this episode, see Edward Earl of Clarendon, *The History of the Rebellion and Civil Wars in England, Begun in the Year 1641* (3 vols., Oxford, 1702–4), III, p. 56. Sanderson's pamphlet had been reprinted before, in Latin, in 1689, 1710 and 1719: it evidently had some currency in academic circles as an exploration of the problems posed by usurped authority.

61. The text is reprinted in *Reasons of the Present Judgement*, pp. 6–51.

62. Richard Blacow, *A Letter to William King, LL.D. Principal of St Mary Hall in Oxford. Containing a particular Account of the Treasonable Riot at Oxford, in Feb. 1747* (London, 1755), p. 5.

63. *An Answer to Mr B[laco]w's Apology, As it respects His King, his Country, his Conscience, and his God. By a Student of Oxford* (London, 1755), pp. 2, 14, 20. This work was 'Printed for W. BIZETT in *St. Clements Church-yard*', the same man who in 1753 had published a print (author's collection) of the Jacobite Alexander Murray with a suitable legend from the opening lines of Horace, Book III, Ode 3 ('Justum, et tenacem propositi virum / Non civium ardor prava jubentium, / Non vultus instantis Tyranni, / Mente quatit solida', translated by Philip Francis: 'The Man, in conscious Virtue bold, / Who dares his secret Purpose hold, / Unshaken hears the Croud's tumultuous Cries, / And the impetuous Tyrant's angry Brow defies'). This was the same William Bizet who had been examined in 1750 on a charge of publishing another seditious print: PRO, SP 36/116/21 (I owe this reference to Richard Sharp).

64. Brasenose College Archives MPP 11 A1.

65. Bodleian MS Top Oxon b 42, f. 129.

66. Bodleian MS Eng misc c 406, f. 177.

67. BL Add MSS 42,506, f. 96. Henry Ellis had been elected as a scholar from Merchant Taylors on 11 June 1796: ibid., f. 95.

68. Brasenose College Archives MPP 25 A1.
69. Edward Bentham, *A Letter to a Young Gentleman of Oxford* (London, 1748), p. 26. Lest there be any doubt, Bentham then printed the oaths of allegiance and abjuration, pp. 29–30.
70. Edward Bentham, *A Letter to a Fellow of a College. Being the Sequel of a Letter to a Young Gentleman of Oxford* (London, 1749), esp. pp. 56–8, 70.
71. The term was not, as today, synonymous with 'fellow', but described both under-graduates and senior members who were supported on the foundation; it there-fore covered the modern categories of 'scholar' and 'fellow' at other colleges. The governing body of Christ Church was, uniquely, not the Students but the Dean and Canons.
72. E.G.W. Bill, *Education at Christ Church Oxford 1660–1800* (Oxford, 1988), pp. 141–5. In this learned and accurate study, Dr. Bill was briefly misled by the letter from 'Philalethes' printed in Amhurst's *Terrae-Filius* (discussed above) into think-ing that the oath of allegiance was taken by all at matriculation, and inferred that, at that early stage, the oaths were disregarded as mere formalities: this was not the case. Students were admitted to their Studentships some time after the university ceremony, in the case of Canoneer Students up to two years after-wards, and they were still commoners on matriculation. I am grateful to Dr. Bill for advice on this point.
73. Clark, *Samuel Johnson*, p. 117; Bill, *Christ Church*, p. 327. For an example of open Jacobitism by another Westminster Student in 1750, however, see ibid., pp. 161–2. Dr. Bill suggests that it is unlikely that any Student was deprived for failing to take the oaths at the accession of George I: ibid., p. 145, n. 3.
74. *A Representation of the Conduct of the Proctors, with respect to the Two Explanatory Statutes proposed by the Vice-Chancellor to Them and the Heads of Houses* [Oxford, 1759], p. 4; *An Answer to the Objections made in Convocation to the Representation of the Conduct of the Proctors* [Oxford, 1759]. Printed flysheets on this question are assembled in a Bodleian volume, shelfmark Gough Oxf. 96.
75. *A Letter to a late Member of the U[niversit]y of O[xfor]d, with Respect to the Two Explanatory Statutes proposed to The C[onvocatio]n* [Oxford, 1759], p. 8.
76. E.g. *A Letter to the Reverend* **** ***** *M.A. Fellow of* ***** *College Oxford, On the Case of Subscription at Matriculation* (Oxford, 1772); *A Collection of Papers, designed to Explain and Vindicate the Present Mode of Subscription required by The University of Oxford, from all Young Persons at their Matriculation* (Oxford, 1772); *Reflections on the Impropriety and Inexpediency of Lay-Subscription to the XXXIX Articles, in the University of Oxford* (Oxford, [1772]).
77. Ward (trans.), *Oxford University Statutes*, I, p. xx; L.H. Dudley Buxton and Strick-land Gibson, *Oxford University Ceremonies* (Oxford, 1935), p. 3.
78. Bodleian Library, Oxford University Archives, SP 12 (Plate 4).
79. See Clark, *Samuel Johnson*, p. 94.
80. Bodleian Library, Oxford University Archives, SP 46.
81. See Clark, *Samuel Johnson*, p. 96.
82. Wetherell to Jenkinson, 20 February 1773: BL Add MSS 38,207, f. 239.
83. Ibid., ff. 240–2.
84. Ward (trans.), *Oxford University Statutes*, I, p. 120; *Parecbolae* (1729), p. 128.
85. *Considerations on the Residence usually required for Degrees in the University of Oxford* (Oxford, 1772), pp. 3, 16, 24. This was routine practice: for over 100 such appli-cations for dispensation in the period from 30 December 1721 to 28 February 1723/4, see Bodleian MS Top Oxon c 69. By contrast, of course, there are no

documentary records of oaths of allegiance or abjuration being tendered to those from whom statutes did not require them.

86. These might have been supplemented by a legacy of £40 in February 1727/8: Reade, *Johnsonian Gleanings*, V, p. 1. The 'formidable library' which Johnson took to Oxford helps 'to rebut the idea of his very narrow circumstances', p. 28. Reade concluded that 'the immediate cause' of Johnson's leaving Oxford was 'probably' melancholia rather than poverty, and acutely observed: 'The extraordinary thing is that Boswell never could learn the truth about Johnson's Oxford career', p. 43. This was indeed remarkable, and suggests that more had been at issue than poverty alone. For Johnson's keeping 'certain subjects . . . off-limits' from Boswell, including 'his having to leave Oxford, his experience teaching school, his collaborating with Chambers', see John B. Radner, ' "A Very Exact picture of His Life": Johnson's Role in Writing the *Life of Johnson*', *AJ*, 7 (1996), pp. 299–342, at 318.

87. Reade, *Johnsonian Gleanings*, V, pp. 48, 153–75, at 160, 168. See ibid., pp. 168–9 for estimates of the expenses of a commoner of Hart Hall for the quarter 21 June–27 September 1723, totalling £7 17s. 1d.

88. Quoted by V.H.H. Green, 'The University and Social Life', in Dame Lucy Sutherland and L.H. Mitchell (eds.), *The History of the University of Oxford*, V, p. 328.

89. [Richard Newton], *A Scheme of Discipline with Statutes Intended to be Established by a Royal Charter for the Education of Youth in Hart-Hall in the University of Oxford* ([?Oxford], 1720), Appendix, p. 1.

90. John Disney (ed.), *The Works Theological, Medical, Political, and Miscellaneous, of John Jebb* (3 vols., London, 1787), III, p. 267.

91. *A Short Account of God's Dealings with the Rev. George Whitefield* (London, 1740), pp. 24, 38, cited in Graham Midgley, *University Life in Eighteenth-Century Oxford* (New Haven, 1996), p. 7. Midgley also gives typical room rents, which might be as low as £3 per annum for a garret, and Johnson's estimates for the cost of furniture, p. 22.

92. Clark, *Samuel Johnson*, p. 117.

93. See below, n. 210.

94. Discussed in Clark, *Samuel Johnson*, p. 118.

95. E.H. Carter, *The Norwich Subscription Books: A Study of the Subscription Books of the Diocese of Norwich 1637–1800* (London, 1937), noted these peaks (p. 90) but added: 'Neither national nor diocesan history offers explanations.' Correlations with moments of national tension, usually over politico-theological issues, now seem likely for most of these high points.

96. Carter, *Norwich Subscription Books*, pp. 94, 117–18.

97. Sir Wolstan Dixie was born in 1701 and succeeded his father in 1713; he died in 1767. In 1722 Anthony Blackwall was appointed headmaster of Market Bosworth school; he swore the oaths on 16 July 1723 before John Kilby, surrogate of the vicar-general (Leicestershire Record Office, Archdeaconry of Leicester subscription books, 1 D 41/34/3 f. 67 v). Blackwall died on 8 April 1730. He was succeeded as headmaster by the Rev. John Kilby (1667–1734), who swore the oaths on 28 September 1730 before John Clayton, surrogate (ibid., f. 72 v). Kilby was headmaster during Johnson's time as usher, from March to July 1732: Johnson's name is not in the subscription books. Samuel Johnson was evidently succeeded as usher by the Rev. Thomas Adderley, offered the appointment in a letter from Dixie dated 15 October 1733 (loc. cit. 1 D 41/35/3); Adderley took the oaths on 27 October 1733 before Joseph Kilbye, surrogate (loc. cit.

1 D 41/34/4, f. 71 v). John Kilby died in August 1734. On 31 December 1734 Dixie wrote to John Crompton, headmaster of Solihull school, inviting him to succeed to Market Bosworth (loc. cit. 1 D 41/35/5); Crompton accepted, and subscribed the oaths on 14 January 1734/5 before Joseph Kilbye, surrogate (loc. cit. 1 D 41/34/4 f. 71 r). See also Reade, *Johnsonian Gleanings*, V, pp. 76n, 232–6. Reade used the subscription books only to establish the dates of Johnson's teaching career, and did not realise their political significance. Nor did he see the significance of the fact that Johnson's name is not in the registers.

98. For this archive see Leicester Museums and Art Gallery, *Handlist of Records of Leicester Archdeaconry* (Leicester, 1954).

99. Lincolnshire Archives, Lincoln. I have examined the subscription books, Sub. VII, VIII; the subsidiary and 'travelling' subscription books, Sub. T. I, II, III; and the Letters testimonial and licences for schoolmasters, Lic/Sch/1. For this archive see Kathleen Major, *A Handlist of the Records of the Bishop of Lincoln and of the Archdeacons of Lincoln and Stow* (London, 1953).

100. Hawkins, *Life*, pp. 20–1.

101. Anthony Blackwall's High Churchmanship is established by his assize sermon, *Duty to God and the Queen. Briefly Expressed in a Sermon Preach'd at St Mary's Nottingham, March the 17th 1703/4* (London, 1704). He was also the author of two substantial works, *An Introduction to the Classics* (London, 1718; 6th edn., 1746) and *The Sacred Classics defended and illustrated* (2 vols., London and Derby, 1725, 1731; 3rd edn., 2 vols., 1737). I shall discuss his work elsewhere.

102. Boswell, *Life*, I, pp. 84–5.

103. 'A State of England', RASP 65/16, printed in Paul S. Fritz, *The English Ministers and Jacobitism between the Rebellions of 1715 and 1745* (Toronto, 1975), pp. 147–55. The list analysed supporters county by county, dividing names into three groups: the first not described; a second, small, category labelled 'Dubious'; and a third, equally small, category of 'Whiggs'. Leicestershire provided eight names, including 'Sir Woolston Dixey', all in the first category. (I owe this reference to Paul Monod.)

104. Lichfield Diocesan Record Office, Lichfield. I have examined the subscription books, refs. B/A/4/2, 14–16, 30–3.

105. Paul Monod, 'A Voyage out of Staffordshire: or, Samuel Johnson's Jacobite Journey', ante, ch. 1.

106. The evidence of the Archdeaconry of Leicester subscription books is inconclusive only because the chronological point at which Johnson's name would have appeared, had he subscribed, comes at the point of transition between two similar folio volumes, 1 D 41/34/3 and 1 D 41/34/4. The last subscription in vol. 3, f. 73 v (before those later added for 1745) is a schoolmaster's, dated 11 December 1731. In vol. 4, the subscriptions for the first time cease to be recorded in a single chronological series and are grouped by profession; the first subscription, at f. 72 v, is a schoolmaster's on 10 April 1733. It might be claimed that this represents a break in the records during which Johnson subscribed, his doing so being recorded in a document now lost (although it would be a desperate argument). This is unlikely on the grounds that: (1) Joseph Kilbye, the surrogate, took the last subscriptions in vol. 3 and the first ones in vol. 4: there was no interruption of the responsible personnel; (2) Kilbye evidently maintained his records with equal care, and in the same form of words, in both volumes; (3) Kilbye did not run out of space in vol. 3. From f. 73, there were blank pages until an index began on f. 91 r, blanks which were partly filled up (ff. 74–5) only

in 1745. Johnson could have signed the usual formula here, had he subscribed; (4) although a page has been removed from vol. 4, before what was later numbered as f. 1, this preceded the entries for subscriptions not of schoolmasters but of surgeons, the first entry being for 14 October 1735 before George Newell, Vicar General. The subscriptions for schoolmasters begin at the opposite end of the book, which has been inverted and completed in reverse order of pages to economise on space, beginning with the subscription on 10 April 1733 before Joseph Kilbye, f. 72 v. There was also a blank page before this subscription, f. 73 r, which could have been used for earlier schoolmasters' subscriptions, had there been any; (5) there is no sign of loose pages having been stuck into either volume but later removed; (6) there were other lengthy gaps, even in the single chronological series combining all the professions: December 1719 to September 1721; June 1724 to October 1725; April 1728 to February 1729; (7) vol. 4 was not a new volume in 1733, for it already contained at the back (ff. 84 v–73 v) material dated 1719–21. Kilbye did not therefore obtain a new volume, perhaps after a delay, when vol. 3 ran out. This makes it unlikely that he abandoned vol. 3, made entries in another volume now lost, and abandoned that within a year for no known reason to begin entries in yet another volume. What is now vol. 4 was already to hand in December 1731, had he wished to use it; (8) the unsupported speculation that Johnson subscribed on a document now lost is inconsistent with the rest of the evidence that points to Johnson's not having taken the oaths. It is impossible to prove a negative with total certainty, but the balance of probabilities is decidedly against Johnson's subscribing between March and July 1732. Here, as elsewhere where evidence is fragmentary, historians seek to discern a common pattern which makes the best sense of the evidence which is available.

107. London Metropolitan Archives, Justices' certificates, Index, WC/R 1, f. 144 v. Dryden's refusal seems not to have been noticed in modern scholarship. Howard Erskine-Hill first alerted me to the possibility of such an event.

108. Dryden to the Duke of Ormonde, 'The first day of Winter, 1698', in Charles E. Ward (ed.), *The Letters of John Dryden* (Durham, NC, 1942), p. 107.

109. Dryden to Mrs Steward, 7 November [?1699], in Ward (ed.), *Letters*, pp. 122–4.

110. Dryden to Mrs. Steward, 26 November [?1699], in Ward (ed.), *Letters*, pp. 128–30; James Anderson Winn, *John Dryden and his World* (New Haven, 1987), p. 508. For Dryden's position as reflected in his writings, see William J. Cameron, 'John Dryden's Jacobitism', in Harold Love (ed.), *Restoration Literature: Critical Approaches* (London, 1972), pp. 277–308.

111. Maynard Mack, *Alexander Pope: A Life* (New Haven, Conn., 1985), p. 265.

112. Howard Erskine-Hill, 'Pope and Civil Conflict', pp. 90–114, at 97, quoting Greater London Record Office (now London Metropolitan Archives) MR/RR/23, f. 3.

113. CLRO Misc MSS 307.5/1–22. For a similar exercise in 1723 required by 9 Geo. I, c. 24 see CLRO Sessions Records 226B.

114. CLRO Abjuration Rolls. I have examined 223B Boxes 8 and 9 (the rolls for January 1735 to October 1757), 223C Box 15 (undated) and 235D (Southwark sessions, 1744–1835). A 'Samuel Johnson' appears in the roll for 13 January 1735/6, but the signature is clearly not that of the lexicographer. By contrast Benjamin Rackstrow, whom I suggest was Johnson's captain in the Trained Bands (see below), signed on 13 January 1747/8.

115. Clark, *Samuel Johnson*, pp. 17, 62, 177.

116. C[harles] S[ackville], *A Treatise Concerning the Militia, in Four Sections* (London, 1752), pp. 11, 62. In true patrician style, Sackville proceeded from a long dissertation (pp. 12–30) '*Of the* ROMAN MILITIA'. A Bill to give effect to his plan failed in the Commons the same year: J.R. Western, *The English Militia in the Eighteenth Century: The Story of a Political Issue 1660–1802* (London, 1965), p. 121.

117. Ian F.W. Beckett, *The Amateur Military Tradition 1558–1945* (Manchester, 1991), p. 51; David Allen, 'The Role of the London Trained Bands in the Exclusion Crisis, 1678–1681', *English Historical Review*, 87 (1972), pp. 287–303; C. Neville Packett, *Her Majesty's Commission of Lieutenancy for the City of London: A Brief History* (privately printed, London, 1987). The Trained Bands of London were not (as has sometimes been suggested) established by the Militia Act of 1757.

118. That this was the criterion for eligibility is suggested by the excuses accepted by the Court of Lieutenancy from defaulters, e.g. on 29 January 1746: 'Ann Nash – Not a Housekeeper . . . John Catlin – Only a Lodger': CLRO, Lieutenancy Minute Book 1744–49, 441/A/7, p. 207. A woman too, if a housekeeper in her own right, was liable to find a substitute.

119. Western, *English Militia*, pp. 52–74.

120. CLRO Lieutenancy Minute Books 1714–44 (441/A/6), 1744–49 (441/A/7), 1749–83 (441/A/8).

121. In 1756, the colonels were: Blue regiment, the Hon. Sir Joseph Hankey, Alderman, President of the Honourable Artillery Company; Orange, the Hon. William Baker, Alderman, Vice President; Red, the Hon. Sir William Calvert, Alderman, Vice Treasurer; Green, the Hon. Thomas Chitty, Alderman; Yellow, the Hon. Sir Samuel Fludyer, Alderman; White, the Hon. John Porter, Alderman: Packett, *Lieutenancy*, p. 68.

122. CLRO Lieutenancy Minute Books, 441/A/7, pp. 143, 234; 441/A/8, pp. 37, 202, n.p.

123. Ibid., 441/A/8, n.p., p. 244.

124. Ibid., 441/A/8, pp. 67, 115, 148, 170–1.

125. CLRO Misc MSS 11.20.

126. CLRO Lieutenancy Minute Book, 441/A/7, pp. 25–9.

127. Johnson to Lewis Paul, 29 December 1755: Johnson, *Letters*, I, p. 116; 'I have been ill for about a fortnight': Johnson to Lucy Porter, 30 December 1755: ibid., p. 118; Johnson to Joseph Wharton, 15 April 1756, ibid., pp. 133–4.

128. Johnson to Richard Congreve, 16 October 1755: Johnson, *Letters*, I, p. 114.

129. Cf. Irma S. Lustig, 'Facts and Deductions: The Curious History of Reynolds's First Portrait of Johnson, 1756', *AJ*, 1 (1987), pp. 161–80.

130. I accept here the review of the medical evidence offered in John Wiltshire, *Samuel Johnson in the Medical World* (Cambridge, 1991), pp. 11–63; see esp. pp. 11–13, 18–20, 24–33, 38–40.

131. Clark, *Samuel Johnson*, pp. 120–1.

132. Johnson to Samuel Richardson, 16 March 1756: Johnson, *Letters*, I, p. 132. In February 1758, Johnson was arrested for debt a second time: James L. Clifford, *Dictionary Johnson: Samuel Johnson's Middle Years* (New York, 1979), p. 191.

133. Donald D. Eddy, *Samuel Johnson Book Reviewer in the Literary Magazine: or, Universal Review 1756–1758* (New York, 1979). A facsimile edition of *The Literary Magazine* is available, ed. Donald D. Eddy (3 vols., New York, 1978).

134. Clifford, *Dictionary Johnson*, pp. 164–76, at 171. Clifford identified Johnson's 'country Tory bias', p. 170.

135. From *The Literary Magazine*, no. 2 (15 May–15 June 1756), pp. 57–64, at 59.

136. Thomas Comber, *A Vindication of the Great Revolution in England In A.D. MDCLXXXVIII* (London, 1758), p. 52.

137. Charles M. Clode, *The Military Forces of the Crown; their Administration and Government* (2 vols., London, 1869), I, pp. 38–40; Tony Hayter, *The Army and the Crowd in Mid-Georgian England* (London, 1978), pp. 38, 81, 103; Paul Kléber Monod, *Jacobitism and the English People 1688–1788* (Cambridge, 1989), pp. 197–8; Western, *Militia*, pp. 147–8.

138. Beckett, *Amateur Military Tradition*, p. 65; Western, *Militia*, p. 158.

139. Clifford, *Dictionary Johnson*, p. 174.

140. Thomas M. Curley, *Sir Robert Chambers: Law, Literature and Empire in the Age of Johnson* (Madison, Wisconsin, 1998), pp. 25–7. Chambers (1737–1803) had been a pupil at Newcastle Royal Grammar School during the '45 and, although Johnson's junior, was still within a shared body of public experience. Curley dates Chambers's first meeting with Johnson to the summer of 1754 and places it in London (ibid., p. 21), but how they met is unknown. The quick and lasting friendship between the two is remarkable, and suggests an affinity not yet fully understood. For their co-operation in the 1760s see below, nn. 185–93.

141. *Literary Magazine*, 4 (15 July–15 August 1756), pp. 171–6, at 171, 176.

142. Review of *Familiar Letters of Dr William Sancroft, late Lord Archbishop of Canterbury, to Mr North, afterwards Sir Henry North of Mildenhall, Bart. both before, but principally after, his Deprivation for refusing to take the Oaths to King William III. and his Retirement to the Place of his Nativity in Suffolk: found among the Papers of Sir Henry North, never before published* (London, 1757), in *The Literary Magazine* no. 14 (May 15–June 15, 1757), pp. 228–33, at 228–9.

143. Ibid., p. 233.

144. It was not in William Prideaux Courtney and David Nichol Smith, *A Bibliography of Samuel Johnson* (Oxford, 1925), pp. 75–7, based on Boswell, *Life*, I, pp. 309–10, or in Eddy, *Samuel Johnson Book Reviewer*, p. 32. Boswell's list was mostly compiled from what he termed 'internal evidence' rather than Johnson's avowal. It is partly corrected by D.J. Greene, 'Johnson's Contributions to the *Literary Magazine*', *Review of English Studies*, 7 (1956), pp. 367–92. Greene suggested: 'There is evidently nothing sacred about the origin of [this] canon to deter the student from recommencing a search of the *Literary Magazine* for items to add to it . . . When it is known that Johnson "contributed largely" to a periodical, the student's method must be to go through the file of that periodical item by item, examining the style and content of each piece; and it seems reasonable that he should work on the premises that if he encounters a piece of writing compatible with Johnson's known styles and interests in the middle of a number that contains many pieces already attributed to Johnson on "internal evidence" only (and their attribution not controverted), there is a legitimate presumption that it too is by Johnson, unless there exist reasons to believe otherwise' (p. 371). Greene re-examined nos. 1–5 of the *Literary Magazine* on those principles, but did not get further.

145. Ruth K. McClure, 'Johnson's Criticism of the Foundling Hospital and its Consequences', *Review of English Studies*, 27 (1976), pp. 17–26.

146. Clifford, *Dictionary Johnson*, pp. 184–5.

147. As Greene showed ('Johnson's Contributions', pp. 371–2), Johnson had more than one prose style: his grandiloquent manner is easily recognised (and par-

odied), but he was also capable of writing functional, everyday prose difficult to distinguish from that of other authors.

148. *The Literary Magazine* 18 (15 September–15 October 1757), pp. 434–6.
149. Samuel Johnson, *The Idler*, 10 (17 June 1758). Perhaps Johnson's own political disillusion is echoed in this passage: 'Many and many a time has *Tom* told me, in a corner, that our miseries were almost at an end, and that we should see, in a month, another Monarch on the Throne; the time elapses without a Revolution; *Tom* meets me again with new intelligence, the whole scheme is now settled, and we shall see great events in another month.'
150. Boswell, *Life*, II, p. 220.
151. Romney Sedgwick (ed.), *The History of Parliament: The House of Commons 1715–1754* (2 vols., London, 1970). Ian R. Christie, 'The Tory Party, Jacobitism and the Forty-Five: a Note', *HJ*, 30 (1987), pp. 921–31, highlights the considerable extent of Jacobite involvement among MPs as late as the Parliament of 1741.
152. *A Letter from S[?tafford]shire, to a Gentleman in Town, Concerning a turbulent and seditious Faction which has lately infested that Part of the Country* (London, 1751), p. 20.
153. [Amhurst], *Terrae-Filius*, pp. iv, vi. In republishing his periodical, Amhurst was bidding for an official reward for his Hanoverian loyalty. He followed these arguments with the Scriptural parable of the labourers in the vineyard, to claim that those (i.e. himself) who had *'borne the* heat *and* burthen *of the day'* should be not less well rewarded than those hired *'at the* eleventh *hour'*, p. viii. Unfortunately, the meaning of the parable was the opposite.
154. John Conybeare, *Calumny Refuted: or, an Answer to the Personal Slanders Published by Dr Richard Newton, in his Letter to Dr Holmes, Vice-Chancellor of the University of Oxford, &c.* (London, 1735), p. 78.
155. Richard Newton, *The Grounds of the Complaint of the Principal of Hart-Hall, Concerning the Obstruction given to the Incorporation of his Society, by Exeter-College and their Visitor . . . In Answer to the Misrepresentations of Dr C[onybear]e . . .* (London, 1735), pp. 59–60.
156. William Bromley, Jr. (?1701–37), son of the Jacobite William Bromley (?1663–1732), MP for Oxford University 1701–32. Bromley Jr. had apparently paid his respects to James Francis Edward Stuart while on the grand tour in 1721: Sedgwick, *HC*, I, pp. 493–5.
157. *An Exact Account of the Poll, As it stood between The Honourable Mr Trevor, and Wm. Bromley, Esq.* (London, [1737]), pp. 9, 37, 39.
158. Richard Newton, *Rules and Statutes for the Government of Hertford College, in the University of Oxford* (London, 1747), pp. 16, 98.
159. [Richard Newton], *The Principles of the University of Oxford, As far as relates to Affection to the Government, Stated* (London, 1755), Advertisement.
160. Clark, *Samuel Johnson*, pp. 182–3. Newton was the subject of a lengthy attack by the undoubtedly Whig Nicholas Amhurst, in the collected edition of his periodical: [Amhurst], *Terrae-Filius . . . To which are added, Remarks upon a late Book, entitled, University Education, by R. Newton, D.D. Principal of Hart-Hall*, pp. 289–335.
161. He is not to be confused with the anti-Walpolian Henry Brooke (?1703–83), playwright and author of *Gustavus Vasa* (1739), a conflation which would make *Gustavus Vasa* seem more securely Hanoverian than, in its proper context, it was. This was the Henry Brooke who described the convicted Jacobite con-

spirator Francis Atterbury, Bishop of Rochester, as 'that great and good man': Henry Brooke to Alexander Pope [November 1731], in Howard Erskine-Hill (ed.), *Alexander Pope: Selected Letters* (Oxford, 2000), pp. 303–4.

162. On Brooke's death in 1752, the ex-Jacobite William Murray reportedly proposed to the Secretary of State, the Duke of Newcastle, that William Blackstone should succeed: Newcastle allegedly disbelieved his political reliability, and gave it to a Dr. Jenner instead: John Holliday, *The Life of William late Earl of Mansfield* (London, 1797), pp. 88–9; Lucy Sutherland, 'William Blackstone and the Legal Chairs at Oxford', in Sutherland, *Politics and Finance in the Eighteenth Century* (London, 1984), pp. 551–62.

163. [Henry Brooke], *A Letter to the Oxford Tories. By an Englishman* (London, 1750), pp. 3–7, 11.

164. [Benjamin Kennicott], *A Letter to Doctor King, Occasion'd by his late Apology; And, in particular, By such parts of it as are meant to defame Mr Kennicott, Fellow of Exeter College. By a Friend to Mr Kennicott, And lately A Member of the University of Oxford* (London, 1755), pp. 118–21.

165. [Kennicott], *A Letter to Doctor King*, p. 121.

166. *The Balance: or the Merits of Whig and Tory, Exactly weigh'd and fairly determin'd. Addressed to All Honest Britons concerned in the Election of Members of Parliament* (London, 1753), pp. 3–4.

167. [Benjamin Buckler], *A Proper Explanation of the Oxford Almanack For this present Year M.DCC.LV* (London, [1755]), pp. 27–8.

168. Clark, *Samuel Johnson*, p. 184.

169. Rev. John Young to Duke of Grafton, 11 September 1761, in Sir William Anson (ed.), *Autobiography and Political Correspondence of Augustus Henry Third Duke of Grafton K.G.* (London, 1898), p. 33.

170. For Westmorland's installation, see Clark, *Samuel Johnson*, p. 102.

171. *A Letter from Albemarle Street to the Cocoa-Tree, on some late transactions* (London, 1764), p. 24.

172. Junius, Letter XXXV, 19 December 1769, in John Cannon (ed.), *The Letters of Junius* (Oxford, 1978), p. 167; cf. pp. 187, 252–3, 480, 490. Denunciations of the Scots and Jacobites were prominent themes of Junius's letters, as they had been of John Wilkes's *The North Briton*.

173. Letter LXI, 14 November 1770, in Cannon (ed.), *Letters of Junius*, p. 207.

174. For which, see J.C.D. Clark (ed.), *The Memoirs and Speeches of James, 2nd Earl Waldegrave, 1742–63* (Cambridge, 1988), p. 59.

175. *Historia Placitorum Coronae. The History of the Pleas of the Crown, By Sir Matthew Hale Knt. sometime Lord Chief Justice of the Court of King's Bench. Now first published from his Lordship's Original Manuscript, and the several References to the Records examined by the Originals, with large Notes. By Sollom Emlyn of Lincoln's-Inn Esq.* (2 vols., London, 1736). Emlyn argued that Hale was 'very far from being of a mind with those, who lookt on every branch of the prerogative as *jure divino* and indefeasible' (I, p. iii), and quoted the Whig bishop Gilbert Burnet in praise of the judge.

176. Donald Greene, *Samuel Johnson's Library: An Annotated Guide* (Victoria, B.C., 1975), p. 64.

177. *The History and Analysis of the Common Law of England. Written by a learned Hand* [Sir Matthew Hale] (London, 1713), pp. 78–9. Hale's authorship was acknowledged in the second edition of 1716. Hale's argument that the presence of a king *de jure* terminated the title of a king *de facto* was the exact opposite of the teaching of Sir Edward Coke, *The Third Part of the Institutes: Concerning High Treason*

and other Pleas of the Crown (London, 1644). After 1688, Nonjurors championed Coke's judgement in *Calvin's Case* (1608) and rejected his different interpretation in the third part of the *Institutes*: Jones, *Conscience and Allegiance*, pp. 206–7, 220–1.

178. This work should not be confused with another by Hale with a similar title. *Pleas of the Crown: or, a Methodical Summary of the Principal Matters relating to that Subject* (London; Printed by the Assigns of Richard Atkins and Edward Atkins Esq; for William Shrewsbury . . . and John Leigh . . . 1678) indeed complained (Preface, n.p.) of the inaccuracies of an earlier edition (London: Richard and Jacob Tonson, 1678); but these are single octavo volumes, brief synopses of the larger work of the same title, and do not contain the passages printed by Harbin.

179. For the editor, Sollom Emlyn (1697–1754), a legal reformer, see *DNB*.

180. Jones, *Conscience and Allegiance*, p. 221.

181. Curley, *Sir Robert Chambers*, p. 39.

182. [George Harbin], *The Hereditary Right of the Crown of England Asserted* (London, 1713), pp. 101, 128, 179, 221–6. Harbin printed the central passage twice, the second time at greater length, and the passage cited here from Hale's *Analysis of the . . . Law of England*.

183. Jones, *Conscience and Allegiance*, pp. 221, 265.

184. Johnson had made much use of Hale's other writings in compiling the *Dictionary*: see Daisuke Nagashima, 'How Johnson read Hale's *Origination* for his *Dictionary*: A Linguistic View', *AJ*, 7 (1996), pp. 247–97. Thomas Curley (*Sir Robert Chambers*, p. 30) suggests that Johnson's interest in the study of law at Oxford began with his support of Chambers for a Vinerian Scholarship (virtually an assistantship to the Vinerian Professor) in 1758.

185. Thomas M. Curley (ed.), *A Course of Lectures on the English Law Delivered at the University of Oxford 1767–1773 by Sir Robert Chambers* (2 vols., Oxford, 1986), I, pp. 7–8, 22; Curley, *Sir Robert Chambers* (1998) adds a wealth of detail on other matters.

186. For Blackstone's acceptance of *de facto* arguments see Jones, *Conscience and Allegiance*, pp. 234–5.

187. Chambers, *Lectures*, I, pp. 268, 270–1.

188. Chambers, *Lectures*, I, p. 270.

189. Chambers, *Lectures*, I, p. 138, noticed by Howard Erskine-Hill in *AJ*, 8 (1997), p. 5.

190. Chambers, *Lectures*, I, p. 155.

191. Chambers, *Lectures*, I, pp. 350–1.

192. Chambers, *Lectures*, I, p. 155.

193. Chambers, *Lectures*, I, pp. 374–5.

194. J.C.D. Clark, *English Society 1660–1832: Religion, ideology and politics during the ancien regime* (Cambridge, 2000), ch. 3.

195. This was Thomas Townshend (1733–1800), MP for Whitchurch, who had resigned from Grafton's administration in June 1768 after an imagined slight and thereafter indulged his resentment.

196. J. Wright (ed.), *Sir Henry Cavendish's Debates of the House of Commons, during the Thirteenth Parliament of Great Britain* (2 vols., London, 1841–3), II, pp. 456–7.

197. Cavendish, *Debates*, II, p. 457.

198. It was first published in 1739 with the name of 'John Brett' as its publisher. There is, however, evidence to suggest that he was 'a man paid to draw fire away from the real principals involved in publication' and to shield them from persecu-

tion: A.D. Barker, 'The Printing and Publishing of Johnson's *Marmor Norfolciense* (1739) and *London* (1738 and 1739)', *The Library*, sixth series, 3 (1981), pp. 287–304.

199. An Unitarian, Francis Webb: Clark, *Samuel Johnson*, p. 231. There is other evidence for Webb's politics. A copy of Algernon Sidney's *Discourses Concerning Government* (London: A. Millar, 1763) is extant with the ownership signature of a Francis Webb; it carries annotations in Webb's hand dated February 1796 in praise of Sidney as 'This exalted Patriot & righteous Martyr for Liberty'. Webb continued: 'Notwithstanding this, I myself have heard in the Reign of George the Third, not only these noble, & divine Discourses depreciated, & the Principles on which they are founded call'd in question; but I have read performances in direct opposition to them, which I have heard highly extoll'd; & seen the Authors of them countenanc'd by those in Power, & not only countenanc'd but applauded in the Senate & rewarded with enormous Pensions.' For permission to quote Webb's notes, I am grateful to the owners of his copy of Sidney, the American Communications Network of Hagerstown, Indiana.

200. Geoffrey Scott and Frederick A. Pottle (eds.), *Private Papers of James Boswell from Malahide Castle* (New York, 1928–34), XII, p. 108.

201. Cited in *AJ*, 7 (1996), p. 142.

202. Richard Hurd (ed.), *The Works of the Right Reverend William Warburton, Lord Bishop of Gloucester* (7 vols., London, 1788–94).

203. Sir John Hawkins (ed.), *The Works of Samuel Johnson LL.D.* (11 vols., London, 1787) had omitted *Marmor Norfolciense*, the Whig Hawkins believing that 'The principles it contained were such as the Jacobites of the time openly avowed': Clark, *Samuel Johnson*, pp. 168, 203–4. In 1788 John Stockdale then edited two further volumes of Johnson's parliamentary debates supplementary to Hawkins's edition; the same year he added a fourteenth volume. Its Preface recorded: 'The reluctance which Dr. Johnson always shewed to giving any information concerning his anonymous works, and his silence to all enquiries on that subject, have left much to conjecture ... there is some reason to believe, that had Dr. Johnson revised his own works for publication, the twelfth and thirteenth Volumes, containing those exquisite models of senatorial eloquence, and probably the first two pieces of the present Volume, would have been excluded.' These two pieces were the virulently anti-Hanoverian pamphlets *Marmor Norfolciense* and *A Compleat Vindication of the Licensers of the Stage*.

204. In 1755 and 1764 the young Richard Hurd had published, anonymously, pamphlets attacking John Jortin and Thomas Leland respectively. In these tracts, termed 'servile and spiteful' by the *DNB*, he had sought the favour of his patron, Warburton, by supporting him in his controversies. In 1789 Hurd was Bishop of Worcester, enjoying royal favour; Samuel Parr, an extreme Whig, had been blocked from preferment and was still only a perpetual curate in Hurd's diocese. Parr now sought to embarrass his bishop by republishing these two of his early works.

205. [Samuel Parr, ed.], *Tracts, by Warburton, and a Warburtonian; not Admitted into the Collections of their Respective Works* (London, 1789), p. ii.

206. *Observations on Doctor Price's Revolution Sermon, and on the Conduct of the Dissenters, and Mr. Pitt, respecting The Repeal of the Test Act, and the English Representation in Parliament, with Remarks On the public, and private Character Of the Minister and His Opponents* (London, 1790), p. 12.

207. Clark, *Samuel Johnson*, p. 164.

208. Hawkins, *Life*, pp. 80–1, 161, 251, 394, 448, 450–1, 504–5, 542. For independent confirmation of Johnson's politics see Katharine C. Balderstone (ed.), *Thraliana: The Diary of Mrs Hesther Lynch Thrale (Later Mrs Piozzi) 1776–1809* (2nd edn., 2 vols., Oxford, 1951), I, p. 192. For Leslie, see Richard Sharp, ' "In the *sound* and *safest* way": Charles Leslie and the Church of England', *Faith and Worship* 45 (1998) and 46 (1999).

209. Howard Erskine-Hill, 'Twofold Vision in Eighteenth-Century Writing', *ELH*, 64 (1997), pp. 903–24, at 920; idem, 'A Kind of *Liking* for Jacobitism', *AJ*, 8 (1997), pp. 3–13, at 6. For further passages by Boswell, now lost, reflecting on the problems raised by Johnson's acceptance of a pension see Allen Reddick in *AJ*, 8 (1997), pp. 413–14.

210. Sir John Hawkins, *A Charge to the Grand Jury of the County of Middlesex* (London, 1780), reprinted in Georges Lamoine (ed.), *Charges to the Grand Jury 1689–1803*, Camden Fourth Series, 43 (London, 1992), pp. 431–44, at 433–4. Hawkins cited, as the recent origin of his 'middle Hypothesis', two essays 'Of the Origin and Extent of Civil Power' in *Miscellanies in Prose and Verse . . . By the late Reverend . . . Mr. Henry Grove* (London, 1739), pp. 42–62 and *An Essay upon Government: or, the Natural Notions of Government, demonstrated in a chain of consequences from the fundamental principles of society . . . By Tho[mas] Burnet* (London, 1716); Hawkins found support in Hooker's *Discourse of Ecclesiastical Polity*.

211. For one such discussion of 'a latitude in subscribing', see 'Strictures on the Articles, Subscriptions, Tests, &c.' in *Tracts, Philological, Critical, and Miscellaneous. By the late Rev. John Jortin, D.D.* (2 vols., London, 1790), I, pp. 417–27.

212. J.E. Crimmins, 'Bentham's Unpublished Manuscripts on Subscription to Articles of Faith', *British Journal for Eighteenth Century Studies*, 9 (1986), pp. 33–44.

213. For a theological discussion see Oliver O'Donovan, *On the Thirty Nine Articles: A Conversation with Tudor Christianity* (Exeter, 1986); for modification of the sense in which subscription was required, *Subscription and Assent to the Thirty-nine Articles: A Report of the Archbishops' Commission on Christian Doctrine* (London, 1968).

214. Clark, *Samuel Johnson*, p. 95.

5
Tory and Whig 'Patriots': Lord Gower and Lord Chesterfield

Eveline Cruickshanks

The general shape of the political world within which Samuel Johnson's early life was set has been a matter of controversy, but it can be illuminated by a study of two men whose lives touched Johnson's own. The careers of Lord Gower and Lord Chesterfield illustrate that early eighteenth-century politics were constructed along party lines expressing a Whig vs. Tory dichotomy. There was political fluidity, for people could change sides in response to events and circumstances; like Lord Gower, they could embrace and later relinquish Jacobitism. The background of Gower's father was one of High Toryism but not of active Jacobitism, whereas Gower himself was a prominent Jacobite after 1715, became less active in the 1730s, but, as head of the Tory party in 1743, was regarded as pledged to the restoration of the Stuarts. The Jacobite overtones and political symbolism of the demonstrations against him after 1744 were aimed at one who had deserted Jacobitism, not one who had abandoned moderate Toryism.

Chesterfield, on the other hand, had a strong Jacobite family background, but being brought up away from his grandfather and father, and under the influence of his kinsman James Stanhope, began his political life as an ardent Whig, calling for the impeachment of all the Tories who concluded the Peace of Utrecht. He was rewarded with high office, but his wealth and talent allowed him to take an independent line on matters such as the Excise Bill in 1733, when he was dismissed. His social rank and prominence among the Whigs in Parliament made him necessary to the ministry at times, but he never clung to office *per se*.

Chesterfield and Gower were united in their dislike of Sir Robert Walpole and their desire for his overthrow. In Parliament, as always, numbers were everything and neither Tories nor opposition Whigs alone were strong enough to vote Walpole down. There was a deep longing in Britain for the implementation of reforms on 'Country' principles and an end to the system of political corruption, which Walpole had not invented but which he had perfected. The Tory and Whig Patriots, headed by Gower, Chesterfield and others achieved immense popularity by advocating such reforms and demanding a foreign policy serving the interests of Britain rather than those of Hanover. The Tories wanted cast-iron guarantees from opposition Whigs not only for these reforms, but, in the light of subsequent evidence, for a Stuart restoration. When a motion for the overthrow of Walpole was made in 1741 without consulting the Tories, they mostly abstained or withdrew. Chesterfield broke the deadlock by obtaining through his kinsman, the Duke of Ormonde, a letter from James III to his Tory friends instructing them to vote against Walpole. In return, James would have required undertakings that his cause would be served by doing this.

The fall of Walpole in 1742 brought great hopes of a new beginning in the country at large and Johnson shared this 'short-lived joy'. Bitter disappointment at promises betrayed made patriotism a dirty word for Johnson and many others. Gower and Chesterfield condemned this political treachery in 1742. Gower presided at the Lichfield races in 1743, which were attended by an envoy from Louis XV sent over to sound opinion before an expedition to restore the Stuarts was launched. Sections of the Whig opposition led by Chesterfield, Cobham, Westmorland and Bedford were regarded as pledged to support a restoration; all but the last were to be consulted on the arrangements to meet the expedition when it landed, and were appointed to Prince Charles Edward's council of regency. It is significant that none of them gave away the plan to the government. Westmorland became a Jacobite at this time, but the others remained Whigs. Chesterfield, it seems, tried to implement promises he had given to Ormonde in 1741 until the expedition led by Prince Charles Edward was damaged and dispersed by violent storms in February 1744 and there seemed no immediate prospect of another attempt being mounted from France. He then turned to the Pelhams and brought Lord Gower over to the new Whig government.

December 1744 and the formation of the 'Broadbottom' administration was meant to bring a Whig/Tory coalition, but it foundered because George II hated the Tories even more than George I had done and refused to give office to more than a handful of them. Chesterfield and Bedford brought Gower over to the Whigs but Chesterfield's hopes that Gower would break up the Tory party by bringing with him a hundred Tories failed and he was replaced as head of the party by the Duke of Beaufort, a staunch Jacobite. Subjected to unprecedented insults and opprobrium for his political apostasy, Gower was given office but not really trusted by the Pelhams, though his sons were integrated into the Whig hierarchy and prospered in the long run. Chesterfield was a very different kind of man. His intellectual sympathies and contacts were with the French Enlightenment and his attitude to Irish Roman Catholics as Lord Lieutenant of Ireland and to making peace with France in 1746 reflected this. A wealthy man, he did not understand what penury was: what he lost in one night's play at the gaming table would have kept Johnson afloat financially for a good while when he was writing his *Dictionary*, hence the damning rebuke he received from Johnson. Gower died a broken man. Chesterfield, in contrast, was celebrated as the epitome of eighteenth-century elegance, wit and good manners.

Lord Gower

John Leveson Gower, 2nd Baron Gower (1709) and 1st Earl Gower (1746) was the grandson of Sir William Leveson Gower, 4th Bt. who was MP for Newcastle-under-Lyme and Shropshire in the reign of Charles II and sat again for Newcastle-under-Lyme from 1689 until his death in 1691. Sir William, who had great estates at Stittenham in Yorkshire, as well as in Shropshire, inherited Trentham, five miles from Newcastle-under-Lyme, where the family built up a powerful parliamentary interest. He was a strong supporter of the Crown and the Church of England after the Restoration of 1660, but hostility to Roman Catholicism led him to support the exclusion of Charles II's brother, James, Duke of York from the succession in 1680. Nevertheless, he was a court candidate for James II's proposed new Parliament in 1688 and, as a result, Trentham was sacked by a Protestant mob at the Revolution. He was one of the Tories in the 1689 Parliament who supported the transfer of the crown to William and Mary.[1]

Gower's father, the 5th baronet, represented Newcastle-under-Lyme from 1692 to 1703 when he was created Baron Gower of Stittenham. He was a High Church Tory, acting in the Commons with Sir Christopher Musgrave, 4th Bt., a Jacobite, and in the Lords with the Earl of Rochester, Queen Anne's uncle. He served as Chancellor to the Duchy of Lancaster from 1703 to 1706. He married Catherine, daughter of John Manners, Lord Roos, a court supporter in the reign of Charles II, who was opposed to James II's policies and became Duke of Rutland with the support of Godolphin in 1703.[2]

Gower was born on 10 August 1694 and was educated at Westminster School and at Christ Church, Oxford, institutions then devoted to High Anglicanism. Succeeding as 2nd Baron Gower in 1709, on 13 March 1712 he married Evelyn, daughter of Evelyn Pierrepoint, 1st Duke of Kingston. Gower dominated the politics of Staffordshire, Johnson's native county and one which Thomas Carte, the Jacobite historian, described to James III as 'entirely affected to Your Majesty'.[3] Affable and handsome, Gower had a large fortune and wide electoral influence in Staffordshire, where he could usually carry one seat at Lichfield and two seats at Newcastle-under-Lyme. 'He had,' Horace Walpole wrote, 'been educated a stiff Jacobite.'[4] During the 1715 Jacobite rebellion, which was fuelled by George I's proscription of the Tory party from office at the national and local level, Kingston, a Whig, was concerned to find that Gower, who was of age, had not attended the House of Lords or waited on George I. Kingston thought Gower had 'too good an understanding to trust his abbey land to a Popish prince'.[5] The fear of owners of monastic lands that a Roman Catholic King or Queen would restore them to the Catholic Church had been a potent factor in English history.

1. William Kent, *The St. Clement Danes Altarpiece*, 1721
(destroyed 1940).

This Print is exactly Engrav'd after ỹ Celebrated Altar-Peice in S.ͭ Clements Church which has
been taken down by Order of ỹ Lord Bishop of London as tis thought to prevent Disputs and
Laying of wagers among ỹ Parishioners about ỹ Artists meaning in it, for publick Satisfaction
here is a particular Explanation of it humbly Offerd to be writ under ỹ Original, that it may be
put up again by which means ỹ Parishes 60 pounds which thay nisely gave for it, may not be Entirely lost
1.ᵗ Tis not the Pretenders Wife and Children as our weak brethren imagin
2.ˡʸ Nor S.ͭ Cecilia as the Connoisseurs think but a Choir of Angells playing in Consort

A	an Organ	E An Angel tuning an Harp	H the other leg judiciously Omitted to
B	an Angel playing on it	the inside of his Leg but whether,	make room for the harp
C	the shortest Joint of the Arm	right or Left is yet undiscoverd	I smaller Angells as appears by
D	the longest Joint	G a hand Playing on a Lute	K their Wings.

2. William Hogarth, *The St. Clement Danes Altarpiece*, 1725, engraving.

3. Jakob Frey, *Queen Mary Clementina*, c. 1725, engraving.

TITULUS II.

De Matricula Universitatis.

§. 3. *De Tempore & conditionibus Matriculationis.*

OMNES & singuli Studentes seu scholares cujuscunque conditionis, intra quindenam postquam ad Universitatem accesserint, coram Cancelario ejusve Commissario matriculandos se sistant; nec, priusquam in Matriculam Universitatis relati fuerint, ullis Universitatis privilegiis aut beneficiis gaudeant. Quod si à Praefecto Domus suae, ejusve Deputato legitime moniti, nihilo secius matriculandos sese non sistant, pro qualibet quindena suae dilationis sex solidis & octo denariis ad usum Universitatis mulctentur.

Quotquot autem in Matriculam Universitatis redigendi accedunt, si decimum sextum suae aetatis annum attigerint, Articulis fidei & Religionis subscribant, & de agnoscendo primatu Regiae Majestatis; nec non de fidelitate Universitati exhibenda; Statutis, Privilegiis, & consuetudinibus ejusdem observandis, juxta formam hactenus usitatam, corporale juramentum praestent.

Quod si infra decimum sextum & supra duodecimum aetatis annum extiterint, Articulis fidei & Religionis duntaxat subscribent, & in Matriculam redigentur.

Quod si duodecimum non excesserint, in Matriculam duntaxat referentur; utrique tamen postmodo ubi ad maturam aetatem pervenerint, qua caetera requisita praestare possint, tum demum ea praestare teneantur sub poena non sistentium se Matriculandos.

The Oath of Supremacy.

I A. B. do Swear, That I do from my Heart Abhor, Detest, and Abjure, as impious and Heretical, that damnable Doctrine and Position, *That Princes Excommunicated or Deprived by the Pope, or any Authority of the See of Rome, may be Deposed or Murthered by their Subjects, or any other whatsoever.*

And I do declare, That no Foreign Prince, Person, Prelate, State or Potentate, hath, or ought to have any Jurisdiction, Power, Superiority, Preeminence, or Authority Ecclesiastical or Spiritual within this Realm.

So help me God, &c.

The Oath at the Matriculation of a Scholar.

TU fidem dabis ad Observandum omnia Statuta, Privilegia, & Consuetudines hujus Universitatis *Oxon.* Ita Deus te adjuvet, tactis Sacro-Sanctis Christi Evangeliis.

The Oath at the Matriculation of a Privileged Person.

YOU shall Swear to Observe all Statutes, Privileges and Customes of this University: So help you God.

You shall farther swear that you will never sue in any Cause of yours before the Mayor and Bayliffs of this Town; nor answer before them as your Judge, so long as you continue to enjoy the Privileges of this University.

4. Oxford University Matriculation Register 1714–40, Oxford University Archives SP12: the oaths required on matriculation.

br:14° Edwin Alcock. è Col: Univer: Cler: Fil:

John Blandy è Col: Div: Jo: Bap: Arm: Fil:

6 Samuel Johnson è Coll: Pembr: Gen: Fil:

Lewis West e Coll: Reg: Arm: Fil:

William Deane e Coll: Woo Cler: Fil:

John Coles e Coll: Reg: pleb: Fil:

Rich: Lewis e Coll: Jesu pleb: fil:

Joh: Boll Lane e Coll: On: Nat: arm: Fil:

7 Guilielmus Pyring ex Aede Christi Generosi filius

Richardus Clarke ex Aede Christi Armigeri filius

Gulielmus Mgilchrist e Col: Bal: Generoti filius   58

vacatione

17 Humphredus Lowe ex Aede Christi Arm: Fil:

24 Maximilian Cole Engraver ——

Term: Hil: 1728/9

Jan: 14 James Jubb Barber

Gulielmus Foulkes ex Aede Xti Doctoris Felius:

24 Emanuel Collins Ex Aula Cerina pleblii filius

Gideon. Murray e Coll: Ball: Baronis Fil:

29 Johannes Tucker e Coll: Ball: Cler: Fil:

Robertus Lodei e Coll: Ball: Generosi Fil:

Y Johannes Jubb e CCC Cler: Fil:

Thomas Mayhew ex Aede Christi Generosi fil:

Bernardus Andreas Woodstock e Coll: Mag: generosi filius

Feb:12 Jacobus Parry e Coll: Merl: Cler: filius

14 Marshall Ayir e Coll: Ball: gen: fil:

Johnas Carter e Coll: Ball: Cler: fil:

15 Gulielmus Gill e Coll: Bal: Gen: fil:

2 Gulielmus Williams e Coll: Mert: Bar: Fil:

5. Oxford University Matriculation Register 1714–40: Samuel Johnson's
   signature.

Three Articles in the 36th Canon.

I. THat the King's Majefty under God, is the only Supream Governour of this Realm, and of all other his Highnefs's Dominions and Countreys, as well in all Spiritual or Ecclefiaftical things or caufes, as Temporal; and that no Foreign Prince, Perfon, Prelate, State or Potentate, hath or ought to have any Jurifdiction, Power, Superiority, Preeminence or Authority, Ecclefiaftical or Spiritual, within His Majefty's faid Realms, Dominions and Countreys.

II. That the Book of Common Prayer, and of Ordering of Bifhops, Priefts and Deacons, containeth in it nothing contrary to the word of God, and that it may lawfully fo be ufed, and that I my felf will ufe the Form in the faid Book prefcribed in publick Prayer, and Adminiftration of the Sacraments, and none other.

III. That I allow the Book of Articles of Religion agreed upon by the Arch-Bifhops and Bifhops of both Provinces, and the whole Clergy in the Convocation holden at *London* in the year of our Lord God, One thoufand five hundred fixty and two: and that I acknowledge all and every the Articles therein contained, being in number Nine and thirty, befides the Ratification, to be agreeable to the Word of God.

PEractâ Præfentationis Formulâ Procurator fenior fingulorum Præfentatorum Subfcriptiones Articulis Fidei & Religionis fic teftabitur.

Nos Procuratores teftamur A. B. C. omnibus Articulis Fidei & Religionis in hoc Libro contentis; Nec non tribus Articulis in Canone tricefimo fexto comprehenfis prius in præfentia noftra lectis fubfcripfiffe.

The Oath of Allegiance.

I A. B. do fincerely Promife and Swear, That I will be faithful, and bear true Allegiance to his Majefty King *George*.
So help me God, &c.

The Oath of Supremacy.

I A. B. do Swear, That I do from my Heart Abhor, Deteft, and Abjure, as Impious and Heretical, that damnable Doctrine and Pofition, *That Princes Excommunicated or Deprived by the Pope, or any Authority of the See of Rome, may be Depofed or Murthered by their Subjects, or any other whatfoever.*

And I do declare, that no Forrieign Prince, Perfon, Prelate, State or Potentate, hath, or ought to have any Jurifdiction, Power, Superiority, Preeminence, or Authority Ecclefiaftical or Spiritual within this Realm.
So help me God, &c.

6. Oxford University Graduation Register 1736–63, Oxford University Archives SP46: the oaths required on graduation.

Kingston's optimism, however, was misplaced. There was strong Jacobite feeling and riots in Staffordshire, when the militia cried 'The Duke of Ormonde for ever and down with the Roundheads'. Carte wrote to James III in 1739:

> I remember the time when after the affair of Preston few people in Staffordshire would drink Lord Gower's health, because he did not rise to support Mr. Forster (though he had in reality sent Mr. Cotes of Woodcote [John Cotes, MP] to Lord Digby on Saturday November 12th, the very day of the action at Preston to appoint with His Lordship and the neighbouring gentlemen a rendez vous on Cannock Heath on Thursday following in order to take the field, had not the surrender happened).[6]

Carte was well informed, but that Gower had been about to join the 1715 rebellion was common knowledge and, many years later, he was taunted with the cry 'who had a foot in the stirrup in 1715?'[7]

Gower attended the House of Lords assiduously after 1715, about seventy per cent of the time.[8] He was not a gifted speaker, but he was active in the Lords, serving as teller in forty divisions between 1715 and 1743.[9] In 1717 he supported the acquittal of Robert Harley, Earl of Oxford, and his release from the Tower. The Earl of Mar (Duke in the Jacobite peerage), who had succeeded Bolingbroke as James III's Secretary of State, forwarded a letter from James to Gower in August 1718. He added that there were good reports of Gower's devotion and that he had referred Gower to Bishop Atterbury and Lord Arran for details of James's marriage and other affairs.[10] In October, Atterbury wrote to him urging him to attend the new session when the repeal of the Occasional Conformity and Schism Acts (Acts promoted by the Tories in the last years of Queen Anne's reign to keep Dissenters out of office) was coming on.[11] At the beginning of the Atterbury Plot (1720–22), Gower wrote to James, assuring him he 'would embrace all opportunities of serving' him 'with the utmost alacrity imaginable'.[12] His name was sent to the Stuart Court in 1721 as the leader in Staffordshire of the proposed general rising in the English counties,[13] though he did not take a central part in the planning of the plot. Lord Bathurst wrote to him in October 1722 asking him to whip in every Tory MP he could to attend Parliament during Bishop Atterbury's trial.[14]

Atterbury's going into exile in 1723 coincided with the pardon and return to England of Henry St. John, Viscount Bolingbroke. After his dismissal as James III's secretary of state in 1716 for failing to provide arms and reinforcements to the Jacobites during the Fifteen, Bolingbroke worked to detach his friends Lord Gower, Lord Bathurst and Sir William Wyndham from James, so as to form a group of Hanoverian Tories who might be able to get back into office. On the accession of George II in 1727 the Tories in a body, including Lord Gower, went to Court in the hope of bringing about an end to the proscription of their party. This cannot be taken as a sign that they meant to abandon Jacobitism for, as in the reign of William III, the Tories believed their status in English society entitled them to a share of offices in their own country and, in any case, they would be better able to help the Stuarts from inside the political establishment than outside it.

Bolingbroke had more success in separating Wyndham after 1720 than Gower, who was included in 1730 among James III's chief supporters in England, together with Sir John St. Aubyn, Lord Barrymore, Sir Charles Kemys Tynte and Watkin Williams Wynn.[15] There was at that time a scheme to restore the Stuarts with the help of Chauvelin, the French foreign minister who was more favourable to the Jacobites than the peace-loving French chief minister, Cardinal Fleury. Captain Hardy, son of the Tory admiral, who went to France first, reported to James III on 7 January 1731 that he was trying to detach Lord Gower and Lord Bathurst 'from some persons whom [it] might be dangerous to trust' (Bolingbroke and Wyndham). On 20 March 1732 Hardy reported to James that Lord Strafford and Lord Arran (Ormonde's brother) were disappointed at Lord Gower and Lord Bathurst not being more forward in the project, though Lord Gower 'gave assurances of his zeal' for James's service.[16] James, however, gave express orders that Gower and Bathurst should be 'associated' with Lords Strafford and Arran in the plan.[17]

Lord Cornbury, son of the Earl of Clarendon, who was in charge of the project, went to see James in Rome with lists of promotions in the event of a successful Restoration. In these, Bolingbroke was to be made a marquess and British ambassador to France, with a pension of £2,000 a year; Lord Bathurst was to be principal secretary and a marquess, while Gower was to be made an earl and a lord of the bedchamber. Some leading Whigs in opposition were to be offered places too.[18] Bolingbroke, whose professions of Hanoverian Toryism had got him nowhere, then put the cat among the pigeons by suggesting that James's eldest son Charles Edward should be restored instead of James and that he should be brought up as a member of the Church of England under the guidance of the Duke of Ormonde. James III angrily refused. The dismissal of Chauvelin and the outbreak of the War of the Polish Succession, in any case, removed the likelihood of French assistance and put an end to the project.[19]

In 1730 Gower became a member of the Honourable Brotherhood, the Tory Club founded by the Duke of Beaufort in 1709. Lord Scarsdale was then President, being succeeded by the Earl of Lichfield in 1736 with Sir John Hynde Cotton, a leading Tory parliamentarian as Vice-President.[20] Gower supported the merchants' petition against Spanish depredations in 1739, declaring that 'trade is essential to the very being of this nation'.[21] After the death of Sir William Wyndham in 1740, the Tories were led in the Commons by Sir Watkin Williams Wynn and Sir John Hynde Cotton, two active Jacobites. Gower, one of the leading Tories in the Lords, took a prominent part in the attack on the administration of Sir Robert Walpole, acting with the Whigs in opposition, with whom he was in closer touch since the marriage of his eldest daughter to the Duke of Bedford in 1737. In January 1741 he supported a secret committee of inquiry into Admiral Vernon's complaints of not being given an adequate number of ships to attack Spanish possessions.[22]

After twenty years of Robinocracy, very many people longed for the reforms advocated by the 'Country' lobby since the 1690s to be put into practice at last. Among the most important were the end of the proscription of the Tories from office; the curbing of political corruption at Westminster and in the constituencies; a Place Act to control the number of office-holders and pensioners in Parliament; the repeal of the Septennial Act; the repeal of the penal laws passed since 1715; a strict inquiry into the abuses of Walpole's administration; a reduction in the numbers of the Army; the pursuit of a foreign policy based on the national interest; the revival of and the inclusion of Tories in the county militia; and new commissions of the peace to include more Tory JPs.[23]

On 12 February 1742, the day after the fall of Walpole, there was a mass meeting of the Opposition at the Fountain Tavern in the Strand. The Duke of Argyll, an opposition Whig who had been in touch with James III through Lord Barrymore, called for a 'Broadbottom' administration to include Tories as well as Whigs. Argyll and Bedford stressed the necessity for prosecuting Walpole, now Earl of Orford, while 'Lord Gower and Sir Watkin Williams Wynn [were] more moderate'.[24] Argyll refused office until his Tory friends were given places, while Sir Watkin Williams Wynn, on his side, pressed for Argyll to be made commander-in-chief of the army. Thereupon the Tories in a body accompanied Argyll to Court to press their demands.

George II expressed surprise at seeing so many new faces, but was concerned when he heard some say they would come only this once.[25] Argyll insisted, Dudley Ryder the Attorney General wrote, that his friends, particularly Lord Gower, Lord Bathurst, Sir Watkin Williams Wynn and Sir John Hynde Cotton, be given places.[26] Argyll agreed to return to office provided Lord Cobham (who, like Chesterfield, had been treating with the Jacobites) should have a regiment and the rank of field marshal and that Bathurst, Gower and Chesterfield would be provided for. George II approved Gower as Lord Privy Seal on 8 March, but refused to have Cotton on the Admiralty Board, whereupon Argyll resigned.[27] Gower continued in opposition as did his brothers Baptist Leveson Gower, MP for Newcastle-under-Lyme, and William, who represented Staffordshire. Gower refused to attend Cabinet meetings and his succeeding Lord Lichfield as Head of the Honourable Brotherhood, the Jacobite Club, which made him the head of the Tory party, did nothing to endear him to Whig ministers.

William Pulteney's ineffectual Place Act in 1742 satisfied no one and a Tory motion for the repeal of the Septennial Act was thrown out. John

Lefebure, the head of the Secrets Department of the Post Office, a Jacobite mole in the Whig establishment, wrote in June 1742: 'The people here are in great ferment against the Administration; the Tories are quite out of the question of being admitted into employment. What all this will end in, we must leave to time'; and four days later he added, 'Patriotism is in great contempt here.'[28] The City of London expressed indignation at the 'unprincipled treachery and corruption' of Bath (Pulteney), Carteret and the New Whigs.[29] Sir John Hawkins wrote that Samuel Johnson 'partook of the short-lived joy that infatuated the public, when Sir Robert Walpole ceased to have the direction of the national councils', but that Johnson soon came to the conclusion that the Patriotism of the opposition had been either 'hatred' or 'ambition'. It was these circumstances which led Johnson to make his celebrated comment: 'Patriotism is the last refuge of a scoundrel.'[30]

Meanwhile Tory negotiations had been going on apace with Louis XV and his ministers, asking them to provide a substantial military expedition (as in the case of William of Orange in 1688) to restore the Stuarts, an expedition to be led by Prince Charles Edward, James III's elder son. James Butler, a kinsman of the Duke of Ormonde and Master of the Horse to Louis XV, was sent over to England to sound the Tories, under the pretext of buying horses. During the Interregnum royalist plots had been hatched at horse races and history was repeating itself. Butler was taken to the most famous of the Tory horse races, the Lichfield races, to meet as many Tories as possible. There were indeed over three hundred peers and gentry present while Butler was there.[31] The Lichfield races had started after the Restoration of 1660 and were held on two days in September, though, in 1743, 233 of the gentlemen present decided to organise a third day.[32] Lord Gower was Patron, and as such he would have met Butler. In the list of supporters of a Stuart restoration drawn up in England for the French in the event of a successful expedition Lord Gower was listed as one of the chiefs in Staffordshire, together with his two brothers. The Duke of Bedford was said to have given assurances of support for a restoration through Lord Gower at this time, but he was not 'trusted with anything before execution'.[33]

In December 1743, finding no more Tories were to be admitted, Gower gave up the Privy Seal and Cobham resigned.[34] In the debate on the Address in January 1744 Gower spoke against taking the Hanoverian troops into British pay.[35] In February 1744 a French expedition of 10,000 troops commanded by Maurice of Saxony, the ablest commander in the French army and a Protestant, and Prince Charles Edward with a commission as Regent of England, embarked at Dunkirk. The plan was well conceived and executed and offered real hope of a restoration. It was not foiled by the British Navy but by the weather, as the transport ships were dispersed and damaged by terrible storms in the Channel, whereupon the expedition was abandoned for the time being.[36] This presumably triggered Gower's political *volte face*.

In November 1744 a message was sent to Chesterfield, Cobham and Gower, ostensibly by Frederick Prince of Wales, but really by George II, offering that the whole Broadbottom would be provided for,[37] but they refused to serve with Lord Granville (Carteret) or under him.[38] In December 1744, after negotiations with Henry Pelham and the Duke of Newcastle, Gower became Lord Privy Seal once again. Sir John Hynde Cotton was made Treasurer of the Chamber, taking the salary but not the oaths. He then sent an express to Louis XV asking for another expedition into England, with more troops than before.[39] Two other Tories were given minor places, but the King refused to admit more, which made the Broadbottom Administration, as it was called, a sham. This time, however, Gower, his brothers Baptist and William and his son, Granville Leveson Gower, Lord Trentham (who was brought into Parliament for Bishop's Castle, a rotten borough), all went over to the Government. Newcastle urged Chesterfield to write to Gower from time to time to make sure he resisted any temptation to return to his Tory allegiance.[40]

In contemporary political parlance, Gower was a rat. Dr. King was outraged:

> my Lord Gower's defection was a great blow to the Tory party, and a singular disappointment to all his friends. For no one had entertained the least jealousy or suspicion of this part of his conduct. The Tories considered him as their chief: they placed the greatest confidence in him, and did nothing without his advice and approbation. He had assured them that he went into employment with no other view than to serve his country, and that many articles tending to a thorough reformation were already stipulated. I had a letter from him (for I lived in some degree of intimacy with him for many years) to the purpose I have mentioned. Soon after I saw him, when he read the articles to me, they were thirteen in number: not one of which was performed or ever intended to be performed. When this was at length discovered, he laid aside his disguise, adhering to the new system, and openly renouncing his old principles.[41]

Speaking of his *Dictionary*, Johnson told Boswell: 'You know, Sir, Lord Gower forsook the old Jacobite interest. When I came to the word *Renegado*, after telling it meant "any one who deserts to the enemy, a revolter", I added "sometimes we say a Gower", but the printer struck it out.'[42]

As a sop to the Tories, and at Bolingbroke's suggestion, Lord Chancellor Hardwicke offered to remodel the commissions of the peace in the various counties to take in more Tories. Hardwicke tried to continue negotiating with the Tories on this matter through Lord Gower. This was too much and Lord Gower was replaced as head of the Honourable Brotherhood by the Duke of Beaufort, 'a most determined and unwavering Jacobite'. Newcastle wrote on 26 March 1745 to Chesterfield, who was then at The Hague:

The Duke of Beaufort has set himself up, and the Tories have taken him, for the head of their party; in consequence of which they have excluded Lord Gower from a negotiation depending about justices of the peace and put it into the hands of the Duke of Beaufort . . . If you write to Lord Gower, for God's sake, preach up firmness towards those who have left him; and moderation and inclination towards those who desire to join with him.

Chesterfield replied: 'I don't much mind the Duke of Beaufort's opposition, which singly as his, and a few other of the red hot absurd Tories, might rather do good than hurt; but then reasonable satisfaction should be given to the others, as to enable Gower to carry off the best, and leave only a marked avowed Jacobite faction behind him.' Chesterfield was worried to see Watkin Williams Wynn, Lord Oxford and Sir John Hynde Cotton adhering to Beaufort and he hoped that Oxford's 'cool good sense' and Cotton's 'sagacity' would make them change their minds and support Gower in return for suitable concessions.[43]

Chesterfield had expected Gower to be able to bring over at least forty Tories, but this did not materialise. Four, Thomas and Charles Gore, John Pitt and George Venables Vernon (who later reverted to opposition) went over with Gower. Gower's brother-in-law, John Proby, remained a Jacobite Tory as did Randle Wilbraham, who had been connected with Gower. Nicholas Fazakerley, whose daughter and heir had married Lord Trentham, did not defect. Chesterfield hoped that Gower might bring over 'a hundred heads of Tories in Parliament' and 'at last break the Tory party so, as to make the other part of it absolutely inconsiderable'. He urged 'such concessions as will satisfy the reasonable and greater part of the Tories in the nation, and so brand the others with Jacobitism and Faction'.[44] These expectations were not realised. Eight new commissions of the peace were issued (excluding Staffordshire), but the Tories were unmollified and no more new commissions were issued.[45]

During the 1745 Jacobite rebellion, Lord Gower was reported to have gone to see George II 'and assured him he had formerly been his enemy and a Jacobite, but he saw the folly of it and that he be no more' and offered to raise a regiment of foot in Staffordshire for him. This was satirised by Sir Charles Hanbury Williams, who advised Gower to think it over:

> And now, dear G . . . , thou man of Pow'r,
> And Comprehensive Noodle;
> Tho' you've the Gout, yet as you're stout,
> Why wa'n't you plac'd in Saddle?
> Then you might ride to either Side,
> Chuse which K . . . you'd serve under;
> But, dear Dragoon, charge not too soon,
> For fear of th' other blunder.

The troops in the new regiment, however, were not all anxious to fight, for when Sir Richard Wrottesley, son-in-law of Lord Gower, raised a troop of yeomanry and set about to join Gower's regiment, his men refused to march any further than the nearest inn, less than a mile from their starting point.[46]

The Tory backlash against Lord Gower and his family and against the Duke of Bedford, who was regarded as having corrupted Gower, was awesome. Gower complained to Bedford that he was being 'persecuted by the gout and Jacobitism'.[47] Although Gower had become lord lieutenant of Stafford-shire, which under normal circumstances gave electoral advantage, he found that Tory candidates were put up against his interest in all Staffordshire con-stituencies. Lord Anson wrote to the Duke of Bedford from Lichfield on 21 June 1747: 'everything has been done that could be thought of against Lord Gower's interest.'[48] Ill from the gout, Lord Gower complained to Henry Pelham in July 1747 that he was persecuted in Staffordshire 'by a set of men that I have lived in the strictest friendship with the best part of my life. I thank God they have now opened my eyes and I hope I have had the good fortune to open the eyes of all the world as to their character and principles.'[49] Sir Richard Wrottesley was defeated for Staffordshire, a county where Gower had lost most of his interest. What success he had was due, Henry Pelham wrote, 'almost entirely to the Whigs'.[50] In violent Jacobite demonstrations at the Lichfield races, described by Paul Monod, the Duke of Bedford was horsewhipped, while Lord Trentham was cudgelled. This 'popular rage and rebellion', it was reported, continued during the whole of the Staffordshire county election. Lord Gower avoided violence against his own person by not attending elections or public places, pleading an attack of the gout.[51]

The culmination of the backlash against Lord Gower took place at the Westminster by-election of 1749–50, when Lord Trentham had to seek re-election after his appointment as a Lord of the Admiralty. The Independent Electors of Westminster, founded as a joint Whig–Tory organisation, had become controlled by the Jacobites. At their annual dinner, the Indepen-dent Electors drank the King's health by 'each man having a glass of water on the left hand, and waving a glass of wine over the water'.[52] The demon-strations against Gower and his family were organised by Alexander Murray, Lord Elibank's brother, and an agent of Prince Charles Edward. An intrigu-ing aspect is that, in the middle of this electoral turmoil, Prince Charles Edward made a secret visit to London in September 1750, when he attended a meeting of about fifty of his supporters presided over by the Duke of Beaufort and the Earl of Westmorland. He entered the Church of England at this time in 'the new church in the Strand', which could be either St. Mary le Strand or Johnson's church, St. Clement Danes.[53]

Gower, Lord Trentham and the Duke of Bedford were depicted in a popular print like a plague of locusts descending upon Westminster.[54] They were hated in Westminster because of their avarice and haughtiness, as well as the practice of Bedford and Gower, two of the largest landowners in Westminster, of turning their tenants out of their houses if they did not vote as directed by Bedford's electoral agent, a brutal character aptly named Butcher.[55] The 'bribery, threats and compulsion' on Trentham's part were denounced as 'scandalous', and some of his supporters were said to have voted up to nine times. Gower was reported to be ill and did not appear in public.[56] Lord Trentham's side denounced the Independent Electors for 'the earnestness with which they opposed all subscriptions and levies for suppressing the last rebellion, their suspected correspondencies, and the indecent [treasonable] healths so often proposed and so publicly drunk at their meetings and assemblies'.[57] Like the rioters at Lichfield, they had taken to wearing the plaid.

The Duke of Bedford was said to have spent £7,000 on the election and the scrutiny demanded on behalf of the opposition candidate, Sir George Vandeput, who had the support of Frederick Prince of Wales as well as of the Independent Electors, was believed to have cost Gower at least as much.[58] Trentham's side urged the voters to 'exert yourselves so as to quash the present growing spirit of Jacobitism and Independency, and thereby save these kingdoms, from those great and worst scourges of providence: popery, the Inquisition and Arbitrary Power'. To this the Independents retorted: 'Ask Lord Trentham, who had his foot in the stirrup in the year 1715?' Trentham was branded as a member 'of a turncoat race', who 'opposed his late and present Majesty with the utmost bitterness, rancour and malevolence, till they were bought off by places to repair their shattered fortunes which they had spent in supporting the cause of the Pretender'.[59] A contemporary noted: 'Sure there never was an election carried on with so much violence on both sides; the scandal and dirt flung upon Lord Gower's family and the Duke of Bedford's is shocking, and is enough to terrify anybody, and make them have some regard, great as they are, how they exasperate an English mob.'[60]

Arraigned before the House of Commons for 'menaces and seditious behaviour' and calling Lord Trentham a scoundrel during the election, Alexander Murray was ordered to apologise to the House on bended knee and, refusing, was sent in custody to Newgate. As soon as Parliament was prorogued, the sheriffs of London released Murray. A vast concourse of people, including Sir George Vandeput, with a banner proclaiming 'Murray and Liberty' took Alexander Murray back in triumph to his brother, Lord Elibank's, house.[61]

Trentham kept his Westminster seat, if not his reputation, and lived to become Master of the Horse, Lord Chamberlain, Lord Privy Seal and Marquess of Stafford. His father, Lord Gower, however, was a broken man. He complained 'of want of confidence' and being kept 'a stranger to every thing that is doing both at home and abroad' by the Pelhams. When in 1750 Gower was proposed as Lord President of the Council, Pelham thought

Gower was too 'broke in spirit and constitution' to undertake such an office. The palsy and a second stroke in 1752 were further blows and Pelham wrote: 'if he lingers on some months and perhaps years more, it will be to him, poor man, a miserable life.'[62] He died on Christmas day, December 1754.

Lord Chesterfield

Philip Dormer Stanhope, 4th Earl of Chesterfield, was born on 22 September 1694.[63] His grandfather, the 2nd Earl, was a royalist during the Interregnum. He married Lady Elizabeth Butler, daughter of the lst Duke of Ormonde, and, after her death, he wed Elizabeth, daughter of Charles Dormer, 2nd Earl of Carnarvon, from whom Chesterfield derived his second Christian name. The 2nd Earl cut a fine figure at Charles II's court, being Lord Chamberlain to the Queen and a colonel of foot. He was notorious for his drinking and gambling as well as successes with women and was beloved by Lady Castlemaine, Charles II's mistress. He was a patron of Dryden, who dedicated his translation of the *Georgics* to him. One of the largest landowners in the Midlands, at the Revolution of 1688 he went to Nottingham to protect Princess Anne, James II's second daughter. A Dutch propaganda list wrongly described him as in arms for the Prince of Orange. As he wrote to the Earl of Danby, who organised the rising in the North, though he had not approved of James II's policies, 'I have ever had a natural aversion to taking arms against my King, which the law justly terms designing the King's death'.[64] Consequently, he was a Nonjuror, refused to abjure the 'pretended' Prince of Wales and was a Jacobite, living in retirement at Bretby in Derbyshire until his death in 1714.

Chesterfield's father was the 3rd Earl, who married Elizabeth, daughter of George Savile, lst Marquess of Halifax, the Great Trimmer. He did not share Halifax's politics, having declared he 'had rather be a plain, honest country gentleman, than a cunning, false, court knave'. A lifelong Jacobite, he was said to have sent money to the Stuart court in exile. He was on friendly terms with Dryden and Matthew Prior, who gave him their portraits. A deeply religious man, he was said to have had a melancholy disposition and he lived a retired life. He did not like his eldest son, who inherited his short stature and deafness in later life, and was 'neither desirous nor able to advise' him.

Philip Dormer, who idolised his grandfather, though he saw little of him, was cared for by his widowed grandmother, Lady Halifax. Educated privately, with a good grounding in classics, by a French Huguenot tutor named Joaneau, he became a fluent speaker of French. At his grandmother's he saw much of Danby, now Duke of Leeds, and other politicians; he acquired the Savile outlook and a sceptical attitude towards revealed religion, rather than the views of his father or grandfather. Our knowledge of his early years is derived mainly from his celebrated *Letters* to his natural son, Philip Stanhope. He entered Trinity Hall, Cambridge in August 1712 at the age of 18, two years later than the usual age, and found the company of many lawyers in his college, who were worldly-wise as well as learned, particularly congenial. He took special pains to learn eloquence from out-standing examples, ancient and modern. Leaving Cambridge in 1714, he went travelling abroad, first to The Hague, where he developed an addiction to gambling, and then on to Antwerp, where he was the guest of the Duke and Duchess of Marlborough. He had intended to go on to Turin, Rome and Venice, but he cut his Grand Tour short on the death of Queen Anne and went to Paris, where at 19 and with no experience he tried to engage fine ladies in conversation, being advised to steer clear of actresses and opera girls. 'Le petit Stanhope', as he was known, was in no hurry to return to England. In France he learned to appreciate the social graces and literary genius of the French, though he distrusted their politics and became well aware of their pro-Jacobite sympathies and the influence in France of the Jacobite exiles.

On Stanhope's return to London, his kinsman, James Stanhope (grandson of the 1st Earl of Chesterfield), Secretary of State, offered to introduce him to the new king, George I. Styled Lord Stanhope, he was brought into Parliament for St. Germans, a Cornish pocket borough, at a by-election in May 1715 on the recommendation of James Stanhope. He had a great admi-ration for Stanhope, whom he called subsequently 'as able and honest a minister as ever served the Crown'. To distinguish himself in Parliament was his aim and, as he wrote, 'from the day I was elected to the day that I spoke I thought nor dreamed of nothing but speaking'. When he made his maiden speech on 5 August, he called for the impeachment of Ormonde (his own kinsman) and denounced as traitors all those who had supported the Peace of Utrecht, whereupon a Tory MP took him aside and threatened to reveal that he was under age if he voted as he had spoken. To avoid being expelled, Stanhope 'made a low bow', left the House and went back to Paris.[65]

Once he was 21, he returned to London and was appointed a Lord of the Bedchamber to George, Prince of Wales through James Stanhope's influence. He spoke and voted for the Septennial Bill in 1716. On the Whig split in the years 1717–20 he followed the Prince by going into opposition. This placed him in an awkward position as he was opposing the measures of James, now Earl Stanhope, as First Lord of the Treasury in the Stanhope–Sunderland administration. This is presumably why he supported Sunder-land's darling scheme, the Peerage Bill, in 1719, which was anathema to the Prince of Wales. Lady Cowper wrote in 1720: 'the Prince has been so rough with little Lord Stanhope about voting in the South Sea affair [the proposal of the South Sea Company to take over the national debt] that he has talked of resigning a good while'. Stanhope's speeches, which were carefully contrived and lacked spontaneity, were cruelly mimicked by another MP, with the result that he hated mimicry for the rest of his life.

Returned for Lostwithiel, another Cornish borough, in 1722, he succeeded Lord Townshend as Captain of the Yeomen of the Guards in 1723 and left the Commons as he did not seek re-election on his appointment to office. He liked Townshend although 'his manners were coarse, rustic and seemingly brutal'. He always disliked Sir Robert Walpole as 'money, not prerogative, was the chief engine of his administration'. At this time, he came to know Alexander Pope and was introduced to Swift by Dr. Arbuthnot, thus coming into contact with a very different intellectual milieu from that of his Whig patrons in Parliament. Severely critical of the Hanoverian dynasty, he admired Arbuthnot as 'a Jacobite by prejudice, and a Republican by reflection and reasoning'. George I, he thought, was a dull German, with an odd taste in mistresses, and unfit to rule over a country much greater than Hanover. He liked George, Prince of Wales, who often consulted him, better, though he thought him stiff and petty with 'all the weaknesses of a little mind, without any of the virtues, or even the vices, of a great one'. He courted Lady Suffolk, the Prince of Wales's mistress, which earned him the enmity of Princess, later Queen, Caroline. Walpole offered him a place in the revived Order of the Bath, which he refused, and derided it as 'one of the toys Bob gave his boys'. This led to his being removed as Captain of the Yeomen of the Guards.

Stanhope returned to Bretby, where he had not been for many years, on his father's illness in 1725, complaining that the inhabitants of Derbyshire were 'utter strangers to the sun' as well as to shoes and stockings. He succeeded his father as 4th Earl of Chesterfield and to the large entailed estates on 28 January 1726. This brought him back to Parliament, when he found his style of oratory more congenial to the House of Lords than it had been to the more rowdy Commons. Handicapped by a head too big for his body and a voice like 'a shrill scream' he compensated by his wit and exquisite manners and boasted of feminine conquests. Horace Walpole found Chesterfield's wit too studied, but it was real enough. A choice example was when Chesterfield ridiculed the genealogical pretensions of many members of the aristocracy by tracing his own pedigree back to Adam de Stanhope and Eve de Stanhope.[66] Lord Hervey, a hostile witness, knew the effectiveness of Chesterfield's wit:

> his propensity to ridicule, in which he indulged himself with infinite humour and no distinction, and with inexhaustible spirits and no discretion, made him sought and feared, liked, not loved, by most of his acquaintances; no sex, no relation, no rank, no power, no profession, no friendship, no obligation were a shield from those pointed, glittering weapons.

A more impartial observer, Speaker Onslow, said that Chesterfield 'was esteemed the wittiest man of his time, and of a sort that has scarcely been known since the reign of Charles II'. His hopes had risen on the accession of George II in 1727 when he stayed as a Lord of the Bedchamber, but he was bitterly disappointed to find Sir Robert Walpole continued as Prime Minister and in great favour with Queen Caroline. In 1728 he was appointed Ambassador to The Hague, where he distinguished himself by the magnificence of his hospitality and by losing immense sums to the Dutch at play. It was there that he met Mlle. du Bouchet, the mother of his natural son, Philip Stanhope. In 430 letters written over thirty years he tried to guide his son towards an ideal demanding 'engaging, insinuating, shining manners, distinguished politeness, an almost irresistible address, a superior gracefulness in all you say and do'.[67] Amorous adventures with high-born ladies, he advised his son, were preferable to love with a low-born woman. In 1730 he negotiated the marriage of William, Prince of Orange, with Anne, the Princess Royal, and was made Knight of the Garter in May. On his return to England he became Lord Steward of the Household. He returned to The Hague to conclude the second Treaty of Vienna which guaranteed the Pragmatic Sanction (the succession of Maria Theresa to the Austrian dominions) and he was relieved of his post in 1732.

Returning to the Lords Chesterfield voted with the Government on the Mutiny Bill and supported an increase in the standing army from 12,000 to 18,000 troops, having too good an opinion, he declared, of the gentlemen of the Army to believe they would ever enslave their countrymen. What brought Chesterfield onto a collision course with Walpole was the Excise scheme in 1733 against which Chesterfield's three brothers (Charles, John and Sir William Stanhope) voted in the Commons. Chesterfield voiced his strongest disapproval of the Excise Bill, and was held by Walpole to be responsible for several further defections in the Commons. The right to search private houses was much resented and prompted William Pitt to denounce it as a violation of the principle that 'every Englishman's house was his castle'. Johnson shared this opinion, describing the excise as a 'hateful tax levied upon commodities . . . by those to whom excise is paid'. The upshot was that the Bill was dropped before it reached the Lords. Walpole was furious and the King threw Chesterfield out. Chesterfield surrendered his white staff saying he was ready to sacrifice everything for the King's service 'except his honour and conscience'.

From then on, Chesterfield's main aim was to bring about Walpole's downfall, working with Lord Cobham and his 'cubs' the Grenvilles and Pitt, who had been turned out at this time, together with Carteret, Pulteney, Sir William Wyndham, Bolingbroke and Frederick Prince of Wales (who often stayed at Chesterfield's house in Bath), in a disparate opposition which advocated 'Country' measures. He further infuriated George II by marrying in 1733 Melusine von der Schulenburg, Countess of Walsingham, the illegitimate daughter of George I by his favourite mistress, the immensely wealthy Duchess of Kendal. Her parents' subsequent morganatic marriage in Hanover was not legal or acknowledged in England. His wife was 40 and a year his senior. She was said to have brought him £50,000 down and £3,000 a year. Until the Duchess of Kendal's death, Lady Chesterfield lived with her mother in a house adjoining his in Grosvenor Square, but he spent little of his time with mother or daughter. He chose this time to take a new mistress: Lady Frances or Fanny Shirley, 'a great beauty'. On the Duchess of Kendal's death in 1743, Lady Chesterfield was defrauded of large legacies because George II burnt the Duchess's will and had also destroyed George I's will. Chesterfield threatened to sue the Crown and was quietened when the King gave him £20,000 in lieu.

In Parliament in 1734 Chesterfield supported a bill to prevent military officers being deprived of their commissions for voting against the Government (as they had been after the Excise Bill) and he opposed increasing the size of the Army or the Navy. In 1736 he published a satirical essay arguing that an army of waxwork dummies would be cheaper and just as useful:

> Let nobody put the Jacobite upon me, and say, that I am paving the way for the pretender, by disbanding this army. That argument is worn threadbare; besides, let those take the Jacobite to themselves, who would exchange the affections of the people for the fallacious security of an unpopular standing army.[68]

His attack on Walpole in 1737 was particularly skilled on the bill to allow the Lord Chamberlain to licence (i.e. censor) plays. Chesterfield described it as an attack not only on liberty but on property: 'Wit, my Lords, is a sort of property; it is the property of those who have it.' It earned him a compliment from Pope in the *Dunciad*. He took a leading part in the debates on Spanish depredations in 1739, advocated war with Spain, and blamed Walpole for conducting a *'languente bello'* against the Spaniards. He was disappointed when Lord Carteret's motion on 13 February 1741 demanding the dismissal of Sir Robert Walpole and a similar motion in the Commons were defeated because the Tories, who had not been consulted, either absented themselves or voted against.

The parliamentary arithmetic was such that without the Tory vote, Walpole could not be overthrown. Horace Walpole wrote that after the failure of the motion for the dismissal of Walpole, 'Lord Chesterfield was despatched to Avignon by the party, to solicit, by the Duke of Ormonde's means, an order from the Pretender to the Jacobites to concur roundly in any measure for Sir Robert's destruction.'[69] In August 1741 Chesterfield went over to France, stopping in Paris where he met Bolingbroke. He then travelled to Avignon to see his kinsman, the Duke of Ormonde. Ormonde, the most respected of the Tory statesmen and the most trusted by James III, lived like a prince, having retained his pay as Captain-General of all the armies of Spain when he retired there in 1736.[70] Avignon, a Papal possession, was an elegant town often visited by Englishmen on the Grand Tour. Chesterfield's purpose was not touristic, however. Through Ormonde, he obtained a letter from James III dated 16/27 September 1741, instructing his friends in England to join those of different principles from themselves in all attacks on Walpole's administration. Walpole said he had proof that one hundred copies of this letter had been distributed to Tories. James III, writing to Ormonde on 20 September 1741, expressed the hope that his letter would be 'attended with consequences better and greater than one can well foresee'.[71] The price tag to this deal, as subsequent evidence reveals, was agreeing to a restoration of the Stuarts.

Chesterfield's background had made him well qualified to know what the Jacobites were after. A dogged Jacobite-watcher, Horace Walpole, commented that his uncle, old Horatio Walpole, was not as gifted as Chesterfield, but that at least he was 'never known to take a trip to Avignon to confer with the Duke of Ormonde'.[72] On his return to Paris, Chesterfield was introduced to the *salon* of Madame de Tencin by Montesquieu and there met Fontenelle and Marivaux. The meeting place of the best writers in France, alcohol and gambling were banned from her house and hot chocolate only was served. This made quite a change from the customs at White's, Chesterfield's club in London. Madame de Tencin was the sister of Cardinal de Tencin, one of James III's greatest friends, and one who was tipped to become Cardinal Fleury's successor as chief minister of France.[73] We do not know if anything besides literature was discussed between her and Chesterfield, but her brother did nothing without consulting her, and the question of a Stuart restoration may have been broached.

The Tories duly voted with the Whigs in opposition to bring down Walpole in February 1742. Bussy, a French diplomat who was a secret agent for the British government, wrote that Chesterfield joined Argyll and Cobham in attacking Pulteney and Carteret for taking office to the exclusion of the Tories, but their efforts were foiled by George II's 'invincible répugnance pour les Tories'.[74] For Chesterfield, to change two or three men only and go on as before was unacceptable. He pressed for an inquiry into Walpole's administration. In February 1743 he opposed the taking of Hanoverian troops into British pay and denounced 'the dirty mercenary schemes of pretended patriots and avowed profligates'. A popular anonymous pamphlet attributed to him and Edmund Waller, published in 1743, was entitled *The Case of the Hanover Forces in the Pay of Great Britain examined. The Interest of Hanover steadily pursued* was ascribed to Chesterfield alone. His attack on the King for spoiling the victory of Dettingen in 1743 by showing open preference to his Hanoverian officers and wearing the yellow sash of Hanover is a good example of his oratory: 'My Lords, the triumphal laurels yet green upon their brows, were soon overshadowed by the gloomy cypress.'[75]

After the meetings at the Lichfield races between Louis XV's envoy and leading Tories in the summer of 1743, Chesterfield and his brother John Stanhope MP were included in the list of supporters of a restoration sent to the French. It was proposed that those who were to meet the expedition when it landed in England should act in concert with 'Lords Chesterfield, Westmorland [a Whig peer who became a Jacobite at this time] and Cobham'.[76] Like Cobham and Westmorland, Chesterfield was included in the Prince's Council of Regency.[77] In January 1744 Chesterfield opposed the Hanoverian troops: 'The crown of three kingdoms, he declared, was shrivelled beneath an electoral cap.' He was reported to have remarked: 'if we have a mind effectually to prevent the Pretender from ever obtaining this crown, we should make him Elector of Hanover, for the people of England will never fetch another King from thence.' All this could not have endeared him to the King, nor presumably to his own wife, but it aroused the enthusiasm of the Duchess of Marlborough, who left him £20,000 in her will.

After the failure of the Jacobite attempt in February 1744, Chesterfield and Bedford led the opposition to the bill to make it treason to correspond with the Pretender's sons. Chesterfield argued that forfeiture for this offence would punish innocent children and that the Jacobites were too cowardly to pose any real threat.[78] Lord Chancellor Hardwicke was shocked to find that instead of applying 'his genius and eloquence in displaying the horrors and miseries of conspiracies, rebellion and civil war', he drew 'a very moving picture of the distress of children disinherited by the crime of their parents'.[79]

On the formation of the Broadbottom Administration in December it was Chesterfield who brought Gower over to the Pelhams and the Whigs, and he engaged for Cobham too. His hopes of breaking the Tory party through Gower, however, were not realised. He was ready to sacrifice the Bath–Granville Whigs ('the victims are at the altar already, let them bleed') and he sent Newcastle 'the numbers and names of our necessary people' to be brought in instead.[80] Chesterfield became Lord Lieutenant of Ireland and was appointed once more Ambassador at The Hague with a mission to try to get the Dutch into a fighting spirit in the war with France, which had recently been declared. This had the advantage of keeping him as far away from George II as possible. Chesterfield had been either utterly cynical in obtaining the Tory vote to overthrow Walpole by promises of support for the Stuarts, or he had come to the conclusion that after the miscarriage of the 1744 expedition there was little prospect of a restoration. Had the attempt succeeded, he would, of course, have been one of the chief beneficiaries. As it was, he could dictate terms to the Pelhams. His tactics, however, did not earn him the public opprobrium Gower and Bedford incurred.

As Lord Lieutenant, Chesterfield was sympathetic to the plight of the native Irish, thinking they were worse used than negroes by their lords and masters. He refused to countenance further draconian measures against Roman Catholics during the '45 and undertook public works to relieve economic distress, which made him popular. In April 1746 he left Ireland due to illness. By then he had managed to ingratiate himself with George II to such an extent that it was the King who suggested Chesterfield should become principal Secretary of State (for the North) in October 1746. His intellectual sympathies were with the French Enlightenment and, like the *philosophe* French foreign minister, the Marquis d'Argenson, he wanted to make peace at this stage. As a result, he was regarded as too francophile by his fellow ministers. Personal differences as well as disagreements with the Duke of Newcastle over foreign policy led to his resignation in February 1748.

In the autumn of 1747, at the suggestion of the publisher Dodsley, Johnson addressed to Chesterfield (while he was still Secretary of State) the plan of his *Dictionary*, having been informed that Chesterfield had expressed himself in terms very favourable to its success. In the conclusion of the Plan, Johnson wrote:

> When I survey the Plan which I have laid before you, I cannot, my Lord, but confess that I am frighted at its extent, and, like the soldiers of Caesar, look on Britain as a new world, which it is almost madness to invade.

Chesterfield, being at the time 'the butt of dedications' made no response beyond sending Johnson £10. Colley Cibber, the poet laureate, claimed that Johnson was kept waiting in Chesterfield's antechamber, while he, Cibber, was admitted, but this was denied by Johnson himself, who told Boswell 'his Lordship's continued neglect was the reason why he resolved to have no connection with him'.

Johnson had expected real help from Chesterfield while the hard work was in progress. Two anticipatory eulogies written anonymously by Chesterfield in *The World* in 1754 were regarded as inadequate by Johnson. In the 28 November issue, Chesterfield wrote: 'I make a total surrender of all my rights and privileges in the English language, as a free-born British subject to the said Mr. Johnson; for the term of his dictatorship.' Adulatory though this was, it was unacceptable to Johnson, who wrote to Chesterfield on 7 February 1755:

> Seven years, my Lord, have now past, since I waited in your outward rooms, or was repulsed from your door; during which time I have been

pushing on my work through difficulties, of which it is useless to complain, and have brought it, at last, to the verge of publication, without one act of assistance, one word of encouragement, or one smile of favour. Such treatment I did not expect, for I never had a Patron before . . . Is not a Patron, my Lord, one who looks with unconcern on a man struggling for life in the water, and, when he has reached ground, encumbers him with help? The notice which you have been pleased to take of my labours, had it been early, had been kind; but it has been delayed till I am indifferent, and cannot enjoy it; till I am solitary, and cannot impart it; till I am known, and do not want it.[81]

Chesterfield affected supreme indifference at Johnson's letter, which he showed to all and sundry.

After his resignation from the Secretaryship, with illness and increasing deafness coming on, Chesterfield devoted himself to the building of Chesterfield House, overlooking the Park, one of the finest houses in the Palladian style in London. Though he had withdrawn from politics, on 20 February 1751 he introduced a bill to reform the calendar, which was promoted by George Parker, 2nd Earl of Macclesfield, President of the Royal Society. The bill, which introduced the Gregorian calendar with the year beginning on 1 January, passed both houses. The popular reaction to 'a calendar amended by a Pope',[82] however, was less than favourable and the popular cry 'Give us back our eleven days' figured prominently in Hogarth's 'Four Prints of an Election', depicting the great Oxfordshire election of 1754. It did, of course, temporarily cause difficulties in commemorating anniversaries and set dates.

In 1755 Chesterfield became a member of the *Académie des Inscriptions* in Paris and he corresponded with Voltaire, Montesquieu, Fontenelle and Crébillon, as well as with Madame de Monconseil, who presided over Parisian intellectual life. Coming out of retirement, Chesterfield showed magnanimity towards Newcastle during the ministerial crisis of 1757 being instrumental in reconciling Pitt and Newcastle to act together in a coalition. He succeeded in curbing the influence of the Duke of Cumberland and in engaging the Prince of Wales (the future George III) in a compromise.[83] Despite his son's, Philip Stanhope's, illegitimacy, Chesterfield succeeded in obtaining diplomatic posts and a seat in Parliament for him. His son's death in 1768 revealed that, in the face of all Chesterfield's advice, the son on whom he had lavished so much care and affection had secretly married a woman of low birth, by whom he had two sons. Chesterfield died on 14 March 1773, leaving Philip Stanhope his godson and a distant cousin as the 5th Earl and heir to Bretby. Within a year of his death, his son's widow sold his letters for publication to Dodsley for £1,500. On reading Chesterfield's letters, Johnson thought Chesterfield had taught his son 'the morals of a whore and the manners of a dancing master'.

Notes

1. Henning, *HC*, II, pp. 736–8.
2. Geoffrey Holmes, *British Politics in the Age of Anne* (London, 1967), pp. 271–2, 276, 516 n. 49.
3. RASP 216/111. I am obliged to Her Majesty the Queen for permission to cite these papers.
4. Horace Walpole, *Memoirs of King George II*, ed. John Brooke (3 vols., New Haven and London, 1985), I, p. 125; II, p. 34.
5. HMC *5th Rep.* I, pp. 188–9.
6. RASP 216/111.
7. *A Genuine and Authentick Account of the late election for the City and Liberty of Westminster* (London, 1749).
8. *Tory and Whig. The Parliamentary Papers of Edward Harley, Third Earl of Oxford, and William Hay, M.P. Seaford, 1716–53*, ed. Stephen Taylor and Clyve Jones (Woodbridge, Suffolk 1998), p. xxxv.
9. Linda Colley, *In Defiance of Oligarchy: The Tory Party 1714–60* (Cambridge, 1982), p. 67.
10. HMC *Stuart* VIII, p. 555.
11. Colley, *Defiance of Oligarchy*, p. 76.
12. RASP 47/41, received May 1720.
13. RASP 65/16.
14. Colley, *Defiance of Oligarchy*, p. 200.
15. RASP 133/151.
16. RASP 151/77.
17. RASP 153/21.
18. RASP 142/99.
19. See Eveline Cruickshanks, 'Lord Cornbury, Bolingbroke and a Plan to Restore the Stuarts, 1731–33', *Royal Stuart Papers*, XXVII (Huntingdon, 1986).
20. Linda Colley, 'The Loyal Brotherhood and the Cocoa Tree: The London Organisation of the Tory Party, 1727–1760', *HJ*, 20 (1977), pp. 92–4. For Cotton as Vice-President, see Cambridgeshire Record Office, Cotton MSS from Madingley: 'list of the Board from the original'.
21. *Parl Hist*, X, col. 883.
22. *Parl Hist*, XI, col. 1016.
23. Cruickshanks, *Political Untouchables*, p. 30; *Gentleman's Magazine* (1742), pp. 29–30, 95–7, 159–61.
24. *Parl Hist*, XII, cols. 411–12 (Secker mss.).
25. Cruickshanks, *Political Untouchables*, pp. 30–1.
26. Harrowby MSS: Ryder diary, 17 February 1742.
27. Cruickshanks, *Political Untouchables*, p. 31.
28. Archives étrangères, mémoires et documents, Angleterre 76 f. 70.
29. Sedgwick, *HC*, I, p. 282.
30. Clark, *Samuel Johnson*, p. 171; Boswell, *Life*, II, p. 348.
31. Cruickshanks, *Political Untouchables*, pp. 41–5.
32. Anne Kettle, 'The Lichfield Races', *Lichfield and South Staffordshire Arch. & Hist. Soc.*, VI, pp. 39–41.
33. Cruickshanks, *Political Untouchables*, pp. 44, 134.
34. John B. Owen, *The Rise of the Pelhams* (London, 1957), pp. 193–4.
35. *Parl Hist*, XIII, col. 532.

36. Cruickshanks, *Political Untouchables*, ch. 4.
37. Owen, *Rise of the Pelhams*, p. 236.
38. Sir G.H. Rose (ed.), *A Selection of the Papers of the Earls of Marchmont* (3 vols., London, 1831) I, p. 88.
39. Cruickshanks, *Political Untouchables*, p. 72; Walpole, *Memoirs of George II*, I, p. 22.
40. BL Add MSS 32,704 f. 25.
41. William King, *Political and Literary Anecdotes* (London, 1818), pp. 46–7, and Clark, *Samuel Johnson*, p. 47.
42. Boswell, *Life*, I, p. 296.
43. Cruickshanks, *Political Untouchables*, pp. 73–5.
44. Owen, *Rise of the Pelhams*, p. 264 and Chesterfield to Gower 2/13 April 1745: PRO 30/29/11, Granville MSS.
45. BL Add MSS 35,602 ff. 50–7.
46. Cruickshanks, *Political Untouchables*, pp. 85–6, 89.
47. Lord Gower to Duke of Bedford, 3 August 1747, Bedford MSS, Woburn.
48. Lord Anson to Duke of Bedford, Lichfield, 21 June 1747, ibid.
49. Pelham MSS, History of Parliament transcripts.
50. Cruickshanks, *Political Untouchables*, pp. 106–7.
51. BL Add MSS 32,712 ff. 117, 288.
52. *Gentleman's Magazine* (1747), p. 150; Cruickshanks, *Political Untouchables*, p. 108.
53. RASP Box 3, folder 1. Letter from Lord Stanhope in *The Times*, 29 December 1864.
54. BM Catalogue of Prints and Drawings No. 3018 'Locusts'.
55. Despatch from Mirepoix, London, 24 October 1750, Archives étrangères, correspondance politique, Angleterre, 427 ff. 301–7.
56. HMC *Du Cane*, pp. 203–4.
57. *Westminster Elections 1741–50* (London, 1750).
58. Sedgwick, *HC* I, p. 287.
59. *A Genuine and Authentick Account* (1749), loc. cit.
60. *A Series of Letters of the First Earl of Malmesbury* (2 vols., London, 1870), I, p. 75.
61. Sedgwick, *HC*, I, pp. 286–7; *Gentleman's Magazine* (1751), pp. 200–2, 282.
62. William Coxe, *Memoirs of the Administration of the Rt. Hon. Henry Pelham* (2 vols., London, 1829) II, pp. 341, 380, 441.
63. Unless otherwise stated, this essay is based on Dobrée's introduction to his edition of *The Letters of Philip Dormer Stanhope, 4th Earl of Chesterfield* (6 vols., London, 1932) and the entry for Chesterfield in the *DNB*.
64. BL Add MSS 19,253 ff. 67–8.
65. Sedgwick, *HC*, II, p. 487.
66. *The Yale Edition of Horace Walpole's Correspondence*, ed. W.S. Lewis (39 vols., New Haven, Conn., 1937–74), XX, p. 181.
67. Dobrée (ed.), *Letters of Chesterfield*, IV, p. 1330; J.C.D. Clark, *English Society 1688–1832* (Cambridge, 1985), p. 101.
68. Clark, *English Society 1688–1832*, p. 145.
69. Walpole, *Memoirs of George II*, I, p. 37.
70. See Eveline Cruickshanks, 'The 2nd Duke of Ormonde and the Atterbury Plot', in *The Dukes of Ormonde 1610–1745*, ed. Toby Barnard and Jane Fenlon (Woodbridge, 2000).
71. Cruickshanks, *Political Untouchables*, pp. 27–8 and RASP 236/27.
72. *Horace Walpole's Correspondence*, ed. Lewis, XIX, pp. 68–9.
73. C. de Coynart, *Les Guérins de Tencin* (Paris, 1918), p. 293. For Tencin's correspondence with Fleury as his eventual successor see M. Boutry, *Une Créature du*

Cardinal Dubois; intrigues et missions du Cardinal de Tencin (Paris, 1902) App. III. See also J. Sareil, *Les Tencins: histoire d'une famille au XVIIIe siècle* (Geneva, 1969).

74. BL Add MSS 34,500 ff. 86–7, copy of despatch from Bussy to Amelot, the French Foreign Minister given by Bussy to Newcastle.

75. P.C. Yorke, *The Life and Correspondence of Philip Yorke, Earl of Hardwicke* (3 vols., Cambridge, 1913), I, p. 326.

76. RASP 250/189.

77. Cruickshanks, *Political Untouchables*, pp. 46–7.

78. *Parl Hist* XIII, cols. 704, 768–74, 854.

79. Yorke, *Hardwicke*, I, p. 328.

80. *Marchmont Papers*, I, p. 87; Owen, *Rise of the Pelhams*, pp. 197, 237.

81. Boswell, *Life*, I, pp. 183–266; Clark, *Samuel Johnson*, pp. 187–8.

82. Walpole, *Memoirs of George II*, I, pp. 35–6.

83. J.C.D. Clark, *The Dynamics of Change* (Cambridge, 1982), p. 387.

6

Samuel Johnson, *Thoughts on the Late Transactions respecting Falkland's Islands*, and the Tory Tradition in Foreign Policy[1]

Jeremy Black

Attitudes to war, international relations and foreign policy have been generally neglected in treatments of eighteenth-century cultural and intellectual life. However, they were an important dimension, and consideration of them is instructive. Such consideration is particularly important as Britain emerged as a leading world power during the century. Protracted periods of conflict played a major role in British society and any approach to British culture that ignores such conflict would be misleading. There was a national debate on questions of foreign policy and it was important to other spheres of political debate.[2]

Johnson is of particular importance in this context because he played a major role in that foreign policy debate. In Sir Robert Walpole's later years as first minister, Johnson took part in the polemical attacks on Walpole's alleged appeasement of Spain. In *London*, published in May 1738, Johnson used Elizabeth I's successful stand against Spain as an ahistorical tool in an assault on Walpolean policy:

> In pleasing Dreams the blissful Age renew,
> And call Britannia's Glories back to view;
> Behold her Cross triumphant on the Main,
> The Guard of Commerce, and the Dread of *Spain*,
> Ere Masquerades debauch'd, Excise oppress'd,
> Or *English* Honour grew a standing Jest.[3]

Thirty-three years later, Johnson wrote the most important defence of British policy in the Falkland Islands crisis.[4] As far as the Falklands dispute is concerned, a powerful case can be advanced that Johnson's emphasis on prudence and caution corresponded with a philosophical Tory attitude towards the limitations of human calculation and interventionism, the latter associated with Whig concepts of the balance of power and the necessity of alliance strategies.[5]

169

This contrast offered a consistency that was different from the role in the public debate of pragmatic responses to quickly changing problems. The contrast can and should be traced back to the definition of Whig and Tory attitudes after the Revolution of 1688, or rather their redefinition in response to the political changes that followed the Revolution. The Williamite moment in British foreign policy was one in which a major disjuncture was followed by a rapid process of state formation, constitutional and governmental change and ideological formulation, all in close association with a perception and policy which indicated not only that France was a major threat, but also that it was necessarily Britain's task to thwart her. By presenting Louis as a threat to both Britain and Europe, and as an inexorable expansionary force, William III could be absolved by his apologists from the charge of causing the war and from responsibility for the burdens and problems that stemmed from it. Furthermore, this could be presented both as in accordance with traditional British interests and as forward looking in offering a vision of Europe freed from the hegemonic threat of French empire.[6] The divine right theory of monarchy was replaced by a divine destiny theory of nationhood.

This Williamite legacy was to dominate British foreign policy until it was abandoned in 1762, when George III refused to sustain the diplomatic assumptions of the Newcastle–Pitt government.[7] Put simply, the sense that Britain had to play a major role on the continent, as opposed to one of episodic intervention, was central to what can be seen as the Whig tradition and practice of foreign policy. Whether in cooperation with France or, more commonly, in opposition to her, the Whig tendency was characterised by interventionism to a degree that exceeded what had been typical over the previous century. The Whigs referred back to Elizabeth I and Cromwell, but Elizabeth had been cautious about full commitment on behalf of the Dutch rebels, and war with Spain had not begun until 1585. The Cromwellian regime had been an atypical British government, with an unusually strong army and navy.

Williamite intervention was more widespread, sustained and expensive than what had gone before. It was a revival of the interventionism of the Hundred Years' War, but one that was wider in scope, and presented as driven by national, not dynastic, concerns. This perception had to be sustained against the reality of the Williamite coup and the Stuart claim. The Williamite diplomatic tradition was one of collective security, a system of mutual guarantees that required continual oversight and frequent intervention. The pursuit of collective security has been attributed to an 'idealistic conception of a stable European states system'.[8] It also owed much to a pursuit of security that was more intense and wide-ranging than had been the case under the later Stuarts.

Sympathy for William, antipathy towards Louis XIV and the persuasive nature of Williamite propaganda have all led historians to neglect this

and, instead, to concentrate sympathetically on the idealistic conception and presentation of his role; but such an emphasis fails to address
the rhetorical strategies of Williamite apologists,[9] the scope for choice in
Williamite policies and the concerns of contemporaries about both foreign
policy and strategy. Victory over France, especially in 1704–8 and 1759, was
a lubricant both for Britain's alliances and for British public support for
interventionist conflicts, but its effects could not counteract indefinitely
domestic divisions and discontents, or for that matter divergent interests
among allies.[10]

Indeed, victory exacerbated both domestic divisions and divergent
alliance interests by raising expectations and enlarging diplomatic and
domestic demands. An anonymous pamphlet of 1712 drew attention to the
trajectory of public opinion:

> If ever hellebore was necessary for the nation, this is the critical minute
> for giving it in large doses. For certainly the brains of the people
> were never so distempered as at present: at one time Spain and the West
> Indies was thought too narrow a spot for empire for such capacious souls.
> The great hopes we had conceived of our successes abroad had heated
> our imaginations, and we were all bent to carry on the war with vigour
> until the Spanish monarchy should be restored entire to the House of
> Austria; but perceiving ourselves short in that reckoning, jaded with
> frequent miscarriages in Spain, finding the enemy recruited to a miracle,
> after several defeats, our selves scarce able to maintain the single province
> of Catalonia, and exhausted with the prodigious charge a war of so
> remote a situation had involved us in, the nation abated much of their
> former warm resolutions, and clamoured for peace.[11]

An awareness of the fickleness of domestic attitudes was to be married in
Tory thought on foreign policy to a sense of the instability of international
affairs. Both were combined in Jonathan Swift's *The Conduct of the Allies*, the
crucial work for any understanding of Tory printed thought on foreign
policy and the point of departure for a consideration of Johnson's relevant
work. The *Conduct* appeared in November 1711, intended to influence the
forthcoming parliamentary session.[12] Its essential theme was that

> no Nation was ever so long or so scandalously abused by the Folly, the
> Temerity, the Corruption, the Ambition of its domestick Enemies; or
> treated with so much Insolence, Injustice and Ingratitude by its foreign
> Friends.

Swift argued not only that the Whigs had mishandled their relations with
Britain's allies, but also that the very alliance system ensured that the
purpose and conduct of the war was wrong:[13]

First, That against all manner of Prudence or common Reason, we engaged in this War as Principals, when we ought to have acted only as Auxiliaries.

Secondly, That we spent all our Vigour in pursuing that Part of the War which could least answer the End we proposed by beginning of it; and made no Efforts at all where we could have most weakened the Common Enemy, and at the same time enriched our Selves.

Lastly, That we suffered each of our Allies to break every Article in those Treaties and Agreements by which they were bound, and to lay the Burthen upon us.[14]

Swift's argument that the alliance inhibited Britain from following her correct policy, naval action, was a standard Tory claim, and was linked to the allegation, expressed for example by Swift in number 20 of *The Examiner* (21 December 1710), that the Duke of Marlborough and the Whig officers had acquired excessive influence and much money, and that their pretensions might have pernicious political consequences.[15] In the *Conduct*, Swift similarly ascribed Britain's concentration on Continental campaigns to Marlborough's influence:

It was the Kingdom's Misfortune, that the Sea was not the Duke of Marlborough's Element, otherwise the whole Force of the War would infallibly have been bestowed there, infinitely to the Advantage of his Country, which would then have gone hand in hand with his own.[16]

He also argued that victory and profit could both have been obtained by a maritime strategy:

And what a noble Field of Honour and Profit had we before us, wherein to employ the best of our strength, which, against all the Maxims of British Policy, we suffered to lie wholly neglected? I have sometimes wondered how it came to pass, that the Style of Maritime Powers, by which our Allies, in a sort of contemptuous manner, usually couple us with the Dutch, did never put us in mind of the Sea; and while some Politicians were shewing us the way to Spain by Flanders, others by Savoy or Naples, that the West-Indies should never come into their Heads. With half the Charge we have been at, we might have maintained our original Quota of Forty thousand Men in Flanders, and at the same time, by our Fleets and Naval Forces, have so distressed the Spaniards in the North and South Seas of America, as to prevent any Returns of Money from thence, except in our own Bottoms. This is what best became us to do as a Maritime Power: This, with any common-degree of success, would soon have compelled France to the Necessities of a Peace, and Spain to acknowledge the Archduke.[17]

Although Johnson described the *Conduct* as 'a performance of very little ability', and his views on foreign policy were much more explicitly Christian than those of Swift, there were nevertheless important parallels in their views on foreign policy, unsurprisingly so as both were Tory writers. Thus the criticisms of the Walpole government's alleged failure to defend maritime interests against Spain in the late 1730s represented another instance of the Tory view that Whig governments failed to defend national interests, specifically by preferring continental interventionism to a 'Blue Water' policy. George I and George II (with marked Hanoverian interests) and their Whig ministers (apparently unwilling to prevent these from dominating British policy) could be seen as successors to William III and Marlborough.[18]

Circumstances both domestic and international were important in the expression of Tory views on foreign policy, not least the question of whether the Tories were in office or not. One of the strongest Tory themes, however, was that of the mutability of human affairs, frequently advanced in direct contrast to Whig attempts to create an acceptable international order. Swift expressed this Tory perspective when he suggested that leaving a Bourbon (Louis XIV's younger grandson, Philip, Duke of Anjou, now Philip V of Spain) on the throne of Spain would not necessarily be fatal, and he was to be proved correct. In 1719, indeed, France, from 1716 in alliance with Britain, attacked Philip V, a neat reversal of earlier Whig phobias. Earlier in the *Conduct*, Swift had offered a very pessimistic assessment:

> How to insure Peace for any Term of Years, is difficult enough to apprehend. Will Human Nature ever cease to have the same Passions? Princes to entertain, Designs of Interest or Ambition, and Occasions of Quarrel to arise? May not we Ourselves, by the Variety of Events and Incidents which happen in the World, be under a necessity of recovering Towns out of the very Hands of these, for whom we are now ruining Our Country to Take them.[19]

This pessimistic account looked forward to *Gulliver's Travels* where the causes of European wars were explained by Swift as 'the Ambition of Princes, who never think they have Land or People enough to govern: Sometimes the Corruption of Ministers, who engage their Master in a War in order to stifle or divert the Clamour of the Subjects against their evil Administration'.[20] Such a system was made unstable by human vice, an approach that accorded with general Tory views, specifically the emphasis on morality. As a result optimistic Whig views on international relations could be dismissed as naive as well as prescriptive. Tories could pride themselves on realism, an appreciation of an international anarchy in which there was no reason to assume that allies would act well. Unable to place trust in the word of princes, or indeed of the republican Dutch, there was no reason for Tories to assume that Britain would be rewarded if she bore a heavier burden than her allies. It was therefore understandable that Swift should urge a recourse to, and reliance upon, national self interest.

Swift's analysis was more accurate than the Whig assumption of lasting, because natural, alliances (in, for example, Hoadly's *Conduct of Foreign Affairs* of 1727, which assumed an immutable alliance between the Protestant powers in Europe). The notion that every state had innate interests which, properly understood, dictated a course of policy to which other states could respond by alliance or enmity, was mechanistic and placed insufficient weight on the personal role of rulers and the unpredictable nature of most policies. As Swift more shrewdly argued in the *Conduct*, 'great Events often turn upon very small Circumstances'.[21]

In essence, there was a conflict between an optimistic Whig assessment of the possibility of establishing consistent policies and creating a world order that was predictable and stable, and a pessimistic Tory realisation of the fallibility of human ambitions and schemes. When Swift wrote in the *Conduct* of the Emperor (Joseph I) sacrificing 'the whole Alliance to his private Passion'[22] for subduing rebellious Hungary, he was showing his support for a pessimistic, or perhaps realistic, assessment of the extent to which Europe was an international system, and thus an assessment of the chances that British ministers could devise a consistent policy through alliance diplomacy. In his *Thoughts on the late Transactions respecting Falkland's Islands* (1771), Johnson stressed the unpredictability and volatility of human affairs:

> It seems to be almost the universal error of historians to suppose it politically, as it is physically true, that every effect has a proportionate cause. In the inanimate action of matter upon matter, the motion produced can be but equal to the force of the moving power; but the operations of life, whether private or publick, admit no such laws. The caprices of voluntary agents laugh at calculation. It is not always that there is a strong reason for a great event. Obstinacy and flexibility, malignity and kindness, give place alternately to each other, and the reason of these vicissitudes, however important may be the consequences, often escapes the mind in which the change is made.[23]

The pessimistic sense that developments, both in individuals and more generally, could not be predicted because they were 'irrational', and that therefore foreign policy risked upset if it sought to create a system based on the views and interests of others, constituted a major theme in Tory thought. The stress on the uncertainty of human affairs reflected a distinct religious, moral, and intellectual position.

Swift stressed the personal basis of policy in a monarchical system, but was also careful to represent what he saw as the social context and consequences of British policy. He offered a conspiratorial account of the monied interest:

> A set of Upstarts, who had little or no part in the Revolution, but valued themselves by their Noise and pretended Zeal when the Work was over, were got into Credit at Court, by the Merit of becoming Undertakers and Projectors of Loans and Funds: These, finding that the Gentlemen of Estates were not willing to come into their Measures, fell upon those new Schemes of raising Mony, in order to create a Mony'd Interest, that might in time vie with the Landed, and of which they hoped to be at the Head.[24]

Similarly Johnson, in his pamphlet on the Falklands, asked,

> how are we recompensed for the death of multitudes and the expence of millions, but by contemplating the sudden glories of paymasters and agents, contractors and commissaries, whose equipages shine like meteors and whose palaces rise like exhalations[?][25]

Aside from the moral revulsion towards those who profited from the sufferings of others, Johnson and Swift also thus offered the classic Tory critique of financial activity and speculation. This looked back on a rich tradition, but one that was in many respects outdated in a society where such activity and wealth were of growing importance; thus trade and commerce created a 'national interest' that Swift and Johnson found it difficult to accommodate. The same revulsion, combined with a sense that society had indeed changed, can be seen in Edmund Burke's cry about the passing of the 'age of chivalry' (although the Rockingham Whigs did not share the government's view of the Falklands crisis).

In his *Life of Johnson*, James Boswell commented on the doctor's anti-Wilkesite pamphlet of 1770, *The False Alarm*:

> It was wonderful to see how a prejudice in favour of government in general, and an aversion to popular clamour, could blind and contract such an understanding as Johnson's, in this particular case; yet the wit, the sarcasm, the eloquent vivacity which this pamphlet displayed, made it read with great avidity at the time, and it will ever be read with pleasure, for the sake of its composition. That it endeavoured to infuse a narcotick indifference, as to publick concerns, into the minds of the people, and that it broke out sometimes into an extreme coarseness of contemptuous abuse, is but too evident.[26]

This verdict could be applied to Johnson's pamphleteering of the entire period. When writing political pamphlets, Johnson adopted the conventions of the genre without difficulties. This led in his *Thoughts on the late*

Transactions respecting Falkland's Islands (1771), the pamphlet that followed *The False Alarm*, to a combination of two contrasting elements, the bitter language of the contempt with which, in Boswell's phrase, he lashed the opposition 'with unbounded severity', and the humanity and scepticism with which he attacked war and confidence in martial victory.

The pamphlet also illustrated another feature of the genre: the combination of often very detailed narrative and the treatment of political issues in moral terms. This approach allowed opponents to be vilified and despised, as in the closing sentences of his pamphlet in which Johnson described the defeated 'Patriot' opposition in a passage that echoed classical themes of order triumphant over reptilian and baser animal disorder:

> To be harmless though by impotence obtains some degree of kindness; no man hates a worm as he hates a viper; they were once dreaded enough to be detested, as serpents that could bite; they have now shewn that they can only hiss, and may therefore quietly slink into holes, and change their slough unmolested and forgotten.[27]

Although powerful, this is scarcely a measured discussion of public affairs or in keeping with the humanity of Johnson's attitudes and energy. The energy of Johnson's language, the vigour of his imagery, clearly lent themselves to polemical pamphleteering. There is, both in the pamphlet and more generally in his career, a struggle, or at least tension, between sets of contrasting elements of suspicion and hope, anger and tolerance, antagonism and humanity.

At the same time, Johnson adopted the conventions of the genre. Political pamphlets were written to attack as much as elucidate, and Johnson knew how to apply the lash, as in his description in the pamphlet of the great 'Patriot' hero, William Pitt the Elder, who had attacked the government's policy over the Falklands as 'supine neglect or wicked treachery':

> This surely is a sufficient answer to the feudal gabble of a man who is every day lessening that splendour of character which once illuminated the kingdom, then dazzled, and afterwards inflamed it; and for whom it will be happy if the nation shall at last dismiss him to nameless obscurity with that equipoise of blame and praise which Corneille allows to Richlieu [*sic*], a man who, I think, had much of his merit, and many of his faults.[28]

Much of this passage was not entirely unreasonable, but it is the bite of the 'feudal gabble' that makes the impact. A comparison of Pitt with a French cardinal, renowned for hypocrisy and autocratic policies, was scarcely flattering in the political culture of the age. Johnson's criticism of 'Patriotism' was also seen in a sentence near the conclusion of *Thoughts*, 'To fancy that our government can be subverted by the rabble, whom its lenity has pampered into impudence, is to fear that a city may be drowned by the overflowing of its kennels.'[29]

More than social conservatism was involved, however. There was also a criticism of the 'Patriot' proto-imperialism that assumed that Britain should extend her sway, that her destiny was one of maritime mastery and colonial acquisitions, a destiny that made conflict with the Bourbon powers of France and Spain necessary and inevitable. Such an analysis has recently received much scholarly attention as a result of interest in questions of urban political consciousness and of national identity.[30]

The young Johnson had supported conflict with Spain in 1738, but his later attitude was markedly different. He had a longstanding hostility to colonialism and oppressive war that probably owed much to his Nonjuring Christian beliefs. In the 1750s and early 1760s he had condemned British policy in the Seven Years' War, and in the early 1760s, like Swift at the close of the War of the Spanish Succession, was in favour of a 'soft' rather than a 'hard' peace, a position very different from that of Pitt and the 'Patriots'. The contrast between the young Johnson and his later writings reflects a tempering of youthful optimism and changes in the political situation. It is difficult to determine which was more important. Pitt himself had in 1750 explained why he had tempered his earlier criticisms of Walpolean foreign policy and become instead an advocate of caution; a position he found it difficult to maintain. Pitt told the Commons how

> upon some former occasions I have been hurried by the heat of youth, and the warmth of debate, into expressions which, upon cool recollection, I have deeply regretted . . . Nations, as well as individuals, must sometimes forbear from the vigorous exaction of what is due to them. Prudence may require them to tolerate a delay, or even a refusal of justice, especially when their right can no way suffer by such acquiescence.

The following year he told the Commons that he had 'considered public affairs more coolly', and had been wrong to criticise Walpole in 1739 over Spanish depredations.[31] Thus Johnson's own shift was neither exceptional nor evidence of hypocrisy.

The *Thoughts* was by turns a reflective work, considering the nature of human society, and a detailed account of a particular crisis. Johnson asserted both a generalised concern for peace and a more specific criticism of those who advocated war without considering the consequences and largely in order to pursue factional ends. The pamphlet begins with a mention of 'the pride of power' and 'the cruelties of war', before offering an essentially static view of international relations that contrasted markedly with the idea of colonial expansion: 'what continuance of happiness can be expected, when the whole system of European empire can be in danger of a new concussion, by a contention for a few spots of earth, which, in the deserts of the ocean had almost escaped human notice?'[32] – a remark that echoed Voltaire's criticism of the British and French for fighting over the barren wastes of Canada during the Seven Years' War (1756–63) and the end of part four of *Gulliver's Travels*.

Instead, Johnson offered a humane prospect, 'that as the world is more enlightened, policy and morality will at last be reconciled, and that nations will learn not to do what they would not suffer'. This reflection was accompanied by an attack on the practice of contraband trade which was essential to British commercial penetration of the protected markets of Spanish America. Walpole's reluctance to support such trade in the face of often brutal Spanish policing had led to bitter opposition criticism in 1738–9, but by 1771 Johnson could advance an argument that Walpole would not have hesitated to endorse. Johnson's attack on contraband trade was an aspect of his criticism of corruption, an echo of Patriot moralising that led him to describe mankind as always struggling with corruption.[33]

Johnson's account of the discovery and settlement of the Falklands was essentially factual, but his reflections made his views clear. 'Indulgence of romantick projects and airy speculations' was contrasted with 'judgment', and Johnson suggested that 'shame of deserting a project' played a major role in leading the government to value possession of 'tempest-beaten barrenness'. Johnson was at pains to stress the moderation of the conduct of the Spaniards, who had a rival claim and had obliged the outnumbered British garrison to surrender on 10 June 1770.[34]

Having discussed the subsequent international crisis, and criticised the opposition's attacks on the ministry for failing to get Spain to renounce their claims, a measure that Johnson presented as impractical, the pamphlet warned that 'To push advantages too far is neither generous nor just'.[35] Johnson judged critically the idea that war with Spain would have measured up to the expectation of its proponents against the background of his view of the uncertainty of human affairs. He presented war as 'the extremity of evil', to be avoided if at all possible, but he also offered a more specific critique.[36] From a distance war could appear heroic, but in recent wars with the Bourbons tens of thousands had died of terrible diseases, helping to exhaust the population while the National Debt rose to the profit of the monied interest alone.

Having claimed that all nations assume that they would win in war and that history teaches otherwise, Johnson raised the specific point about the response from other countries if Britain fought Spain, a view vindicated by subsequent British isolation in the War of American Independence (1775–83). Johnson went on to argue, correctly, that attacks on Spanish America might well be unsuccessful, in large part because of the problems of operating in the tropics, a conclusion he ably supported by reference to the unsuccessful attack on Cartagena in 1741.[37] That had at the time been blamed by the opposition on a failure of governmental support, but Johnson in 1771 rejected the entire 'Patriot' argument that Spanish America would fall easily. In contrast, a letter in the *Gentleman's Magazine* of December 1770 claimed that the Spanish empire could be attacked readily and that Buenos Aires, Lima and Vera Cruz would fall easily.

In the latter section of the pamphlet, Johnson advanced conservative views on the nature of Georgian political society. He contrasted those whose opinions were worth heeding with 'the rabble . . . the cits of London, and the boors of Middlesex' who applaud 'contempt of order, and violence of outrage . . . rage of defamation and audacity of falsehood'. Aware that war would be dangerous for the stability of the ministry, a conclusion that the political crises of 1710, 1742, 1744, 1756–7 and 1782 supported, Johnson also argued that foreign nations would be overly affected by reports of discontent in Britain, discontent that Johnson presented in a very harsh light as 'the insolence of Common Councils . . . the howl of Plebeian patriotism . . . the chain of subordination broken'.[38] Johnson thus adopted a position that was similar to that of the Walpole ministry at the time of the outcry over Spanish depredations upon British trade, one that linked continual political opposition to social insubordination and the encouragement of foreign rivals, and that reflected the profound ambivalence in Georgian political thought about both the notion of a loyal opposition and the acceptability of extra-parliamentary pressure.

Johnson drew on government information for his pamphlet. Lord North laid before Parliament on 4 February 1771 the papers about the affair and they were soon after published by John Almon. Johnson would have had access to them through his friend Henry Thrale, MP for Southwark, or through his printer, William Strahan MP, who was a loyal supporter of North. Thomas Bradshaw MP, who was close to senior governmental circles, wrote in 1773 that the piece had been written 'under the special direction of Lord North',[39] an expression that had appeared in the daily press less than three weeks after its publication. A sentence that Johnson added when he revised the pamphlet in 1776 for his collected *Political Tracts* may indicate that he had access to 'inside' information from the ministry: 'To all this the Government has now given ample attestation, for the island has been since abandoned, and perhaps was kept only to quiet clamours, with an intention, not then wholly concealed, of quitting it in a short time.'

The pamphlet is impressive because Johnson discussed his views of the specific merits of the government's case in the perspective of a developed view of human affairs that reflects both an idealised hostility towards war and selfishness in international relations and an historically grounded awareness of the problems, political, economic and moral, of conducting an aggressive foreign policy. It certainly bears comparison with contrary views. The *North Briton* of 13 October 1770 argued that Tories deliberately sought to favour France, the *Whisperer* charged the government with betraying the interests and honour of the nation, while the *Public Advertiser* of 17 January 1771 employed a familiar device of opposition writing throughout the century, the appeal to the supposed example of Elizabeth I. The issue of 13 February carried a letter accusing the ministry of craven surrender to France. On the other hand, the government was not without press support. 'C.P.G.', writing in the *Westminster Journal* of 1 December 1770, attacked popular prejudice and, in contrast to the general claim that the Bourbons could not be trusted, argued that their friendship should be cultivated, adding 'We know very well that Jack Helter-Skelter says, damn the Spaniards, we shall soon give them a belly-full, and bring home their treasure by ship-load after ship-load. Better to cultivate their friendship, and supply them with the manufactures of Great Britain.'

Johnson had to repeat the achievement of Swift, and of Israel Mauduit who had successfully attacked a well-entrenched and popular 'Patriot' view in his 1760 pamphlet *Considerations on the Present German War*.[40] Johnson's task was harder both because he was not writing against the background of an expensive, albeit successful, war that many wished to end and because, again unlike Swift and Mauduit, there were no allies and no land war upon which to focus discontent. Pro-government writers in peacetime faced the problem that it was difficult to advocate a prudential policy, one that urged caution, a balanced assessment of risks and opportunities, and countenanced war only as a last resort. This was particularly hard after the triumphant conclusion of the Seven Years' War.

Johnson's *Thoughts* was one of the most intelligent defences of this viewpoint, but it is one that has received insufficient attention because it did not accord with notions, triumphal or otherwise, of Britain's inevitable rise to oceanic mastery. The pragmatic and prudential dimension of the public debate needs to be recovered. In the case of Johnson's *Thoughts*, the absence of a sense of Britain's inevitable rise is linked both with traditional Tory refrains, especially the impermanence of human achievements and actions and the dangers of popular politics, and a more optimistic hope that international relations could become more rational, moral and peaceful. These aspects were potentially contradictory but were held in place by the cumulative nature of the pamphlet.

In his *Life of Johnson*, Boswell claimed that in the *Thoughts* Johnson 'successfully endeavoured to persuade the nation that it was wise and laudable to suffer the question of right to remain undecided, rather than involve our country in another war', and Boswell wrote of 'the earnestness with which he averted the calamity of war'. It is understandable that Boswell should have emphasised the impact of writings and of his subject, but it is important not to exaggerate the potency of print. Swift had claimed credit for the Commons defeat of the 'No peace without Spain' motion (the Whig demand that war continue until the Habsburg candidate gained Spain) and his pamphlet was used as a source for the Tory speeches, but a certain amount of scepticism is in order as peace was clearly coming anyway. The same is true with regard to Mauduit's claim that he was responsible for a shift away from interventionism.

In 1771 the possible impact of Johnson's pamphlet was lessened by the Bourbon climbdown and the avoidance of war. Pro-ministerial writing had therefore to explain the terms of the settlement, rather than defend a reluctance to fight or to continue fighting. Far from decrying the value of forceful behaviour, the North ministry was presenting itself as having succeeded in a confrontation whose ethos Johnson attacked. They had negotiated with Spain while arming for war, as Pitt the Younger's ministry was again to do successfully in 1790 in the Nootka Sound crisis.[41] There is no sign that the political nation lost its interest in an aggressive international stance.

Johnson's theme of opposition to imperial expansion was to be lost, but it was of importance during the eighteenth century as British commentators considered how best to respond to imperial opportunities and expansion. Gibbon shared Johnson's opposition to war and martial glory, his disapproval of imperial expansion, and his moralism.[42] Johnson's early support for war, as in his *Marmor Norfolciense*, was replaced by a more critical view of conflict.[43] This was a response to his own greater experience of life and also to his political repositioning as a supporter of the established order, rather than a critic aghast at its hypocrisies and weaknesses.

The morality of international relations was a vexed problem for contemporary writers, as was to be shown with the First Partition of Poland in 1772.[44] To write in moral terms on such subjects was difficult, but that was the prevailing language of political writing, and Johnson's path was eased by the pessimism and sense of transience that was such an integral part of Tory thought. Johnson's views on foreign policy were part of his consistent Christian politics and an aspect of his hostility to bland rationalism. They reveal his preference for the teachings of an experience that showed that human effort could not produce a perfect society.

Notes

1. I am grateful to Jonathan Clark, Grayson Ditchfield and Bill Gibson for their comments on an earlier draft.
2. Jeremy Black, *A System of Ambition? British Foreign Policy 1660–1793* (London, 1991).
3. [Samuel Johnson], *London: A Poem, In Imitation of the Third Satire of Juvenal* (London, 1738), lines 25–30. For the public debate see, most recently, Philip Woodfine, *Britannia's Glories: The Walpole Ministry and the 1739 War with Spain* (Woodbridge, 1998), pp. 128–53.
4. For the international background see, most recently, H.M. Scott, *British Foreign Policy in the Age of the American Revolution* (Oxford, 1990), pp. 140–56.
5. Jeremy Black, 'The Tory View of Eighteenth-Century British Foreign Policy', *HJ*, 31 (1988), pp. 469–77.

6. Jeremy Black, 'The Revolution and the Development of English Foreign Policy', in Eveline Cruickshanks (ed.), *By Force or By Default? The Revolution of 1688–89* (Edinburgh, 1989), pp. 135–58.

7. Jeremy Black, *America or Europe? British Foreign Policy 1739–63* (London, 1997).

8. Ragnhild Hatton, *War and Peace 1680–1720* (London, 1969).

9. For these see, in particular, Manuel Schonhorn, *Defoe's Politics: Parliament, Power, Kingship and 'Robinson Crusoe'* (Cambridge, 1991) and Tony Claydon, *William III and the Godly Revolution* (Cambridge, 1996). More generally see Jeremy Black, 'Confessional State or Elect Nation? Religion and Identity in Eighteenth-century England', in Tony Claydon and Ian McBride (eds.), *Protestantism and National Identity: Britain and Ireland, c. 1650–c. 1850* (Cambridge, 1998), pp. 53–74.

10. Jeremy Black, *Britain as a Military Power 1688–1815* (London, 1999).

11. *The Present Negotiations of Peace Vindicated from the Imputation of Trifling* (London, 1712), pp. 3–4.

12. J.A. Downie, 'The Conduct of the Allies: The Question of Influence', in C.T. Probyn (ed.), *The Art of Jonathan Swift* (London, 1978), pp. 108–28.

13. D. Coombs, *The Conduct of the Dutch: British Opinion and the Dutch Alliance during the War of the Spanish Succession* (The Hague, 1958). For the background, John Hattendorf, *England in the War of the Spanish Succession: A Study of the English View and Conduct of Grand Strategy, 1701–1713* (New York, 1987).

14. *The Prose Works of Jonathan Swift*, ed. Herbert Davis et al. (16 vols., Oxford, 1939–68), VI, pp. 15–16.

15. Swift, *Prose Works*, III, p. 45. On the Duke see, most recently, J.R. Jones, *Marlborough* (Cambridge, 1993).

16. Swift, *Prose Works*, VI, p. 23.

17. Swift, *Prose Works*, VI, p. 22.

18. For the debates see, most recently, Robert Harris, *A Patriot Press: National Politics and the London Press in the 1740s* (Oxford, 1993) and Woodfine, *Britannia's Glories*.

19. Swift, *Prose Works*, VI, p. 55.

20. Swift, *Prose Works*, XI, pp. 245–6.

21. Swift, *Prose Works*, VI, p. 23. For a reassertion of Whig views, H.M. Scott, 'The Second "Hundred Years War", 1689–1815', *HJ*, 35 (1992), pp. 443–69. See, in contrast, Jeremy Black, 'The Theory of the Balance of Power in the First Half of the Eighteenth Century: A Note on Sources', *Review of International Studies*, 9 (1983), pp. 55–61. A recent valuable approach, from a continental perspective, is provided by Heinz Duchhardt, *Balance of Power und Pentarchie 1700–1785* (Paderborn, 1997), pp. 7–19.

22. Swift, *Prose Works*, VI, p. 34.

23. [Samuel Johnson], *Thoughts on the late Transactions respecting Falkland's Islands* (London, 1771), pp. 33–4.

24. Swift, *Prose Works*, VI, p. 10.

25. [Johnson], *Thoughts on the late Transactions*, p. 44.

26. Boswell, *Life*, II, p. 112.

27. [Johnson], *Thoughts on the late Transactions*, p. 75.

28. [Johnson], *Thoughts on the late Transactions*, p. 37.

29. Sotheby's, *Catalogue of the Lyttelton Papers* (London, 1978), p. 141; [Johnson], *Thoughts on the late Transactions*, p. 73.

30. Nicholas Rogers, *Whigs and Cities: Popular Politics in the Age of Walpole and Pitt* (Oxford, 1989); Kathleen Wilson, *The Sense of the People: Politics, Culture and Imperialism in England, 1715–1785* (Cambridge, 1995).

31. *Parl Hist* XIV, cols. 694, 801.
32. [Johnson], *Thoughts on the late Transactions*, pp. 1–2.
33. [Johnson], *Thoughts on the late Transactions*, p. 10.
34. [Johnson], *Thoughts on the late Transactions*, pp. 14, 18, 24–5.
35. [Johnson], *Thoughts on the late Transactions*, p. 38.
36. [Johnson], *Thoughts on the late Transactions*, p. 41.
37. Richard Harding, *Amphibious Warfare in the Eighteenth Century. The British Expedition to the West Indies, 1740–1742* (Woodbridge, 1991).
38. [Johnson], *Thoughts on the late Transactions*, pp. 53, 56, 58, 72.
39. BL Add MSS 35,505 f. 220.
40. K.W. Schweizer, 'Foreign Policy and the Eighteenth-century English Press: The Case of Israel Mauduit's "Considerations on the present German war"', *Publishing History*, 39 (1996), pp. 45–53.
41. Jeremy Black, *British Foreign Policy in an Age of Revolutions 1783–1793* (Cambridge, 1994), pp. 225–56.
42. Jeremy Black, 'Gibbon and International Relations', in Rosamond McKitterick and Roland Quinault (eds.), *Edward Gibbon and Empire* (Cambridge, 1997), pp. 217–46.
43. [Johnson], *Thoughts on the late Transactions*, pp. 1, 41 and *The Patriot. Addressed to the Electors of Great Britain* (London, 1774), pp. 19–20.
44. D.B. Horn, *British Public Opinion and the First Partition of Poland* (Edinburgh, 1945).

7
Johnson and Scotland

Murray G.H. Pittock

Samuel Johnson's attitude to Scotland and its inhabitants has traditionally been assessed in terms of caricature hostility. From Boswell's reported confession to being a Scotsman who 'cannot help it', via the infamous definition of 'Oats' in the *Dictionary* ('meant to vex', as Johnson admitted), to the Great Cham's crowning comparison of the troublesome Irish fly and the bloodsucking Scots leech, Johnson's outlook appears consistently prejudiced and insular: 'he considered the Scotch, nationally, as a crafty, designing people, eagerly attentive to their own interest', colonials comparable to 'Cherokees' and even 'ouran-outangs'.[1] What is there left to explain?

A great deal is the answer, as some more recent critics have understood, taking as their key text that fascinating paradox the *Journey to the Western Isles* (1775), a thoughtful record of a long and trying journey by an ageing man to a country he was supposed universally to despise and detest, but which he ended up dignifying. For Pat Rogers, Johnson chose his tour as a rite of passage for his Grand Climacteric at sixty-three, as a kind of reverse Grand Tour and as a homage to the 'lapsed nationhood' overthrown in the Rising of 1745.[2] In Rogers's view, therefore, age and decline, the opposition of native vigour to foreign manners and the metonymic loss of Scotland and the Stuarts, are all subtexts to the language and itinerary of the Tour. On this reading, Scotland, far from being merely despised, stands for something critical in the life and values of Johnson himself.

Whatever one's view of these accounts, each of them implicitly recognises an important thing about Johnson: the extent of his interest in Scotland, and the number of references he makes to it. To some degree this can be explained by the interposing voice and influence of Boswell, but although this can account for Johnson's teasing of his biographer (and Scotland is not the only subject on which he teases), it cannot altogether explain the depth of intellectual attention Johnson gave the country, especially when he sojourned there. In this essay, I suggest three major reasons for Johnson's Scottish interests: the state of the country as a proxy for the state of the Church, its locus as the major source for the Jacobite debate, and its monitory significance as a warning that the decline Scotland has experienced has threatened England too, and might do so still. Here the Grand Tour idea put forward by Rogers is interesting in its suggestive implications; for just as Italy was in the eighteenth century an awful example of the state to which a great civilisation might be reduced, so in its lesser way Scotland serves the same purpose for Johnson: a ruined seat of Renaissance learning.

The peculiarity of Johnson's interest in Scotland strikes us immediately if we stand back from it. His knowledge of and interest in its history was profound. Englishmen who disliked and belittled Scotland were not difficult to find in the eighteenth century, but their typical state was one of ignorance: they knew little of Scotland, and cared less. That this was an appealing position in Johnson's time can be seen from the conflation of Highland and Lowland Scot, flea-ridden savage and ingratiating Edinburgher in the political cartoon tradition in which 'Sawney' (Alexander) on his 'Boghouse' is a synecdoche for the Scottish character in general, uncivilised, militant, and voracious for sexual mischief and a full belly.[3] The political and later the perceived economic threat posed by the Scots led to the same kind of collectivist ethnic caricature of them as intruders and immigrants as afflicted the Irish in the nineteenth century.[4]

Although Johnson can adopt this mode, he nearly always does so in teasing exchanges. Elsewhere he displays a considerable understanding of Scottish history and culture, and does so in terms that emphasise not its backwardness, so much as its decay. As Jonathan Clark points out, like Thomas Ruddiman (1674–1757), whom Johnson admired,[5] himself one of the last scions of Scoto-Latin and Episcopal culture, Johnson 'was predisposed to see Scots society in decay'. Again and again it is evident from the language and encounters of the Tour that 'Johnson like Ruddiman believed that the decline of learning went together with the advance of Presbyterianism'. In opposition to this advance, Ruddiman had himself been involved in the '15, and one of his sons was transported for his part in the '45.[6] Johnson himself 'pointedly refused to enter a Presbyterian church' while in Scotland,[7] while in his *Dictionary* the illustrations of the meaning of 'Presbyter' and 'Presbyterian' are drawn from Samuel Butler (1613–80), Jonathan Swift (1667–1745) and Charles I, all among its most decided opponents.

In these circumstances, it is little wonder that Aberdeen, Ruddiman's city, made such a favourable impact on Johnson:

the scene at Aberdeen had made such an impression upon him that he often said, on his return to London, to Dr. Dunbar [Professor of Philosophy at King's] that if he ever removed from the capital, he would incline to fix in Aberdeen. 'What', said the professor, 'in preference to Oxford?' 'Yes sir', replied Johnson, 'for Aberdeen is not only a seat of learning, but a seat of commerce, which would be particularly agreeable.' This he so often repeated that Dunbar used to tell him he had secured apartments for him in the King's College, which flattered him much.[8]

This puts a rather different perspective on the oft-quoted gibe on the best prospect for a Scotsman. What may underlie Johnson's attitude here? Aberdeen (particularly Old Aberdeen, the Aulton, till 1891 a separate burgh) was the city at the heart of Scottish Episcopalian territory: in 1708, an estimated 40 per cent or more of Scots were Episcopals in Aberdeenshire, Angus and Mearns, and over 50 per cent in neighbouring Moray and Ross.[9] As Gordon Donaldson notes in his important thesis on 'the conservative north' of Scotland, in 1690 only four clergy from 200 in the synods of Aberdeen, Banff, Moray and Ross 'conformed to Presbyterianism'.[10]

Old Aberdeen itself had long resisted the Reformation; and it was for this reason, perhaps, that King's College Chapel, unspoilt unlike so many of the ruins of episcopacy lamented by Johnson, retained the earliest ecclesiastical wood interior remaining in Scotland, a tribute to local joinery and the city's contacts with medieval Flanders. The environs too bore witness to the 'conservative north'. Aberdeen's 'Sang Schule' was the longest continuing survivor in any Scottish burgh; King's was the home of the Aberdeen Doctors, who had opposed the Covenant, of James Sharp, the Archbishop of St. Andrews murdered in 1679 and of Dr. Arthur Johnston (1577–1641), the Latin Royalist poet, whose works Johnson admired and unsuccessfully sought to buy while in the city: of his *Deliciae Poetarum Scotorum* Johnson noted that it 'would have done honour to any nation'.[11] Johnston dedicated a version of the Psalms to Archbishop Laud in the 1630s, thus pointing up Aberdeen's loyalism to High Church Episcopacy;[12] his contemporary, William Forbes (1585–1634), opined that 'many of the differences between the Church of Rome and the Protestants were merely superficial' and that 'Purgatory, Praying for the Dead, the Intercession and Invocation of Angels and Saints' were all practices which could be derived from Scripture.[13] In 1684, the agent of the Episcopalian administration in Edinburgh described Aberdeen as 'the onlie toune in Scotland most conforme to the government both in principle and practice'.[14] Indeed, when Johnson visited Old Aberdeen, the image of Our Lady on the cross by the Town House was still *in situ* (apparently it did not finally disappear until the 1790s).[15] Just across the High Street from King's, the old kirkyard of St Maria ad Nives (founded, like King's itself, by Bishop Elphinstone) was still in use in Johnson's time as a Catholic burying-ground.[16] Most notably, the Jacobite William Drummond, whom Johnson thought a 'very worthy man'[17] and breakfasted with on the northern tour in 1773, had recently acted as publisher for the Scottish Communion Office of 1764, one of the major liturgical texts of Nonjuring Episcopalianism. Drummond published both octavo and duodecimo editions, and a third was prepared in 1765 under the supervision of Bishop Forbes, ardent patriot, Jacobite and author of *The Lyon in Mourning*.[18] It is noteworthy that Johnson apparently made Drummond's acquaintance when the latter was still in hiding from the authorities in the 1740s: he had possibly served as a gentleman volunteer in the Perthshire Horse, whose leader, his namesake Major-General the Viscount Strathallan, had possibly died leading his cavalry in a heroic if vain counter-attack against the Government advance at Culloden, and had thus, together with Brigadier Stapleton's Irish troops, prevented a total massacre.[19] If such (or, indeed, the possibility that he served as Captain in Perth's Regiment) were indeed Drummond's antecedents, he was a real-life Jacobite hero, who had followed a chief of his name 'under his patriarchal care . . . to the field upon an emergency', as Johnson put it.[20]

These are all circumstances which go some way to explain Johnson's reported appetite for rooms in King's. Although while in Scotland he does not appear to have attended any Scottish Episcopalian liturgies, instead visiting the licensed chapels presided over by those ordained by English and Irish bishops, his pointed snubbing of Presbyterian services and clear sympathy for Episcopacy are steadily and frequently evident. The Scottish Episcopalian church had been effectively outlawed after the 1745 rising, and the orders of Scottish bishops were no longer recognised: public worship under their authority was almost itself an act of sedition. Nevertheless, even in the licensed chapels, members of the congregation would take snuff and fidget during prayers for King George,[21] and Johnson may well have encountered behaviour of this kind.

Such a context lends colour to Pat Rogers's assessment of the *Tour*'s 'cultural Jacobitism' with Johnson's emphasis on the 'ravages left behind by the Reformation' and his particular regret for the condition of Scotland's cathedrals. In this, he was travelling in the footsteps of Laud, who had described the debris of 1560 as 'deformation'. As Rogers puts it: 'Almost the only buildings which Johnson describes with approval . . . are the vestiges of the old religion and learning, destroyed by the progress of the Reformation.'[22]

In the ruined cathedrals of Scotland, Johnson may have seen an image of the damage wrought to Lichfield Cathedral in the 1640s. North of the Border lay a warning for England: Johnson's fierce opinion that those who wished to 'melt the lead of an English cathedral' should swallow it can only have been exacerbated by the presence north of the Tweed of the descendants of a regime of cathedral despoilers. Indeed, the stolen lead from Elgin and Aberdeen cathedrals is described as a 'cargo of sacrilege'.[23] In Scotland the result of the wars of the Three Kingdoms was permanent victory for sectarian iconoclasts: small wonder Johnson disliked them. He had just viewed the scars of that war on a recent visit to the 'cathedrals of Winchester, Exeter, Ely and Norwich', and in Iona in particular he was to see 'the connection between the ruins and the intellectual and religious decay of society'. To Johnson, John Knox (1505–72) was 'a flesh-and-blood villain' who had, in Thomas Curley's words, had a profound influence on 'a culture's demise and a people's degradation'.[24] Johnson had accused Knox of having 'set on a mob, without knowing where it would end';[25] perhaps in Johnson's own mind its end was in the greedy place-seekers of the 1760s and 1770s. The Great Cham indeed links the Scot-on-the-make directly to the Reformation, replying to Boswell's musings on the Union by suggesting that the Scots could '*go home*' and take their Presbyterianism 'into the bargain', for 'We should have had you for the same price, though there had been no Union': here the longstanding link between Presbyterianism and venality (made by anti-Union Scots Jacobites from the role of 'English gold' in 1707 on) is implicitly present. Indeed, to James Kerr's reported objection to the Union that 'Half our nation was bribed by English money', Johnson snarled, 'Sir, that is no defence: that makes you worse.' It is arguable that in Johnson's eyes, the simony of the Scots, who had famously sold their king in 1647 and their country sixty years later, was still being reflected in the greed of contemporary place-seeking, itself only the latest manifestation of an established tendency to betray King and Country. The Scots had, on this reading, failed to defend Mary's Catholic crown ('never talk of your independency, who could let your Queen remain twenty years in captivity') and sold Charles's Episcopalian one, over which Lord Auchinleck (who thought his guest 'a *Jacobite fellow*') and Johnson argued.[26] As Eithne Henson notes, 'Johnson's devotion to Mary Stuart is central to his Jacobite sympathies, whatever their strength.'[27]

The betrayal of Mary (itself intrinsically linked to the Reformation) marked the onset of Scotland's degradation. 'Degradation' is the key word here: Scotland was to Johnson not primarily a barbarous, backward culture, but a culture in decline: a salient distinction. Taken to see the High Kirk of St Giles, icon of the Reformation and the Covenant, Johnson remarked to William Robertson, the leading moderate Presbyterian, 'let me see what was once a church'. The metonymy of these reported conversations is clear: Johnson is on tour to see what was once a nation, 'if we allow the Scotch to be a nation' he observed in 1779.[28] Nationality was a question on which Johnson was more alert than many modern theorists: in *Taxation no Tyranny* (1775) he memorably demonstrates the relative nature of the right to secede by comparing Cornwall's claims to nationhood with those pretended to by the American colonies. In this case too, Johnson's distaste for economic self-interest and the hypocrisy accompanying it (in American attitudes to slavery as in Scots' pride in nationality) is evident.

The inclination to Episcopalianism Johnson notes in the Hebrides[29] must have predisposed him in their favour, and may also connect with his favourable comments to Mrs. Thrale on the learning to be found there among the tacksman class. He certainly deals with the western islands more kindly than with the rest of Scotland; notably, the only city he comments on favourably himself (though Boswell reports kind words on Edinburgh) is Glasgow (described as 'opulent and handsome') which 'is the only episcopal city whose cathedral was left standing in the rage of Reformation'.[30] At Inch Kenneth, Johnson favourably remarks on the features of the 'chapel' which had survived the Reformation:

> The altar is not yet quite demolished; beside it, on the right side, is a bas-relief of the Virgin with her child, and an angel hovering over her. On the other side still stands a handbell, which though it has no clapper, neither a Presbyterian bigotry nor barbarian wantonness has yet taken away.[31]

In such terms is the message of decline summed up: a few remote relics of a nobler age saved from bigotry and neo-barbarism. The silent bell of which only the shell remains can no longer sound for the elevation of the Host, just as the spoliated ruins of cathedrals once full of sacrament and worship are left as the bones of the broken body of the Scottish nation: '*Ponti inter strepitus sacri non munera cultus / Cessarunt; pietas hic quoque cura fuit*': 'Amid the thunder of the sea the offices of holy religion did not cease; here also the true faith was pursued'.[32] The metonymy of King and Church into country is one of the most powerful messages of Johnson's writing on the Tour.

Part of Scotland's declension is, as Rogers implies, to be found in the defeat of the Stuart dynasty: Scotland had, from the period 1650 to 1750, been engaged in felling 'the ancient oak of loyalty', as Edwin Muir was later to put it.[33] At St. Andrews, Johnson commented of James VI's reign that 'there was then abundance of learning in Scotland . . . lost . . . during the civil wars'; Scottish learning in his own time, he observes, is but 'widely and thinly spread'. Although Johnson's attribution of 'the spirit of learning' to the reformer George Buchanan perhaps shows admiration overcoming judgement, the tenor of his endorsement of the culture of James VI, that champion of Episcopacy, is notable; and it is voiced at the seat of the 'ruins of religious magnificence', seat of the deposed Archbishop, and site of the murders of both Cardinal Beaton in 1546 ('murdered by the ruffians of reformation') and Archbishop Sharp in 1679, alike victims of Presbyterian extremists.[34] Johnson comments to Mrs. Thrale that St. Andrews, with its 'poor remains of a stately cathedral' was yet 'once the see of the Primate of Scotland'.[35] In the *Journey* itself, he goes on to note that the decline of St. Andrews reflects its loss of 'archiepiscopal preeminence' and opines that the falling number of students is a consequence of the fact that 'there is no episcopal chapel in the place'. St. Andrews is in consequence a city with 'an university declining, a college alienated, and a church profaned and hastening to the ground'. It is 'pining in decay and struggling for life'.

In his indignation, Johnson compares Knox to Alaric the Visigoth, who sacked Rome in 410 AD.[36] The comparison of the sack of St. Andrews to the sack of Rome not only makes an explicit alignment between Presbyterianism and barbarism, but also (especially in the context of the comments on Cardinal Beaton) exhibits an implicitly pro-Catholic sympathy evident elsewhere in Johnson's work: Rome, like St. Andrews, is a seat of religious primacy attacked by barbarians (we may remember that it was a Pope who turned back the prospect of Attila's further depredations forty years later). Boswell's *Life* repeatedly reports pro-Catholic sentiments, from 'I would be a Papist if I could' to Johnson's description of any Protestant conversion from Catholicism as hardly likely to 'be sincere and lasting', since so much of the Church would have to be given up. 'There is no idolatry in the Mass', he insisted and explicitly in Boswell's record endorses Catholicism's superiority to Presbyterians who 'have no church, no apostolical ordination'. By implication then, Catholic ordination is apostolic, a sentiment entirely in conformity with the *Catechism of the Catholic Church* (para. 857), and indeed with the Anglican tradition embodied in Laud, who called the Reformation 'that miserable rent in the Church of Christ' and described the Church of Rome as 'a true church'.[37] In this vein Johnson observes that 'the blackest midnight of popery is meridian sunshine' to the Scottish Reformation.[38]

At Arbroath, Johnson's appreciative comments on the majestic Abbey are in keeping with this.[39] Shortly afterwards, on their visit to Lord Monboddo (whose father had been tried for his part in the Rising of 1715), Johnson remarked to Monboddo's son that his Latin was so good that 'When King James comes back, you shall be in the "Muses' Welcome!"' *The Muses' Welcome* had been published in 1617 to welcome King James VI back to Scotland; Johnson had already used it as a touchstone of Scottish learning in the Episcopalian period; the implication is that only the return of King James can restore learning worthy of Monboddo's son. Since in general Jacobite policy was to restore Episcopalianism the contiguities of Johnson's thought are at the least suggestive.[40] As Jonathan Clark remarks, Scoto-Latin poetry was itself 'a cultural movement which defined itself against Covenanting religion from the 1630s; this theme became intertwined with the dynastic one'.[41] Long before the famous night in Charles Edward's bed (one shared by Thomas Pennant and thus not necessarily political) and the encounter with Flora MacDonald,[42] Johnson's language and outlook on the Tour is politically provocative. They remain so: 'Your ancestors did not use to let their arms rust,' he observes to Sir Alexander MacDonald,[43] while to Mrs. Thrale he writes 'you may guess at the opinions that prevail in this country, they are, however, content with fighting for their king, they do not drink for him' – this last observation being a clear-cut gibe at the Welsh and English Jacobites, following on from that made by Charles Edward himself in 1745.[44] Johnson arguably goes yet further in speaking of the chiefs as suffering 'the heavy hand of a vindictive conqueror',[45] a statement which can refer to little other than the bloody aftermath of Culloden and the presence of occupying troops throughout northern Scotland.

Boswell's displaced Jacobitism surely had its part to play in this: it had already been evident in his cult of Corsican independence in the 1760s. In the first paragraph of the dedication of his *Journal of a Tour*, he cites Pasquale Paoli, the Corsican national leader whom he had been proud to bring to Scotland only two years before his journey with Johnson.[46] On it, he sought to find 'simplicity and wildness' in the Scottish West as he had done in Corsica; and he did so by following an 'itinerary . . . devised so as to make sustained contact with the prince's flight through the heather'. As Rogers argues, Boswell's tracing of the 'role of an adventurous partisan' in Scotland echoed that undertaken in Corsica almost a decade before. Furthermore, Rogers suggests a parallel in Boswell's mind between Charles as 'the Wanderer' and Johnson as 'the Rambler'.[47] Whether or not this was the case, Boswell's own links with Jacobitism were more than sentimental, not least in his correspondence with Andrew Lumisden, Secretary to Prince Charles: 'my very worthy and ingenious friend, Mr. Andrew Lumisden', as Boswell calls him. Boswell interestingly notes that Johnson was termed an '*honest man*' in Scotland, a term which the biographer glosses as 'an expression of kindness and regard', but which in fact was an established code-word for Jacobitism (not that there would be any necessary political implication at such a date, but presumably Episcopalians rather approved the sentiments Johnson expressed which were also reported by Boswell: 'What have your clergy done, since you sunk into presbyterianism?').[48]

Whatever Boswell's more romantic sentiments may have been, Johnson's observations are very precise, and thus are strongly suggestive of his own direct engagement with the society he was visiting. For example, he notes that swordsmanship is not widespread in the Highlands,[49] despite the already established cultural construct of the Jacobite Highlander as opposing muskets with the broadsword. In fact, as Johnson notes, swordsmanship was an elite activity of the heroic class: most of those who fought in 1745 bore muskets and pistols like their adversaries. On the other hand, although he is careful to examine the Highland view that the 'most savage clans' live 'next the Lowlands',[50] in the end he dismisses it as an example of Highland opinions of Lowland degeneracy. Interestingly, the most recent research shows that although Johnson's view was understandable, the Highlanders he spoke to were most likely right, for broken and landless men pushed to the frontier of magnate territories caused much of the trouble there.[51]

Johnson's well-known disparagement of Ossian is of course also matched by a lively sympathy with the inhabitants of the Gaeltachd he was reputed to despise: indeed, Johnson's 'Last Word on Ossian' consisted of a ghost-written piece for the Gaelic scholar William Shaw (1743–1831).[52] In 1757, Johnson had encouraged the learning of Irish Gaelic,[53] and in 1766 he famously wrote a letter to the Jacobite William Drummond in support of Scots Gaelic, where Johnson states that 'I am not very willing that any language should be totally extinguished': this view was credited as being influential in ensuring the provision of Gaelic scriptures.[54] On the Tour, Johnson was 'dissatisfied at hearing of racked rents and emigration'[55] and of the forcible teaching of English, so that in schools where 'their language is attacked on every side . . . the natives read a language which they may never use or understand'.[56] He shrewdly notes the laws against dress and drily marks their exception: that 'to allure them [the Highlanders] into the army, it was thought proper to indulge them in the continuance of their national dress' and notes that 'To hinder insurrection, by driving away the people, and to govern peaceably, by having no subjects, is an expedient that argues no great profundity of politics.'[57]

The sense of decline identified by Johnson in Scotland in general is prevalent in the Highlands also, Johnson remarking that 'the clans retain little now of their original character' of 'antiquated life'. Although he is to some extent an agent here of the outlook and vocabulary of Primitivism (as perhaps in the encounter with the women's 'harvest song',[58] which one is tempted to read as a model for Wordsworth's 'Solitary Reaper'), in other ways the decline marked in the Highlands by Johnson is one which is general throughout Scotland. In an interesting political manifestation of his deep-seated Latinity, Johnson notes of the Highlands after 1745 that 'where there was formerly an insurrection, there is now a wilderness'.[59] The echo is unmistakable: *'solitudinem faciunt, pacem appellant'* ('they make a wilderness and call it peace'). The speech of Calgacus at Mons Graupius is revisited, and his prophecy fulfilled by Culloden, where the last Scottish patriots, as Calgacus was the first, were destroyed, and the *Pax Britannica* achieved what the *Pax Romana* could not, the desolation of northern Scotland. Lord Lovat, that ardent nationalist, had subsequently called from the scaffold in the words of Horace *'Dulce et decorum est pro patria mori'*.[60] Tacitus, Johnson's source, was also the source for the Roman republican rhetoric of Charles Edward in the 1740s and beyond that for the characterisation of the Jacobite leader, Viscount Dundee, as 'last and best of Scots' by Archibald Pitcairne (1652–1713) in the elegy translated by Dryden. Johnson had in fact talked to Boswell about Tacitus' sentiments on Scotland the previous year, so we know the topical echo was in his mind;[61] he had also perhaps made the same allusion in his 1769 reference to Scotland's 'desart'.[62] In this desolated land 'the malignant influence of Calvinism has blasted ceremony and decency', effacing 'the monuments of papal piety'.[63] Johnson makes an apparently obligatory reference to 'papal superstition' to soften this essentially pro-Catholic point: we may term it obligatory because he also argues that the inhabitants have experienced 'the decay of religion' and were 'more devout' in past times.[64]

Thus Johnson's hostility to Scotland and the Scots should be read through the political prism of their perceived double betrayal of King and Church. Statements which are apparently bald assertions of English superiority can be extensively qualified by their context. For instance, here is the Great

Cham on the benefits of Union: 'Till the Union made them [the Scots] acquainted with English manners, the culture of their lands was unskillful, and their domestick life unformed; their tables were coarse as the feasts of Eskimeaux, and their houses filthy as the cottages of Hottentots.'[65] Here surely is the colonising voice of English superiority at its most pronounced. And yet on the same page, Johnson notes that 'the politer studies were very diligently pursued' in Scotland up to almost the middle of the seventeenth century (is he thinking of the National Covenant of 1638?) and, yet more tellingly, that 'they [the Scots] must be for ever content to owe to the English that elegance and culture, which, if they had been vigilant and active, perhaps the English might have owed to them'. This is a very telling remark, which forcefully endorses Johnson's repeatedly implied view that Scotland's inadequate civilisation is not innate, but, dreadfully, *chosen*. This is a country which has willingly allowed 'its universities to moulder into dust', where 'the episcopal cities . . . fell with their churches' in the 'waste of reformation'.[66] It is true that Johnson regarded the Highlands as in a different case,[67] and made occasional gibes elsewhere, but none the less the overall sense is that of a missed opportunity. In this context, the Macphersonian reliance on orality and unprovided and unspecified ancient texts to boost Scottish self-image through the tales of a heroic past is itself a sign of decline from the learning of a past age.

Scotland's example has a monitory force in English culture, where Johnson displays many of the same concerns. In 'On the Fireworks for the Peace of Aix-la-Chapelle', for example, he condemns the show as mere frippery, 'a trifling profusion, when so many sailors are starving, *and so many churches sinking into ruins*' (emphasis added). The ruination of churches is a sign of national decline which is by no means unique to Scotland.[68] As John Vance points out, Johnson was 'quite different from those of his century who saw something stylish in decayed buildings'. His fears for England's churches are reflected in his view of Iona as displaying 'the connection between the ruins and the intellectual and religious decay of society'.[69] The country which Johnson fears will 'groan distrest' in 'To Posterity' (from *Marmor Norfolciense*) by the tramplings of the Hanoverian horse, is foreshadowed in the vindictive conquest of Scotland by the same dynasty and its clerical allies (the Lutheran religion of George I was a Nonjuring debating point). The Lyon who suffers is of course the symbol of the Scottish royal line: the Lyon is another name for the King of Scots. The Stuart line is the line of the Lyon, and the title of course survives today in that of the Lord Lyon. As Howard Erskine-Hill has pointed out, the source of Johnson's 1739 emblem 'appears to be Otto Hamerani's fine Jacobite medal of 1721, or later depictions deriving from it': hence the centrality of the Stuart line to *Marmor*.[70] What Scotland is, England may become: we must weigh the present balance between 'the Rocks of *Scotland*' and 'the *Strand*' against the potential of Inch Kenneth, where '*Quo vagor ulterius*' ('who would wander further'). The death of the 'bonny Traytor' (almost exclusively a Scots adjective, as Johnson notes in the *Dictionary*) will leave his country a wilderness indeed. Interestingly, Johnson's use of the term 'gaping Heir' in line 48 of *The Vanity of Human Wishes* derives from a couplet in Dryden's translation of Juvenal's *Satire III* ('I neither will, nor can Prognosticate / To the young, gaping Heir, his Father's Fate'), which itself leans heavily on the opening couplet of 'The King Shall Enjoy His Own Again' ('What Booker doth prognosticate, / Concerning kings and kingdoms' fate'). Within the Juvenalian paradigm as well as the Tacitean, Johnson can hint (and sometimes more than hint) at the Jacobite language of decay and disappointment. He has, after all, just been discussing 'rival Kings' and 'dubious Title'. The borrowing from Dryden is especially apposite.[71]

Johnson's vision of and relationship to Scotland and its status are far more complex, and reverberate more deeply than the common summary of them would allow. His prejudices and antipathy are based at least as much on religion as on nationality: in their Presbyterianism, Scots have destroyed their nation, pulled down their cathedrals, sold their king and lost their bishops. Their simony is the subject of Johnson's contempt: but it was also condemned by Robert Burns, Edwin Muir and many other writers. The lost opportunity of Scotland is a fitting sign of the mortality of nations and the vanity of human wishes. It was thus on yet another level a suitable backdrop for Johnson's Grand Climacteric; and it is not for nothing that much of Scotland's modern literature is concerned with the theme of renewal.

Notes

1. Boswell, *Life*, II, p. 321; IV, p. 168; Pat Rogers, *Johnson and Boswell: The Transit of Caledonia* (Oxford, 1995), p. 103; Clark, *Samuel Johnson*, p. 66.
2. Rogers, *Johnson and Boswell*, pp. 5, 31, 145.
3. Murray G.H. Pittock, *Celtic Identity* (Manchester, 1999), p. 32, plate 14.
4. Pittock, *Celtic Identity*, pp. 27–8, 33–5, 55, plates, 2, 3, 5, 6, 7, 10.
5. Boswell, *Life*, II, p. 216.
6. Clark, *Samuel Johnson*, pp. 34, 36, 239.
7. John Cannon, *Samuel Johnson and the Politics of Hanoverian England* (Oxford, 1994), p. 22.
8. Norman Page (ed.), *Dr Johnson: Interviews and Recollections* (Basingstoke, 1987), p. 115.
9. Jean McCann, 'The Organisation of the Jacobite Army, 1745–46', unpublished PhD thesis (University of Edinburgh, 1963), pp. 137, 146–7; Murray G.H. Pittock, *The Myth of the Jacobite Clans* (Edinburgh, 1995), p. 47.
10. Gordon Donaldson, 'Scotland's Conservative North in the Sixteenth and Seventeenth Centuries', in *Scottish Church History* (Edinburgh, 1985), pp. 191–203, at 191–2.
11. Barry Baldwin, *The Latin & Greek Poems of Samuel Johnson* (London, 1995), p. 3.
12. *Musae Latinae Aberdonensis* (3 vols., Aberdeen: New Spalding Club, 1892–1910), I, p. xxiii; II, p. 241.

13. William Watt, *A History of Aberdeen and Banff*, The County Histories of Scotland (Edinburgh and London, 1900), p. 218; D. Macmillan, *The Aberdeen Doctors* (London, 1909), pp. 173–4.

14. Aberdeen City Archives, Calendar of In Letters Volume 7 (1682–99), Letterbox Index.

15. William Kennedy, 'An Alphabetical Index of the first 67 Volumes of the Council Register' (2 vols., 1818), II, p. 311 (Volume 18), Aberdeen City Archives; Agnes Mure Mackenzie, *Scottish Pageant* (3 vols., Edinburgh, 1946–9), III, p. 103.

16. Alexander MacDonald Munro (ed.), *Records of Old Aberdeen* (2 vols., Aberdeen: New Spalding Club, 1899, 1909), II, pp. 31, 44–5; Kennedy Index (1818), II, p. 355; *Passages from the Diary of General Patrick Gordon of Auchleuchries AD 1635–AD 1699* (Aberdeen: Spalding Club, 1859), p. 148n.

17. Boswell, *Life*, II, p. 27.

18. John Dowden, *The Scottish Communion Office 1764* (Oxford, 1922), pp. 78–9n.

19. Cf. Alasdair Livingstone of Bachuil et al. (eds.), *Muster Roll of Prince Charles Edward Stuart's Army 1745–46* (Aberdeen, 1984), pp. 54, 67.

20. Boswell, *Life*, I, p. 409.

21. John Davidson, *Inverurie and the Earldom of the Garioch* (Edinburgh and Aberdeen, 1878), p. 335.

22. Rogers, *Johnson and Boswell*, p. 166.

23. Samuel Johnson, *A Journey to the Western Islands of Scotland*, ed. Mary Lascelles (New Haven, 1971), pp. xxxiv, 20. (Citations to Johnson's *Journey* are from this edition.)

24. John A. Vance, *Samuel Johnson and the Sense of History* (Athens, Georgia, 1984), pp. 28, 74, 78–80.

25. Samuel Johnson and James Boswell, *A Journey to the Western Islands of Scotland; The Journal of a Tour to the Hebrides*, ed. R.W. Chapman (London, 1974), p. 198.

26. Boswell, *Journal*, pp. 184–5, 415, 419.

27. Eithne Henson, *'The Fictions of Romantick Chivalry': Samuel Johnson and Romance* (Rutherford, N.J., 1992), p. 196.

28. Boswell, *Journal*, 185; Boswell, *Life*, III, p. 387.

29. Johnson, *Journey*, p. 104.

30. Johnson, *Journey*, p. 159.

31. Johnson, *Letters*, II, p. 105.

32. Samuel Johnson, 'Insula Sancti Kennethi', discussed in Baldwin, *Latin & Greek Poems of Samuel Johnson*, p. 106.

33. Edwin Muir, *Scotland 1941* (London, 1960), pp. 97–8.

34. Johnson, *Journey*, p. 6; Boswell, *Journal*, pp. 196, 198; Boswell, *Life*, II, p. 363.

35. Johnson, *Letters*, I, p. 55.

36. Johnson, *Journey*, pp. 6, 8, 9.

37. *Catechism of the Catholic Church* (London, 1994); Charles Carlton, *Archbishop William Laud* (London, 1987), pp. 40–1.

38. Boswell, *Life*, II, pp. 103–6; IV, pp. 289–90.

39. Johnson, *Journey*, p. 11.

40. Boswell, *Journal*, pp. 196, 210.

41. Clark, *Samuel Johnson*, p. 21.

42. Cannon, *Samuel Johnson*, p. 63.

43. Boswell, *Journal*, p. 256.

44. Johnson, *Letters*, I, p. 83.

45. Johnson, *Journey*, p. 89.

46. Boswell, *Journal*, p. 155.
47. Rogers, *Johnson and Boswell*, pp. 7, 140.
48. Boswell, *Journal*, pp. 287, 328, 338.
49. Johnson, *Journey*, p. 114.
50. Johnson, *Journey*, p. 36.
51. Cf. Allan Macinnes, *Clanship, Commerce and the House of Stuart* (East Linton, 1996), p. 33.
52. Thomas M. Curley, 'Johnson's Last Word on Ossian', in J.J. Carter and Joan Pittock (eds.), *Aberdeen and the Enlightenment* (Aberdeen, 1987), pp. 375–431.
53. Ibid., p. 376.
54. Boswell, *Life*, II, p. 28.
55. Boswell, *Journal*, p. 255.
56. Johnson, *Journey*, pp. 57, 103.
57. Johnson, *Journey*, pp. 89, 97.
58. Boswell, *Journal*, p. 62.
59. Johnson, *Journey*, p. 97.
60. Boswell, *Life*, I, p. 101.
61. Baldwin, *Latin & Greek Poems of Samuel Johnson*, p. 99.
62. Boswell, *Life*, II, p. 75.
63. Johnson, *Journey*, pp. 57, 65.
64. Johnson, *Journey*, pp. 65–6.
65. Johnson, *Journey*, p. 28.
66. Johnson, *Journey*, pp. 7, 23, 24.
67. Johnson, *Journey*, pp. 43–5.
68. *Yale Edition*, X: *Political Writings*, ed. Donald J. Greene (New Haven, 1977), pp. 114–15.
69. Vance, *Samuel Johnson and the Sense of History*, pp. 75–6, 79.
70. Howard Erskine-Hill, *Poetry of Opposition and Revolution: Dryden to Wordsworth* (Oxford, 1996), p. 128.
71. *The Poems of Samuel Johnson*, ed. David Nichol Smith and Edward L. McAdam (2nd edn., Oxford, 1974), pp. 68, 87–8, 116–17, 197; James Hogg, *The Jacobite Relics of Scotland* (Paisley, 1874), p. 1.

Part III
The Cultural Allegiance

8
Samuel Johnson and the neo-Latin Tradition

David Money

This essay discusses several aspects of Johnson's use of Latin, and seeks to place it in context. In his age the reading and composition of Latin literature flourished to an extent that is now often forgotten. First, some of his own considerable output of Latin poetry is considered. Then I examine the surviving evidence for neo-Latin works in Johnson's own collections of books, both in the sale catalogue (as edited by Donald Greene) which gives us an idea, albeit imperfect, of the scope of his library at his death, and also in the much earlier list of the books he owned as an undergraduate. Even in those early years he possessed a variety of fascinating Latin works; one or two of these are analysed at some length, together with several contemporary translations, for the light that they can shed on Johnson's appreciation of neo-Latin culture (as well as their own intrinsic interest). Finally we turn to another side of the wider neo-Latin context, to look at the vast range of new Latin that was printed and reprinted in Johnson's lifetime; only then can one attempt to assess the place of neo-Latin in eighteenth-century culture, and Johnson's own place in that Latin tradition. This is a large and varied topic; in the present essay, there is room to consider only a few parts of it. For further examples, and a wider context, the reader is asked to turn elsewhere.[1] Johnson's overall achievement as a Latinist may seem remarkable in isolation; it is less so, in comparison with some actual, or near-contemporaries (particularly, I would argue, the major lyric writer Anthony Alsop).

Johnson's Latin

Because of Johnson's vernacular reputation, a fair number of scholars have looked at Johnson's Latin (while neglecting that of many other eighteenth-century authors). I would wish to add an overview, and contribute a few specific ideas to the debate. The recent edition by Barry Baldwin[2] has much that Johnsonians will find invaluable; and also some details that may mislead them. For example, he is not a wholly reliable guide to metre, an essential aspect of neo-Latin poetry that is understandably alien to non-classicists.[3] Baldwin's useful bibliography lists a number of articles on Johnson's Latin.

Let us, then, examine some of the chief poems, starting with *Gnothi Seauton*, 'Dictionary' Johnson's outpouring of personal emotion on the completion of his laboriously revised fourth edition.[4] Howard Weinbrot rightly calls this poem 'riveting', raising questions which the private, tormented poet is unable to answer.[5] Wiesenthal, perhaps less plausibly, sees the poem's form as innovative – seeing, in effect, *Gnothi Seauton* as a 'lyric' idea in hexameter form.[6] There may be some boldness in the choice of form: yet great flexibility in the use of poetic forms is characteristic of British, and other, neo-Latin. There is a tendency among scholars to assume Johnson's Latin is original, or characteristic of his own poetic genius, when in fact he may be doing exactly the same as any other neo-Latin author might do; this is noticeable in Baldwin's general approach, as well, which can detect a Johnsonian 'style' in perfectly normal Latin (while castigating others for failing to spot faint classical echoes).

Gnothi Seauton is a melancholy poem; one cannot win either way, whether working or idle (lines 24ff.) – a significant theme for Johnsonian studies in general. Does this melancholy come close to madness? It may perhaps be worth exploring a possible connection to a relevant ancient model. Baldwin notes rather petulantly that 'none of these writers take any account of Horace, *Epistles* 1. 3. 6, "quid studiosa cohors operum struit? Hoc quoque curo" '.[7] Presumably (as not infrequently with Baldwin's parallels) this previous scholarly neglect results from the almost complete irrelevance of the passage in question; the meaning, tone and general message in Horace are completely different from Johnson's 'dolorum / Importuna cohors'. Horace means a real group of men (humorously called a military cohort); Johnson makes troops out of his troubles. Having pointed out the tenuous parallel, Baldwin does not explore any possible implications. If, by chance, Johnson *is* recalling Horace, in what tone does he do so? Is he melancholic? Or is he lightening melancholy by a humorous allusion to lively young men, who are writing the *res gestae* of their commander – the sort of hack-work for a patron that Johnson himself would despise:

> What Works of Genius do the Youth prepare,
> Who guard his sacred Person?[8]

Baldwin's predecessors also allegedly 'overlook' Horace, *Satires* [= *Sermones*] 2. 3. 14–15, the Siren of idleness; though Fleeman aptly cites Sloth's opiate fumes.[9]

Again, Baldwin does not follow up the comparison. Yet it is not so much the coincidence of a single word, 'desidia', but a deeper relationship between these poems that bears examination. Horace's satire is long: its central theme is madness. We begin with the dangers of idleness, of writer's block and bitter self-criticism – Johnsonian themes also. The presentation of human folly is light-hearted (though still with sharp points to make), and through a discussion Horace has with the Stoical busybody Damasippus – a figure wholly at home in the eighteenth century, explaining his interest thus:

> When I had lost all Business of my own,
> And at th' Exchange my ship-wreck'd Fortunes broke,
> I minded the affairs of other Folk.[10]

He became also an art-dealer and dilettante: 'In rare Antiques full curious was my taste'; he 'bought a Statue for five hundred Pound. / A perfect Connoisseur at gainful Rate.' The Florence or Rome of the Grand Tourists, and Johnson's London, were as full of such people as Horace's Rome. One Stertinius has given him advice on the nature of madness, 'quid sit furere' (line 41). The melancholy nature of men's obsessions is remorselessly exposed:

> Come all, whose Breasts with bad Ambition rise,
> Or the pale Passion, that for Money dies,
> With luxury, or Superstition's Gloom . . .[11]

The miser 'credidit ingens / Pauperiem vitium' (lines 91–2):

> Long as he liv'd, he look'd on Poverty,
> And shun'd it as the Crime of blackest Dye . . .

For everything is subject to gold: 'quas qui construxerit, ille / Clarus erit, fortis, justus – [D:] Sapiensne? – [S:] Etiam et rex, / Et quidquid volet' (lines 96–8):

> And he who piles the shining Heap, shall rise
> Noble, brave, just – [*Damasippus*] – You will not call him wise.
> [*Stertinius*] Yes; any thing; a Monarch, if he please.

The 'gen'ral massacre of gold', and crowd of suppliants 'Athirst for wealth, and burning to be great' that we find in Johnson's Juvenalian satires are not far away; in his *London*, 'all are slaves to gold'. The aged miser, a stock figure of such satire, is well depicted by Horace; yet this terrifying madness is far from rare:

> By few, forsooth, a Madman he is thought,
> For half Mankind the same Disease have caught.[12]

The doctor (lines 161ff.) is another Horatian figure with links to Johnson's attitudes; physical ill-health, as well as mental torment, much concerned him, as we see in his Latin poems to Dr. Lawrence, discussed below. As for ambition:

> That Glory ne'er may tempt ye, hear this Oath,
> By whose eternal power I bind ye both,
> Curs'd be the Wretch, an object of my Hate,
> Whoe'er accepts an Office in the State.[13]

The 'Sons of Luxury' (line 224ff.) are no better. Indeed, the picture of waste and folly, pearls dissolved in vinegar, again dramatically illustrates this mental derangement. The aged Johnson was to make a similar point in his chilling, Swiftian 'Short Song of Congratulation' on a youth's coming of age.[14]

At the end of this very extended Horatian satire on madness and folly (a work of roughly the same scale and importance as Juvenal 3 or 10), Horace turns on his informant: 'Good Stoic, mind your own.' Damasippus retorts by twitting him with 'Those thousand furious passions for the Fair –'.[15] But Horace has the final say: 'Thou mightier – Fool, inferior Ideots spare.' 'O major, tandem parcas insane minori' (line 326), which Johnson no doubt read with Francis's note: 'The Poet begins this Line, as if he designed to compliment Damasippus with a Superiority of Wisdom, but he soon undeceives his impertinent Moralist, and breaks off the Dialogue with returning him the Title of Madman. If this Remark is not a little too refined, we are obliged to Mr. Dacier for it.' It is not, indeed, too refined; and it illustrates the very considerable subtlety and playfulness with which Horace satirises the mad. Juvenal could not quite attain it; nor could Johnson. My purpose is not so much to stress the many ways in which Horace's satire underlies both Juvenal's later work, and Johnson's imitation of Juvenal, as to think about those Horatian features that Johnson is *not* willing to borrow. Horace can laugh at himself, call himself mad (lines 305–6) before rounding on his tormentor. Johnson himself is too much of the Stoic. And he is distinctly uncomfortable with madness.

The same applies to some of the Juvenal that Johnson leaves out of *The Vanity of Human Wishes*; the old man in Juvenal is presented far more harshly, as preyed on by real 'dementia'.[16] Johnson's old man may be a bore, whom 'scarce a legacy can bribe to hear', and whose petulant daughter and extravagant son 'mould his passions till they make his will'. They would have had thin pickings from Juvenal's more ghastly relic, who has forgotten the names of his servants, his children, and even the friend he dined with yesterday: 'nam codice saevo / heredes vetat esse suos, bona tota feruntur / ad Phialen; tantum artificis valet halitus oris.'[17] This savagely funny picture, entirely appropriate to the eighteenth century, is smoothed out by

Johnson; the mistress's artful mouth, good (one supposes) for more than talking, becomes no more than a spoilt daughter's. Is the madness too much for him? In the case of the scholar, he does indeed warn one of sloth and melancholy, with personal feeling; but he avoids Juvenal's harsher tone; and he would not want anyone to think of, and laugh at, his own verse, as some might, if he had followed Juvenal's mention of Cicero's 'ridenda poemata'.[18]

Returning to *Gnothi Seauton*, and considering its relation to Horace *Sermones* 2. 3, we may observe both significant similarities and equally striking differences. He, like Horace, wants to know himself; but he shies away from the madness that the robuster Roman may ridicule. Horace's enquiry stems from a lack of poetic inspiration; Johnson too knows not whither he should turn, and lacks the force to rise to poetic heights. For Johnson, there is no poetic marble to sculpt ('si marmoris absit / copia', lines 38–9): instead, both Juvenalian 'res angusta' – real poverty – and a mental poverty that is dangerously close to Horatian madness. Horace's poem might speak clearly to the eighteenth century (it is perhaps surprising that Pope didn't select it for imitation); to Johnson, the message was perhaps too loud for comfort.

Johnson's *Marmor Norfolciense* is a fascinating example of the use of Latin for Jacobite politics. The Latin version is in vigorous Leonine hexameters;[19] the pamphlet itself stresses that the lines are to be read as such, when it refers to 'the first four lines' (p. 16), meaning the first eight, as printed. Kaminski notes that 'the diversity of its structure betrays Johnson's conscious artistry and marks the work as a minor *tour de force*'; 'there is a dark cast to the Latin poem that is still evident at times even in the more decorous English version'.[20] Baldwin inevitably adduces classical 'parallels', without much further discussion. The Virgilian elements are not in fact confined to superficial 'tags'. The theme of *discordia* (from invasion, or civil war – or madness) is central to the *Aeneid*, and to our little *Marmor*. Dryden's Virgil, with its political and iconographic complexities, is in the background.[21] Virgil is particularly relevant to the central image of cowardly red serpents (i.e. Hanoverian soldiers) devastating the land. 'The particular mention of the colour of this destructive viper,' says the pamphlet's bumbling critic, 'may be some guide to us in the labyrinth . . . when . . . I heard of the multitude of lady-birds in Kent, I began to imagine that these were the fatal insects . . .' (p. 19). Baldwin briefly notes a Virgilian snake (*Aeneid* 2. 471: his p. 67, n. on line 10): there Pyrrhus is compared to a poison-eating, hissing snake in a new skin. But Johnson's snakes are 'haud pugnaces', 'of no fighting race', as is stressed in the pamphlet (p. 20): 'they will threaten, indeed, and hiss . . . but have no real courage' – the author thus incites the sufferers to resistance, rather than cowardly and ruinous submission. This sort of snake is *unlike* those one expects to meet in similes: though a snake will die, in the fourth 'Messianic' Eclogue (an obviously inspiring text for those seeking the return of a Stuart golden age); and we find fantastic colours there too, including bright red rams roaming the meadows.[22]

The sneaky 'snake in the grass', more deadly than brave, is another relevant Virgilian idea: 'latet anguis in herba' (*Eclogue* 3. 93). And in *Georgics* 4 a huge hidden serpent causes the death of Eurydice (and the despair of the poet Orpheus, so influential on his literary descendants). Shortly thereafter we meet the terrifying Furies, with a permanent wave of blue snakes.[23] Without attempting an exhaustive search, one might venture to suggest that literary snakes are more often blue than red. Thus an unwary Greek is surprised, as one who meets an angry snake's '*caerula* colla':

> He starts aside, astonish'd when he spies,
> His rising crest, blue neck, and rolling eyes;
> So from our arms, surpriz'd Androgeos flies.[24]

But the chief Virgilian serpents (ignored by Baldwin) are those that so foully consume Laocoon and his sons: and they, unlike most other snakes, are red. They have 'iubae sanguineae', 'flaming [lit.: bloody] crests' and blood-red eyes (*Aeneid* 2. 206–7, 210). The watchers are 'exsangues' (212), bloodless with fear. So the British lion, in *Marmor*, finds its blood sucked away by the Hanoverian horse. 'That a weaker animal should suck the blood of a stronger without resistance is wholly improbable' (pamphlet, p. 25); nor is a treacherous horse often the cause of disaster – except in *Aeneid* 2, when that infamous wooden horse, vainly attacked by Laocoon, and defended by red snakes, is brought into the city by an unsuspecting Trojan populace. Troy has stood for Britain before. It seems highly likely that a reader familiar with Virgil (as most were) might recall the episode while reading Johnson. He might lament Laocoon's modern equivalents, those who fought bravely, but unsuccessfully, for the old Stuart order, and against the Trojan Horse of Hanover, as the nation was 'plundered, starved, and devoured by vermin and by reptiles' (pamphlet, p. 20). Whatever one may think of Johnson's later position, *Marmor* cannot but be Jacobite; classical allusion helps to reinforce the message.

Blood opens the hexameter poem to Dr. Lawrence, 'Sanguine dum tumido'.[25] It is Johnson's own, suffusing his eye, and the poem perhaps reveals a degree of self-obsession, worrying in melancholy verse about his own symptoms, before moving to philosophy. There is a huge quantity of eighteenth-century Latin verse addressed to doctors, by doctors, or about medicine, generally more cheerful in tone – even when unpleasant symptoms call for sympathy.[26] It is perhaps surprising, given Baldwin's enthusiasm for dredging up large quantities of classical parallels, from the reasonably relevant to the rather tenuous, that he here misses one of the clearest and most striking of Johnson's allusions to Horace. Line 9, 'Sunt qui curriculo timidi versantur in arcto', alludes to Horace, *Carmina* 1. 1. 3: 'Sunt quos curriculo . . .' (an extremely familiar passage, from a great programmatic ode). *Curriculo* means a race, or race-course (or, as an adverb, 'at full speed'); it can also mean a chariot, or the course of our lives (*vitae curricu-*

lum is found in Cicero: who does not know and loathe its modern usage?). A phrase many might wish to forget, it constantly reminds us of the competitive, and ultimately vain, nature of business and academic life. So too for Johnson, and Horace: we are back to the theme of *The Vanity of Human Wishes*. Both are interested in people's different career choices; Horace is rather happier to forgive the foibles of others, while stressing his own aims are different. At the start of his collection of *Odes*, he has the enthusiasm of Johnson's young scholar: if he succeeds, his head will strike the heavens, not just Bodley's dome. The difference is that, by the end of that collection, he has actually made an everlasting memorial.

All, according to Johnson's eighth line, have a single love for truth (though various ways of searching). He ignores the less thoughtful part of mankind. There is stress on experience, and such practical men as merchants and seafarers (both regular Horatian examples), and certain types of philosopher. He gives the example of the tides: 'Scire vices ponti facile est' (line 15), 'to know the changes of the sea is easy'. The tides may be reducible to tables, and easy for the expert: the sea's other changes certainly are not, and no real sailor, or landsman with genuine maritime affinity, could have written what Johnson did. With reference to line 22, Baldwin cites Virgil, *Georgics* 2. 175, but without discussion of its context. Virgil's following line is 'Ascraeumque cano Romana per oppida carmen' – 'And old Ascraean verse in Roman cities sing'.[27] That is very similar to what Johnson himself, and other neo-Latin writers, are doing, as they renew classical forms in modern Britain. The end of the poem, after Lucretian concern with causes, takes us back to Horace's first ode. Johnson's final word, 'metam' (goal, winning-post, boundary) recalls 'metaque . . .' (*Carmina* 1. 1. 4), continuing Horace's image of the charioteer at the Olympic games, eager for rewards that the poet thinks are vain. Overall, Johnson's poem stands in a long tradition of British Latin; 'themes' (set exercises) on philosophical topics were a standard part of education, that an accomplished poet could turn to good account. Milton's *De Idea Platonica* is a good example of the genre.

Johnson periodically turned to poetical exercises: we find him playing with numbers, in his *Geographia Metrica* (Baldwin, p. 152) and elsewhere. One might compare Gray's desire to write Latin poems on beetles; in neither case was the project carried through to produce anything of real interest – as it might have been, for such works as Cowley's *Sex Libri Plantarum* (which Aphra Behn helped to translate) remind us that neo-Latin was seen as a perfectly suitable medium for major vernacular authors to approach the genuine excitements of natural philosophy. Cowley was a Fellow of the Royal Society and a Latin playwright, as well as an English and Latin poet.[28] Johnson's efforts are far less interesting than Cowley's (and for personal rather than public use). Such too are his translations from Greek. His selections from the *Anthology* covered some by Hipponax – which Baldwin misunderstands by failing to identify the metre as scazontes, limping iambics (the satirist Hipponax's invention); the metre found favour with Catullus, and many neo-Latin authors, including Milton.[29]

Johnson's Latin odes are relatively few in number, especially compared to the lyrics of such major predecessors as Alsop, but do comprise some of his finer writing (as well as some less impressive moments). Kaminski finds the mythological stanza that ends *Ad Urbanum* unsatisfactory, thinking that the subject cannot sustain such exalted treatment: 'so much pomp for so little reason' coming 'dangerously close to bathos'.[30] *In Theatro* (Baldwin, pp. 71–5) is somewhat better. In the third stanza, there is an elegant chiasmus, before a clear Horatian allusion:[31] 'Inter aequales, sine felle liber / Codices . . . inter / Rectius vives . . .'. The learned Crispus' equals are free, and without bile; there may be punning on *liber* as both 'free' and 'book', appropriately for a citizen of the Renaissance republic of letters; the books, too, may be his equals. The Horace ode to which he alludes contains the firmest advice on moderation (with the famous phrase 'aurea mediocritas', the golden mean). The overall theme of Johnson's ode, the avoidance of activities inappropriate to one's age, is thoroughly Horatian; we should also recall, in particular, *Carmina* 4. 1, where the fifty-year-old Horace ('circa lustra decem') tries to resist Venus. But there Horace subverts his own initial opposition: he has fallen in love again, with the boy Ligurinus.

Crispus' concern for truth ('veri studiosus', line 10) reminds us of the search in the hexameters to Lawrence, discussed above. Who is this Crispus? Baldwin notes the name at Horace, *Carmina* 2. 2. 3. Might there be an allusion, not just to 'Horatian colour' (his p. 74), but to the content of that ode? There we find another crucial Horatian, and Johnsonian, theme: avarice, and the need to use wealth in moderation:

> Gold hath no Lustre of its own,
> It shines by temperate Use alone.[32]

Johnson's ending, 'sapienter uti / tempore' (lines 15–16) is a similar message; *sapienter*, 'wisely', also picks up on the final stanza of the 'Rectius vives' ode, with the same word at *Carmina* 2. 10. 22 – 'Wisely contract your swelling Sail', fit advice for the victims of *Vanity*. The fourth stanza of Horace's Crispus ode, with its dropsy and 'watry Languor', also sounds a Johnsonian note of medical melancholy. And Johnson would certainly approve the mental firmness and robust independence of Horace's ending:

> Who can a treasur'd Mass of Gold
> With firm, undazzled Eye behold.

Another very famous Horatian ode is also behind *In Theatro* lines 11–12, 'sua quisque carpat / Gaudia gratus': the little poem 1. 11, with Johnson's *carpat* recalling 'carpe diem':

> Instant the fleeting Pleasure seize,
> Nor trust to-morrow's doubtful Light.

Johnson has a quite Horatian emphasis on the shortness of time; one must use it wisely, but for 'Gaudia', joys of some kind or other. The alcaic ode to Dr. Lawrence ('Fateris ergo . . .': Baldwin, pp. 117–19) has an effective use of repetition in the final stanza ('Permitte . . .'). In urging him to trust in God, 'summo . . . Patri', he echoes the final stanza of *Skia* (discussed below). He also echoes Horace: 'Permitte divis cetera':[33] leave the rest to the gods – the message of 'carpe diem', and in a Christian form, of *The Vanity of Human Wishes*: 'But leave to Heav'n the measure and the choice.'

The various Horatian comparisons we can make are given added force by the fact that Johnson, and very many of his readers, knew Horace intimately. The contemporary versions that I have been quoting, from *A Poetical Translation of the Works of Horace* by the Rev. Mr. Philip Francis (5th edn., 1753), were read and much respected by Johnson, who observed that 'the lyrical part of Horace never can be perfectly translated; so much of the excellence is in the numbers and the expression. Francis has done it the best; I'll take his, five out of six, against them all.'[34]

The two Skye odes[35] are perhaps his best lyrics. Is there any hint of romantic Jacobitism here? 'Cura exulat', in *Skia* line 5 – care, but also the thing or person one cares for, is exiled. Might that hint at the Pretender?[36] Wiesenthal sees a 'fundamental change in the Horatian structure'.[37] What he means is presumably the lack of a personal addressee. Is that so vital a change? And does not Johnson's ode, in any case, have an addressee in the vocative in the fourth line, the island of Skye herself (personified, perhaps, as the female nymph, 'Skia')? Skia's cave is as welcoming, and, in the end, as unsatisfying, as Pyrrha's cave in Horace, *Carmina* 1. 5. Skia, the nymph or island, is most welcome to the sailor ('grata', line 3; albeit also 'nebulosa', cloudy),[38] offering a 'virentem . . . sinum' (a green bay, on a coast, or lap, on a lady); Pyrrha – definitely nymph rather than rock – no doubt has good uses for her 'sinus', as she accepts the attentions of her naïve and temporary lover, that unnamed, beardless boy who reeks with needless aftershave. She is 'vacuus' and 'amabilis' (line 10; herself an open cave?), and her cave itself is described with the adjective Johnson uses for Skia ('grato . . . sub antro', line 3). Johnson's Skye cannot provide perfect peace, for only God can do that. Pyrrha's cave is no safe refuge, for she herself will turn stormy, and the unpractis'd youth 'fidem / Mutatosque Deos flebit, et aspera / Nigris aequora ventis . . . nescius aurae / Fallacis' (lines 5–7 and 11–12): and, in the popular version of Philip Francis, 'How soon behold with wondering Eyes / The blackning Winds tempestuous rise, / And scowl along the Main.' Horace's rich and subtle poem depends on a constant comparison of the girl and the forces of nature: 'simplex munditiis' (Francis's 'with careless Art' is a fair stab at the famously untranslatable phrase), her moods are deceptive. So too may Johnson's poem gain something from the island's femininity, an effect more easily gained in Horatian Latin than in English. Though far older and wiser than Horace's boy, he may flirt with Skia, as with the romantic Jacobitism of Flora's isle; and as with Mrs. Thrale herself in the second Skye ode.

Indeed, the sentiments of 'Permeo terras . . .' may be read with some ironic force, in the context of Horace's Pyrrha. Johnson's final stanza stresses Thrale's *fides* (repeated, lines 17 and 18). 'How often', as Francis might have put it, would an older man, 'Of alter'd Gods, and injur'd Truth / With Tears, alas! complain?' – when Mrs Pyrrha Piozzi proved that loyalty had its limits. The Ovidian theme of exile may permeate the poem. It is also reminiscent of Anthony Alsop's several magnificent exile poems, and others where he wonders what absent friends are up to.[39] Johnson uses repetitions (characteristic of Alsopian sapphics), in his third and fourth stanzas.

Returning to *Skia*, we may make a further instructive comparison, with Thomas Gray's 'Alcaic Ode, written in the Album of the Grande Chartreuse, in Dauphiny, August 1741'. Baldwin briefly notes the comparison, p. 100 (though saying it was written in 1740). Gray's ode seems to offer a good parallel for Johnson's choice of addressee: it is the place itself that he calls upon – strictly speaking, its *Religio* (line 1) or *Numen* (line 4), whatever form that mystical concept might take. And Gray does so with all the formality of Horace addressing a distinguished patron or deity, over three whole stanzas, the opening 'O Tu . . .' (line 1) and the greeting, 'Salve' (line 11) being separated by a long and impressive parenthesis. Johnson's greeting, by contrast, is on a much more domestic scale. Gray claims that he feels nearer to God himself, in these wild and dangerous mountains: 'Praesentiorem et conspicimus Deum . . .' – amid sheer drops, and crashing torrents, and the alliterative greyness of the groves ('. . . nemorumque noctem', line 8, a fine end to the stanza). Johnson's picture is less melodramatic, although he too deploys with skill the standard techniques of Latin lyric (which we find regularly in Alsop's more prolific and more sophisticated writing, and indeed in many other neo-Latinists). Thus his first, descriptive, stanza bristles with alliteration (especially of 'p', in lines 1, 2 and 4), and has a neat chiasmus in the second line.

In Gray's final stanza, the address to *Pater* is strikingly similar to Johnson's *Rex Summe*; both turn to God for peace from mental storms. For Johnson, it is God alone who can both raise up and calm these tempests, and ancient Stoicism will not serve; one cannot create one's own Juvenalian *mens sana* (recalling the theme of *The Vanity of Human Wishes*). In Gray's final lines, 19–20: '. . . Tutumque vulgari tumultu / Surripias, hominumque curis'. Freedom from care had also been the subject of Johnson's second stanza. The waves that are prominently placed at the end of Johnson's central and final stanzas ('. . . fluctus', lines 12 and 20) also end Gray's crucial penultimate stanza: 'me resorbens / In medios violenta fluctus'. Gray and Johnson can both use neo-Latin to express deeply personal emotion.

Johnson's books

The importance of neo-Latin for Johnson's life goes beyond his own use of the medium. He not only wrote, but also read it keenly and throughout his life. Greene examined the evidence for his mature library.[40] Neo-Latin books are certainly in evidence. Greene estimated that, due to the imperfections of the sale catalogue, we should multiply the number of books in each category by four to obtain a very rough estimate of Johnson's total holdings in that field. We can thus do little more than guess at the full range of his Latin: but Greene's calculation might suggest a total of 100 or so neo-Latin works, of all nations, and with much prose as well as verse.[41]

I propose to list some of the relevant titles, and examine one or two of them in greater detail, as particularly interesting examples of the neo-Latin culture in which Johnson participated. Some of these works are now (to say the least) rarely read by scholars. Yet many of them are of the greatest interest, both for their historical significance, and for the intrinsic quality of their writing, which is fully equal to that of the vernacular work which does tend to engage the close attention of those scholars not obsessed by their own theoretical navels. Britain's past intellectual culture can present a serious challenge to modern scholarship. That culture, though in some ways similar to ours, was also profoundly different in its linguistic expectations. Most educated people were effectively bilingual, familiar with classical Latin, and able and willing to read whatever neo-Latin caught their imaginations, sometimes also enjoying some elegant new translation alongside the original.

The list included several widely circulated continental works of the early seventeenth century, such as Alciatus, *Emblemata*, edited by C. Mignault (Leiden, 1608); Schottus, *Adagia* (Antwerp, 1629);[42] Folengo's macaronics (Venice, 1613); Vida's *Poemata*; and Cardinal Barberini (Urban VIII), *Poemata* (Antwerp, 1634) – a very elegant book, with the Cardinal's poetry offered the distinction of large and beautiful italic type by the great Plantin press; since Urban was Pope at the time of publication, this honour is hardly surprising. Johnson is notorious for neglect of the aesthetic qualities of books, and can hardly have been impressed by the beauties of this one; nevertheless, he certainly held in his hands an object that would have reminded him of the primacy of neo-Latin in seventeenth-century European culture. There are a number of significant Latin works by French authors, e.g. Rapin, *Hortorum Libri IV* (Paris, 1665) a didactic continuation of Virgil's *Georgics*; also some of Gruter's very significant anthologies of Continental Latin: his *Delitiae* of French Latin poets, and of other nations. He also had the didactic poem on painting by DuFresnoy, in Mason's new translation of 1783.[43]

The chief of Scottish Latinists, as Johnson himself acknowledged,[44] was George Buchanan, whose poems, and *Opera* (Edinburgh, 1715), naturally appear in the list. He also owned a fascinating collection of religious paraphrases (by Arthur Johnston, and others), entitled *Poetarum Scotorum Musae Sacrae* (Edinburgh, 1739), edited by his own sometime friend William Lauder, who was later disgraced for his literary forgery, in attempting to prove Milton's plagiarism of continental neo-Latin writers. A concern for such learned adaptations of the Bible is also reflected in his possession of a distinguished Greek equivalent, James Duport's Psalms (Cambridge, 1666); we may note that Johnson's copy probably had the frontispiece (extant in some copies) with a grand engraving of Charles II, together with a set of loyal verses. Duport, successively Vice-Master of Trinity and Master of Magdalene, was a staunch supporter of monarchy and of Latin composition, with whose views Johnson will have found himself often in sympathy. He also had Duport's *Homeri Gnomologia* (Cambridge, 1660). More recent neo-Latin prose scholarship is represented by Lowth's highly influential *De Sacra Poesi Hebraeorum*, of 1753. Indeed the list of modern Latin prose, both Renaissance and contemporary, is extensive, including work by Erasmus, Lipsius, Strada and Lambinus; letters by Bembo and Casaubon; medical and scientific works by Boerhaave, and by Archibald Pitcairne. This last author was highly significant as a Latin poet, and fierce Jacobite, as well as a physician; Johnson knew Pitcairne's Latin, and his politics – and certainly admired the verse, albeit less so than Buchanan's far more massive achievement.[45]

As one might expect, the mature Johnson's library illustrates his wide reading in neo-Latin literature; it is perhaps more surprising to find the same breadth of reading in the necessarily smaller, but still most impressive, collection of books which he owned as a relatively impecunious Oxford undergraduate.[46] Out of a collection of over 100 volumes, there is a substantial proportion of neo-Latin works. We find both Joseph Scaliger, *Poemata*, and J.C. Scaliger, *Poetices Libri Septem* (the latter being the chief of Renaissance literary treatises). There is More's *Utopia*, and the *Colloquia* of his friend Erasmus; Vida, *Ars Poetica* (with Pitt's translation); Buchanan, *Poemata*; Barclay's *Argenis*, and *Satyricon*; and Bonefon, *Pancharis*. Other modern Latinists appear in the *Italorum Poemata Selecta*,[47] that presumably is Francis Atterbury's 1684 *Anthologia* (later re-edited by Pope: as discussed below). As well as familiar classical authors, there is the late antique *Itinerarium* of Rutilius Namatianus. The young Johnson read Milton and Salmasius in Latin, and Hugo Grotius; among his collection of English poets was Edmund Smith's works, which included Latin poems pirated from Alsop (and likely to fascinate an Oxford student).[48] He had the *Musae Anglicanae*, in two volumes – a most important anthology of recent British (mainly Oxford) writing.

The young Johnson also owned Claude Quillet's major didactic poem on parenthood, the *Callipaedia*, together with Rowe's translation – not necessarily because he was hoping to get practical advice, but for the sheer quality of the Latin. Let us examine some aspects of Quillet's masterpiece, and its reception in eighteenth-century England – focusing particularly on his marvellous attack on English revolutionary licence in book IV.

A seventeenth-century Frenchman, Quillet still had a large English readership. A fine edition (perhaps that owned by Johnson) was printed in London in 1708/9, by J. Bowyer. There are two different English translations of 1710 (testimony to the interest roused by Bowyer's reprinting of the Latin text in the previous year); one also contains, like Bowyer's edition, the related *Paedotrophia* of St-Marthe, and is entitled *Callipaediae; or, an Art how to have Handsome Children . . . Now done into English Verse.*[49] The rival translation, 'by several hands', has a slightly different title: *Callipaedia: or the Art of Getting Pretty Children.*[50] (I refer to them here as 'H', for *Handsome*, and 'P' for *Pretty*.)

The third version of Quillet was probably written a little later in the same decade; it is often referred to as Rowe's (and appears thus in the list of Johnson's books), although in fact Rowe was responsible only for part of the first book, which he shared with Mr. S. Cobb MA. The second book was taken by Mr. Sewell, the third by Cobb, and the fourth, from which we are here quoting, was another joint effort, by Cobb and Mr. Diaper.[51] The title here is: *Callipaedia: or, the Art of Getting Beautiful Children* ['B' for short]. Rowe himself died in 1718, his funeral being conducted by Atterbury (as we learn from the *Life* by G. Sewell, p. vi); he was chiefly famed for his plays, and translation of Lucan. Some of Rowe's miscellaneous poems suggest both his robust sense of humour and his own occasional use of original neo-Latin: a nice example, in both English and ten lines of Latin elegiacs, is the epigram 'On a lady who shed her water at seeing the Tragedy of Cato' (the English may well be by Pope, the Latin is almost certainly Rowe's).[52]

Here is Quillet's attack on the English (p. 72, in Bowyer edn.):

> Anglos immanes, Regumque a caede cruentos
> Repperies: plebem effraenem, sanctisque rebellem
> Legibus, et varia cum Relligione furentem.
> Unusquisque sibi Vates, sibi quisque Sacerdos
> Hic audit proprium Genium, sequiturque proterve;
> Proque animi libito Superis imponit honorem . . .
> Et si qua antiquas convellat opinio mentes,
> Hanc subito arripiunt, et toto pectore firmant.
> Nec tamen omni laude carent; hos nautica virtus
> Ornat, et immensi divina peritia Ponti.

There is a reasonably close translation in 'H' (p. 134):

> At Calais if you cross the Streight, you'll find
> The Cruel *English* from the World disjoin'd.
> Cruel indeed, with Royal Blood defil'd,
> A Rabble, Rash, Untameable, and Wild.

> With holy Lunacy they're all possest,
> And ev'ry Man's a Prophet, or a Priest.
> Honour's with them Religion's only Guide,
> And each that fatal Rule pursues with Pride ...

Naturally enough, one might expect all this to go down poorly with an English audience. The difficulty of the fourth book is thus addressed in the Rowe version ('B', end of preface): '... the Character he gives of our own Nation was in the Time of the Civil War; which makes that severe Censure agree very well with those Days of Villany and Confusion'. It is translated accordingly ('B', p. 127):

> If then from Calais you design to land
> On *England's* vile, inhospitable Strand,
> There shall you find a race of monstrous Men,
> Where mangled Princes strew the *Cyclops* Den,
> A false, ungrateful, and rebellious Brood,
> New from a slaughter'd Monarch's Sacred Blood:
> They break all Laws, all Fancies they pursue,
> And follow all *Religions*, but the *True*:
> All there are Priests, each differently prays,
> And worships Heaven ten thousand various ways:
> If by the Mob the canting Fool's admir'd;
> The Brother's gifted, and the Saint's inspir'd:
> Hence the *Fanaticks* rave, and wildly storm,
> Convert by *Pistol*, and by *Pike* reform ...
> ... Yet we must do the Sons of *England* Right,
> Some Stars shine thro the Horror of the Night:
> For Navigation, and for Skill renown'd,
> In sailing the Terraqueous Globe around ...

But not all lovers of Quillet were so confident of their readers' magnanimity. In the preface to 'P' (sig. B3v) we find:

In his Fourth Book, where the various Customs of the several parts of Europe are describ'd, the Lines that concern Great-Britain, are wholly alter'd, even in opposition to the Original; for our Nation being at that time, when Quilletus wrote, overrun with the Confusion and Disorders of a Civil War, 'twas thought improper to make that unsettled State the Measure and Standard of a Publick and National Character. Here 'twas high time to leave the Enemy and the Frenchman: It being a plain Breach of good Nature and good Breeding, as well as the Rules of Art, to draw a Beauty with the Small Pox, or in a High Fever, and to shew that, as her Picture and Likeness, to all her Admirers.

And in practice we get a splendid and quite shameless piece of patriotic bombast, which returns to some semblance of translation only when we come to England's naval eminence, which Quillet did find it possible to mention with praise. It may have seemed to some contemporaries (as, I am sure, to even the averagely patriotic modern reader) to get more and more hilariously absurd as it goes on. Yet, being composed at the height of Britain's successes in the War of the Spanish Succession, after six years of victories (and in ignorance of the forthcoming Tory peace, and of Marlborough's eclipse), it accurately reflects how many readers will have felt about their country, feeling no incongruity in ascribing such sentiments to a supposedly impartial neo-Latin observer from a previous generation. It is perhaps worth quoting in full, as much to illustrate the thoroughness of the transformation of Claude Quillet to John Bull, as for its unintentional comedy:[53]

> Remote from *France* (the *Channel* flows between)
> White Cliffs, tall Tow'rs, and glittering Spires are seen:
> A lovely Isle adorns the Subject Seas,
> Rich in the Product of a Godlike Race,
> All brave and stout as *Mars*, as *Venus* fair,
> Gentle in Peace, and terrible in War:
> Great amidst Changes, fix'd in high Renown,
> No other Victors but themselves they own;
> What Nation can such Troops of Victors boast,
> Reviving all that *Greece* and *Rome* have lost?
> All court their Love, or to their Valour bow:
> No Bounds their Arms, no end their Triumphs know,
> Fond of their Laws, and willing to obey,
> They temper Freedom with Imperial Sway:
> Brave as in Fight, in Arts and Counsels great,
> They add new Strength and Beauty to the State;
> Religion, free from Pomp, yet still Divine,
> Does in the purest, brightest Colours Shine;
> All hearts and Eyes she conquers with her Charms,
> And with her Love the willing People warms;
> Plenty and Riches crown the smiling Plains,
> Till'd by a Race of strong industrious Swains.
> Proud *Neptune* bends beneath their awful Sway,
> And all the Winds and Waves their Sails obey,
> Beneath whose Lofty Tow'rs the Billows foam,
> Conveying endless Wealth and Plenty home,
> Or carrying dread and hostile Arms afar,
> That speak in Thunder and in Flames make War:
> *Tethys* and *Jason*, and the Grecian Band

> Of *Argonauts*, for Naval Valour fam'd,
> Must yield to these, whilst on their fruitful shores
> They empty, from both Worlds, the noblest Stores.
> Far hence, the Dutch, a mingled Nation lye
> Averse to Kings, and fond of Liberty.

And now, at last, we are back with Quillet, who also compares Britons to Argonauts, and continues with the fierceness of the Dutch in defence of freedom:

> Non Anglum Tiphys superet, non fortis Iason;
> Non quemcumque tulit velis audacibus Argo.
> Quid referam angusto divisos aequore Belgas,
> Non Celtis multum absimiles; nisi regia sceptra
> Odissent, cara pro libertate feroces?

Quillet's Latin, though of an earlier generation, remained vigorously alive in Johnson's England. Another item on the list, 'Landesii Poemata', is of particular interest for the influence it may have had on Johnson's youthful compositions, and more enduring attitudes. The same volume was later owned by Dr. Hall, the nineteenth-century Master of Pembroke: 'some peculiarities of the style . . . may be traced'.[54] This work was by a living continental Latinist, the Frenchman André Deslandes.[55] Deslandes had achieved international prominence as a neo-Latin poet by his early twenties, no more than fifteen years before Johnson's own arrival in Oxford. He could therefore provide an example for an ambitious young author: a reminder that a contemporary might still achieve as much as any of the great figures of the Renaissance, most of whom were already 'classics' from the very different society of fifteenth- or sixteenth-century Italy. Deslandes' preface, indeed, seems to foreshadow some of Johnson's later attitudes to the profession of letters, with its sturdy self-confidence and contempt for the views of fools; and the young Johnson will have perused it with sympathetic interest. Deslandes knows what he does well, and says so: 'Insaniunt *mehercle* qui omnibus student placere' [Those who are keen to please everyone are quite mad] – a sentiment with which Johnson himself might readily have agreed. Deslandes offers the example of the so-called detractors of Virgil:

> Non olim defuere, qui Virgilium arguerint. Habebatur tamen Virgilius poetarum facile princeps.[56] Sunt et hodie qui Bavii et Maevii stolidam garrulitatem curiose imitantur: Homines invidi, male cordati, et qui delicatiores litteras vix primis labris degustarunt. Horum judicis quis sanus reformidet? Mihi quidem gratulor et diu gratulabor, qui viris tantum politioribus placuerim. Carpant me tenebriones insulsi, turpiculi scurrae . . .
> [There were once people who censured Virgil; yet he was taken to be easily the chief of poets. Today, too, there are those who diligently imitate the

foolish loquacity of a Bavius or a Maevius;[57] these are envious, bad-hearted men, who have scarcely tasted the more dainty titbits of literature. What sane man would be frightened of their judgement? As for me, I can indeed congratulate myself (and will long continue to do so), if I please only more polished gentlemen. Let tasteless tricksters and dirty little dandies carp at me!]

Deslandes has a particular fondness for hendecasyllables: he provides three books of them, more than thirty pages in the London edition.[58] This metre is particularly associated with Catullus (and his Renaissance imitators); Catullan vocabulary is, unsurprisingly, prominent – and handled with precocious verve. The first poem of book 2 might particularly have attracted Johnson, for there he addresses his own library: 'Ad meam bibliothecam':

> Salvete aureoli precor libelli,
> Meae deliciae, meae lepores . . .

[Be well, I pray, my golden little tomes – my sweet delight, my store of wit . . .]; he then proceeds to enumerate some of the delights he has in store, from ancient poets through to an interesting range of neo-Latinists, including 'jocose' Cotta, 'blandior' Bembo, the modest Muse of Marcantonio Flaminio, and finally:

> Amoenisque jocans Rapine in hortis.
> Omnes denique vos quibus negatum est
> Includi rigido nimis phaleuco.

[. . . and Rapin, joking in your pleasant gardens; and all of you, at last, whose names won't fit in this too-rigid metre of mine.][59] There is also a book of *Sylvae*, with some further light-hearted pieces; the young Deslandes is not afraid to address with familiarity the great and good in the international republic of letters, as in his 'Nugarum laus satyrica, ad Isaacum Newtonum' [satirical praise of trifles: to Isaac Newton]. His third book of hendecasyllables had also praised Abraham De Moivre, 'insignem Matheseos cultorem' and correspondent of Newton.[60] In the same book he returns to the sharpness of the preface, with 'Ad Zoilum, qui me scripto ineleganti carpserat . . .' and 'Ad sciolos quosdam . . .', both counter-attacks against the sort of dull scholarly criticism that he despised. Johnson will have read these neo-Latinists, and learned much.

Johnson in context

Alexander Pope offers a fascinating comparison with Johnson. Although Johnson, unlike Pope, did compose a significant amount of original Latin, it was Pope rather than Johnson who managed to produce a major neo-Latin volume, by editing the works of earlier, chiefly Italian, Latin poets; the young Johnson made ambitious plans to publish similar works; but these never came to fruition.[61] For Pope, the neo-Latin anthology was a work of personal piety, for he was revising the important *Anthologia* of his friend Francis Atterbury (the exiled Jacobite leader, who had, with John Freind and others, also been in Alsop's circle). Atterbury's work dated from 1684, over fifty years before Pope's revision of 1740: thus a work of Atterbury's youth was thought worthy of Pope's attention in maturity. This anthology is not the least interesting of Pope's major projects (though it has as yet received very little attention from modern experts on Pope). It reminds us of the vital place of neo-Latin in British culture, and in Pope's own literary concerns. A thorough analysis and edition, highlighting the reasons for Pope's often major changes to Atterbury's original, would be welcome.[62]

Neo-Latin is not infrequently political, and sometimes subversive. Some of the finest eighteenth-century Latin writers were Jacobite: Alsop was one, William King another, Pitcairne a third.[63] Those who did have sedition to preach found Latin a valuable medium: potentially ambiguous, probably uncensored, but still hard-hitting and much-read. There is no room here to discuss the major issue of neo-Latin libraries; Johnson's interest was shared by numerous private and institutional collectors. One should perhaps emphasise that it was *not* a simple matter of owners of neo-Latin books being Jacobite: on the contrary, all educated people were likely to read them. And there were a number of major Whiggish writers of Latin (such as Addison; or William Hogg).[64]

This is a rather different matter from the question of 'Anglo-Latin Toryism' which has been raised in recent debates. 'Anglo-Latin' can be taken to mean a number of things. A general interest in, and debt to, the classics might be taken as a sign of 'Anglo-Latin' culture, in the broadest sense. In this sense most educated people, of whatever political opinions, might be termed participants. Translation of classical Latin into English may also be counted. And most of this writing can be considered part of 'polite literature'.[65] But there is also a more restricted sense, that may offer a more helpful defini-tion: that of active participation in the writing (and also reading, and translation into English) of original neo-Latin poetry. Though far from exclusively 'Tory', neo-Latin *was* a convenient medium for politically sensi-tive, or indeed blatantly seditious, writing; that others shared a general clas-sical culture does not detract from this point.[66] Perusal of some of Alsop's poetry (e.g. 1. 11, 3. 1, 3.3) should make clear the particular vitality of Jacobite Latin. It could also produce some tremendous bawdiness, as from time to time in Alsop, and regularly in the less sophisticated Benjamin Loveling, who also imitated Persius in English for political ends.[67]

Latin could also be used successfully for large-scale poetry. Johnson might have done so, but never quite managed it. In comparison to Johnson, we might adduce the substantial *De Animi Immortalitate* of Isaac Hawkins Browne (1754), with several English versions, one by Soame Jenyns (who earned Johnson's scorn elsewhere: yet his translation is far from contemptible. It was readable, popular, and serious).[68] I would definitely consider it comparable in quality and stature to Johnson's major (but shorter) English poems, *London* and *The Vanity of Human Wishes*.

Some new neo-Latin works attained much immediate, and lasting, popularity, evidence of a lively culture. Such was Holdsworth's comic gem, *Muscipula* [Mouse-Trap], a great success in 1709 – the same year as Quillet had caught readers' imaginations. It even spread to the colonies: there is a translation by R. Lewis, printed by W. Parks at Annapolis, Maryland, in 1728: 'the smallest attempt to cultivate polite Literature, in Maryland, has been received with such ample Testimonies of Candor and Generosity . . . ' (end of preface, p. xiii). There follow English dedicatory verses to the Governor of Maryland, Benedict Leonard Calvert:

> . . . This FIRST ESSAY
> Of Latin Poetry, in English Dress,
> Which MARYLAND hath publish'd from the Press . . .
> . . . But all Translators must with Grief confess
> That while they strive in English to express
> The pleasing Charms of Latin Poesy,
> They lose its genuine Life, and Energy:
> Some Grace peculiar thro' each language flows
> Which other Idioms never can disclose.

The Bodleian copy of Lewis's translation was sent by Calvert, the dedicatee, to 'my good friend' the Oxford Nonjuror Thomas Hearne, with Calvert's note, 'hae nugae, seria ducent' [these trifles will lead to serious things].[69] This lively satire on the Welsh had an enduring reputation, well into the period of Johnson's own literary activity: 'No modern piece of Latin poetry was ever received better, being soon diffused in several editions, and appearing in three English translations, one in blank verse and two in rime. Nor did its run continue onely for some time after its first appearance; but, being a true classical composition, is still constantly read with the highest delight and admiration' (London edn., 1749, p. iv).

Considerations of space preclude a more detailed survey here. But I would like briefly to stress two further indicators of the range of the neo-Latin context: first, the many hundreds of Johnson's contemporaries who published splendid verse in university commemorative collections;[70] and second, the variety and quality of work to be found in anthologies – not only Pope's Italians, but also the Englishmen of the *Musae Anglicanae*, and, towards the end of Johnson's life, of Edward Popham's major collection, which amused polite and learned society in Bath and London.[71] Many of

Johnson's themes are found in Popham's poets, at greater length and with equal or greater verve. Religion is well represented, and the biblical paraphrases of Burton or Jortin surpass Johnson's religious Latin. Daily life shows all its pleasures (including theatre, smoking, football, billiards). Public events and heroes are celebrated, as are physicians (comparable to Johnson's Dr. Lawrence). Accomplished Horatian lyrics share space with other genres, the whole filling hundreds of pages (three volumes, in one version of Popham's collection).

How does Johnson's own Latin compare with the work of this vast array of predecessors and contemporaries? His performance is occasionally impressive, but far from the massive superiority that we might expect from the most prominent and most learned literary figure of his age. To speak of the 'Age of Johnson' might make sense in vernacular terms, as a reflection of his overall greatness; but it would be virtually meaningless for neo-Latin literature, in which Johnson is no more than a practitioner of average merit and productivity. That is not to say his work is poor; just that the general standard is high. And, while Johnson may not mean much to the neo-Latin tradition, Latin clearly meant much to him. His Latin poetry is a vital part of his poetic output, which no Johnsonian scholar can afford to ignore. Had his great energies been more consistently devoted to the art, it is possible to imagine Johnson as a really major Latin (or indeed English) poet, a colossus of modern epic or lyric; but it was not to be, and he remained a talent of the middle rank, with that part of his potential largely unfulfilled. His temperament, and financial circumstances, perhaps made such single-minded Latinity impossible to achieve. Rarely, too, can scholarship of his high order be combined with the highest levels of poetic creativity; few major British neo-Latin poets were very serious classical scholars, or vice versa.[72] Let us read and respect both Johnson's Latin, and that of his contemporaries.

Notes

1. See D.K. Money, *The English Horace: Anthony Alsop and the Tradition of British Latin Verse* (British Academy, Oxford, 1998). Ch. 8, 'After Alsop', contains discussion of Johnson, some of which is drawn on for the present paper. The bibliography suggests some other primary and secondary sources that may be of interest to Johnsonians.
2. Barry Baldwin, *The Latin & Greek Poems of Samuel Johnson: Text, Translation, and Commentary* (London, 1995).
3. Mistakes noted in Money, *English Horace*, pp. 218–21. N.b. especially Baldwin's failure to identify correctly iambics (his p. 96), anapaests (p. 122), trimeters (p. 142), or hexameters (pp. 151, 153); or to print Greek properly (p. 47): surprising from a classical publisher.
4. Baldwin, *Poems of Samuel Johnson*, pp. 75–86 (other scholars' discussions cited, p. 79).

5. H.D. Weinbrot, 'Johnson's Poetry', in G. Clingham (ed.), *The Cambridge Companion to Samuel Johnson* (Cambridge, 1998), pp. 34–50 ('Post Lexicon . . .' [i.e. *Gnothi Seauton*] at pp. 43–4).

6. A.J. Wiesenthal, 'On the literary value of Samuel Johnson's Latin verse', *Humanistica Lovaniensia*, 28 (1979), pp. 294–301, at 295.

7. Baldwin, *Poems of Samuel Johnson*, p. 84 (on lines 27–31).

8. The translation is Francis's (discussed further below).

9. Baldwin, *Poems of Samuel Johnson*, p. 84 (on lines 24–5); *The Vanity of Human Wishes*, line 150.

10. Horace, *Sermones* 2. 3, lines 18–20: '. . . aliena negotia curo'; Francis's version (and text) is used in this and the following extracts.

11. Lines 78–9: 'argenti pallet amore; / Quisquis luxuria, tristive superstitione' – a fine and memorable four-word hexameter.

12. 'Nimirum insanus paucis videatur; eo quod / Maxima pars hominum morbo jactatur eodem' (lines 120–1).

13. Lines 179–81: 'ne vos titillet gloria . . .' – another wonderful phrase: glory as tickling temptress.

14. Discussed by Weinbrot in Clingham (ed.), *Cambridge Companion*, pp. 44–5.

15. Of both sexes: 'Mille puellarum, puerorum mille furores'; not a chiasmus to be decently rendered.

16. Juvenal 10. 233.

17. 'He forbids his own kin to be heirs, in a savage will: everything goes to his mistress – such is the power of a professional's breath', Juvenal 10, lines 236–8.

18. Juvenal 10. 124; see further Money, *English Horace*, p. 220. For extended discussion of *The Vanity of Human Wishes* in context: H.H. Erskine-Hill, *Poetry of Opposition and Revolution* (Oxford, 1996), pp. 139–66.

19. Baldwin, *Poems of Samuel Johnson*, pp. 63–8 (who does not use the standard term, Leonine, though aware that the lines make up hexameters with internal rhyme, p. 67). 'Leonine' (though of different derivation) might suit the beleaguered British lion. For Jacobite medallic parallels, etc., see Erskine-Hill, in *AJ*, 7 (1996), pp. 11–12.

20. Thomas Kaminski, *The Early Career of Samuel Johnson* (Oxford, 1987), pp. 100–1.

21. Cf. Erskine-Hill's concept of the 'twofold vision', in *ELH*, 64 (1997), pp. 903–24, esp. 915–17.

22. Virgil, *Eclogue* 4. 24, 43–4; Baldwin notes 'mood' and language from *Ecl.* 4 later in *Marmor* (but not here): his p. 67.

23. Virgil, *Georgics* 4. 458–9, 482–3.

24. Virgil, *Aeneid* 2. 380–2 (Dryden's translation, lines 512–14).

25. Baldwin, *Poems of Samuel Johnson*, pp. 86–91.

26. As for example in Alsop 2. 16: Money, *English Horace*, p. 311.

27. Virgil, *Georgics* 2. 176 (Dryden's trans., line 246); Ascraean = Hesiodic.

28. See Money, *English Horace*, pp. 50–2 (Cowley), 208–18 (Gray).

29. *Ad Salsillum . . . Scazontes*. See now J.K. Hale's selection of Milton's Latin for *Bibliotheca Latinitatis Novae*: Assen, Van Gorcum, 1998. Johnson's scazontes: Money, *English Horace*, pp. 222–3.

30. Kaminski, *Early Career*, pp. 17–18.

31. Horace, *Carmina* 2. 10 (as Baldwin notes, without further discussion, p. 75).

32. Horace, *Carmina* 2. 2, 1–2 ('Nullus argento color est avaris . . .'); Francis's trans. (as below, for lines 23–4).

33. Horace, *Carmina* 1. 9. 9 (line 13, especially, is very similar to 1. 11).

34. Boswell, *Life*, III, p. 356 (16 May 1778).

35. *Skia* ('Ponti profundis . . .'): Baldwin, *Poems of Samuel Johnson*, pp. 97–102; and 'Permeo terras . . .', pp. 103–6.

36. See analysis at Money, *English Horace*, p. 222. Nothing is provable; but I do see a possible hint. For such nuances, cf. Erskine-Hill, 'A kind of *Liking* for Jacobitism', in *AJ*, 8 (1997), pp. 3–14.

37. Wiesenthal, 'On the literary value of Samuel Johnson's Latin verse', 299; he misnumbers the Leuconoe / 'carpe diem' ode, p. 298: it is 1. 11, not 'ix'.

38. Perhaps punning too on Skia as shadowy and mysterious, from the Greek (a connection Baldwin notes only in another context, p. 106).

39. See Money, *English Horace*, pp. 173–83, etc.: especially discussions of Alsop 2. 6, 2. 9, 2. 10, 2. 11, 2. 12, 2. 23. Thrale's family life recalls that of Alsop's friend Sir John Dolben. Savage people: 2. 12. 9–12, etc. (cf. Johnson's 'Permeo . . .', 5–8).

40. Donald Greene, *Samuel Johnson's Library: an annotated guide* (Victoria, BC, 1975: E.L.S. monograph no. 1).

41. Though one must stress this can only be the roughest of guides: it could easily have been as few as 70 or as many as 150.

42. I.e. *Paroimiai Hellenikai. Adagia sive proverbia* . . . ; Johnson had one of several early seventeenth-century editions.

43. On DuFresnoy and his translators, see my article on didactic poetry, 'A symphony in Gray and Browne . . .' in *Kleos*, 4 (Bari, 1999), pp. 141–54 and forthcoming work there cited by Y.A. Haskell and others.

44. Cf. Boswell, *Life*, V, p. 58 (cited Baldwin, *Poems of Samuel Johnson*, p. 100; also p. 2, etc.).

45. Cf. Money, *English Horace*, pp. 142–9, with several Jacobite examples discussed.

46. Reade, *Johnsonian Gleanings*, V: Johnson's undergraduate library, pp. 213–29.

47. Ibid., p. 216.

48. Money, *English Horace*, p. 106.

49. This is ESTC t077305; London, J. Morphew, 1710.

50. This is ESTC t077310; London, B. Lintott, 1710; attributed to W. Oldisworth in subsequent editions.

51. Information taken from 3rd edition: London, W. Feales, 1733; bound up with Rowe's *Miscellaneous Works*. This is a variant copy of ESTC t019838.

52. N. Ault and J. Butt (eds.), *Alexander Pope: Minor Poems* (Twickenham edn., VI, 1964, repr. London, 1993), pp. 99–100: 'Upon a [Tory] Lady . . .'.

53. 'P', pp. 63–4: book 4, lines 675–708.

54. Reade, *Johnsonian Gleanings*, V, p. 220.

55. A.F. Deslandes ('Landesius'), 1690–1757; *Poetae Rusticantis Literatum Otium: sive Carmina Andreae Francisci Landesii* (2nd edn., London: B. Lintott, 1713). A third London edition followed in 1752 (including an iambic poem on the death of Malebranche, d. 1715).

56. A phrase used also of Johnson's favourite Scottish Latinist, George Buchanan, 'prince of poets'.

57. Opponents of Virgil, famously satirised in the *Eclogues*.

58. Phaleucorum liber primus, pp. 12–25; secundus, 26–37; tertius, 38–43.

59. On this topos, cf. R. Kassel, 'Quod versu dicere non est', *Kleine Schriften* (Berlin, 1991), pp. 131–7; also Alsop 2. 14. 1–2: Money, *English Horace*, p. 307.

60. Cf. Money, *English Horace*, p. 162.

61. E.g. his plan to edit Politian, 1734 (Boswell, *Life*, I, p. 90), for which he borrowed – and never returned – a 'very old and curious edition' from Pembroke.

62. I have provided a brief analysis: *English Horace*, pp. 101–4.

63. The issue is discussed extensively in Money, *English Horace*.

64. Hogg deserves attention: cf. Money, *English Horace*, p. 141 for a Williamite effusion, one of many.

65. Cf. L.E. Klein, *Shaftesbury and the Culture of Politeness* (Cambridge, 1994): a Whig, philosophical politeness coexisted with a reading of elegant neo-Latin. NB also Thomas Kaminski's essay in the present volume and idem, 'Rehabilitating "Augustanism": on the Roots of "Polite Letters" in England', *Eighteenth Century Life*, 20 (1996), pp. 49–65.

66. Thus M. Caldwell, 'Dr. Clark and Mr Holmes: speculation in Johnsonian biography', *AJ*, 8 (1997), pp. 133–48 (a regrettable article: Caldwell's rather pointless list, p. 141; and *which* Hill or Philips does he mean?).

67. Cf. forthcoming work by R.A. Kennedy and D.K. Money; on his English: C.S. Dessen, 'An Eighteenth Century Imitation of Persius, *Sat.* 1', *Texas Studies In Literature and Language*, 20 (1978), pp. 433–56.

68. See my *Kleos* article, cited above; *English Horace*, pp. 212–17.

69. From Horace, *Ars Poetica* 451 (on the need for ruthless criticism); the *seria* were originally *mala*.

70. See Money, *English Horace*, chapter 9.

71. See brief survey, Money, *English Horace*, pp. 227–8; Leicester Bradner, *Musae Anglicanae* (New York and London, 1940), pp. 292–6. I hope to offer more detail elsewhere.

72. For Alsop's one scholarly effort (despised by his opponent, Bentley) see Money, *English Horace*, ch. 4; Bentley's own poetry is negligible (cf. Boswell, *Life*, IV, 23–4: 'forcible verses of a man of strong mind, but not accustomed to write verse'). Two who combined poetry and scholarship were Michael Maittaire, and Joshua Barnes: prolific classical editors, but no Bentleys.

9
Some Alien Qualities of Samuel Johnson's Art

Thomas Kaminski

In recent decades scholars of the visual arts have demonstrated rather convincingly that aesthetic responses are largely conditioned by one's previous experiences of art. In other words, we recognise something as artful only when we have been schooled, either formally or informally, in its techniques.[1] Thus the Impressionist painters, whose artistry is immediately recognisable to modern viewers, often seemed crude or ridiculous to their contemporaries, especially to their 'academic' contemporaries.[2] Our modern taste, though, has been trained to respond to their paintings, and we may even have been taught to see the natural world differently through their eyes. Conversely, when an artistic movement has had its day, the skills of reading its cues and interpreting its symbols can be lost, leaving the art with a distant, alien feel. Thus Egyptian art will often seem to us inscrutably formal; and the mosaics of Ravenna, which represented the height of artistic sophistication in their day, can seem naive, even simplistic, coming as they do in the wake of the great realistic achievements of the Greco-Roman tradition.[3]

What I have said of the visual arts applies equally to literature. In reading the literature of the past we are generally confronted with the problem of applying our modern expectations to works created by authors with very different aesthetic assumptions. Samuel Johnson, I wish to argue, poses a particularly difficult case. Some characteristics of his artistry are so alien to the modern taste that they are frequently (in some cases almost universally) overlooked. This can be true even in the case of readers who find Johnson's moral vision rich and compelling and who admire him as a prose stylist or a poet. In this essay, I will survey some of the artistic techniques that Johnson employed in both his prose and his poetry, especially those that seem to me far removed from the modern taste and that modern critics often seem to miss. Although the body of the essay may appear somewhat desultory as I move from one brief passage to another, I shall try to redeem myself at the end by discussing some of the basic assumptions that underlie these alien qualities.

I will start with a passage that is familiar to every serious reader of Johnson, the introductory paragraph of *Rambler* 60:

> All joy or sorrow for the happiness or calamities of others is produced by an act of the imagination, that realizes the event however fictitious, or approximates it however remote, by placing us, for a time, in the condition of him whose fortune we contemplate; so that we feel, while the deception lasts, whatever motions would be excited by the same good or evil happening to ourselves.[4]

To a modern reader, the beginning of this passage may seem to contain a critical ambiguity: 'all joy or sorrow for the happiness or calamities of others' might imply the possibility of feeling joy for the calamities of others and sorrow at their good fortune. Such sentiments were by no means unheard of in the eighteenth century, as evidenced by Swift's adaptation of one of La Rochefoucault's maxims near the beginning of the 'Verses on the Death of Dr. Swift':

> In all distresses of our friends
> We first consult our private ends,
> While nature, kindly bent to ease us,
> Points out some circumstance to please us.[5]

But the remainder of Johnson's sentence eliminates the possibility of such a reading. Our own feelings, Johnson tells us, are guided by an act of the imagination that places us in the condition of some other person, allowing us to experience for a time the feelings appropriate to that condition. An enterprising critic might find in this passage an ingenious strategy on Johnson's part, perhaps calling it 'entrapment', a term that had a brief vogue about a decade ago. That is, Johnson lures you into a morally compromised response, forcing you to acknowledge that you might, in a Swiftian manner, feel joy at the calamities of others, but then, as the sentence proceeds, makes you realise the impropriety of such feelings. But ambiguities of this sort played a much smaller role in Johnson's scheme of literary valuations than they do in ours, and when compared with the elegance of an artfully constructed period, they would have seemed trivial.

Johnson, of course, would often have encountered similar syntactic patterns in classical prose. Note the arrangement of words in the following sentence from Seneca's essay *De Vita Beata*:

> Ne quid aut bonum aut malum existimes, quod nec virtute nec malitia continget.[6]
> [You should not consider anything either a good or an evil that will not be the result of either virtue or vice.]

The Latin passage possesses the same potential for linguistic (and moral) ambiguity as Johnson's English sentence; but for Seneca, 'good' is clearly the result of 'virtue' and 'evil' the result of 'vice'. To interpret the passage otherwise is to do violence to Seneca's intention and his art. Johnson no less than Seneca would have dismissed the potential for ambiguity in his own sentence, for he would have assumed an audience attuned to and appreciative of his artful arrangement of words.

With this passage still in mind, let me turn next to what I call the 'disguised concreteness' of Johnson's *Rambler* style. It is a commonplace that Johnson favoured the general over the particular; it is not the task of the poet, as we all know, to number the streaks of the tulip. And so we readily acknowledge the high level of abstraction in Johnson's prose, especially noticeable in the Latinate diction of the *Rambler*. Unfortunately, our assumptions about the 'abstract' quality of Johnson's diction can prevent us from recognising the fundamental concreteness of his style. The passage that I have just been discussing offers us an illustration of this underlying concreteness. When Johnson writes of 'an act of the imagination that realizes the event however fictitious, or approximates it however remote', he expresses two very specific, totally concrete ideas. The word 'realize' here means 'to bring into being' (its primary definition in the *Dictionary*), and the word 'approximate' means, according to its Latin root, 'to bring near to'. Thus 'to realize the fictitious' is to make real to us things that are made up, and 'to approximate the remote' is to bring close to us things that are far off. The diction may seem Latinate and abstract, but the root meanings of 'realize' and 'approximate' should convey to the attentive reader highly specific, concrete actions.

Johnson was of course compiling the *Dictionary* at the same time that he was writing the *Rambler* essays, and as William Wimsatt pointed out many years ago, the experience of compiling the one had a profound influence on the style of the other.[7] In the *Dictionary*, Johnson often gave a literal translation of a Latin root as one of the definitions of a word, even if this meaning was not in common usage. He justified this practice in the 'Preface': 'The original sense of words is often driven out of use by their metaphorical acceptations, yet must be inserted for the sake of a regular origination. Thus I know not whether *ardour* is used for *material heat*, or whether *flagrant*, in English, ever signifies the same with *burning*; yet such are the primitive ideas of these words, which are therefore set first, though without examples, that the figurative senses may be commodiously deduced.'[8] In the *Ramblers*, these 'primitive ideas' are often present just beneath the surface of the prose, providing concrete images that support the broader general meaning of a passage. Wimsatt was the first modern critic to comment on this characteristic of Johnson's style. As he said in *Philosophic Words*, 'Johnson reminds us that *rectitude* is straight, *simplicity* simple, *asperity* rough, the *obdurate* hard, the *insipid* tasteless; that *superfluities* run, and that *plentitude* is full.'[9] The Latin word *acerbus* means 'bitter', and for Johnson the 'exacerbation' of misery is never just some indistinct worsening of it, but the increase of its bitterness and pain. And when he says in *Rambler* 172 that flattery can 'obtund remorse', he has created a metaphor, for *obtundo* is the Latin word for dulling or blunting something sharp; and the root of the word 'remorse' (*mordeo*) means to bite. Remorse, then, has sharp teeth, but flattery can dull their edge and keep us from feeling their smart.

In another sentence from *Rambler* 60, we can see Johnson's disguised concreteness operating at its finest. Asserting a 'uniformity in the state of man', he says, 'We are all prompted by the same motives, all deceived by the same fallacies, all animated by hope, obstructed by danger, entangled by desire, and seduced by pleasure.'[10] The remarkable quality of this sentence lies in the concrete images embedded in its participles. To 'prompt' is not merely to suggest or encourage, but literally to move something forward; and to 'animate' has, in its Latin root, a much greater force than in its pallid English counterpart – it means 'to give life to'. (Once again, this is Johnson's primary definition in the *Dictionary*.) Thus we are all moved forward by the same incitements; and hope actually breathes life into our intents. Each of the last three participles contributes to a single image – an interrupted journey. To 'obstruct' is to place obstacles in the way, to 'entangle' (the only Germanic participle of the group) is to catch in a snarl, and to 'seduce' is to lead aside. Danger piles obstacles in our path, desire catches us in its snarls, and pleasure leads us from the road. It is, of course, the journey of life. In fact, if we fail to perceive the concrete images in the roots of Johnson's words, some of his phrases, like 'deceived by fallacies'[11] and 'seduced by pleasure', seem otiose or tautological. It is only when we recognise 'the primitive meanings' of the Latinate words that clear images force themselves on the reader and bring the prose to life.

If we turn now to Johnson's poetry, we find many of the same tendencies towards disguised concreteness, but these images are often used in the service of even more subtle or complicated forms of poetic figuration. Because these qualities of Johnson's language often go unperceived, many modern readers find his poetry dry and lifeless, admirable perhaps for its sententiousness and instructive exempla, but more or less devoid of the qualities that constitute 'real' poetry. It was not long after Johnson's death, of course, that many of the techniques that he employed ceased to be valued or even recognised. Coleridge's famous censure of the opening of *The Vanity of Human Wishes* as 'mere bombast and tautology as if to say "Let observation with extensive observation observe mankind extensively"' is well known.[12] Johnson's partisans leap to his defence by noting that 'observation' here is personified, but even that justification often seems lukewarm. I wish to bolster that defense a bit by adding a classical context – not a source, but a stylistic parallel.

When Johnson says, 'Let observation with extensive view, / Survey mankind, from China to Peru', the personification is brought into being by the use of the active verb 'survey'. Abstractions are only abstractions until they are given something to do. Coleridge thought the lines tautological because surveying is to some extent implicit in the concept of observing; but in joining an abstract noun with a concrete active verb, Johnson employed a highly compressed form of figurative language that he would have found in one of the classical writers he most admired, Juvenal. Here are a few lines from the Tenth Satire:

> Quosdam praecipitat subjecta potentia magnae
> Invidiae, mergit longa, atque insignis honorum
> Pagina;[13]

[Power, exposed to great envy, overthrows certain men; a long and distinguished list of public offices sinks them.]

Notice that each of the clauses contains an image in its verb. *Praecipitat* means, literally, to throw something headlong; *mergit* suggests dunking something under water. It is of course common for verbs of all languages to lose their imagistic force. The word I used above to translate *praecipitat*, 'overthrow', is a good example. English speakers do not generally feel the physical sense of 'throwing over' in the verb. Roman poets, though, in their highly compressed poetic idiom, often isolated a verb in such a way that brought its imagistic force back to life.[14] In this example, then, we must see 'power' (*potentia*) throwing men headlong from the heights, and feel the list of a man's achievements (*pagina*), perhaps through its very weight or awkwardness, dragging him beneath the surface.[15] This sort of two-word figure is precisely the technique that we encounter at the beginning of the *Vanity*. Johnson has not merely offered us a tautology; rather, he has isolated a concept that is necessary to his study of human nature ('observation') and given it an appropriate activity. The general statement gains in impact through the visual image it is intended to stimulate in the reader's mind. Coleridge may indeed have recognised what Johnson was doing, but a shift in taste had occurred since Johnson's day, and he either could not or would not value such writing.

By this discussion of the figurative tradition behind Johnson's lines I do not wish to suggest that the opening couplet of the *Vanity* is great poetry; it is not. There are, though, some astonishing things in that poem. Let me choose a single couplet, the concluding lines of Johnson's passage on Xerxes, to demonstrate what Johnson can achieve within the constraints of conventional diction and neoclassical form.[16]

Johnson's portrait of Xerxes has surprisingly little in common with Juvenal's. A different set of issues engages each author, and the two treatments differ greatly in both tone and technique: Juvenal is all derisive irony, Johnson instructive example. Each passage, though, achieves its climax with the aftermath of the battle of Salamis. In the *Vanity* Xerxes reaches 'Th' insulted sea' (which earlier he had lashed) and escapes in a 'single skiff'. Here is Johnson's depiction of the scene:

> Th' incumber'd Oar scarce leaves the dreaded Coast
> Through purple Billows and a floating Host.[17]

The structure of the lines is thoroughly conventional: each noun has a single modifier; and two of the nouns ('billows' and 'host'), like two of the adjectives ('dreaded' and 'purple'), are drawn from the standard poetic vocabulary of the day. And yet the lines seem cryptic. Why is the oar encumbered? What is this floating host? The answer is in Juvenal, who had provided an image both graphic and concise. Xerxes escapes

> Nempe una nave cruentis
> Fluctibus, ac tarda per densa cadavera prora.

> (ll. 185–6)

[with one ship amid bloody waves, its prow slow through the dense bodies.]

If we re-read Johnson's highly conventional couplet in terms of Juvenal's graphic description, we recognise a powerful visual picture painted with a few suggestive brush-strokes: the oar is encumbered by dead bodies, the sea turned purple with blood. Few modern readers, I suspect, actually *see* these images, for modern prejudices against conventional language tend to blur its pictorial qualities. Such language, though, often contains a set of visual cues by which the attentive reader, his imagination at the ready, can construct an entire scene.[18] Note that Johnson mentions only the oar, but that is all we need; it implies the skiff. Pictorially it functions like some exaggerated element in a baroque painting. And thematically it focuses our attention on the appropriate detail, for the encumbering of the oar is at the center of the couplet's significance.

This use of a single concrete noun to suggest a larger picture is another technique that we find elsewhere in Juvenal, in this case at the fall of Sejanus. In his most concise yet powerful manner, he says,

> Sejanus ducitur unco
> Spectandus.

> (ll. 66–7)

[Sejanus is led by the hook so that he might be viewed.] This line, also cryptic I expect to modern readers, depicts in the briefest possible manner the horrific practice of dragging a corpse through the streets, a large hook thrust through the neck or up under his chin. The verb in this case (*ducitur*) is very bland, throwing maximum force onto the concrete noun at the end of the line, *unco* (hook). And just as *unco* carries a strong visual impact, *spectandus* bears equally strong social force: Sejanus's body is to be 'viewed' in this manner by the populace so that they might learn the appropriate lesson. In four words Juvenal has compressed a remarkable amount of image and commentary. For the English neoclassical poet, as for the Augustan and post-Augustan Roman poets, abundance of detail was not necessary for a picture, just the appropriately chosen detail. Johnson's oar, like Juvenal's hook, focuses attention on the most important matter at hand, and the reader's imagination does the rest.

In addition to the visual impact of the lines, Johnson has elaborated his couplet in other remarkable ways. The phrase 'floating host' would have been a fitting description for the mighty Persian fleet before the battle of Salamis; it takes on a powerful irony when we realise that it is now an army of corpses. Johnson's 'purple billows' echoes Pope's glorious image of the sun rising 'o'er the purpled Main' at the beginning of the second Canto of *The Rape of the Lock*; and could any colour be more fitting than purple for the regal progress of Xerxes, even in retreat? But now the waves are purple with blood. And finally, the word 'incumbered' constitutes a bilingual pun. In various Latin authors, including both Virgil and Juvenal, *incumbere remis* is the common term for 'plying oars'.[19] In Johnson's phrase, then, the 'incumbered' oar is simultaneously strained at by the rowers and impeded by the bodies in the water.

Modern readers are always in danger of missing the richness of such a couplet because of the conventionality of its language. But conventionality has a sophistication of its own for those who refuse to dismiss 'poetic diction' as empty verbiage and who read not just the words but the tradition behind them. As I have tried to show, this couplet is highly pictorial, its few details combining to stimulate in the reader's imagination an image not unlike a history painting. Even a skilled reader may require a glance at Juvenal's handling of the scene in order to bring the picture into perfect focus, but this simply affirms the importance of the literary tradition to a full appreciation of Johnson's poem. In addition, the couplet's 'diction', far from being merely decorative, is highly suggestive, each detail calling to mind subsidiary contexts that enrich its meaning. The conventional, then, is richly poetic, if only we know how to see its images and to hear, with our mind's ear, its echoes.[20]

Let me now pass from the merely difficult to the esoteric: Johnson's skilful appropriation of a passage from Ovid in one of his own Latin poems. To the vast majority of modern readers, Johnson's Latin poetry is not only 'alien' but literally incomprehensible; but even to their small readership these poems have more and less obvious poetic effects. Like all neo-Latin poets Johnson made extensive use of classical sources, sometimes creating a verbal echo that enriched the meaning of his own lines, sometimes merely mining ancient texts for authentic forms of expression. But in the example I wish now to examine he went beyond the typical uses of source materials, turning a bit of Ovidian wit into an artful tribute to a friend.

Late in his life Johnson sent a brief verse letter to his friend and physician Dr. Thomas Lawrence, titled 'Nugae anapaesticae in lecto lusae. Medico Aeger S[alutem]', or 'Anapestic Trifles Playfully Composed in Bed; a Sick Man [Sends Greetings] to his Doctor'. The poem is written in short lines of brisk metre, and it recounts the relief Johnson experienced after being bled by Lawrence. As the poem nears its close, Johnson praises Lawrence as the first among physicians (*gentis / Medicae Princeps*) and offers the following heart-felt wish for his well-being:

> Votaque fundam
> Ne, quae prosunt
> Omnibus, artes
> Domino desint.[21]

[And I shall pour forth prayers that those arts that benefit all others may never fail you, their master.]

And yet, the unaffected sincerity of these lines conceals a splendid example of neo-Latin artifice – the skilful adaptation of a passage from Ovid's *Metamorphoses*. The speaker in the original is Apollo, the inventor of medicine, lamenting that he can do nothing to treat the pains of love he feels for Daphne:

> Hei mihi, quod nullis amor est medicabilis herbis:
> Nec prosunt domino, quae prosunt omnibus, artes![22]

[Alas, that love cannot be cured by herbs! Nor are those arts of any use to me, their lord, that benefit all others!]

Johnson's verses consist of an artful rearrangement of Ovid's second line, and his adaptation of the content is richly appropriate: Apollo is the father of medicine, Lawrence the first among physicians; and whereas Apollo could not heal himself, Johnson prays that the same may never befall Lawrence. The shape of Ovid's line is truly elegant, with the repetition of *prosunt* constituting what Dryden would call a 'turn'.[23] Johnson's short lines disrupt that elegance somewhat, but the authentic personal feeling they convey, combined with the ingenious nature of the adaptation, more than makes up for the diminished formal perfection.

Before leaving this poem, I wish to note one other issue of interest. The Roman poets were extremely sensitive to metre. Ancient literary criticism devoted vastly more attention to it than does modern criticism, and the original Augustans were almost obsessed with 'perfecting' Latin verse. For neo-Latin poets, of course, Latin metres were largely a matter of rules. No vestige of the authentic ancient pronunciation of the language remained, and no one knew (indeed, to this day no one can really be sure) precisely how a Roman verse sounded. But a mastery of the technical requirements of classical metres was necessary for any poet who sought to gain esteem as a Latinist. In addition, transposing poetry from one metre to another was a game that Horace himself had played in his satires, where he adapted several of Terence's iambic lines to his own dactylic hexameters.[24] Those of Johnson's contemporaries who caught his adaptation of Ovid's line (and it is difficult to estimate how many did) would certainly have admired the skilful manner in which he refashioned a dactylic hexameter into three 'anapestic' lines.[25] In the title of the poem Johnson suggested that he was merely 'playing with trifles'; he obviously found amusement at a highly refined level.

Finally, I wish to address a slightly different kind of issue, not a bit of hidden artistry, but the problem of aesthetic response in a genre that Johnson held in high esteem but that we tend to find flat and unsatisfactory – allegory. In *Rambler* 121 Johnson declared allegory to be 'perhaps one of the most pleasing vehicles of instruction'.[26] (Lest anyone quibble about what Johnson meant by a 'vehicle of instruction', let me note that he was referring to *The Faerie Queene* and clearly had the highest forms of poetry in mind.) And we know that at some period between 1756 and 1760 he told Bishop Percy that he thought 'The Vision of Theodore' was 'the best thing he ever wrote'.[27] It is not clear whether he said this before or after he wrote *Rasselas*, but the obvious inference is that he preferred 'The Vision' to *London*, *The Vanity of Human Wishes*, and the *Ramblers*. We can, of course, try to explain away this statement – 'The Vision' is perhaps more clearly didactic than these other works, and thus preferable on moral, though not necessarily on artistic, grounds. Or quite simply, Johnson was teasing Percy and probably did not mean it. But we must always beware of bending Johnson's statements to our own view of the way things *should* be. And we should be especially careful in the case of allegory, for Johnson's contemporaries held his allegorical works in high esteem.[28] In our own day these works have fallen so far from favour that even Donald Greene, a champion of the fugitive and the unappreciated in Johnson's writings, put none of the *Rambler* allegories in his selection of Johnson's works.[29]

Modern critics are liable to account for the loss in popularity of such writings either by doubting the sincerity of those who praised them or by despising their taste. Johnson's readers knew, the argument might go, that the didacticism of such works fits the contemporary assumptions about what art should be, and so they praised allegories even if they did not derive aesthetic pleasure from them. There is probably some truth in this. But before we begin to feel superior, we should consider how many educated people today admire Ezra Pound's *Cantos* and James Joyce's *Ulysses* without getting much aesthetic pleasure from either of these works, and how many people listen respectfully to the music of Schoenberg or Webern, bored or confused, with no real aesthetic response. These readers or hearers pay homage to the works largely because of modern (or 'modernist') assumptions about what art should be. And, then, let us also remember that many people have acclimatised themselves thoroughly to the artistic idioms of these authors or composers and respond to their creations authentically. The same, we must assume, was true of eighteenth-century audiences. And I find it far less surprising that someone might derive rich aesthetic pleasure from Johnson's allegory on 'Patronage' (*Rambler* 91) than that anyone should enjoy either Pound or Webern. So I am unwilling to dismiss the possibility of true aesthetic response to Johnson's allegories.

How, then, are we to reimagine this kind of aesthetic response, so different from our own? When we turn to Johnson's allegories themselves, any reader should find one sort of intellectual satisfaction: they are truly ingenious. One is frequently surprised by the way Johnson introduces his personified abstractions and by the skill with which he gives each its appropriate characteristics. In eighteenth-century terms, then, these works display a great deal of 'invention'. In addition, personification, their primary figurative mode, was held in the highest esteem by that century. With the onset of Romanticism, though, personification lost its privileged position, yielding to the symbol as the most powerful form of poetic figuration. The personifications in Johnson's allegories are themselves 'symbolic', but they are different in kind from such open-ended symbols as Blake's 'Sick Rose' or Coleridge's albatross, any explanation of whose meaning inevitably seems partial. In contrast, Johnson's personified abstractions represent clearly defined categories of experience; they are both limited and knowable, the product of careful observation. As such they often seem too intelligible to the modern reader, mechanical rather than suggestive, artifice rather than art.

Johnson, of course, would have prided himself not only on the ingenuity and clarity of his personifications, but on the overall truth of his symbolic narratives. If the personifications were elaborated with sufficient skill, they would reveal the forces that drive human behaviour. For Johnson, as for many of his contemporaries, the value of the allegories almost certainly lay in their generality, their apparent applicability to all men in all circumstances. The universality of his symbolic scheme was the source of part of its beauty and all of its usefulness. Such generality, of course, encounters dual antagonisms today: modern (and especially 'postmodern') thinkers have called into question the very existence of a universal human nature; and our modern aesthetic sensibilities seem to crave the depiction of individual experience in all its distinguishing detail. But it seems fair to assert that for the contemporaries of Johnson who praised his allegories, the generality of the works must have contributed to their overall *aesthetic* merit. In so far as the personifications seemed congruent with one's own experience of the world, or indeed provided a better explanation of men's actions than the reader's limited experience had done, the allegories would seem to embody fundamental truths and perhaps contribute to a feeling of moral certainty. These may seem to us intellectual rather than aesthetic satisfactions, but that very dichotomy is largely rooted in Romantic aesthetics.

If we truly wish to understand the appeal of Johnson's allegories, we must first doubt the universality of our own aesthetic responses and then entertain the possibility of the 'rationally pleasing' as an aesthetic category. To some extent we already accept this notion. There is an undeniable beauty to the workings of mathematics ('Euclid alone has looked on Beauty bare'); and modern readers certainly employ rational criteria when they find a narrative unsatisfying because of its lack of probability. The first of these rational responses is of course non-literary, and the second low on our scale of literary judgements; but this merely shows that our training as readers (in the largest cultural sense) has taught us to discriminate between different kinds of aesthetic responses and to value certain effects over others. In fact, a few minutes' reflection should lead us to expect the 'rationally pleasing' to be an integral part of eighteenth-century literary responses. Its intellectual bases lay in any number of seventeenth-century attempts to bring reason to bear on various aspects of life. As modern readers we are likely to be suspicious of the claims of 'reason' in literary matters, and as literary historians we know the unsatisfying nature of much of the literary criticism that initially arose from these intellectual movements. (The tyranny of the dramatic unities comes immediately to mind, as well as the names Dennis and Rymer.) Nevertheless, we must assume that some of these rationalist impulses became thoroughly assimilated into the cultivated modes of thought of the day and that many an eighteenth-century reader would have been puzzled by an attempt to separate the rational from other aspects of aesthetic response. Under these circumstances, the pleasure that many readers received from Johnson's allegories would seem not only authentic but predictable.

This discussion of the 'rationally pleasing' may open a window on another alien aspect of eighteenth-century literary practice, the demand for moral instruction. To modern readers this too seems highly artificial, the imposition of extrinsic moral criteria on the neutral materials of art. But we must consider that for Johnson as well as for many of his readers, the demands of morality and religion were not 'extrinsic criteria' at all, but the fundamental propositions of human life; and any depiction of 'nature', however close it might seem in its external details, must inevitably have appeared flawed if it disguised or misrepresented what they understood to be the true meaning of things. These readers could easily have made exceptions for the works of classical antiquity, whose authors laboured in ignorance of these fundamental truths; but modern literature could plead no such special tolerance, and the critique of such works on moral grounds must have seemed for many readers almost instinctual, devoid of any hint of the quasi-mechanical application of external values that we tend to attribute to these efforts. In fact, aesthetic judgements are never made in a moral vacuum, and even today we constantly impose our own 'moral' criteria on the reading of literary texts. (For a long time these were couched in a sanctified aestheticism; now they more frequently appear disguised as sociological or political imperatives.) In so far as Johnson's allegories not only offered certain rational satisfactions but also conformed to a widely held moral view of the world, they would have seemed all the more satisfying as aesthetic objects.

Here, then, is a working model for conceptualising the aesthetic appeal of Johnson's allegories. Their primary characteristics are ingenuity and propriety, the ingenuity with which the personifications are first imagined and then assembled into a narrative, and the propriety with which the qualities attributed to each abstract concept are made to fit its personification. Most important, these artistic components come together to illustrate human actions and motivations in a convincing and satisfying manner. And finally, such works almost certainly appealed to an authentic aspect of eighteenth-century aesthetic experience, which I have termed the 'rationally pleasing'. Of course, the validity of the rational as an aesthetic category was already being challenged in Johnson's own day by the rise of 'sensibility', and Romanticism swept it away completely. But I think it a form of hubris to assume that what fails to please now could never have truly pleased and that our modern sensibilities are more authentically alive to literary excellence than those of an earlier age, an age whose readers included Samuel Johnson himself. Johnson's allegories are in fact a window into a distant and alien literary taste, a taste quite different from our own, but one that is at least as understandable as a modern claim to enjoy Pound or Webern.

In concluding, I wish to offer some general reflections on the disparate materials that I have been examining. The first point of interest is Johnson's sense of language. By this I do not mean to suggest a 'theory' of language, for I doubt that Johnson consciously had one, and I certainly would not try to infer such a theory from the few brief passages that I have adduced here. Nevertheless, when Johnson is being artful, he employs words with a particular sensitivity to their histories, both etymological and literary. As I have already shown, he often brings vividness to English abstractions by calling our attention to their Latin roots, a practice that acknowledges simultaneously a word's concrete 'primitive' meaning and its modern, more general, acceptation. And in his poetry he continually exploits the resources of conventional language, that is, language with a literary past. For the 'conventional' poet, the literary tradition within which he works offers not only a body of approved 'diction', but a series of literary contexts as well. The merit of such poetry arises from the skill with which the poet manipulates both language and context either to say new things or to say old things in a new way. Thus Johnson's phrase 'purple billows', with its suggestion of royalty and its echo of Pope's 'purpled main', creates a darkly ironic context for the scene before the reader, a sea reddened with blood. Johnson's scene in fact differs little from Juvenal's, but he has exploited the resonances of English poetic diction to create a new impact.

To the extent, though, that Johnson seems more responsive to the historical and traditional qualities of language, he seems correspondingly less affected by the broadly evocative or the vaguely suggestive. It seems fair to say (without any derogation from his abilities as a reader or a poet) that the aesthetic category of the 'rationally pleasing' operated with respect to language as well as to such matters as allegory. It often reveals itself as a concern for various kinds of 'correctness'. We find this most clearly in his criticism of Shakespeare's language, summed up in the famous comment that 'Shakespeare never has six lines together without a fault'.[30] Modern readers, for whom Shakespeare rather than Virgil provides the standard of literary excellence, take unabashed pleasure in his rampant figuration. We find sublimity in a phrase like 'take arms against a sea of troubles' where Johnson and his contemporaries recognised a mixed metaphor.[31] For them the propriety of a figure was valued more highly than its evocativeness. The Romantics, of course, inferred from this that the entire age suffered from an impoverished sense of language and that their rational restrictions on meaning inhibited a 'true' appreciation of metaphor. Perhaps, but perhaps not. For readers like Johnson, the ability to convey meaning clearly and distinctly and the careful use of figurative language formed part of an integrated response to literary language. As I have shown in Johnson's handling of the couplet on Xerxes, the traditional resources of literary language were very rich, and they afforded poets a great variety of potential poetic effects. Johnson's couplets, like those of Dryden and Pope before him, could be both 'correct' and highly evocative. We should also remember that the idea of the 'sublime' was reclaimed for seventeenth-century Europe by Boileau, one of the most 'correct' poets of the most 'correct' age of the most 'correct' nation. In fact, no inherent conflict exists between correctness and suggestiveness; the issue is whether the suggestive is sought in accord with certain traditional literary canons or in violation of those canons. Genius can operate under either set of conditions.

Even in this brief discussion, though, I am in danger of placing too much stress on 'the rational', for it was but one component of Johnson's literary taste. And much that I have located under that heading would have seemed to Johnson indistinguishable from the purely aesthetic. In many of the areas that we have been examining, especially the skilful manipulation of conventional language and the restricted use of figures of speech, Johnson would have found sufficient justification for his aesthetic responses in the literary practice of the ancient Augustans. Virgil and Horace had taught several generations of poets (French as well as English) how to achieve effects of great subtlety and power while working within a tightly defined literary tradition. From them one learned the importance of using a vocabulary 'appropriate' to each genre, as well as care, delicacy, and elegant control in the handling of metaphor. Restraint and propriety, then, were not merely the product of seventeenth-century rationalism but the lessons learned from the most respected poet of the day – Virgil, that is, not Shakespeare.[32]

When we consider Johnson as an imitative writer, perhaps the most surprising aspect is his overall independence. Outside his formal imitations, one rarely catches him filching a line directly from a classical source.[33] Ben Jonson, Milton and even Pope plunder the ancient texts with far greater abandon. But if Johnson has few direct borrowings from the Roman writers, he has many stylistic affinities with them. He seems to have assimilated many of their rhetorical and poetic techniques, making these his own and employing them with individuality and skill. One thus finds stylistic analogues in Seneca and Juvenal rather than closely imitated passages. And even in a direct imitation like *The Vanity of Human Wishes* Johnson rarely attempts to redo Juvenal in Juvenal's own manner. None of this should be surprising. His praise of the great Scots neo-Latin poet George Buchanan was that he had 'fewer *centos*' – that is, scraps of language taken from other authors – 'than any modern Latin poet'.[34] Johnson valued Buchanan's originality of expression over any number of spurious echoes of ancient texts. The tradition provides the author with a wealth of resources, but from all these riches he must still make something new.

Finally, except for my comments on Johnson and allegory, I have been chiefly concerned in this essay with matters of style, that is, with the surfaces of Johnson's poetry and prose. If the definition of art is the imitation of nature, I have touched on few of art's fundamental qualities here. And if art's primary purpose is to instruct, as Johnson surely believed it was, I have concerned myself with matters of only secondary importance. But Johnson also tells us (in his own particular adaptation of Horace) that 'the end of poetry is to instruct *by pleasing*'.[35] All the artistic techniques that I have analysed were intended to engage readers or to delight them. Of course, it is part of Johnson's greatness as a writer that his meaning is generally accessible even to those who miss these subtleties of art; his observations on life were certainly intended to be available to anyone with a competent grasp of English (though I suspect that a word like 'adventitious' puzzled the common reader in Johnson's own day nearly as often as it does in ours). But Johnson clearly had a special kind of reader in mind as he wrote, one at least competent in Latin and exposed to a variety of classical authors. He expected this reader to recognise the images implicit in English abstractions, to hear with pleasure the resonances of conventional diction, to catch the force of a highly condensed personification whose vividness rests in a single active verb, and, on rare occasions, to note and admire a passage skilfully adapted from Ovid. In addition, and for this a classical education was not required, this reader should have found the rational and the aesthetic largely in accord. Where is such a reader to be found today? And how confidently can any of us claim truly to read Johnson when we are so poorly equipped to recognise the elements of his art?

Notes

1. See Erwin Panofsky, 'The History of Art as a Humanistic Discipline', originally published in 1940 and reprinted in *Meaning in the Visual Arts* (Chicago, 1982), pp. 1–25; and Sir Ernst Gombrich, *Art and Illusion: A Study in the Psychology of Pictorial Representation* (2nd edn., Princeton, 1961). Panofsky discusses the 'cultural equipment' necessary to interpret a work of art created under an alien aesthetic (pp. 14–19), and Gombrich examines such issues as the need to 'learn to read' unfamiliar images and the expectations that we bring to any work of art (pp. 53–62). Gombrich develops these issues extensively in the section called 'The Beholder's Share' (pp. 181–287).
2. For some early responses to the Impressionists, see Joyce Cary, *Art and Reality* (New York, 1958), pp. 67–70.
3. See Gombrich, *Art and Illusion*, pp. 120–45.
4. *The Rambler*, ed. W.J. Bate and Albrecht Strauss, vols. III–V of *Yale Edition* (New Haven, 1969), III, pp. 318–19.
5. *Jonathan Swift*, ed. Angus Ross and David Woolley (Oxford, 1984), p. 514, lines 7–10.
6. *Moral Essays*, ed. John W. Basore, Loeb Classical Library (3 vols., London, 1951), II, pp. 140–1. Both the Latin text and the translation are from this edition.
7. *Philosophic Words* (New Haven, 1948), pp. 70–93.
8. *Samuel Johnson*, ed. Donald Greene (Oxford, 1984), p. 317.
9. P. 107. As Wimsatt's examples show, the Latin roots of English abstractions are generally highly concrete; it is this curious relation between the two languages that Johnson exploits for his artistic purposes. Perhaps the first person to comment directly on this aspect of Johnson's style was Robert Burrowes in his 'Essay on the Stile of Doctor Samuel Johnson' (1787), cited by Wimsatt in his earlier *Prose Style of Samuel Johnson* (New Haven, 1941), p. 66.
10. *Yale Edition*, III, p. 320.
11. 'Deceived' has in its root a sense of being 'caught'.
12. *The Collected Works of Samuel Taylor Coleridge* (16 vols., Princeton, 1969–), *Lectures 1808–1819: On Literature*, ed. R.A. Foakes, V, pt. 1 (1987), p. 292.
13. Lines 56–8. I have quoted the passage from the Delphin *Juvenal*, ed. Prateus (Paris, 1684; London, 1691), which was one of the editions that Johnson used for his own translations of Juvenal. See Edward and Lillian Bloom, 'Johnson's *London* and its Juvenalian Texts', *HLQ*, 34 (1970–1), pp. 1–23. Subsequent quotations from the Tenth Satire are also from this edition. The translations are my own.
14. Wimsatt (*Prose Style*, p. 66) suggests that through his use of etymologies Johnson revivifies dead metaphors, a phenomenon similar to that which I am discussing here.
15. Something more must be said of the subtlety of Juvenal's technique here. We expect the great man's 'power' to 'overthrow' his enemies, but ironically that

power destroys the one who wields it. There is something paradoxical about this, but Juvenal clarifies the situation through the participial phrase *subjecta . . . magnae / Invidiae*: power falls when it is 'exposed to great envy'. ('Exposed' is in fact a rather loose translation for *subjecta*, which may suggest being 'subject to' or 'cast down before' envy.) In a mere six words Juvenal has sketched out a complex picture of the dangers of power by focusing our attention on the clash of two general terms, *potentia* and *invidia*.

16. In limiting myself to the analysis of a single couplet, I hope I will not be mistaken for the pedant in Hierocles (to use Johnson's own allusion), who showed a brick as a specimen of the excellence of his house. The *Vanity* is a great edifice, and its power can only be appreciated by a view of the whole; but Johnson's 'art' in that poem is elaborated couplet by couplet, brick by brick, if you will. And no broad generalisations about the poem's structure or its impact will further the exploration of my topic, the often unrecognised qualities of Johnson's art.

17. *The Poems of Samuel Johnson*, ed. David Nichol Smith and Edward L. McAdam, (2nd edn., Oxford, 1974), p. 127, lines 239–40.

18. Far too little attention has been paid to the process of seeing images in eighteenth-century poetry. A good introduction to the topic is Lawrence Lipking's 'Quick Poetic Eyes: Another Look at Literary Pictorialism', in *Articulate Images*, ed. Richard Wendorf (Minneapolis, 1983), pp. 3–25.

19. See, for example, Virgil, *Aeneid*, 5. 15, and 8. 108; and Juvenal, *Satires*, 15. 128.

20. Although I have pointed out several places where Johnson employs images or figurative language in a manner similar to Juvenal, I do not wish to give the impression that Johnson merely adapted Juvenal's poetic techniques to English verse. These examples merely provide a glimpse into a stylistic tradition and thus a context for appreciating the art of certain passages. But as poetic stylists, Johnson and Juvenal were in fact very different. Johnson is much more likely to use personification, while Juvenal more often heaps his verses with the rummage and refuse of daily life. Their differences far outweigh their similarities.

21. *Poems*, pp. 231–2, ll. 27–30.

22. *Metamorphoses*, 1. 523–4. I have taken the text from the variorum edition of Ovid's *Opera* edited by Borchard Cnipping (Leiden, 1670). This is the sort of edition that Johnson was most likely to have read. Modern editions differ from this text by reading *sanabilis* for *medicabilis*. The translation is my own.

23. For Dryden's discussion of 'turns', with special emphasis on Ovid, see *The Essays of John Dryden*, ed. W.P. Ker (2 vols., Oxford, 1926), II, pp. 108–10, 219, 257.

24. See Horace's *Satires*, 2. 3. 262–8.

25. Johnson did not originally court the esteem of his contemporaries with this poem; he seems to have contemplated no audience beyond Dr. Lawrence, to whom he sent the original without making a copy. Two months later, though, he wrote to Lawrence's daughter requesting that she make a copy for him: see the headnote in *Poems*, p. 231. Finally, since I have stressed the importance to neo-Latinists of metrical skill, it is only fair to point out, as R.W. Chapman has noted, that lines 11 and 13 of the poem (not quoted above) are not metrically correct: see Johnson, *Letters*, ed. Chapman, 3 vols. (Oxford, 1952), II, p. 471.

26. Quoted in Bernard L. Einbond, *Samuel Johnson's Allegory* (The Hague, 1971), p. 26. I rely heavily on Einbond throughout this portion of the essay.

27. Boswell, *Life*, I, pp. 192, 537. Einbond (p. 56) discusses the dates between which the statement must have been made.

28. Einbond (pp. 9–10) gathers a significant body of contemporary praise for

Johnson's allegories, as well as a number of nineteenth- and twentieth-century dismissals of them.

29. By Johnson's allegories I mean 'The Vision of Theodore' and the following numbers of the *Rambler*: 3 ('Criticism'), 22 ('Wit and Learning'), 33 ('Rest and Labour'), 67 ('Hope'), 91 ('Patronage'), 96 ('Truth and Falsehood'), and 102 ('The Ocean of Life'). No. 65 is an oriental tale with an allegorical explanation added at the end. *Rambler* 44, an allegory of 'Religion and Superstition', was written by Johnson's friend Elizabeth Carter. Greene includes 'The Vision of Theodore' in his collection for the *Oxford Authors* (Oxford, 1984), but none of the *Rambler* essays listed above.

30. Boswell, *Life*, II, p. 96. Johnson seems particularly concerned with two matters in Shakespeare, neither of which gives modern readers the least concern: whether the level of diction is appropriate to the seriousness of a given passage, and whether an attentive reader can assimilate (or will tolerate) Shakespeare's abundant, sometimes chaotic, figuration.

31. Johnson's comment on this line tells us a great deal about both his own responses and those of his contemporaries: 'Mr. Pope proposed "siege". I know not why there should be so much solicitude about this metaphor. Shakespeare breaks his metaphors often, and in this desultory speech there was less need of preserving them.' Johnson does not censure the passage, but he does not revel in its suggestiveness either. He tolerates it on pragmatic grounds. See *Johnson on Shakespeare*, ed. Arthur Sherbo, vols. VII and VIII of the *Yale Edition* (New Haven, 1968), VIII, p. 981.

32. The influence of the ancient Augustans on English literature has been a matter of some dispute in recent years. For a discussion of the development of Augustan literary values during the seventeenth and eighteenth centuries, see my article 'Rehabilitating "Augustanism": On the Roots of "Polite Letters" in England', *Eighteenth-Century Life*, 20 (1996), pp. 49–65.

33. At this point I am referring primarily to Johnson's writings in English. As I mentioned above, one of the fundamental characteristics of neo-Latin poetry was a certain responsiveness to the poetic language of ancient texts. But even there Johnson often seems strikingly independent. See his praise of George Buchanan below.

34. Boswell, *Life*, II, p. 96.

35. From the 'Preface to Shakespeare', *Yale Edition*, VII, p. 67 (emphasis added).

10

'Elevated Notions of the Right of Kings': Stuart Sympathies in Johnson's Notes to *Richard II*

Matthew M. Davis

Scholars involved in the great debate over Johnson's politics have gone over most of Johnson's writings with a fine-tooth comb.[1] They have scrutinised not only Johnson's political writings, but also his poems, letters, travel writings and biographies. However, neither side has paid any substantive attention to Johnson's 1765 edition of Shakespeare.[2] In this essay I wish to correct this oversight by drawing attention to some politically suggestive notes on *Richard II*. These notes are fragmentary and sometimes difficult to interpret, but they nevertheless suggest that Johnson was substantially more sympathetic to the Stuarts, up to and including James II, than supporters of the Hanoverian Johnson have been willing to admit.[3]

A number of Johnson's notes on *Richard II* are politically suggestive. The first such note occurs in Act II, scene ii of Johnson's edition.[4] In this scene the moribund John of Gaunt upbraids Richard for governing England poorly and 'deposing himself':

> Why, Cousin, wert thou Regent of the world,
> It were a shame to let this Land by lease;
> But for thy world enjoying but this Land,
> Is it not more than shame to shame it so?
> Landlord of *England* art thou now, not King.
> Thy state of law is bondslave to the law.[5]

In the eighteenth century the last line of this passage became a textual crux. Bishop William Warburton, a previous editor, had argued that Shakespeare could not have had the concept of absolute sovereignty in mind when he wrote the line in question. Warburton glossed the line as follows:

State of law, i.e. *legal sov'rainty*. But the Oxford editor [Thomas Hanmer] alters it to *state o'er law*, i.e. *absolute sov'rainty*. A doctrine, which, if our poet ever learnt at all, he learnt not in the reign when this play was written, Queen *Elizabeth*'s, but in the reign after it, King *James*'s. By

239

bondslave to the law, the poet means his being inslaved to his *favorite* subjects.

(30)

Johnson liked to boast that he would never contradict a bishop, but in this case he did just that.[6] Against Warburton's interpretation, Johnson set his own, which was in many ways a restatement of Hanmer's position:

> This sentiment, whatever it be, is obscurely expressed. I understand it differently from the learned commentator, being perhaps not quite so zealous for *Shakespeare*'s political reputation. The reasoning of *Gaunt*, I think, is this: *By setting thy royalties* to farm *thou hast reduced thyself to a state below sovereignty, thou art now* no longer king but landlord of England, *subject to the same restraint and limitations as other landlords; by making thy condition* a state of law, *a condition upon which the common rules of law can operate*, thou art become a bondslave to the law; *thou hast made thyself amenable to laws from which thou wert originally exempt.* Whether this interpretation be true or no, it is plain that Dr. *Warburton*'s explanation of *bondslave to the law*, is not true.

(30)

Warburton had tried to distance Shakespeare from any understanding of the concept of absolute sovereignty. He had declared that Shakespeare could not have known of this doctrine in the 1590s when he wrote *Richard II* because the doctrine was not promulgated until the reign of the first Stuart King, James I. Johnson rejects Warburton's reading out of hand. He asserts that Gaunt is indeed referring to the king's being above the law. We may say that Johnson corrects Warburton because he wishes to establish the true meaning of Shakespeare's text, but we should recognise that the textual meaning that Johnson seeks to establish also has political ramifications. If Shakespeare was able to articulate the doctrine of absolute sovereignty in the 1590s, this proves that the Stuarts did not invent that doctrine, as many Whigs liked to claim.[7] Johnson's note, therefore, functions not only as a partial clarification of the text but also as a partial vindication of the Stuarts.

In his note Johnson suggests that one of the reasons why he disagrees with Warburton is that he is 'perhaps not quite so zealous for Shakespeare's political reputation'. This is a tantalising remark, but it is not immediately clear how we ought to read it. Does Johnson mean that Warburton cares about Shakespeare's politics, but he himself does not? This reading seems unlikely. As we shall see, Johnson returns again and again in his notes to political issues, and especially to issues of absolute sovereignty and hereditary, indefeasible right. He clearly shares Warburton's interest in Shakespeare's political ideas. If there is a difference between the two men it must lie in the points of view that they bring to bear on those ideas. Johnson thinks Warburton's point of view is clear: he evinces a 'zealous' desire to save Shakespeare's contemporary political reputation by distancing the playwright from the doctrine of absolute sovereignty and pinning the responsibility for that doctrine on the Stuarts. In what may be a significant understatement, Johnson describes himself as 'perhaps not quite so zealous' in this crusade.

At this point it may be useful to pause to ask how Johnson's point of view might have differed from Warburton's. If we confine ourselves to religious questions this is not an easy question to answer. Warburton was a great champion of the Anglican Church, but so was Johnson. Warburton defended the Test Act and the alliance between Church and State, but so did Johnson.[8] However, one area of disagreement, political or dynastic rather than religious, does seem possible.

Warburton was a strong supporter of the Hanoverian regime. He had in fact preached several sermons against the 'vile unnatural rebellion' of 1745.[9] In these sermons Warburton praised 'his excellent Majesty KING GEORGE' and attacked all four of the Stuart kings, as well as 'the Pretender' (285–6). He blasted James I and Charles I for 'aim[ing] at a despotic power', and he ripped into Charles II and James II for championing 'Popery' and claiming 'a power of dispensing with the laws' (319). He spoke scornfully of 'the pretender's . . . imaginary title, founded on I know not what jargon of indefeasible hereditary Right for the King, and passive obedience and non-resistance for the Subject: A title, which the much provoked resentment of an injured People hath long since with the highest justice dissolved and abrogated' (285).

Johnson's devotion to the Hanoverians has been doubted recently, and was doubted in his own lifetime.[10] Sir John Hawkins observed that, although Johnson was pensioned by George III, he had 'very little claim to the favour of any of the descendents of the house of Hanover'.[11] Critics of *Taxation No Tyranny* complained that Johnson was 'an inveterate foe to the Royal Family upon the throne',[12] and a man who had always 'written of the Revolution and the House of Hanover' with 'singular virulence'.[13]

Certainly Johnson did not share Warburton's high opinion of George II. On one occasion, he 'burst out into an invective against George the Second, as one, who, upon all occasions was unrelenting and barbarous'.[14] On another occasion 'he roared with prodigious violence against George the Second'.[15] In *The False Alarm* (1770) he took a shot at George II and his predecessors by referring to George III as 'the only king, who, for almost a century [i.e. since the Stuart era], has much appeared to desire, or much endeavored to deserve' the favour of his subjects.[16]

On the other hand, Johnson had a number of good things to say about the Stuart monarchs whom Warburton condemned, particularly the last three. As Phillip Mahone Griffith has shown, Johnson venerated Charles I as a pious martyr unjustly murdered by a usurping parliament.[17] He hailed Charles II in conversation as 'the best King we have had from his time till the reign of his present majesty [George III], except James the Second, who was a very good King'.[18] Johnson was not blind to the faults of the individual Stuart monarchs, but he never vilified the four Stuart kings in the sweeping language that Warburton and other Whigs frequently used.[19]

Warburton was scornful of the idea that kings were in any way 'above' the law, but Johnson was sometimes willing to defend a version of this idea. In conversation he once asserted that the King's agents might be prosecuted, but not the King himself: 'in our constitution, according to its true principles, the King is the head; he is supreme; he is above everything, and there is no power by which he can be tried'.[20] Johnson based his argument on practical considerations rather than on an appeal to divine right, and he went on to admit that there is always the possibility of a revolution, but his fundamental contention that 'there is no power by which [the King] can be tried' is strikingly similar to Gaunt's belief that the King is not a 'bondslave to the law'.

Warburton dismissed the Stuarts' appeal to divine hereditary right as meaningless 'jargon', but Johnson may well have been more sympathetic. Mrs. Thrale described Johnson's political views in her diary: 'He is a Tory in what he calls the truest sense of the Word; and is strongly attached to the notion of Divine & Hereditary Right inherent in Kings: he was therefore a Jacobite while Jacob existed, or any of his Progeny was likely to sit on the Throne.'[21] Mrs. Thrale knew Johnson as well as anyone, and it is hard to imagine why she would falsify in a diary entry. This is therefore a very strong piece of evidence.

Johnson's views concerning the '45 are not easy to reconstruct. However, they may well have been substantially different from the views outlined by Warburton. On his Scottish tour Johnson chatted amiably with a number of participants in the rebellion, including the famous Flora MacDonald.[22] In one of his letters to Mrs. Thrale he remarked approvingly, 'These are not Whigs.'[23] In his published journal Boswell refused to refer to Charles Edward Stuart as 'the prince' because he was 'quite satisfied that the right which the House of Stuart had to the throne is extinguished'. Johnson was less inhibited in his letters to Mrs. Thrale. He repeatedly referred to Charles as 'the Prince' and even boasted of having spent the night 'in the bed, on which the Prince reposed in his distress'.[24] Johnson later called the '45 'a noble attempt'.[25] Sir John Hawkins noted that, for many years, the members of the Ivy Lane Club avoided calling the Jacobite rebels 'traitors' while Johnson was in the room: 'we all saw the prudence of avoiding to call the then late adventurer in Scotland, or his adherents, by those names which others hesitated not to give them, or to bring to remembrance what had passed, a few years before, on Tower-hill'.[26] I think this comment deserves more attention than it has so far attracted.[27] Hawkins is not reprinting the observations of another person; he is describing what he himself witnessed. Nor is he describing a particular episode, in which Johnson might well have been 'talking for victory' as opposed to urging his actual opinions. Rather,

Hawkins is summarising a pattern of behaviour that continued for six or seven years. The Ivy Lane Club met on Tuesday evenings from the winter of 1749 until, probably, 1756. During all that time, Hawkins implies, Johnson frequently exhibited Jacobite sympathies – and was belligerent enough about these sympathies to frighten the other members of the club into silence.[28] In short, if Johnson and Warburton did differ politically, it is possible that they differed on the dynastic question, for Warburton was zealous to defend the Hanoverians who had promoted him while Johnson may well have been 'not quite so zealous'.

But let us return from such biographical speculations and examine another one of Johnson's notes on *Richard II*. In Act III, scene ii, Richard boasts that he cannot be deposed:

> Not all the water in the rough rude sea
> Can wash the balm off from an anointed King;
> The breath of worldly men cannot depose
> The Deputy elected by the Lord.
>
> (54)

Johnson uses this boast as evidence in his debate with Warburton:

> Here is the doctrine of indefeasible right expressed in the strongest terms, but our poet did not learn it in the reign of King *James*, to which it is now the practice of all writers, whose opinions are regulated by fashion or interest, to impute the original of every tenet which they have been taught to think false or foolish.
>
> (54)

In this note Johnson does more than just reiterate his earlier claims against Warburton. He broadens his attack by identifying Warburton with other Whiggish writers who opportunistically blame the Stuarts for 'every tenet which they have been taught to think false or foolish', including the central tenet of Jacobitism, the indefeasible right of kings. Johnson is taking arms against a sea of Whiggism, and his word choices in doing so are intriguing. He could easily have criticised those who blame the Stuarts for 'every false and foolish tenet'. Instead he criticises those who blame the Stuarts for 'every tenet *which they have been taught to think* false or foolish'. In other words, Johnson declines to join his voice with the voices of those who think that indefeasible right is a false and foolish tenet. In political terms, he declines to join the Whigs in denouncing the Jacobites. This does not prove that Johnson was himself a Jacobite, or that he accepted the Jacobite doctrine of indefeasible right, but it does suggest that Johnson viewed this doctrine with much less hostility than the Whigs.[29]

Johnson also renews his historical argument with Warburton in this note: he uses Shakespeare's Elizabethan play to argue that the doctrine of divine right pre-dates the reign of James I. Here Johnson steps into the midst of a political controversy. Whigs such as Locke, Burnet and Kennett liked to argue that divine right was a recent development.[30] Locke characterised it as a novelty of 'this latter age', an invention of Caroline divines.[31] Jacobites and Nonjurors denied these claims and attempted to prove the antiquity of divine right and the doctrines associated with it. Abednego Seller traced the doctrines of passive obedience and non-resistance to the Reformation in order to show that these 'were not innovations of clever Stuart policy but had been basic tenets of the [Anglican] Church from its beginnings'.[32] George Harbin traced a hereditary line to William the Conqueror in order to establish the strictly hereditary nature of the English monarchy.[33] And Charles Leslie (whom Johnson once called 'a reasoner . . . not to be reasoned against') defended the divine right of kings by tracing it all the way to Biblical times: 'the notion of Kings having their power from God, was long in the world before either the Reformation or Popery. All the ancient Fathers are full of it. And they took it from the Holy Scripture, where it is abundantly testified.'[34] Johnson's note on indefeasible right cannot be conflated with these explicitly Nonjuring tracts: asserting the antiquity of a doctrine is not the same as asserting the truth of that doctrine. But if the parallel is partial, it is nevertheless remarkable: Warburton joins his fellow Whigs in asserting that indefeasible right is a recent innovation; Johnson joins the Nonjurors in denying this claim. Whether or not Johnson was himself a Nonjuror, there can be little doubt that his note would be more pleasing to Nonjurors and Stuart sympathizers than to Whigs.

In his second fusillade against Warburton Johnson echoes a charge he had made a few years earlier in *The Gentleman's Magazine*. In 1760 Johnson had reviewed William Tytler's book on Mary Queen of Scots and the so-called 'casket letters'. Tytler had attempted to show that the letters that had been used to discredit Mary Stuart were forgeries. Johnson agreed wholeheartedly, and his agreement with Tytler led him into another tirade against Stuart-vilification:

> It has now been fashionable, for near half a century, to defame and vilify the house of Stuart, and to exalt and magnify the reign of Elizabeth. The Stuarts have found few apologists, for the dead cannot pay for praise; and who will, without reward, oppose the tide of popularity? Yet there remains still among us, not wholly extinguished, a zeal for truth, a desire for establishing right, in opposition to fashion.[35]

In *The Politics of Samuel Johnson* Donald Greene denies that these remarks reveal any special sympathy for the Stuarts. Greene insists that Johnson is simply questioning intellectual fashions and trying to establish the historical truth.[36] There is no question that Johnson is doing these things, but the fashions he is questioning happen to be Whiggish fashions, and the version of historical truth he is trying to establish happens to be the version championed by the Jacobites. Hume had written in Johnson's own day that the innocence of Queen Mary was a political touchstone for 'furious' Jacobites. The Scottish philosopher thought that any man 'who maintains the innocence of queen Mary, must be considered [as a Jacobite] beyond the reach of argument or reason'.[37] Since Johnson maintained Mary's innocence, it is no surprise that Hume considered Johnson 'a keen Jacobite' and a man of 'antiquated notions'.[38]

Jayne Elizabeth Lewis has recently reminded us of the political context of the debate over the casket letters. She has shown that Tytler's book and the debate about the authenticity of the casket letters in general were strongly informed by political and dynastic issues. Lewis explains that scepticism about the authenticity of the casket letters generally correlated with sympathy for the Stuarts:

> As they exposed the stains upon Mary's character, the letters helped to justify the recent break in the succession of the English throne; the letters themselves were therefore claimed by the anti-Jacobite cause . . . [and] used to justify the Hanoverian succession. In turn, to discredit the letters [as Tytler and Johnson did] would be to sympathize with the Stuart cause . . . By the 1760s it was clear that any discussion of Mary Stuart carried some reference to the continuing conflict between . . . 'republican writers, equally averse to monarchy and to the House of Stuart' and 'writers attached to the ancient constitution of their country and to the family of Stuart.'[39]

In short, if Hume and Lewis are correct, then Johnson's support for Tytler's thesis may well have had the political implications that Greene denied. And if Johnson's review of Tytler's book displays Stuart sympathies, the same would seem to be true of his note on Shakespeare's play, for these two comments are remarkably similar. In the Tytler review Johnson complains about writers who are motivated by 'reward' or 'fashion' to defame the matriarch of the Stuart clan; in the Shakespeare note he complains about writers who are motivated by 'interest' or 'fashion' to blame the Stuarts for all doctrines 'which they have been taught to think false or foolish'. Both comments suggest that Johnson was, at the very least, angered by the Whiggish interpretation of English history he saw developing around him.

In Act IV, scene ii Johnson returns once again to his debate with Warburton concerning divine right. By this point in the play things are going badly for Richard. Bolingbroke has declared his intention to 'ascend the regal throne', and most of Richard's supporters have abandoned him. However, the Bishop of Carlisle remains loyal and speaks on Richard's behalf. Carlisle asks rhetorically,

> What Subject can give Sentence on his King?
> And who sits here, that is not *Richard*'s Subject?
> . . . shall the Figure of God's Majesty,
> His Captain, Steward, Deputy elect,
> Anointed, crown'd, and planted many years,
> Be judg'd by subject and inferior breath,
> And he himself not present? O, forbid it!
> That, in a christian climate, souls refin'd
> Should shew so heinous, black, obscene a deed.
>
> (76–7)

In his endnote on *Richard II* Johnson explains that this is a speech 'in defence of King *Richard*'s unalienable right, and immunity from human jurisdiction' (105). Once again Johnson's word choices are intriguing. He does not write of 'King Richard's *supposedly* unalienable right' or 'King Richard's *absurd and exploded claim* to immunity from human jurisdiction'. In other words, he passes up another easy opportunity to voice his disapproval of the doctrine of indefeasible right.

Johnson also writes that Carlisle's speech is 'extracted . . . with very little alteration . . . from the Chronicle of *Hollingshead*' (105). Holinshed is indeed Shakespeare's primary source, but the alterations that Shakespeare made to the original are in fact more interesting and substantive than Johnson's note would suggest. As various critics have observed, Shakespeare intensifies the emphasis on divine right.[40] In Holinshed Carlisle is upset that Richard is tried *unheard*; in Shakespeare he seems to be upset that the king should be tried *at all*. Holinshed's Carlisle asserts that there is no man among those present who is 'worthy or meet to give Judgment upon so worthy a Prince as King *Richard*'.[41] Shakespeare's Carlisle asks a much more sweeping question: 'What Subject can give Sentence on his King?' Shakespeare also heightens the religious element of Carlisle's complaint. Holinshed's bishop does not mention God; Shakespeare's bishop speaks of the King as 'the Figure of God's majesty, / His Captain, Steward, Deputy elect'. It is possible that Johnson did not notice these differences; he may simply have been echoing Charlotte Lennox's observations on Shakespeare's use of Holinshed. However, it is also possible that Johnson was consciously taking sides in an ongoing debate over the presence or absence of divine right sentiments in Holinshed and other historians. Nonjurors such as George Harbin and George Hickes liked to argue for the presence of such sentiments; they presented the historical Carlisle as an early advocate of divine right.[42] Whigs denied these claims; they maintained that the historical Carlisle '[did] not insist on the Unalienable, Indefeasible Right of King Richard, nor assert, that the states were not authorized to proceed against him, but that they did not give him a fair hearing'.[43] Johnson suggests that Shakespeare 'extracted' divine right sentiments, 'with very little alteration', from Holinshed; he is therefore closer to the Nonjurors on this issue than he is to the Whigs.

Johnson was obviously very interested in Carlisle's speech because he commented on it not only in the endnote we have been examining but also in a footnote, where he launches the third phase of his campaign against Warburton:

> Here is another proof that our authour did not learn in King *James*'s court his elevated notions of the right of kings. I know not any flatterer of the *Stuarts* who has expressed this doctrine in much stronger terms. It must be observed that the Poet intends from the beginning to the end to exhibit this bishop as brave, pious, and venerable.
>
> (77)

Here Johnson makes an explicit and interesting connection between Carlisle and the defenders of the Stuarts. The phrase 'flatterer of the Stuarts' does not sound especially flattering, and, taken in isolation, it might lead us to think that Johnson is distancing himself from the Stuarts. However, the note as a whole clearly functions as a vindication of the Stuarts rather than as an accusation of them: Johnson is suggesting, once again, that even the most outspoken supporters of the Stuarts were only repeating ideas that were available and widely accepted in the Elizabethan era.

What is more, the single phrase that might seem to suggest disapproval is situated among a number of other phrases that seem to suggest approval. Although Carlisle plays a very minor role in the play – he appears in only two scenes and speaks only about sixty lines – Johnson hails him as 'brave, pious, and venerable . . . from the beginning to the end'. Johnson also writes respectfully of Carlisle's 'elevated notions of the right of kings'. Unlike the verb 'to flatter', the verb 'to elevate' has strongly positive connotations. According to Johnson's *Dictionary*, it can mean not only 'to raise up aloft', but also 'to exalt; to dignify'. When Johnson speaks of Carlisle's 'elevated' notions of indefeasible right he may therefore be praising those notions as exalted or dignified concepts.

What is most remarkable about this note, however, is that Johnson imputes 'elevated notions' of the right of kings not only to Carlisle but also to 'our author': Shakespeare did not learn '*his* elevated notions of the right of kings' during the reign.[43] James I. At first it is hard to know what to make of this statement. Is Johnson merely saying that Carlisle's notions can be traced to Shakespeare in the same sense that every character's notions can be traced to the author? Or is he suggesting that Shakespeare actually shares Carlisle's views? The third sentence of the note suggests that Johnson indeed identified the politics of the author with the politics of the character. In this sentence Johnson notes, with evident approval, that Shakespeare has not only made Carlisle 'brave, pious, and venerable' but has also *intended* to do so. Had Shakespeare wished to show indefeasible right in a bad light, Johnson implies, he would not have depicted the chief spokesman for that doctrine as an ideal prelate.[44]

If we look at a few more notes, we can see that Johnson actually has a clear-cut, unusual and rather one-sided interpretation of this play. A number of earlier critics, including Nahum Tate and Charles Gildon, had argued that Shakespeare paints a dark and unfavourable portrait of Richard II.[45] On the other hand, many critics after Johnson would argue that Shakespeare is neither for nor against Richard and takes no stand on the issue of the divine right of kings. Matthew Black speaks for many modern critics when he describes *Richard II* as an 'impartial recreation of a political impasse':

> It is full of conflicting political ideas: the idea of divine right of kings, the subject's duty of passive obedience, the dangers of irresponsible despotism, the complex qualities of an ideal ruler. But which of these ideas were Shakespeare's own is impossible to discern. On politics as on religion he preserves as always 'the taciturnity of nature'.[46]

Johnson would have disagreed with these comments; he thought he could discern which political ideas were Shakespeare's own. However, Johnson would also have disagreed with the Tate–Gildon reading of the play, for he believed that Shakespeare shared Carlisle's 'elevated notions' of the rights of kings and was therefore sympathetic not only to Carlisle but also to the doctrine that Carlisle enunciates and the king whom he defends.

Johnson's royalist or pro-Ricardian reading of the play flashes out in several of his notes. In IV. iv Carlisle warns that the deposition of Richard will have dire consequences: 'The woe's to come; the children yet unborn / Shall feel this day as sharp to them as thorn.' Johnson was moved by this couplet, and he evidently believed that it revealed Shakespeare's own opinions: 'This pathetick [i.e. emotionally moving] denunciation shews that Shakespeare *intended* to impress his auditors with dislike of the deposal of Richard.'[47] Elsewhere Johnson argues that Shakespeare tries to engage the reader's sympathies for Richard by painting a favorable portrait of him:

> It seems to be the design of the poet to raise *Richard* to esteem in his fall, and consequently to interest the reader in his favour. He gives him only passive fortitude, the virtue of a confessor rather than of a king. In his prosperity we saw him imperious and oppressive, but in his distress he is wise, patient, and pious.

(55)

Here Johnson imputes to the declining Richard exactly the traits that Gildon had denied him. Gildon thought Shakespeare had made Richard 'Poor, Low, Dejected, [and] Despairing'.[48] Johnson insists that Shakespeare has made him 'wise, patient, and pious'. A few pages later, in another note on III. iv, Johnson makes a similar point. He characterises Richard as 'preparing to submit quietly to irresistible calamity' (60). And again, in III. vi, Johnson claims that Shakespeare sought to present Richard as a paragon of 'submissive misery, conforming its intention to the present fortune, and calmly ending its purposes in death' (66).

Now anyone who has read Shakespeare's play is likely to find Johnson's comments a bit odd. Richard may be passive in his failure to act, but he is certainly not passive in his use of language. Nor is he 'patient' and 'quiet'. In fact, Richard frequently unpacks his heart in lengthy and impassioned soliloquies. Shakespeare gives him more lines than Romeo or Juliet, more lines than Lear or Cleopatra, and many of these lines are emotional almost to the point of hysteria.[49] As Leopold Damrosch has pointed out, Johnson's interpretation is one-sided: 'Johnson's notes to *Richard II* take no notice of the king's maudlin and histrionic self-pity; Johnson wants a figure of Patience worthy of the *Rambler*, and accordingly he finds one.'[50] Damrosch points out that Johnson consistently blames Shakespeare for the verbal excesses of Richard. On several occasions Johnson condemns wordplay for counteracting pathos, but 'he fails to see that the speaker [in these cases] is not Shakespeare but Richard, in whom such rhetorical showmanship is entirely in character'.[51] This approach is evident in one of Johnson's notes on III. vi, where Richard, soon to be deposed, launches into convoluted wordplay on 'head' and 'heart':

> . . . I'll be bury'd in the King's high way,
> Some way of common Trade, where Subjects' feet
> May hourly trample on their Sovereign's head;
> For on my heart they tread now, whilst I live;
> And, bury'd once, why not upon my head?

> (66)

Johnson grumbles in his note, 'Shakespeare is very apt to deviate from the *pathetic* to the *ridiculous*. Had the speech of Richard ended [earlier] it had exhibited the natural language of submissive misery, conforming its intention to the present fortune, and calmly ending its purposes in death' (66). Here once again we see that Johnson's interpretation of *Richard II* differs dramatically from the dominant modern interpretation. Whereas modern critics tend to assume that Shakespeare wishes to portray Richard as an hysterical rhetorician, Johnson assumes that Shakespeare wishes to portray Richard as a paragon of 'submissive misery', but undermines his own intentions by pursuing the luminous vapours of wordplay. Indeed, Johnson evidently thinks it is Shakespeare's tendency to deviate from pathetic speech into ridiculous wordplay that vitiates the play's overall emotional impact and keeps it from 'much . . . affect[ing] the passions'.[52]

Damrosch argues that Johnson has committed the original sin of literary criticism: he has looked at Shakespeare's play and found precisely what he wished to find. This argument is substantially persuasive; many of Johnson's comments on *Richard II* really do seem to tell us more about Johnson than they do about Shakespeare. However, it may be that Johnson is finding what he wishes to find not only in a moral sense but also in a political sense, that he sees Richard II not only as 'a figure of Patience worthy of the *Rambler*', but also as figure of patience worthy of Charles I, as he appears in that famous royalist tract *Eikon Basilike, the Portraiture of His Sacred Majesty in His Solitudes and Sufferings*.

It was not uncommon for Englishmen to draw a parallel between Richard II and Charles I. During the Civil War parliamentary propagandists cited the deposition of Richard as a precedent for their efforts to depose Charles.[53] Royalists, on the other hand, had to reject all such precedents. Johnson may well have been familiar with some of the pamphlets in which this parallel is discussed, for he had read deeply in the fugitive tracts of the 1640s while preparing the catalogue of the Harleian Library. If Johnson was familiar with and accepted the parallel, it would almost certainly have made him more sympathetic to Richard II, for he was deeply sympathetic to Charles I. Johnson referred to the Commonwealth government as 'a manifest usurpation'.[54] The Long Parliament was a 'detestable band' that had 'destroyed the church, murdered the King, and filled the nation with tumult and oppression'.[55] Cromwell was a 'tyrant' who 'could do nothing lawful'.[56] On the other hand, Johnson venerated Charles I as a martyr and model of Christian patience. He believed that *Eikon Basilike* was from the king's own hand, and he cited this relatively short work more than 350 times in the *Dictionary*.[57] Johnson also admired Charles' unfortunate prelate, Archbishop Laud.[58] Indeed, Johnson's comments on Richard II sometimes seem to echo Laud's comments on Charles I. Laud famously remarked that Charles was a good Christian but not a good king: he was 'a mild and gracious prince who knew not how to be, or be made, great'.[59] As we have seen, Johnson thinks that Shakespeare's Richard displays 'only passive fortitude, the virtue of a confessor rather than a king'. In short, it is possible that veneration for the deposed Charles I and his supporter Archbishop Laud encouraged Johnson to turn a sympathetic eye on the deposed Richard II and his supporter Bishop Carlisle, as depicted in Shakespeare's play. But is there any hard evidence that Johnson would have been familiar with the parallel between Charles I and Richard II? As it happens, there is. Even if Johnson had not encountered the parallel in Civil War era pamphlets, he would have encountered it in Zachary Grey's *Critical, Historical, and Explanatory Notes on Shakespeare* (1754), a work he cited frequently in his own edition of Shakespeare. Grey had inserted a note on the speech near the end of *Richard II* (V. iii) in which York describes the people's cruel treatment of the deposed Richard:

> No joyful tongue gave him his welcome home;
> But dust was thrown upon his sacred head;
> Which with such gentle sorrow he shook off,
> His face still combating with tears and smiles,
> The badges of his grief and patience.
>
> (89)

Grey drew a parallel between Richard II and Charles I, but he wondered if it was appropriate to make Richard sound like Charles: 'I don't find that this suits, in all respects, the character of King *Richard the Second*. Had Shakespeare survived the reign of King *Charles the First*, I should have imagined that this was an encomium upon him, for his remarkable patience.'[60] Johnson approvingly reprinted several of Grey's notes, but it is no surprise that he did not reprint this one, for, as we have seen, Johnson accepted the similarity which Grey denied. He saw both the historical Charles I and the fictional Richard II as paragons of 'grief and patience'. For Johnson, both kings were models of 'submissive misery'. Both were 'wise, patient, and pious' men 'submit[ting] quietly to irresistible calamity'.

Johnson may also have drawn a parallel between Richard II and the other deposed Stuart King, James II. Such parallels were quite common in the late seventeenth and early eighteenth centuries. Ironically enough, they can be traced all the way to James II himself. On 27 November 1688, as William of Orange and his army were advancing on London, James told an assembly of lords 'that it would appear that the Prince of Orange came for the crown, whatever he pretended; but that he would not see himself deposed; that he had read the story of King Richard II'.[61] But James *was* deposed, and in subsequent years his deposition was often compared with the deposition of Richard II. I have found this parallel treated in more than half a dozen Nonjuring pamphlets,[62] in several Whig responses to these pamphlets,[63] in poems by Dryden and Theobald,[64] in *The Craftsman*,[65] in *Cato's Letters*,[66] in Thomas Hearne's diary,[67] and in Hume's *History of England*.[68] In virtually every case the parallel is politically charged. Those who wish to justify the revolution of 1688–89 typically point to the non-lineal accession of Henry IV in 1399 as a precedent for the non-lineal accession of William and Mary in 1689. On the other hand, Jacobites and Nonjurors tend to point to the arguments advanced against the deposition of Richard II and insist that these arguments were equally valid in the case of James II. The Jacobites and Nonjurors even use the vocabulary of the 1690s to describe the events of 1399: for instance, they hail Richard's great defender, Carlisle, as a 'Nonjuror' to Henry IV and a 'deprived bishop'.[69]

Johnson was unquestionably familiar with the parallels drawn by Jacobites and Nonjurors, and he even approved of them sufficiently to quote one example in his *Dictionary*. If we wish fully to understand the political context of his comments on *Richard II* we need to spend a few paragraphs familiarising ourselves with these parallels as well.

One of the Nonjurors who used the parallel between Richard II and James II effectively was George Hickes. In his *Vindication of Some Among Ourselves From the False Principles of Dr. Sherlock* (1692), Hickes attacked his former companion-in-arms William Sherlock for abandoning the Nonjuring cause and taking the oath of allegiance to William and Mary. Sherlock had originally insisted that James II had an indefeasible right to the throne and that the English people had no right to depose him. However, he eventually changed his mind and took the oath of allegiance. He attempted to justify his apostasy by arguing that William and Mary had a 'providential' right to the throne, and that the Nonjurors' appeal to divine right 'contradict[ed] the general Sense, and Practice of Mankind in all Revolutions'.[70] In his *Vindication* Hickes attempted to refute Sherlock's claims by examining a series of historical events, including the deposition of Richard II:

> But from this Usurpation let us pass to that of *Henry* IV, who was set up by Providence, and the Estates of the Realm, who took upon them to depose *Richard* II, and place Henry on his throne. But *Henry* being conscious to himself that he wanted Legal Right, though he had all the Right that Providence could give him, yet not daring to trust to such an airy Tit[l]e, nor his false pretenses of being the right Heir, caused *Richard* to be murdered; but between his Deposition and Murder, Thomas Merks Bishop of *Carlisle*, a Brave and Godly Prelate, preferring his Duty before his Safety, took the courage to make a Speech in Parliament, against the validity of *Richard's* Deposition, and the Justice of *Henry's* Election; and if you please, Doctor, to read this Speech as it is at large in our Historians, you will find, in spight of all your prejudice, that he was a very *Wise and Considering Man, and entirely of these Mens* [the Nonjurors'] opinion, and produced those Reasons for it which you say, *Contradict the general sense of Mankind in all Revolutions*.
>
> (17)

Hickes then gives a point-by-point summary of the Bishop of Carlisle's arguments. Carlisle insisted on the doctrines of passive obedience and indefeasible right: 'a king may not be deposed by his Subjects for any imputation of negligence and tyranny' (18). He also argued that '*Henry* had no Title', and he ran though a list of reasons why:

First, Not as Heir to *Richard*, which he pretended; for then he ought to stay till King *Richard* was dead; but then if K. *Richard* was dead, it was well known there were Descendents from *Lionel* Duke of *Clarence*, whose Offspring had been declared in the High Court of Parliament, next Successor to the Crown, in case K. *Richard* should die without Issue. Secondly, Not by Conquest, because a Subject can have no right of Conquest against a Sovereign . . . Nor thirdly by *K. Richard's Resignation*, because he made it in Prison where it was exacted of him by force . . . Nor last of all, by Election, for (saith he) we have no Custom that the People at pleasure should elect their king . . . much less can they make good or confirm that Title which is before Usurped by violence.

(18)

Carlisle concluded 'that Richard still remaineth our Sovereign Prince, and . . . it is not lawful for us to give judgment upon him' (19). In short, Hickes and the other Nonjurors held that the situation in the 1690s was exactly analogous to the situation in 1399; they believed that William and Mary had no genuine title and that James II remained the sovereign prince. For these men the Bishop of Carlisle was not only an 'Heroic Prelate', he was also a precursor, a sort of Nonjuror before there were Nonjurors.

Hickes's parallel between Richard II and James II clearly caught John Dryden's attention. In his 'Character of a Good Parson; Imitated from Chaucer, and Inlarg'd', the deposed laureate added twenty-three lines in which he followed Hickes's argument closely. In these lines Dryden identifies Chaucer's good parson with the Bishop of Carlisle, but he also makes a connection between the late fourteenth century and the late seventeenth century by putting many of the Nonjurors' arguments into the mouth of Carlisle. Dryden imagines the Devil tempting Carlisle, asking him to swear allegiance to Henry IV, just as the Nonjurors had been asked to swear allegiance to William and Mary:

> The Tempter saw him too, with envious Eye;
> And, as on *Job*, demanded leave to try.
> He took the time when *Richard* was depos'd:
> And High and Low, with Happy Harry clos'd.
> This Prince, tho' great in Arms, the Priest withstood:
> Near tho' he was, yet not the next of Blood.
> Had *Richard* unconstrain'd, resign'd the Throne: ⎫
> A King can give no more than is his own: ⎬
> The Title stood entail'd, had *Richard* had a son.[71] ⎭

The parallels here would have been too obvious for Dryden's readers to miss. Dryden's parson denies Henry's claim to the throne, just as the Nonjurors denied the claims of William and Mary. The parson points out that Henry is not the 'next of Blood'. The Nonjurors made the same point about William and Mary and their successors. The parson argues that Richard's resignation was constrained. The Nonjurors insisted that James had not abdicated but had been driven away.[72] But the strongest proof that Dryden has James II in mind comes in the last line of the passage quoted above, where Dryden writes, 'had Richard had a son'. Richard II did not have a son, but James II did. By adding these five words, Dryden makes it clear that his lines refer not only to Richard II but also to James II.[73] Dryden even draws attention to the complication of the parallel by extending this crucial couplet into a triplet. He then goes on to list several possible justifications for the deposition of Richard II, all of which the 'good parson' Carlisle rejects in proto-Nonjuring fashion:

> Conquest, an odious Name, was laid aside,
> Where all submitted; none the Battle try'd.
> The senseless Plea of Right by Providence,
> Was, by a flatt'ring Priest, invented since:
> And lasts no longer than the present sway;
> But justifies the next who comes in play.
>   The People's Right remains; let those who dare
> Dispute their Pow'r, when they the judges are.
>   He joined not in their Choice; because he knew
> Worse might, and often did from Change ensue.
> Much to himself he thought, but little spoke:
> And, Undepriv'd, his Benefice forsook.

Dryden runs through the same justifications for deposition that Hickes had run through in his *Apology*: the argument that conquest begets right, the argument that success is an indication of providential right, and the argument that the king's right depends on the voice of the people. Dryden's Carlisle rejects all these arguments, just as Hickes and the other Nonjurors rejected them. When Dryden writes of the 'flatt'ring priest' who invented the notion of providential right, he is clearly referring to the same William Sherlock whom Hickes attacked in his *Apology*. In short, Dryden has taken over the substance of Hickes' argument and versified it. 'The Character of a Good Parson' is, as Howard Erskine-Hill has pointed out, 'a summation and rejection of the various arguments of the 1690s for accepting the Williamite settlement . . . [and] a Catholic convert's tribute to the Anglican Non-Juror position in support of the *de jure* king'.[74]

These connections between Richard II and James II help to explain why Shakespeare's *Richard II* was seldom performed in the years after the Glorious Revolution: plays about deposed kings were political dynamite. In 1719, when he revived an altered version of the play, Lewis Theobald anticipated that viewers might make the connection that Hickes and Dryden (and many others) had made. In his prologue Theobald denied that he meant to draw any such parallel:

> If recent Times more fresh Examples bring,
> How we can *murther*, or *depose* a King,
> Fearful of Censure, and offended Law,
> The Muse presumes no *Parallels* to draw;
> Nor aims to make the sullen, factious Stage
> Bellow with *Anti-Revolution* Rage.
> From *Richard's* Ruin, only, she intends
> To wound your Souls, and make you *Richard's* Friends.[75]

The fact that Theobald felt the need to make such a disavowal proves that the parallel between Richard II and James II was common intellectual currency during the early eighteenth century – and was often used to stir up '*Anti-Revolution* Rage'.

Johnson may have known Theobald's prologue. He was familiar with Theobald's Shakespeare criticism and with English literary history during Theobald's lifetime. He may also have known Hickes's pamphlet. Hawkins noted that Johnson censured Sherlock and other Williamite and Hoadleian divines as 'worthless men' while praising Hickes, Leslie, Brett and other Nonjurors.[76] Indeed, Hawkins believed that the Nonjurors had exercised a major influence on Johnson's own thinking: 'Johnson in his early years associated with this sect of nonjurors, and from them, probably, imbibed many of his religious and political principles.'[77]

On one point, however, there is no need for speculation: Johnson certainly knew Dryden's poem. He cited 'The Character of a Good Parson' at least forty-five times in the *Dictionary*, and five of his quotations are taken from the politically charged sections quoted above.[78] In several cases Johnson used these quotations to illustrate words with dynastic and political significance. For instance, Johnson gave several definitions of 'to ENTAIL', including '1. To settle the descent of any estate so that it cannot be by any subsequent possessor bequeathed at pleasure', and '2. To fix unalienably upon any person or thing'. He then used Dryden's telltale triplet to illustrate the word: 'Had Richard unconstrain'd resign'd the throne, / A king can give no more than is his own: / The title stood *entail'd*, had Richard had a son.' Under BENEFICE, Johnson appended, 'Much to himself he thought, but little spoke, / And, undepriv'd, his *benefice* forsook.' Under 'UNDEPRIVED' he quoted the second of these two lines again. Under 'to CLOSE with' he added, 'He took the time when Richard was depos'd, / And high and low *with* happy Harry *closed*.' Finally, under the noun 'PLAY', defined as a synonym for 'office', Johnson had his amanuensis copy out Dryden's Hickes-inspired attack on Sherlock's concept of providential right:

'The senseless plea of right by providence / Can last no longer than the present sway; / But justifies the next who comes in *play*.'

Johnson made a point of excluding from his *Dictionary* all material that he believed to be ideologically inappropriate. Dryden's poem pays tribute to the Nonjuring bishops who refused to swear allegiance to William and Mary, it rejects the arguments that were routinely used to justify the revolution of 1688–89, and it implies that the Hanoverian kings had no bona fide right to the throne. Yet Johnson evidently did not feel that the poem was inappropriate. This is highly suggestive in and of itself. It lends a certain amount of support to Thomas Edwards's claim that Johnson made his *Dictionary* 'a vehicle for Jacobite and High-flying tenets'.[79] However, these quotations are also valuable because they help us better to understand the political context of, and possibly even the motivations for, Johnson's sympathetic attitude towards Shakespeare's Richard and Carlisle.

Let us review what we have established so far: Johnson knew that Nonjurors and Stuart loyalists like Dryden often drew parallels between Richard II and James II and between the Bishop of Carlisle and the Nonjuring bishops. In his notes on *Richard II* Johnson draws a similar parallel between Carlisle and the defenders of the Stuarts. In a few notes he defends the Stuarts, and in a number of others he reveals a pronounced fondness for Shakespeare's Richard II and Carlisle. Hickes and other Nonjurors hailed their precursor, Carlisle, as 'brave', 'godly' and 'wise'. Johnson salutes this proto-Nonjuror as 'brave, pious, and venerable'. What then shall we conclude? If, as Hume and Lewis have suggested, sympathy for Mary Queen of Scots often correlates with a liking for Jacobitism; and if, as I have suggested, sympathy for Richard II and admiration for Carlisle often correlate with a liking for the Nonjuring cause, do we not have some grounds for suspecting that Johnson had at least 'a kind of liking' for both causes?

Several of Johnson's other notes seem to point towards the same conclusion. On more than one occasion Johnson draws respectful, nonjudgemental attention to the trappings of divine right kingship, including the king's reverence-inspiring sceptre (7) and his 'oil of consecration' (80). Johnson also refers to Richard II as 'the deposed Prince' (83) and Bolingbroke as 'the usurper' (79). This is not the language of neutrality: according to the *Dictionary*, a usurper is 'one who seizes or possesses that to which he has no right. It is generally used of one who excludes the right heir from the throne.'

This pattern of naming is visible not only in Johnson's notes on *Richard II* but also in his notes on the subsequent plays in the tetralogy. In Act IV, scene xi of *2 Henry IV* Bolingbroke, now Henry IV, rejoices that his son's claim to the throne will be more secure than his own: 'for what in me was purchas'd / Falls upon thee in a more fairer sort; / So thou the garland wear'st successively.' In his note on this line Johnson draws a potentially inflammatory generalisation: 'Every usurper snatches a claim of hereditary right as soon as he can' (333). This was a point that Nonjurors such as Charles Leslie and George Harbin liked to make. Leslie pointed out that, 'Usurpers after they [have] got into *Possession*' always 'Pretend some *Right* besides *Posses-sion*'.[80] When it comes to hereditary right, Harbin observed, 'even those who had it not did claim it . . . never was [there] any king in England who would not have preferr'd Hereditary Right to all other titles; the Constitution of England is therefore hereditary':[81] Johnson was keeping suspicious company. Nor was this the first time he had made this politically sensitive observa-tion. In his trenchant and possibly Jacobitical 1739 pamphlet *Marmor Nor-folciense*, Johnson had allowed his bumbling commentator to stumble upon the same point: 'how common it is for intruders of yesterday, to pretend to the same title with the ancient proprietors, and having received an estate by voluntary grant, to erect a claim of "hereditary right".'[82] One critic of *Marmor* attacked this last remark as a 'Jacobitical' libel on 'the first illustri-ous Heroes of the Brunswick Line'.[83] It would certainly be possible to read Johnson's Shakespeare note as something similar; indeed, one might argue that the Shakespeare note is stronger evidence, since Johnson is speaking in his own person rather than through a persona. At the very least, one wonders whether a devoted Hanoverian would repeatedly draw attention to the dynasty's Achilles' heel.

The issue of lineal inheritance crops up again and again in Johnson's notes. In II. vi Johnson points out a passage in which Shakespeare 'seems to have used [the word] *heir* in an improper sense'. Johnson reminds his readers that an heir is 'one that *inherits by succession*' and not 'one that *suc-ceeds* [only] in order of time, not in order of descent' (40). Johnson's imme-diate goal is to clarify the passage in question, but his note raises some politically touchy issues. Bolingbroke had succeeded Richard II in order of time, but not in order of descent; and, as we have seen, his succession was cited as a precedent for William and Mary and the Hanoverians, who also inherited in order of time but not in order of descent.

The issue of lineal succession comes up again in II. x, when Bolingbroke claims a right to his dukedom: 'Wherefore was I born? / If that my cousin King be King of England. / It must be granted, I am Duke of Lancaster.' Johnson sees immediately that Bolingbroke's argument is based on inheri-tance. He paraphrases: 'To what purpose serves birth and lineal succession? I am Duke of *Lancaster* by the same right of birth as the King is King of *England*' (47). What Johnson does not say, but what he clearly understood, is that this principle of lineal succession cuts both ways. If a duke can claim an indefeasible hereditary right to his dukedom, then a king can claim an indefeasible hereditary right to his kingdom. Bolingbroke may be able to appeal to 'lineal succession' when reclaiming his dukedom, but his own principle militates against him and in favour of Richard as soon as he claims the kingdom. It is clear that Johnson understood all this because he drew precisely the same parallel between common inheritance and royal inheritance in a political debate he had with his Whig friend John Taylor in 1777:

> Sir, you are to consider, that all those who think a King has a right to his crown, as a man has to his estate, which is the just opinion, would be for restoring the King who certainly has the hereditary right . . . And you must also consider, Sir, that there is nothing on the other side to oppose this; for it is not alledged by any one that the present family has any inherent right.[84]

This was an explicitly Jacobitical argument.[85] The only questions are whether Boswell accurately recorded Johnson's comments and whether Johnson was urging his sincere opinions or merely 'talking for victory'.

The last note that I wish to consider occurs in III. vi, when Richard foresees his deposition and prophesies that Bolingbroke's usurpation will bring misery upon future generations:

> But ere the Crown, he looks for, live in peace,
> Ten thousand bloody crowns of mothers' sons
> Shall ill become the flow'r of *England*'s face,
> Change the complexion of her maid-pale peace
> To scarlet indignation; and bedew
> Her Pasture's grass with faithful *English* blood.
>
>   (63–4)

Although the sense here is fairly clear, Johnson chooses to draw additional attention to the passage by adding a paraphrase in which he explains that Richard is prophesying about the consequences of revolution: 'though he should get the *crown* by rebellion, it will be long before it will *live* in peace [and] be so *settled* as to be firm' (64). In conversation Johnson often spoke as if he felt the same way about the revolution of 1688–89. Whereas Whigs often spoke of the revolution as a 'settlement', Johnson often spoke of it as an event that had *un*settled the nation. In the aforementioned debate with Taylor, he argued that the English people 'have grown cold and indifferent on the subject of loyalty' precisely because everyone agrees 'that this King has not the hereditary right to the crown'.[86] In 1783 Johnson and General Oglethorpe discussed current 'disturbances'. Oglethorpe complained that 'Government is now carried on by corrupt influence, instead of the inherent right of the king'. Johnson replied, 'Sir, the want of inherent right in the King occasions all this disturbance.'[87] In March 1784 Johnson discussed these same 'disturbances' with Boswell:

> He talked with regret and indignation of the factious opposition to the government at this time, and imputed it, in a great measure, to the

Revolution. 'Sir, (said he, in a low voice, having come nearer to me, while his old prejudices seemed to be fermenting in his mind,) this Hanoverian family is *isolée* here. They have no friends. Now the Stuarts had friends that stood by them so late as 1745. When the right of the King is not reverenced, there will not be reverence for those appointed by the King.[88]

If Boswell's conversational records may be trusted (which is of course a hotly contested question) we can say that Johnson saw the events of 1688–89 in substantially the same way that Shakespeare's Carlisle saw the events of 1399. He saw the revolution as an event that unsettled governmental authority and civil order for years to come.

Johnson's notes on *Richard II* do not prove that Johnson was a Jacobite and a Nonjuror, but they do suggest that the Tory Johnson had at least 'a kind of liking' for both causes. Johnson's uncritical comments on absolute sovereignty and indefeasible right, his distinction between himself and Warburton, his favourable review of Tytler's book on Mary Queen of Scots, his sympathy for Richard II and admiration for the proto-Nonjuror Carlisle, his *Dictionary* citations from Dryden's 'Character of a Good Parson', his cryptic comments on usurpers and lineal succession, and his highlighting of the unsettling consequences of revolution – these are all 'atoms of probability' and they all suggest that Johnson was substantially more sympathetic to the Stuarts, the Jacobites and the Nonjurors than supporters of the Hanoverian Johnson have so far been willing to admit.[89]

Notes

1. For the debate, see the introduction to this volume.
2. Donald Greene mentions the subject briefly in 'Johnson: The Jacobite Legend Exhumed, A Rejoinder to Howard Erskine-Hill and J.C.D. Clark', *AJ*, 7 (1995), pp. 57–135. On p. 61 Greene points out that Parliament had confirmed the deposition of Richard II in 1399. Greene writes, 'Johnson, in his annotations to Shakespeare's plays . . . does not, so far as I can recall, enter any emphatic protest against [this] flagrant [breach] of hereditary "title".' While it is true that there are no 'emphatic protests' in Johnson's notes, there are a number of suggestive remarks.
3. For a different reading of the same evidence, see Warren L. Fleischauer, 'Dr. Johnson's Editing and Criticism of Shakespeare's Lancastrian Cycle', unpublished dissertation (Western Reserve University, 1951), pp. 109–36.
4. The scene divisions in Johnson's edition often differ dramatically from those in modern editions.
5. *The Plays of William Shakespeare* (8 vols., London, 1765), IV, p. 30. All subsequent citations will be to volume IV of this edition and will be given parenthetically. Johnson's notes are also available, in slightly modernised form, in the *Yale Edition* VII–VIII: *Johnson on Shakespeare*, ed. Arthur Sherbo (New Haven, 1968).
6. Boswell, *Life*, IV, pp. 197–8, 274.
7. See G.V. Bennett, *White Kennet* (London, 1957), p. 103.

8. See William Warburton, *The Alliance between Church and State* (London, 1736); Robert M. Ryley, *William Warburton* (Boston, 1984); J.C.D. Clark, *English Society 1660–1832* (Cambridge, 2000), pp. 103–5. In *The Religious Thought of Samuel Johnson* (University of Michigan Press, 1968), Chester Chapin compares Johnson's and Warburton's religious views and finds many similarities (pp. 122–6). One crucial difference between Warburton and Johnson, however, is that Warburton was a strong Erastian, whereas Johnson evidently wished to preserve the independence of the Church. See Allen Reddick, *The Making of Johnson's Dictionary* (2nd edn., Cambridge, 1996), pp. 141–69 and 'Johnson Beyond Jacobitism: Signs of Polemic in the *Dictionary* and *The Life of Milton*', *ELH*, 64 (1997). Also relevant are Johnson's opinions on Warburton and the 'factious' skills of Hanoverian bishops: see Boswell, *Life*, V, p. 80 and II, p. 352.

9. *The Works of the Right Reverend William Warburton, D.D.* (12 vols., London, 1811), IX, p. 304. All subsequent citations are to this volume of this edition and will be given parenthetically. Johnson seems to have known at least some of Warburton's sermons: see Donald Greene, *Samuel Johnson's Library: An Annotated Guide* (Victoria, 1975), p. 115.

10. The modern case is summarised in Clark, *Samuel Johnson* and Howard Erskine-Hill, 'The Political Character of Samuel Johnson', in *Samuel Johnson: New Critical Essays*, ed. Isobel Grundy (London, 1984), pp. 105–36. For contemporary newspaper comments on Johnson's politics, see Helen Louise McGuffie, *Samuel Johnson in the British Press, 1749–1784* (New York and London, 1976).

11. Hawkins, *Life*, p. 393.

12. *The Pamphlet entitled 'Taxation No Tyranny,' candidly considered, and it's Argument, and pernicious Doctrines, Exposed and Refuted* (London, 1775), p. 7.

13. *Tyranny Unmasked. An Answer to a late Pamphlet, Entitled Taxation No Tyranny* (London, 1775), p. 7.

14. Boswell, *Life*, I, p. 147.

15. Boswell, *Life*, II, p. 342.

16. Johnson, *Political Writings*, ed. Donald J. Greene (New Haven, 1977), *Yale Edition*, X, p. 342. At least two replies to this pamphlet cited this passage as evidence of Johnson's Jacobitism. See [John Wilkes], *A Letter to Samuel Johnson, L.L.D.* (London, 1770), pp. 51–4, and *The Middlesex Journal* for 6 February 1770.

17. Philip Mahone Griffith, 'Samuel Johnson and King Charles the Martyr: Veneration in the *Dictionary*', *AJ*, 2 (1989), pp. 235–61.

18. Boswell, *Life*, II, p. 341.

19. For a breakdown of Johnson's reservations about each of the Stuart kings, as well as a different take on Johnson's politics in general, see John A. Vance, *Samuel Johnson and the Sense of History* (Athens, Ga, 1984), pp. 47–50.

20. Boswell, *Life*, I, pp. 423–4. Compare [George Hickes], *A Word to the Wavering* (London, 1689), pp. 5, 7; [Jeremy Collier], *Vindiciae Juris Regii* (London, 1689), p. 40; and [Anon.], *Letter to the Author of a late paper Entituled, A Vindication of the Divines of England* (London, 1689). The first two items are Nonjuring works arguing that the king is above the law; the third is a Hanoverian reply denying the proposition.

21. *Thraliana; The Diary of Mrs. Hester Lynch Thrale (later Mrs. Piozzi) 1776–1809* (2 vols., Oxford, 1942), I, p. 192. This passage was first noted by J.C.D. Clark in 'Religious Affiliation and Dynastic Allegiance in Eighteenth-Century England: Edmund Burke, Thomas Paine and Samuel Johnson', *ELH*, 64 (1997).

22. Clark discusses this episode and the Scottish tour in general in *Samuel Johnson*, pp. 219–25.
23. Johnson, *Letters*, II, p. 91.
24. Boswell chose to refer to Charles Edward as 'the grandson of the unfortunate King James the Second' (*Life*, V, p. 185 and n. 4). For Johnson's terminology, see Johnson, *Letters*, II, pp. 80, 83, 90.
25. Boswell, *Life*, III, p. 162.
26. Hawkins, *Life*, p. 250; Clark, *Samuel Johnson*, pp. 177–8.
27. Clark cites this passage (*Samuel Johnson*, pp. 177–8) but does not comment on it in detail.
28. For the club and its dates, see Hawkins, *Life*, pp. 219ff, 361ff.
29. The Victorian critic Charles Knight went one step further. Knight thought that Johnson 'rejoic[ed]' to find passages in *Richard II* that supported his own absolutist political assumptions: *The Comedies, Histories, Tragedies and Poems of William Shakespeare* (12 vols., London, 1842), IV, pp. 500–4.
30. John Neville Figgis, *The Divine Right of Kings* (2nd edn., Cambridge, 1922), p. 20, n. 1.
31. John Locke, *Two Treatises of Government*, ed. Peter Laslett (Cambridge, 1963), I, s. 3, p. 176. See Mark Goldie, 'John Locke and Anglican Royalism', *Political Studies*, 31 (1983), pp. 61–85.
32. [Abednego Seller], *History of Passive Obedience Since the Reformation* (London, 1689–90). The quoted summary is from G.M. Straka, *Anglican Reaction to the Revolution of 1688* (Madison, Wisc., 1962), p. 27.
33. [George Harbin], *The Hereditary Right of the Crown of England Asserted* (London, 1713). Harbin asserts that 'All Hereditary Titles, that were ever received in this Island, were united in the Person of King James I' (p. 13). Compare Johnson's remark: 'the house of Stuart succeeded to the full right of both the houses of York and Lancaster, whose common source had the undisputed right' (Boswell, *Life*, III, p. 157).
34. For Johnson's assessment of Leslie, see Boswell, *Life*, IV, pp. 286–7. The Leslie passage is quoted in Figgis, *Divine Right of Kings*, p. 20, n. 1.
35. This review originally appeared in *The Gentleman's Magazine* (October, 1760), pp. 453–6. It is reprinted in Donald Greene (ed.), *Samuel Johnson* (Oxford University Press, 1984), pp. 551–7. I quote from Greene's text.
36. Greene, *The Politics of Samuel Johnson* (2nd edn., Athens, Ga, 1990), pp. 181–3. See also Vance, *Samuel Johnson and the Sense of History*, pp. 45–6.
37. David Hume, *History of England* (6 vols., Indianapolis, 1983), IV, p. 394, Note 'M' to chapter 39.
38. Quoted on p. 7 of Howard Erskine-Hill, 'A Kind of *Liking* for Jacobitism', *AJ*, 8 (1996), pp. 3–14.
39. Jayne Elizabeth Lewis, 'Mary Stuart's "Fatal Box": Sentimental History and the Revival of the Casket Letters Controversy,' *AJ*, 7 (1996), pp. 446–7; see also Lewis, 'Hamilton's "Abdication", Boswell's Jacobitism and the Myth of Mary Queen of Scots', *ELH*, 64 (1997), pp. 1069–90.
40. Edmund Malone has a note on this in his edition: *The Plays of William Shakespeare* (21 vols., London, 1821), XVI, p. 129. See also A.R. Humphreys, *Shakespeare: Richard II* (London, 1967), p. 37.
41. The relevant passages from Holinshed are quoted in a book that Johnson cited frequently in his edition of Shakespeare, Charlotte Lennox's *Shakespear Illustrated* (3 vols., London, 1753), III, p. 105.

42. [Harbin], *The Hereditary Right of the Crown of England Asserted*, pp. 64–70. [Hickes], *Vindication of Some among Our Selves Against the False Principles of Dr. Sherlock* (London, 1692), pp. 13ff. (quoted extensively below).

43. [Anon.], *The British Liberty Asserted: Being a Full Answer To a late Book Entitul'd The Hereditary Right of the Crown of England Asserted* (London, 1714), p. 29. But cf. White Kennett, *Letter to the Lord Bishop of Carlisle* (London, 1713).

44. Johnson's associate, George Steevens, held the same opinion: 'Shakespeare has represented the character of the bishop as he found it in Holinshed, where this famous speech (which contains, in the most express terms, the doctrine of passive obedience) is preserved. The politicks of the historian were the politicks of the poet.' Quoted in Malone (ed.), *Plays of Shakespeare*, XVI, p. 129.

45. Tate thought Shakespeare had 'painted' Richard 'in the worst Colours of History, Dissolute, Unadvisable, devoted to Ease and Luxury' (quoted in *Shakespeare: The Critical Heritage*, ed. Brian Vickers [2 vols., London, 1974], II, pp. 322–3). Gildon expressed a similarly unfavourable view: 'Shakespeare has drawn Richard's Character [as] Insolent, Proud, and Thoughtless in Prosperity, and full of the Notion that he cou'd not any Way forfeit his Crown being the Lord's Annointed – the common flattery by which Kings are perverted into tyrants – but then Poor, Low, Dejected, Despairing on the Appearance of Danger. In Distress always dissembling Complyance in all things, but never sincere in performance when the Danger is over' (*Critical Heritage*, II, p. 247).

46. Matthew W. Black, Introduction to *Richard II* in *William Shakespeare: The Complete Works*, ed. Alfred Harbage (New York, 1969), p. 634. See also Humphreys, *Shakespeare: Richard II*, p. 37. Charles Knight seems to have been the first to praise Shakespeare for his 'lofty spirit of impartiality' (IV, pp. 501–4), and it is significant that Knight defined his own appreciation of Shakespeare's impartiality in opposition to Johnson's views.

47. P. 83. I have altered the emphasis in this quotation to highlight the *intention*.

48. Quoted in Vickers, *Critical Heritage*, II, p. 247.

49. Line counts are based on tables in Alfred Harbage, General Introduction to *William Shakespeare: The Complete Works*, p. 31.

50. Leopold Damrosch, Jr., *Samuel Johnson and the Tragic Sense* (Princeton, 1972), pp. 228–9.

51. Damrosch, *Tragic Sense*, p. 229.

52. P. 105. Cf. Johnson's remarks on Shakespeare's puns in the *Preface* (*Yale Edition*, VII, p. 74) and in his notes on individual plays (ibid., VIII, pp. 649, 862 and 1045).

53. Howard Erskine-Hill, *Poetry of Opposition and Revolution* (Oxford, 1996), p. 48.

54. Johnson, *Lives of the Poets*, I, pp. 116 and 101–28 *passim*.

55. Johnson, *Lives of the Poets*, I, p. 269.

56. Johnson, *Lives of the Poets*, I, p. 116.

57. Griffith, 'Samuel Johnson and King Charles the Martyr', pp. 235–61. For a more sceptical analysis, see Vance, *Samuel Johnson and the Sense of History*, pp. 48–9.

58. See 'The Vanity of Human Wishes', lines 165–74 and *Johnsonian Miscellanies*, ed. G.B. Hill (2 vols., Oxford, 1897), I, p. 120.

59. Quoted in Griffith, 'Samuel Johnson and King Charles the Martyr', p. 239.

60. Zachary Grey, *Critical, Historical, and Explanatory Notes on Shakespeare* (2 vols., London, 1754), I, pp. 319–20.

61. S.W. Singer (ed.), *Correspondence of Henry Hyde, Earl of Clarendon* (2 vols., London, 1828), II, p. 211, quoted in Erskine-Hill, *Poetry of Opposition and Revolution*, p. 48.

62. [Hickes], *A Word to the Wavering*, p. 6; [Hickes], *Vindication of Some among Our-selves*, pp. 13ff.; [Jeremy Collier], *Vindiciae Juris Regii*, pp. 7–8; [John Kettlewell], *The Duty of Allegiance Settled Upon its True Grounds* (London, 1691), pp. 12, 29, 37; [George Harbin], *Hereditary Right of the Crown of England Asserted*, pp. 64–70; [Charles Leslie], *The Finishing Stroke. Being a Vindication of the Patriarchal Scheme of Government* (London, 1711), pp. 218–19. Howard Erskine-Hill notes several additional examples in 'Literature and the Jacobite Cause: Was There a Rhetoric of Jacobitism?' in *Ideology and Conspiracy: Aspects of Jacobitism, 1689–1759*, ed. Eveline Cruickshanks (Edinburgh, 1982), p. 54 and note 34. See also Erskine-Hill, *Poetry of Opposition and Revolution*, pp. 47–9.

63. See, for example, White Kennett, *Letter to the Lord Bishop of Carlisle* (London, 1713), and its two sequels, William Higden's *Defense of the View of the English Con-stitution* (London, 1710), pp. 39ff., and an anonymous response to Harbin, *The British Liberty Asserted* (London, 1714), pp. 26–43. The author of this last pam-phlet recognises that Harbin's 'panegyricks' on Carlisle 'are so many Eulogies on those Disaffected Prelates [who refuse] to pay Allegiance to their Majesties King William, Queen Mary, and Queen Anne' (p. 28).

64. Both poems are cited below.

65. 2 July 1737. See Jonathan Bate, *Shakespearean Constitutions: Politics, Theatre, Crit-icism 1730–1830* (Oxford, 1989), pp. 69–70.

66. Ronald Hamowy (ed.), *Cato's Letters* (Indianapolis, 1995), pp. 109, 413.

67. Hearne, *Collections*, V, p. 195; IV, pp. 24, 46–7; VIII, p. 143.

68. Hume, *History of England*, II, pp. 319–21. Hume's comments seem to be those of a moderate Whig. He admires Carlisle for his loyalty to the king, but he also qual-ifies his admiration significantly: 'some topics, employed by that virtuous prelate, may seem to favour too much of the doctrine of passive obedience, and make too large a sacrifice of the rights of mankind' (319). Volume 2 of Hume's *History* appeared in 1761; the late date indicates the staying power of the Richard II–James II parallel.

69. See [Harbin], *Hereditary Right of the Crown of England Asserted* (London, 1713), pp. 74–80; these connections are recognised and disputed in *The British Liberty Asserted*, pp. 27ff.

70. [Hickes], *Vindication of Some among Our-selves*, p. 13. All subsequent references will be parenthetical. There is some question about whether Hickes drew on an actual historical source or merely invented arguments for Carlisle in order to suit his purposes. For background information on Sherlock and 'providential' theories, see ch. 6 of Straka's *Anglican Reaction to the Revolution of 1688*.

71. John Dryden, *Poems of John Dryden*, ed. James Kinsley (4 vols., Oxford, 1958), IV, p. 1739.

72. Johnson himself wrote that 'king James was frighted away' (*Lives of the Poets* II, p. 35). See Howard Erskine-Hill, 'The Political Character of Samuel Johnson: *The Lives of the Poets* and a Further Report on *The Vanity of Human Wishes*', in *The Jacobite Challenge*, ed. Eveline Cruickshanks and Jeremy Black (Edinburgh, 1988), pp. 161–76, but also Dustin H. Griffin, 'Regulated Loyalty: Jacobitism and Johnson's *Lives of the Poets*', *ELH*, 64 (1997), pp. 1007–27.

73. See Erskine-Hill, *Poetry of Opposition and Revolution*, p. 48.

74. Erskine-Hill, *Poetry of Opposition and Revolution*, p. 46; see also Alan Roper, *Dryden's Poetic Kingdoms* (New York, 1965), pp. 170–5; Austin C. Dobbins, 'Dryden's "Char-acter of a Good Parson": Background and Interpretation', *Studies in Philology*, 53 (1956), pp. 51–9.

75. Quoted in Vickers, *Critical Heritage*, II, p. 356. The 'murdered king' is, of course, Charles I. See also Margaret Shewring, *King Richard II* (Manchester, 1996); John Loftis, *The Politics of Drama in Augustan England* (Oxford, 1963), pp. 81–2; and Michael Dobson, *The Making of the National Poet* (Oxford, 1992), pp. 94–9.
76. Hawkins, *Life*, pp. 80–1. See also Boswell, *Life*, V, p. 337.
77. Hawkins, *Life*, pp. 448–51.
78. The information in this paragraph was obtained through a series of searches of the Cambridge University Press CD-ROM of Johnson's *Dictionary* (ed. Anne McDermott). Johnson also quoted, under 'RIGHTFULLY', a passage from Dryden's *Preface to the Fables* which discusses 'The Character of a Good Parson': 'Henry, who claimed by succession, was sensible that his title was not sound, but was rightfully in Mortimer.'
79. Edwards is quoted in Clark, *Samuel Johnson*, p. 186. Clark notes some other seemingly Jacobitical quotations (pp. 184–7). However, as Robert DeMaria, Jr. has pointed out ('The Politics of Johnson's Dictionary', *PMLA*, 104 (1989), pp. 64–74), Johnson's *Dictionary* also contains a number of quotations from Locke's *Second Treatise*. A systematically Jacobitical dictionary would presumably have excluded such a source.
80. [Charles Leslie], *The Constitution, Laws, and Government of England, Vindicated* (London, 1709), p. 28.
81. [Harbin], *Hereditary Right of the Crown of England Asserted*, p. 13.
82. *Yale Edition*, X, p. 28. For Clark's argument that *Marmor Norfolciense* is a Jacobite pamphlet, see *Samuel Johnson*, pp. 56–7, 159–65, 230–1.
83. Quoted in Clark, *Samuel Johnson*, pp. 163–4.
84. Boswell, *Life*, III, pp. 155–7.
85. Charles Leslie made a similar argument in *The Finishing Stroke*: 'Has the *Crown* no *Right* at all? Or, has every body in the Nation a *Right* to *Recover* what is *Unjustly* taken from him, except the *King* only? If so, your *King* is in a worse Condition than the meanest of his *Subjects*' (137). For another analogous argument, see Kettlewell, *Duty of Allegiance*, pp. 5, 17. For a later Whig reply to this line of argument, see *The Spirit and Principles of the Whigs and Jacobites Compared* (London, 1745), pp. 29–31.
86. Boswell, *Life*, III, p. 156.
87. Boswell, *Life*, IV, pp. 170–1.
88. Boswell, *Life*, IV, pp. 164–5.
89. I would like to thank those who have read this paper and provided useful criticisms: Martin Battestin, Michael Bundock, J.C.D. Clark, Susan Davis, Howard Erskine-Hill, Allen Reddick, Steven Scherwatzky, and Patricia Meyer Spacks. Thanks are also due to The Folger Shakespeare Library, the Beinecke Library, and the University of Virginia Library.

11

A Jacobite Undertone in 'While Ladies Interpose'?

Niall MacKenzie

Neither Charles XII of Sweden nor Charles Edward Stuart prospered in the face of opposition for as many years as has the idea that the two figures are united through allusion in *The Vanity of Human Wishes*. First proposed in 1984,[1] this idea has gained credibility in proportion with the violence of resistance offered it.[2] By the end of the 1990s, scholars as suspicious of Jacobite readings as John Cannon, Paul Korshin and Lawrence Lipking had expressed cautious openness to the thought that the Jacobite Prince of Wales is being evoked through a sort of loose 'emotional typology' in Johnson's portrait of 'Swedish Charles'.[3] The subsequent discovery[4] of evidence pointing to a persistent and articulate tradition of analogy between the two Charleses, going back to the start of the 1745 uprising and still active (indeed, resurgent) during the last months of 1748 when Johnson wrote his poem, may prove decisive for some waverers.[5] I will take as my starting point the assumption that the case for a flickering Jacobite allusion in lines 191–222 of the *Vanity* has been proved. Here I want to show that the parallel (which no one suggests is complete) extends to lines 211–14, where after suffering a crushing military defeat,

> The vanquish'd hero leaves his broken bands,
> And shews his miseries in distant lands;
> Condemn'd a needy supplicant to wait,
> While ladies interpose, and slaves debate.[6]

At the first level of meaning, Johnson refers to Charles XII's defeat at Poltava in 1709, his abandonment of a scattered army and flight to Bessarabia, and his ignominious sojourn there as a less than fully welcome guest of the Ottoman Emperor – all as recounted in Voltaire's bestselling biography and other accounts. But in the shifting penumbra of more recent historical connotation which surrounds the *Vanity*, we discern, around these lines, Culloden; Charles Stuart's escape from the Highlands where the remnants of the rebel army remained very much in the lurch; and his two-year stay in

France (October 1746–December 1748) of which the final, much discussed stretch was unfolding even as Johnson worked on his poem. The phrase 'While ladies interpose' clinches this reading of the lines before us. So I believe, and so I hope to demonstrate.

Petticoat patronage

On 26 May 1746[7] Louis XV's minister for foreign affairs wrote a strange, half-menacing, half-wheedling letter designed to prevent anything very unpleasant from befalling Louis's ally, Charles Edward Stuart, whose defeat at Culloden one month earlier the French official had just been able to confirm.[8] He reminded the leaders of the British government[9] of the affection and kinship which bound Louis XV to the Stuart Prince; he referred to the world-famous magnanimity of George II, which surely would not fail to shine in this instance; he expressed his confidence that 'Le Caractere de la Nation Britannique'[10] would lead to the generous treatment of a Prince whose 'Vertus Heroiques'[11] had made him the wonder of the age, whatever one's politics. He darkly intimated what consequences might follow if the King his master were given anything to imitate other than 'des Exemples d'Humanité, de Douceur, et de Grandeur d'Ame'.[12] The foreign minister also put in a good word for the Prince's followers, urging mildness towards those 'Personnes de tout Etat, et de tout Sexe, qui . . . ont suivi les Etendards, qui viennent de succomber sous les Armes Angloises . . .'.[13]

René-Louis de Voyer de Paulmy, Marquis d'Argenson, was an enlightened, literary man whose independence of mind was to ensure the brevity of his employment as Louis XV's foreign affairs minister. He will figure again in our discussion, so this word of introduction is apposite. What should hold our attention for the moment, however, is his phrasing in reference to the defeated Jacobite party. '[L]es Personnes de tout Etat, et de tout Sexe . . .'. This is an example of what might be called *conspicuous inclusion*. The writer's going out of his way to recognise the role of women (or their perceived role) in the uprising is significant. He does not emphasise their role. He does not set it above that of men. But the mere rhetorical gesture of recognition suggests that this was an arresting feature of the 1745 rebellion, in a contemporary's perception. In the eighteenth century, even putting women on an equal footing with men was, in a sense, to give special attention to them.

The conspicuous inclusion of women is a ubiquitous feature of eighteenth-century commentary on Jacobitism. A quasi-Scriptural account of the Jacobites' early progress in the '45 says: 'it came to pass in the eight [*sic*] Month . . . in the Year 1745, That the Young Man landed at *Moidart*. . . . And the Hearts of all Men were turned towards him, and the Hearts of all the Women.'[14] A Whig report on the Battle of Culloden, giving an account of both sides' losses, organises its data under headings such as 'Rebel Officers taken', 'Rebel officers killed', and, matter of factly, 'Rebel Ladies taken'.[15]

A print revelling in the aftermath of that battle includes, amid a scene crowded with incident, the detail of a grenadier attacking four rebel ladies.[16] (An odd concession to Jacobite imputations of a chivalry deficit among Whigs.) In 1715, a memorable scene from *Casablanca* was foreshadowed in Edinburgh when a government officer ordered his drummers to drown out a crowd's spontaneous performance of the Jacobite anthem 'The King Shall Enjoy His Own Again'; the drummers were answered, it was said, by 'a generall hissing of both sexes'.[17]

Why not just 'a generall hissing'? 'General' implies women as well as men. Why take the extra rhetorical step of specifically including the other sex, in addition to the men who are the default focus of any eighteenth-century representation? The answer lies in a curious aspect of eighteenth-century culture. Women were believed to have a special weakness for Jacobitism. At a certain level of crude generalisation or satirical cliché, saying that women were predisposed to Jacobitism was like calling sailors drunken, Frenchmen fops, Tories given to fox-hunting, etc. Whigs in general accepted this idea of women being particularly susceptible to the Stuarts just as Jacobites celebrated it. From the Whig viewpoint (which always allowed that a sound upbringing or virtuous character could overcome such unfortunate tendencies[18]), the association of women with the Stuarts served to trivialise Jacobitism's moral and intellectual underpinnings; women were also regarded as high-risk for Catholicism.[19] A less substantial, more stylistic agenda underlay the Jacobite flaunting of their appeal to female opinion: creating an aura of sex appeal is not a twentieth-century innovation in the arts of political persuasion. The conspicuous inclusion of women in descriptions of Jacobite activity, then, reflected and reinforced widely held contemporaneous perceptions of the gender profile of Jacobite support.

Such perceptions deeply informed the literary and pictorial after-images of Prince Charles's failed revolution that were circulating in London in the late 1740s. Jacobite heroines of the '45, real or imaginary, including Lady Seaforth, Flora MacDonald and Jenny Cameron, were depicted in portrait prints.[20] Few visual images that aspired to any kind of general evocation of the late uprising excluded some reference to the supposed contributions of women. None of this period's popular histories of the rising – none, at any rate, that I have seen, and I have been looking for a long time – neglects at least to allude to the Prince's female partisans; many popular histories evince a special fascination for this side of the '45. Jenny Cameron, 'the Pretender's mistress', was the subject of a range of bestselling pseudo-biographies.[21] (Her shadow flits across *Tom Jones*, published within weeks of the *Vanity*.) One opuscule that dealt with the Jacobites' 'Petticoat Patronage', the sensationalising (tongue-in-cheek?) *Female Rebels* of 1747,[22] incidentally also articulates the popular analogy between Charles Stuart and Charles XII (as has been observed elsewhere[23]). Large numbers of armed women flocked to the banners of each Charles, according to *The Female Rebels*, which then develops the parallel between the two royal overreachers. Some may take an unworthy pleasure in juxtaposing the following paragraph from *The Female Rebels* with such recent insights of Johnsonian scholarship as 'Charles XII was not really very similar to Bonnie Prince Charles'[24] and '[Charles XII] and Charles Edward [Stuart], after all, share scarcely more than a Christian name . . .'.[25]

> Besides the Similitude of Names, without any Affront to either, I think we may observe a great Affinity in many Things between these two Adventurers; they were both young, and neither wanted Courage, but both seems [sic] to be actuated by the chimerical Dictates of Ambition; they despised Danger, and abhorred all kind of effeminate Delicacy; they both undertook Expeditions which none but Madmen would have thought of; and both for a Time had Success, which none without the Gift of Prophesy could hope for or foresee: Both gained Glory, but lost their Ends; and succeeding [sic] in nothing but in involving their native Country in Ruin, Blood, Poverty and Desolation: The one lived in a Blaze and died in a Ditch, the other traversed the Island of *Britain* like a Meteor, and fled in a Fog.[26]

Interposing, in one way or another, is an essential function of petticoat patronage in the mid-eighteenth-century mythology of she-Jacobitism. Flora MacDonald, later the theme of so much poignant reflection on Johnson's visit to Skye, had interposed to save Prince Charles after Culloden. Ladies Seaforth and MacIntosh had interposed to raise their husbands' clans, when their husbands had proved too timid. Lady Kilmarnock had doomed her husband by interposing in his deliberations, overruling his quaverings and sending him away to join the rebels. Lady Cromarty had interposed with George II, winning his mercy and preserving her condemned husband's life.[27] Lady Ogilvy's maid interposed to effect her mistress's escape from captivity[28] (a remarkable stunt which recalled the most celebrated of all Jacobite jailbreaks – Lady Nithsdale's springing her husband from the Tower in 1716. Manuscript narratives which circulated among eager Jacobite nuns framed the Nithsdale caper as 'an exercise in gender solidarity . . . an episode of exhilarating female intervention in the process of power . . .'.[29]) Jenny Cameron was represented not only as Charles's bedroom companion and fierce champion on the battlefield, but as an interposer in his counsels to whose 'Advice in all important Occasions, he was principally indebted for his several Successes in the Course of that Rebellion'.[30]

To risk a quick glance down alleyways we have no time to explore, such representations owed more to the symbolic traditions which informed Jacobite culture than to any reality of a national crisis in female loyalty. Having said that, I must emphasise that women do seem to have played a higher profile role in the Jacobite counterculture than in mainstream political life. It is striking, if you go over the list from Astell to Winchilsea, how many early eighteenth-century writers subsequently enrolled into the proto-feminist canon had at least dabbled in Jacobitism. Striking, but not surprising given the mutual gravitation of marginalised groups. Political undergrounds are not congenial to rigid gender prescriptions, and Jacobitism is far from being the only conspiratorial movement in history to which conspicuous numbers of women contributed as harbourers, infiltrators, recruiters, couriers, encipherers, makers and distributors of propaganda, and so on. On the Continent, houses of British and Irish nuns were among the principal 'anchoring points' of Jacobite ghettoes.[31] British and Irish nunneries were also (as in the Royalist diaspora of the mid-1600s[32]) centres of conspiratorial activity, and of the symbolic reinforcement of the exiled dynasty's claims and the émigré community's sense of national identity.

At the level of policy and patronage, independent, feminist-inspired programmes of research have been showing how elite women exercised considerable influence in high-level politics throughout the early modern period, through their interventions in the informal or 'extra-institutional'[33] territory of 'social politics'.[34] There are grounds for suspecting that in the unsettled and insecure, and in a sense permanently 'extra-institutional' realm of the Jacobite diaspora, women enjoyed even wider influence as cultivators of informal contacts, negotiators of marriages, mediators of patronage and lubricators of conspiracy. Certainly Bolingbroke thought so, with his griping about the 'female managers' who (mis)directed Jacobite affairs;[35] and the Marquis d'Argenson supplies a telling instance of conspicuous inclusion when he writes that during the '45, Jacobite influence in France was maintained through the relentless lobbying of waves, 'semblables à ceux de la Manche qui nous sépare de l'Angleterre, des seigneurs, des valets, des femmes, des moines, [et] des aventuriers . . .'.[36]

During the late 1740s, as Prince Charles showed his miseries in France and (briefly) Spain, there were no more significant figures in his political and personal life than the members of a loose network of sympathetic French or *émigrée* women, including the Duchesse d'Aiguillon, Charles's friend the Princesse de Talmont and the redoubtable Marquise de Mézières (*née* Eleanor Oglethorpe) who, with her daughters the Princesse de Montauban and the Princesse de Ligne,[37] sustained a small industry of Jacobite patronage and plotting. In the foregoing pages I have tried to show that the *Vanity* was addressed to a cultural environment in which the Stuart cause appeared to depend on its meddlesome, but compensatingly devoted, female fifth column; my suggestion is that this context gives Johnson's 'While ladies interpose' a generalised Jacobite resonance.

Our focus moves now to Paris in 1748 to see whether there might be any specific reference to contemporary affairs at this point in Johnson's poem.

An 'English Tragedy'

One of the great themes of coffeehouse talk, in London as in Paris, in the autumn of 1748 when Johnson wrote the *Vanity* concerned Prince Charles's falling out with Louis XV. For two years, from Charles's arrival in France after the collapse of his Scottish adventure, the Prince had been fruitlessly lobbying the French and other governments ('Condemn'd a needy supplicant to wait') for support in a further dash for the British Crown. So long as Europe had remained at war there was a chance his persistence might pay off. But by midsummer 1748, it had become plain to everyone that the peace agreement adumbrated at Aix-la-Chapelle would be ratified, and that it would include an undertaking by the French government not to harbour the Stuart pretender or his sons. This was a far cry from the blanket amnesty for all Jacobite prisoners and recalcitrants which had been demanded of Britain in a French peace proposal two years earlier,[38] and a grave, if not unforeseen, disappointment to the Jacobite party in France.

To Prince Charles, the French government's acquiescence in this clause was insulting beyond endurance. From his viewpoint that government had strategically and materially profited from,[39] without decently sustaining, his expedition to Scotland, and had since his return to Paris displayed less than his due measure of gratitude. Expelling him from the kingdom, at the say-so of the illegitimate regime in London, was in this narrative the climactic act of treachery from a government which had been consistently trifling with a gallant and steadfast ally. Meek compliance in such circumstances did not come naturally to this Prince; nor was it a course of action likely to enhance his public image in Britain – and every indication is that the course which Charles did pursue was calculated to commend him to a British audience.[40]

That course involved two stages. In mid-July, Charles issued a protest against the proceedings at Aix-la-Chapelle which, despite concerted efforts to suppress it, 'quickly became a bestseller'.[41] Having made his position clear in this spirited bit of rhetoric, the Prince then simply tuned out. He ignored all the government's polite efforts to dislodge him. He remained deaf to talk of golden parachutes, opulent hideaways in Switzerland. Deadlines came and went, the Aix-la-Chapelle treaty with France signed on 18 October was in immediate violation because of Charles's refusal to move, and still the Prince acted as though nothing was amiss. His behaviour during these last five months of 1748 brings to mind the modern Hollywood celebrity or star of popular music who, embroiled in a contract dispute with his studio or record label, seeks to confound that former benefactor through extravagant spending and high levels of public debauchery. Earlier in the year, Charles's household intake of oysters had stood at fifteen dozen every two days; of wine, two hundred bottles a week.[42] Now Charles raised his style of entertainment, accelerated his accumulation of debts and stepped up his schedule of appearances before the public whose enthusiasm for the hero of the

'45 had not dimmed. Every day he drew crowds during his promenades in the Tuileries gardens, accompanied by a picturesque retinue of Highlanders. When he showed up, several times a week, at the Opéra or the Comédie Française, the Prince was thunderously applauded for minutes on end. The increasing tension in his stand-off with Louis XV only added a transgressive *frisson* to Charles's popularity. When the government began to hint that it might use force to bring him into line, the Prince encouraged rumours that he would never be taken alive, that he and his guards were at all times armed to the teeth, and that his house was equipped to withstand a siege.[43]

At other points in his career, Charles had consciously sought to bring into focus the popular analogy between himself and Charles XII. At the beginning of the '45 'he affected to imitate the Example of *Charles* the XII of *Sweden'*, according to a (hostile) eyewitness history, 'marching all the Day on Foot, and every River they were to cross, he was the first Man that leap'd into it; he dined with the Soldiers in the open Field, and slept on the Ground wrapp'd in his Plaid'.[44] Thomas Kaiser's study of the French view of the uprising has shown that the connection between the two Charleses was 'a common trope' in the propaganda that made its way back to, or was produced on, the Continent.[45] One French pamphlet of 1745, probably based on a draft prepared in Britain, has the London mob crying, '*Vive le Fils de Jacques, plus brave que Georges, & aussi grand que Charles XII'*. (According to the same source, 'Les Dames, sont pour lui [Prince Charles], de nouvelles Amazones . . .'.[46]) A piece of spin control issued after the Battle of Culloden has the Prince withdrawing to the mountains 'où il est résolu de se défendre comme Charles XII. Roi de Suede, préférant comme il le dit souvent, *de mourir jeune les armes à la main dans sa patrie, & être enterré dans les tombeaux des Rois ses peres, que d'aller vivre oisif un siecle dans une terre étrangere* [. . .]'.[47] (The same source claims that 'les Dames [i.e. of London] sont déclarés ouvertement de sentimens & d'effet pour le Heros d'Ecosse . . . & un grand nombre d'elles persécutent leurs maris & leur amans de lever l'étendard dans Londres en sa faveur . . .'.[48]) Swedeifying the Stuart Charles seems to have been part of the Jacobite propagandistic programme – not an aim that was steadily pursued over long durations, perhaps; and not one which sought to imply a common destiny for the two heroes, to be sure; but a symbolic resource which was activated in apposite circumstances, always in the knowledge that European audiences would recognise the limited but powerful resemblance between the Swedish King and the Stuart Prince.[49]

This period that we have been looking at, these last five months or so of 1748, mark one of those occasions when Prince Charles deliberately conjured the image of Charles XII around himself.[50] The Swedish King was the inspiration, or at any rate an important model, behind all the Prince's talk of sieges and last stands, behind this effort to harden his image as a desperate and dangerous customer, for all his graces. The connection did not go unnoted:

1. 'Il [Prince Charles or, as he was known in France, Prince Edward] voulait imiter Charles XII, et soutenir siège dans sa maison, comme Charles XII fit à Bender' (the Marquis d'Argenson, 4 July 1748).[51]

2. '[T]he Foreign Ministers residing at the Court of France have been informed of every Thing that has pass'd in this Affair, which employs all the Conversation both of the Court and the Publick. They compare the Conduct and Obstinacy of this young Prince to that of Charles the XIIth of Sweden during his Sojourn at Bender' (*The York Courant*, quoting or paraphrasing a report from London dated 22 November 1748 (OS), three days before Johnson signed a receipt for the rights to the *Vanity*).[52]

3. '[T]he Foreign Ministers ... have been inform'd of all that has pass'd in this Affair. The Steadiness and Resolution of this Prince is compar'd to the Behaviour of the late King of Sweden at Bender' (*The Northampton Mercury*, quoting or paraphrasing the *London Evening Post*, 28 November 1748 (OS)).[53]

4. 'This steddy Conduct, which they little expected, appeared extravagant to the [French] Court: They were astonished at his attempting to oppose the Will of the King. Such an Opposition made them believe, that, after the Example of *Charles* the XII. he would stand a Siege in his own House' ('a French Lady at Paris', i.e. Prince Charles himself at Avignon, *c*. January 1749).[54]

5. 'Some People compare his Conduct in this Point with that of *Charles* XII. King of *Sweden* at *Bender*, and imagine that, had he been attacked in his own House, he would have defended himself in it as that Prince did' ('a Gentleman residing at *Paris*', early 1749).[55]

6. '[The Prince's house was stocked with] a considerable number of firearms, and some barrels of powder, because he ... proposed (like *Charles* XII. of *Sweden*. ...) to defend himself, if they had attempted to arrest him there ...' (*The Gentleman's Magazine*, issue for December 1748).[56]

In early December the French authorities' patience ran out. Charles was arrested coming out of his carriage in front of the Opéra, and after a brief captivity was escorted to the Savoyard border. Our next examples refer to that event:

7. 'Permettez moi ... de vous dire combien je suis affligé qu'un de mes héros, le prince Edouard, ait essuyé à Paris, l'aventure de Charles XII, à Bender' (Voltaire, privately).[57]

8. 'It coming on rain while he [Charles] walked, he left the Tuilleries, [having been warned of his impending arrest] and at stepping into his coach the two chiefs spoke to him again and told him if he had a mind to make a Bender of it, as the king of Sweden, he would not want assis-

tance; at which he thanked them, but bid them not be uneasy' (manuscript newssheet circulating in England, December 1748).[58]

It might be objected – it has been objected – that the bulk of the foregoing examples are inadmissible to any discussion of Johnson's intentions in the *Vanity*, having appeared only 'after Johnson had written his poem'.[59] (The cut-off for the *Vanity*'s composition is 25 November (OS)[60] (6 December (NS)) 1748, four days before the Prince's arrest.) But the point about these examples is that they record and extend the idiom in which the Prince's affairs had been discussed since at least the beginning of July, as the Marquis d'Argenson's entry in his journal indicates. These published examples represent the freezing into print of patterns of oral speculation and rumour which had flourished during precisely the period when Johnson was writing the *Vanity*. That published examples of the Charles XII analogy should survive in such easy abundance from December and January 1748–9, suggests that it had been a frequently occurring motif in that oral culture of gossip and conjecture.

The Prince's stand-off with the French King had been watched and commented on, as I have said, with keen interest on both sides of the Channel. For a particular news story to monopolise public attention for a season was not, in the eighteenth century, any more unusual than it is today. But this story's climactic moment, the Prince's arrest and forcible expulsion, produced a reaction in Paris that was, up to that point in Louis XV's reign, unique. '[A]rguably the most famous, and certainly the most glamorous, man in Europe',[61] Charles's celebrity had sustained, and extended itself through, a vibrant traffic in memorabilia – prints, medals, snuffboxes, portrait rings, plaster busts, watchpapers and a wide range of related ephemera. In our world, Alberto Korda's iconic photograph of Che Guevara perhaps approximates to the type of irresponsible glamour which attended the image of Charles Edward Stuart in the late 1740s. Described as 'le heros des halles',[62] the Prince's popularity on the streets of Paris was enormous; fear of a riot was one reason why 1,200 soldiers were deployed overall in his capture. (The other reason being fear of resistance by Charles's immediate circle of bodyguards and hangers-on. The overkill with which the government went about apprehending the Prince added to popular sympathy for him as well as to the sense that, like Charles XII, he was not a man to be lightly tangled with.) Upon Charles's arrest, a high-megaton blast of public outrage shook the capital, the fall-out from which – the *libelles*, the dirty songs, the prints and graffiti, the police informers' reports of *mauvais propos* and *bruits publics* – is still being recovered, sifted and analysed.[63] The verdict of modern scholarship is that 'l'affaire Charles-Édouard' marked 'an acute crisis of legitimation' for the French monarchy, permanently coarsening popular attitudes towards the Crown.[64] Robert Darnton calls this affair 'the greatest news story of the era'.[65]

All of this relates to the *Vanity*'s line 214 in the following way: in the summer and autumn of 1748, part of the political 'folklore' concerning Prince Charles was that he moved in a distinctly feminised milieu in Paris, that his steps were dogged at all times by a devoted constituency of female admirers, and that, in his defiance of Louis XV, he was relying on advice and encouragement from a group of influential lady friends.

I have already spoken of an 'idiom' in which the Prince's affairs were discussed at this time. I am not referring to an exotic Jacobite cant, impenetrable to outsiders; by 'idiom' I mean the loose set of rhetorical habits – the banalities, even, such as the analogy with Charles XII – in which public opinion voiced itself, no matter from what political direction. This rhetoric, together with the understanding of events which underlay it, is what I mean in my unscientific use of the term 'political folklore'. When Johnson was writing the *Vanity*, Prince Charles's differences with the French government were the hottest news story in western Europe.[66] Necessarily shut off from full knowledge of what was happening in the counsels of Versailles and among the leadership of '[l]e parti jacobite-édouardiste',[67] the public had to make do, in its discussions of this subject, with whatever droplets might be leaked by one side or another, with the ideas put about by propagandists and rumour-mongers, and with the kind of idle gossip that always flowers where intense curiosity coexists with scarcity of information. In this way, a general picture was formed of the Prince's political situation in Paris, and it is to that picture that my 'political folklore' refers. In its main elements, this folklore was the same in London as in Paris. Predictably, much of this folklore was shaped by such long-established beliefs about the Stuarts as their special appeal to the female sex. During the period when Johnson was working on the *Vanity*, one of the most definite features of this political folklore finds precise description in Johnson's image of the exiled hero languishing 'While ladies interpose'.

Of the mid- to close-range observers whose accounts of the Prince Edward Affair are available to us, the most scrupulous in his attention to detail and his monitoring the fancies of public opinion is the Marquis d'Argenson himself (by this time out of government service, and looking on with cool *schadenfreude*). As early as 4 July 1748 he records the impression that the Princesse de Talmont was whispering political advice in the Prince's ear, relative to the Aix-la-Chapelle problem.[68] On 18 November d'Argenson writes that Charles's intransigency is taking its strength from the Princesse '[qui] le gouverne avec folie et fureur'.[69] La Talmont was not an uninfluential player in Versailles politics, being on good terms and frequently closeted with her cousin the Queen.[70] But by 24 November, alarmed by word that her role in making a nuisance of the Prince is going to get her banished from Court, she is said to be trying to reconcile the Prince to his change of addresse. 'Véritablement,' d'Argenson writes, 'c'est d'elle que venait le premier conseil pour tenir bon ici et ne point sortir; mais depuis, voyant que cela retombait sur elle, elle lui en a donné de contraires; mais il n'était plus temps, la tête anglaise était allumée.'[71] As Charles's appointment with destiny draws near, d'Argenson concludes: 'Mme. de Talmond a joué toujours le plus grand rôle dans cette affaire.'[72]

Mme. de Talmont is not the only female 'jacobite-édouardiste' whom d'Argenson implicates in this affair. Speculating on the repercussions the affair is likely to have at Court, he foresees the banishment of the Princesse and (rumour has it) 'deux autres dames . . . encores'. Moreover, 'je crains bien pour Mme. de Mézières. . . . Mme. de Montauban [one of the Marquise de Mézières's daughters and, like her mother and sister, a seasoned Jacobite intriguer] me dit . . . qu'elle évitait, depuis un mois, de venir à Paris par la prévoyance de toute cette bagarre'.[73] Meanwhile, 'La comtesse de Lismore, femme du ministre de Jacques III, est enfermée chez elle, et ne voit personne, excepté le nonce du pape . . .'.[74] These were dangerous times for Jacobite ladies in France.

D'Argenson also contributes to our sense that the Prince was thought to be surrounded by women wherever he went, and to be aware of women as a specially devoted section of his international audience. '[C]e prince aimé ici du beau sexe', is how the Marquis describes Charles three days before his arrest.[75] Three days before that, d'Argenson writes: 'Il est venu des femmes d'Angleterre uniquement pour le voir à nos spectacles; elles n'ont passé que deux jours à Paris et sont retournées sur-le-champ à Londres.'[76]

The journal of the former foreign minister discloses a well-informed elite perspective on the Prince Edward Affair. Is there any consistency between the impressions which d'Argenson received and the political folklore down at street level even in Paris, much less London? As we shall see, the answer is yes. But first, another effusion from the Marquis's pen requires our attention. The comments I have quoted referring to Charles's remarkable popularity among women, and his reliance on female advisers, have been taken from a tangled mass of gossip and speculation recorded by the Marquis, as events unfolded, with little discrimination. Given a chance to reflect on the whole episode and to impart some kind of artistic shape to it, did d'Argenson think the Prince's connection with women (or for that matter with Charles XII) worth emphasising?

The French monarchy's 'Charles Edward problem' embodied a conflict between ideology and national interest which fired the Marquis d'Argenson's imagination to the point where he actually wrote a play about it. *La Prison du Prince Charles Edouard Stuardt* survives in manuscript at the Quai d'Orsay. This prose 'tragédie angloise à l'imitation de Shakespear', more recently described[77] as an early 'experiment in historical realism', has never been published in full. The glimpses which are available[78] suggest a slow-going, clotted piece of work which displays little talent for the theatre[79] but which further establishes its author as a sharp literary portraitist and as a man attuned to every vibration of court gossip, popular *propos* and backstairs politics. Given d'Argenson's avowed 'imitation' of Shakespeare, we wonder if the 'prison' of his title does not establish a literary allusion beyond its straightforward reference to the Prince's place of confinement which is the setting of the final scene. Is d'Argenson also evoking Hamlet's 'Denmark's a prison' and thereby implying something seriously out of joint, some ominous corruption at the centre of the French state? The play follows the response of the Prince and his circle to the Aix-la-Chapelle treaty, and the response of Louis and his ministers to their response, over the last eight months of 1748. It was written in 1749, but clearly is designed to catch the attitudes and rhetoric of the historical moment in which it is set.

Sorting out, in the quiet of his study and with benefit of hindsight, what were the salient themes of the great news story which had preoccupied Frenchmen during that time, d'Argenson produced a work which heavily underlines the influence of Charles XII as an historical reference point and psychological prop for Prince Charles,[80] and the influence of interposing ladies in determining the Prince's fate. The Swedish motif, in fact, is introduced by the one of the ladies who bestride this play, the Princesse de Talmont, when she haughtily asks who will dare try to force her lover away:

> [Q]ui osera le chasser? . . . [I]l a l'exemple de Charles XII, quand il resta parmi les Turcs; il est plus brave encore que Charles XII, et, en vérité, le ministère français n'est pas moins stupide que les Turcs.[81]

Thus introduced at Act I, scene iii, the Swedish King's 'example' reverberates through d'Argenson's curious literary experiment. Charles is portrayed as openly identifying himself as a throwback to the dashing Swede while the darker implications of that identification gather like shadows around him. Some of the reactions which have greeted the Jacobite gloss on Johnson's 'Swedish Charles' were anticipated and answered by the modern recoverer of d'Argenson's play:

> It is evident that d'Argenson saw in Charles Edward the kindred spirit of Charles XII and that he tried to do for him what his friend Voltaire had so successfully done for the Swedish King. The resemblance today appears far-fetched. Preston Pans is not Narva, Culloden does not look to us like Pultava, Paris is a far cry from Bender and the death of Charles XII at Frederickshall does not recall in the least the end of the Stuart Pretender in Rome. But d'Argenson and his contemporaries could feel that the two 'têtes de fer' had much in common. The point of view of the Marquis is of considerable interest to us, for it was that of many fair-minded, informed and thoughtful Europeans. He had a great advantage over later historians: he was not influenced by hindsight. He presents the Young Chevalier as people saw him in the late 1740s.[82]

What then about the ladies in d'Argenson's exercise in historical realism *avant la lettre*? His *dramatis personae* gives a separate group identification to 'Des femmes du peuple de Paris'.[83] The published fragments of the play do not reveal much about the role of that group, but from the one published scene on which they do intrude (heckling the soldiers who have arrested Charles)[84] it is plain that the women of Paris are represented in this play as feistily supportive of the Prince.

Among the named characters, the Princesse de Talmont, the Duchesse d'Aiguillon, the Marquise de Mézières and the Marquise's 'confidante' Mistress Foley all figure prominently in the play, whispering, plotting, pulling strings, making defiant speeches and sometimes tearing out each other's hair in their struggle to direct the future of the House of Stuart. The importance of the female characters in this drama is signalled by the opening scene which is given to a *tête-à-tête* between the Princesse de Talmont and the Duchesse d'Aiguillon (an exchange which ends in a catfight – perhaps d'Argenson's theatrical instincts were not so stunted after all). In the Princesse de Talmont we have one of the two female machiavels of the cast, the other being the Marquise de Mézières who is determined to prevent Charles from severing the Stuarts' lifeline to the good graces of Louis XV. 'Des ma jeunesse,' she says, 'la maison des Stuardts a été le centre de mes désirs et tout le sujet de mes méditations.'[85] The Marquise is an old hand at 'social politics'. 'J'entretiens des amis partout,' she says, 'mes sentiments dînent dans un camp et soupent dans l'autre; je m'attache plus a ceux qui peuvent parvenir qu'a ce qui est arrivé; je connois touttes les beauttés de la cour et de la ville qui peuvent parvenir au poste de favorite.'[86] This formidable lady's rival for direction of the Prince's course is no less a force to be reckoned with: 'Je prevoys que made de Tallemont deffendra son heros du bec et des ongles; elle le couvrira de son aegyde,' says a duly cowed male character.[87] The air of menace arising from the Princesse's pride and possessiveness induces the same character to recall the gender-bending image of the Jacobite amazon: 'je ne voys pas jour a marier le Prince edoüard. Made de Talemont ne le souffriroit pas. Elle appelleroit en duel quiconque pretendroit a sa main.'[88]

Prince Charles himself is not portrayed in d'Argenson's play as a patsy or cypher. He is an arrogant but not altogether unsubtle young man whose strong sense of his own destiny cohabits with vulnerabilities and blindspots which lay him open to the influence of the more experienced women who, for their own crossed purposes, want to manage his response to the Aix-la-Chapelle crisis. This triangle of wills, Prince Charles, the Princesse de Talmont, the Marquise de Mézières, is the fundamental structure which d'Argenson saw in Jacobite decision-making in Paris during the suspenseful autumn of 1748. That the Marquis d'Argenson, the observer whose record excels all others in detachment and depth of knowledge, should thus privilege the feminine dimension of the Prince's experience in France makes the Jacobite reading of 'While ladies interpose' very hard to resist.

Fine if the *Vanity* were written in Paris. Is there any evidence that this idea of the Prince being coddled and guided by women was current in London?[89] In its issue for December, the *Gentleman's Magazine* noted that Charles, during a mysterious disappearance earlier in the autumn, had 'passed, it seems, this time . . . at the hotel of the Princess *Talmont*, the Queen's cousin . . .'.[90] The *York Courant*, in its issue of 6 December (OS), reported: 'A certain Princess of the Court has receiv'd Intimation not to appear there 'till further Orders, for testifying her warm Approbation of [Charles's] Refusal to leave France.'[91] The *Northampton Mercury* had carried a similar report in its issue the day before, and on 12 December (OS) added: 'It was the Princess of Talmont, Wife of a Palatine of Poland, and related to the Queen, that receiv'd Orders not to appear at Court, for having openly commended, in Preference of his Majesty, the Conduct of the Pretender's eldest Son . . .'.[92] I have not had an opportunity to check every relevant newspaper. But the alliance between Charles and the Queen's cousin appears to have been as persistent a motif in the coverage of this story as the allusion to Charles XII at Bender.

In 1749, Dr. John Burton published his *Genuine and True Journal of the Most Miraculous Escape of the Young Chevalier*.[93] The first detailed history of the Prince in the heather, this book goes on to give 'A short Account of What befel [*sic*] the Pr. in *France*';[94] that 'short Account', which reuses material appearing in other Jacobite publications of 1749, should be regarded as an expression of the political folklore of 1748–9. It includes a humorous anecdote which, through conspicuous inclusion, emphasises the feminisation of the Prince's milieu. The Prince commissions a service of plate, 'to the Value of 100,000 Crowns',[95] from the King's goldsmith. The plate is to be ready on a particular day. When the King places an order which conflicts with the Prince's, the goldsmith asks the Prince for more time. The Prince refuses, insisting he must have the plate on the day specified. In great agitation, the goldsmith explains his problem to the King, who is delighted. Assuming the Prince is on such a rigid timetable because he is preparing to leave the country, the King not only permits his goldsmith to execute the Prince's order first, but pays the Prince's bill! Punchline:

> [T]he Pr. was . . . far from any such Intention. . . . – This fine Service of Plate was on the Score of a grand Entertainment he made; at which were present the Princess of *Talmont*, a near Relation to the Queen; the Marchioness *de Sprimont*; Madam *de Maiseiuse*; the Duke *de Bouillion*; and above thirty others of the Nobility of both Sexes. . . .[96]

Another publication which solidified in print, in 1749, the airy café talk and streetcorner gossip of late 1748, was *An Authentick Account of the Conduct of the Young Chevalier, from his First Arrival in Paris . . . to the Conclusion of the*

Peace at Aix-la-Chapelle.[97] Here is the author dividing the Prince's enemies from his friends in France:

> [Those at Court most] skilled in Politicks, think the Acquisition he aims at would be of Prejudice to the Good of their Country [note the propagandist's appeal to British patriotism here]. . . . Of this latter Class are all the Ministry, and most of the Princes of the Blood: But the rest of the *Noblesse*, the greatest Part of the Commonality, and all the Ladies in general, are as strong *Jacobites* as the most sanguine of your *Nonjurors*. . . .'[98]

An Authentick Account offers several illustrations of this general she-Jacobitism, repeating the tale that 'The Princess *Talmont* herself spoke so largely of [the Prince's cause] . . . in the King's Presence, that she was forbid the Court . . .',[99] and telling us that

> When [Charles] came to the *Opera* or *Comedy*, the Attention of the whole Audience was fixed upon him, regardless of what was presented on the Stage: The Moment of his Entrance into the Box, a general Whisper in his Favour ran from one Side of the Theatre to the other; and few of the fair Sex but let fall Tears of mingled Pity and Admiration. . . .[100]

So far I have asserted that these publications of December 1748 and early 1749 captured in print the motifs of an oral political folklore that Johnson would have been within earshot of before the end of November. I have not proven this. It is not easy, at the distance of two hundred and fifty years, to demonstrate the content of a preliterary rumour except by pointing to its ultimate literary manifestation. We know that Londoners, in October and November 1748, were talking about Prince Charles's troubles in France; they must have said something. We know that when written and printed material pertaining to that subject begins to appear in English in December and January, it puts an emphasis on ladies who interpose. The logical conclusion is that those ladies figured in the gossip of the preceding months.

But for those who demand to be shown some printed work that Johnson himself might have seen before finishing the *Vanity*, one item has come to light. *A Remarkable Dialogue Which Lately Happened in the Gardens of Luxembourg . . . &c.* is an urbane piece of Jacobite propaganda, published in 1748, which brackets together three essays.[101] The first is a dialogue between a Jacobite Nonjuror and an openminded, honourable Whig – not 'one of your *modern Time-servers*'[102] – who comes to realise that more unites than separates their two parties. The second essay reviews the life and character of Prince Charles, the third throws some stones at the treaty drafted at Aix-la-Chapelle. That third essay offers internal evidence on which the whole pamphlet might be dated to sometime between the signing of the Aix-la-Chapelle preliminaries in April and the treaty's ratification in October. The summer of 1748, then, give or take.[103] *A Remarkable Dialogue* conveys a distinct sense of being part of an orchestrated Jacobite propaganda campaign, framing the Prince's disagreement with the French Court in just the way the Prince wanted that disagreement to be seen in Britain. He is, again, the hearty Englishman set down amid treacherous strangers: 'He loves plain Eating, and every thing that looks like *English*; can smoak his Pipe, and drink [his] Share of whatever falls in his Way [an understatement], but prefers good Malt Liquor to most others. . . .'[104] The old 1745 language of hardship-sharing in which the Charles XII analogy had often been couched (though not the analogy itself) is recalled:

> he underwent as many uncommon Hardships and Fatigues in the cold Climate of *Scotland*, and exposed himself as much as the meanest Man about him; lived in common as they did, and was generally the first, on all Occasions, ready to jump in and wade through Waters and Moors, sometimes up to his Armpits, which added Life and Spirit to all that belonged to him.[105]

Here in this pamphlet, in short, are all the themes, deftly arranged, which the main switchboard of Jacobite propaganda wanted to get across to British audiences in the summer of 1748. *A Remarkable Dialogue* had appeared probably before Johnson started working on the *Vanity*, certainly before he had finished it. In three places, *A Remarkable Dialogue* spotlights the Prince's petticoat patrons. Upon his safe return to France, we are told in the biographical essay,

> if their old Monarch *Louis the Great* had been raised from the Dead, there could scarce appear more Joy, or greater Numbers of People crowd after him wherever he went: And, as for the Ladies, they coveted nothing more than an Opportunity of subscribing half what they had in the World to do him Service.[106]

On his first appearance at Court,

> the Queen, with all the Ladies at Court, being very curious to hear something of his Sufferings and Escapes, she impatiently laid hold of him; but, in answering her Questions, the Subject soon became too serious and affecting to be withstood; and her Majesty, with all that were present, burst into Tears, . . . lamenting the incredible Hardships he had suffered, and admiring the Hero, . . . who had been able to support himself under such a Torrent of Calamities. . . .[107]

But it is the first emergence of the Prince's-ladies motif which most forcefully strikes the reader, coming as it does in the opening lines of the banter between Whig and Nonjuror, affording the pamphlet's first memorable image, and setting the lighthearted tone of the ensuing dialogue:

> *Whig.* [the dialogue begins,] Sir, your Servant! I hope you are well To-day; I thought you would be here this pleasant Morning, at your usual Amusements.
>
> *Nonjuror.* I am your's Sir! You know we poor *Exiles* have little else to do but saunter about, read News, and see what is like to become of our *unfortunate distressed Country*: But, pray, where have you been this Morning? You seem to have walk'd a good deal.
>
> *Whig.* Why, Sir, to tell you the Truth, I have been almost two Hours in the Gardens of the *Tuilleries*, endeavouring to keep pace with your young Gentleman the *Chevalier*, as well as Thousands more who are following him; but never in my Life did I behold such another Walker: In short, he flies insensibly, without taking the least pains; and, o' my Conscience, to see the whole Company sweat, the Ladies with their large Hoops, and long Robes, striving to have as many full Sights of him as they can, and speaking of him in such Raptures, with their different comical Gestures, make it quite entertaining.[108]

We have seen *A Remarkable Dialogue* suggest that the French Queen took a special interest in Charles upon his return from Scotland. This suggestion is elaborated in accounts from 1749. Having just arrived back in France,

> After staying about a Quarter of an Hour with the King, [Charles] passed to the Queen's Apartment, who welcomed him with all imaginable Demonstrations of Good-Will and Satisfaction. . . .
>
> [T]he Sincerity of the Queen's Professions admits no Doubt. Her Majesty and the Princess *Sobieski* [Charles's mother] had passed some Years of their Youth together; they had contracted the most intimate and lasting Friendship with each other; and it is natural to suppose the favourite Son of a Person who had been so dear to her, and who was so much the Resemblance of his Mother, cannot be indifferent to her. It has been with a Kind of maternal Tenderness she has always looked upon him; and I have been told by several about her Majesty, that whenever he came to Court . . . she used to keep him in Conversation for whole Hours together, and make him recite to her, and the Ladies who were with her, his Adventures, the Detail of which seldom failed of drawing Tears from her Eyes; nor were the young Princesses, one of them especially, less affected with the melancholly Story.[109]

There was a political reality behind this idea of the Queen standing up for Charles's interest at Versailles: Charles's interest was bound up with that of the so-called *parti dévot*, centred on the Queen and engaged in a bitter political chess-game with the other main faction at court, the circle of Mme. de Pompadour. Charles's humiliation marked a victory for the Pompadour group, and in the ensuing public outcry the King's mistress received her full share of the blame. '[I]t is properly at this shameful period [when Prince Charles was arrested and expelled],' Moufle d'Angerville later claimed, 'that began the general contempt for the Sovereign and his mistress, which continued increasing to the end.'[110]

La Pompadour's perceived responsibility for Charles's undoing is important to our discussion because there are two ways of reading Johnson's 'interpose'. According to Voltaire's life of Charles XII, the Swedish King's political hopes, during his stay in the Ottoman Empire, rested with the women of the *seraglio* who intrigued busily in his favour, starting with the Sultan's mother who 'prenait hautement dans le sérail le parti de ce prince: elle ne l'appelait que son lion'.[111] Most readers have assumed that Johnson's phrase, in its application to Charles XII, refers to these women who interpose in his favour. But another woman who figures prominently, if briefly, in this part of Voltaire's history is the Czarina. Voltaire goes in to the colourful background of this 'paysanne devenue impératrice'[112] before describing her diplomatic initiative in July 1711 which saves a Russian army from destruction on the River Pruth, leaving Charles nauseous with frustration. *Interpose* is an ambiguous verb in a context like ours. It can mean blocking someone's designs as easily as interceding on his behalf. Johnson's Yale editors gloss 'While ladies interpose' as referring to the Czarina.[113] I should think Johnson's meaning not reducible to either side, but rather takes in those who support as well as she who thwarts Charles: the proud warrior has become a plaything of female busybodies. The reference to the Czarina, however, I think is a subdued or secondary one next to those ladies whose positive interventions strike us more forcefully in the Voltairean and other source texts.

As it applies to Charles XII, then, the phrase 'While ladies interpose' sustains an alternating current of historical reference – to friend as well as foe. The same kind of double reading can be carried through to Prince Charles's experience in France. On the one hand, Charles not only had the Queen, her cousin and other powerful ladies on his side but, indeed, 'all the Ladies in general'. On the other hand, a few ladies of enormous influence parted from the generality to combine against him – not just Mme. de Pompadour but Mme. de Puysieux, a confirmed anti-Jacobite who was married to d'Argenson's successor as minister for foreign affairs. Shortly after the Prince's arrest, d'Argenson records an apocryphal exchange which had got back to the Prince and tickled him: 'quelqu'un dit au prince que Mme. de Puisieux avait gagné deux cents louis, sans dire à quel jeu; il répondit: *Dites deux cents guinées*.'[114] Further in the diplomatic background, the ultimate author of the Prince's misfortune was popularly identified as Maria Theresa of Austria.[115]

These contrary ladies give my Jacobite reading of 'While ladies interpose' the same duality of reference that we have seen in the phrase's application to Charles XII. But they were not, before Prince Charles's arrest at least, anywhere near as prominent in the political folklore surrounding the Prince as were the Prince's petticoat patrons. As with the Czarina, those ladies who interpose against Charles's interest occupy a secondary position in the Jacobite gloss which I suggest for this phrase.

'[T]he greatest news story of the 1740s' in France[116] was also pretty big news in England. In its issue for December 1748, the *Gentleman's Magazine* offered a long report on the Prince's arrest in the front section of the magazine[117] in addition to a paragraph under 'Foreign History',[118] reprinted a piece of verse commenting on the affair from the *Westminster Journal*,[119] and published Charles's father's letter admonishing the Prince to cooperate with his hosts[120] (the French government had released this as damage control). In its issue for November, the *Gentleman's Magazine* had said: 'We have repeated accounts from *Paris* of the obstinacy of the pretender's son' and proceeded to describe the alleged comings and goings of messengers between Louis and Charles and to relay some gossip as to Charles's motivations.[121] In its issue for October, the *Gentleman's Magazine* had published the diplomatic correspondence relating to the French government's efforts to prepare a haven for the Prince at Fribourg.[122] (These efforts had caused a diplomatic ruffle in which Horace Mann, in one of the letters which passed between himself and Horace Walpole on the subject of Charles's 'extravagance',[123] thought he saw the makings of a French 'trick'; Mann regretted that Charles's removal from French territory had not been insisted upon as a 'preliminary to all other preliminaries'.[124])

The *Gentleman's Magazine* is a good source for what Johnson can be expected to have known. But there are many other measures by which to gauge the attention the Prince Edward Affair commanded in Britain. The *York Courant* is a fairly representative provincial newspaper. It came out once a week. If we look at just the period October 1748 to January 1749, we find references to Prince Charles in the following issues of the *York Courant*:[125] 4 October, 11 October, 18 October, 25 October, 1 November, 15 November, 22 November, 29 November, 6 December, 13 December, 20 December, 27 December, 3 January, 10 January, 17 January, 24 January and 31 January. That is to say, during the period under review every issue but one (8 November) of this provincial newspaper reported on the Prince Edward Affair. The news section of the *York Courant* comprised gleanings from three separate posts over the preceding week – Friday's, Sunday's and Tuesday's – with the result that in some issues readers were bombarded with two or even three updates on how matters stood with the Prince. The same is true of the other paper I have examined, the *Northampton Mercury*.[126]

Charles's loss of political footing in France – this latest phase of his exilic 'miseries' – was the great conversational theme of the hour. The patchiness of the printed material relating to this subject from before about the first week of December (NS), when Johnson parted from his manuscript, is itself a sign of the subject's immediacy as news when Johnson was writing his poem; the subject had only begun to pass from orality into print. But it has been possible to reconstruct the political folklore through which the man on the street watched the Prince's game of cat and mouse with Louis XV. No aspect of that folklore was more marked than the set of related ideas concerning Charles and his female connections. He was said to be constantly surrounded by women. He was said to draw comfort in adversity (and perhaps to miscalculate the strength of his position) from the public devotion of 'all the Ladies in general'. He depended, it was said or implied, on the influence of women (such as his friend who was 'a near Relation to the Queen') in his ever more fraught dealings with the Court. He was said to have fallen under the sway of female advisers. Johnson could have selected any detail from the biography of Charles XII to round off his image of the thwarted overreacher in exile. His focusing on the ladies who are the refugee prince's comfort, distraction and (for as long as they can manage it) shield exemplifies the subtle conspiracy between topical allusion and universality in *The Vanity of Human Wishes*.

In my reading, the Jacobite suggestiveness of the *Vanity*'s lines 211–14 reaches its point of maximum intensity in the first half of line 214 and peters out over the rest of that line. An allusive *diminuendo* can perhaps be detected, however, in the image which the last half projects: 'and slaves debate'. *Slave* was a common epithet for the subjects of French absolutism. The fussings and frettings of nervous French ministers over what to do with the obstinate Prince are part of the political folklore which emerges from contemporaneous accounts of the Charles Edward Affair.[127] An anecdote found in print in early 1749 has Charles reply thus to the Comte de Maurepas, who warns him that the King's ministers are determined to see the Aix-la-Chapelle treaty enforced: '"The Ministers! The Ministers! (cried the Pr. with the greatest Disdain). If you will oblige me, *Monsieur le Count*, tell the King, that I am born to break all the Schemes of his Ministers."'[128] In this story, which recurs in the Jacobite press,[129] there is a nobility in Prince Charles's self-destructive *hauteur* and directness, even in defeat, which contrasts rather favourably against the duplicity and hidden purposes of the politicians in whose power an unjust Fortune has placed him. A similar contrast is evoked in Johnson's picture of the proud but fallen hero's fate being decided by a 'slaves['] debate'.

The temptation to relate Voltaire's shifty Turks to the French ministry of 1748 might have been especially keen if Johnson had read *A Remarkable Dialogue*. This pamphlet, in its mini-biography of Prince Charles, plays heavily on the Jacobite theme of tartan heroism, the idea that the Scottish Highlands are Britain's last bastion of native valour and incorruptibility. '[W]hat an Indelible Infamy and Reproach must it be to others, of high Birth and Education,' the author writes, 'to hear of such . . . noble Constancy of Mind, and generous Behaviour' as was displayed by those faithful clansmen who refused to sell their Prince out during his wanderings after Culloden.[130] *Unlike some in Britain in 1745–6*, the author did not need to add – and unlike a certain government across the Channel in that very summer or autumn of 1748. When Charles was hiding out in the mountains, we are told in *A Remarkable Dialogue*,

> He had with him for a time six of his own Party, all brave Fellows, and such as he could entirely depend upon in every respect; and having several Occasions to consult them upon Ways and Means, not of raising Money [never!], he called them his little Parliament, tho' only one of them could speak *English*, who was Interpreter in all Debates. . . .[131]

This image of Charles's 'little faithful Council'[132] unrolls into a running joke across the next several pages, extending to the naming of one of his stalwarts 'his *Chief Secretary*, or the first Lord of his Council'.[133] I think we have here more than a random play on the romance of the Prince in the heather. As we have seen, *A Remarkable Dialogue* appeared probably as part of a propaganda campaign designed to 'spin' the Prince's conflict with his French hosts. I think this image of the Prince's little parliament of simple but unswerving hillmen was designed to impress on the reader a suitably unenticing idea of their antithesis, the smiling villains who lurked in the corridors of Versailles, plotting treachery. Compared with such dignity and worth as was attributed to Charles and his Highland supporters, the French ministers were 'slaves' indeed. It is possible in this context to see the faintest of allusions to Louis's ministry in Johnson's quibbling Turks: a merging of orientalism with Francophobia.

On its face, the *Vanity*'s line 214 – 'While ladies interpose, and slaves debate' – corresponds roughly to books five and six in Voltaire's *Histoire de Charles XII* (the section which concludes with the Bender episode that Prince Charles had been recalling throughout the summer and autumn of 1748). A recent summary of this section of Voltaire's work runs as follows: 'Voltaire . . . describes Charles's bedraggled retreat to Turkey and, thereafter, the Sultana's intervention on his behalf, and his unsatisfactory tenure in a place where women, a eunuch, and various subaltern Turks discuss what to do with the ungrateful and troublesome infidel.'[134]

This judicious reduction of Voltaire's account to its essentials clarifies how neatly Prince Charles's experience in Paris matched that of Charles XII at Bender. *Bedraggled* is a good word for the Prince's near-run skedaddle through the Highlands and Hebrides back to France. He was not yet an 'infidel' in the French perspective, but ever since the public relations nightmare of his brother's becoming a cardinal (July 1747) it had been rumoured everywhere that Charles might convert, or at least take a Protestant bride. Voltaire's 'subaltern Turks' find their epigones in those ministers of state to whom Louis XV handed the thankless task of dealing with a guest who could certainly be described as 'troublesome' and arguably as 'ungrateful' (although he would turn the adjective around). Like the Sultana and the other ladies of the *seraglio*, the Queen and a host of high-placed Jacobite women struggled to steer their royal visitor through the treacherous waters of local politics. So far, only a eunuch seems to be wanting to make the symmetry complete. Given Jacobite propaganda's stress on the Stuarts' sex appeal and the corresponding insufficiencies of those who opposed them, we should not be surprised to find a 'eunuch' ranged against Prince Charles somewhere in this mix. I am pleased herewith to reveal a previously overlooked detail in Charles Edward Stuart's 'tragédie angloise'. Of the Prince's enemies at court, d'Argenson writes in his journal on 11 December 1748, none is more dangerous than 'M. de Maurepas; celui-ci le haïssait depuis longtemps, et l'a desservi sous main avec toute la malice d'un eunuque qu'il est'.[135]

Notes

1. Howard Erskine-Hill, 'The Political Character of Samuel Johnson', in *Samuel Johnson: New Critical Essays*, ed. Isobel Grundy (London, 1984), pp. 107–36.
2. See especially Howard D. Weinbrot, 'Johnson, Jacobitism, and Swedish Charles: *The Vanity of Human Wishes* and Scholarly Method', *ELH*, 64 (1997), pp. 945–81; idem, 'Who Said He Was a Jacobite Hero?: The Political Genealogy of Johnson's Charles of Sweden', *Philological Quarterly*, 75 (1996), pp. 411–50. An ambitious but incomplete bibliography of the debate on this matter can be found in the references of the work cited in note 4 below.
3. John Cannon, *Samuel Johnson and the Politics of Hanoverian England* (Oxford, 1994), p. 55; Paul J. Korshin, 'Afterword', *ELH*, 64 (1997), pp. 1091–1100; Lawrence Lipking, *Samuel Johnson: The Life of an Author* (Cambridge, MA, 1998), pp. 87, 324 n. 3. The phrase 'emotional typology' is Jayne Elizabeth Lewis's, applied by Korshin (p. 1096) to the case of the Charles–Charles analogy. (See Lewis, 'Hamilton's "Abdication", Boswell's Jacobitism and the Myth of Mary Queen of Scots', *ELH*, 64 (1997), pp. 1069–90.)
4. Niall MacKenzie, ' "A Great Affinity in Many Things": Further Evidence for the Jacobite Gloss on "Swedish Charles" ', *AJ*, 12 (2001), forthcoming.
5. But not for everyone. See the reply by Howard Weinbrot, scheduled to appear alongside ' "A Great Affinity" ' in the same volume of *AJ*. One awaits with delicious suspense this document, which is expected to prove the insight of John Philips's fictitious clergyman: 'in Controversy, the more the Adversary is wounded, the more troublesome he grows, and will needs have the last Word': J. Philips, *The Inquisition. A Farce. As It Was Acted at Child's Coffee-House, and the King's-Arms Tavern, in St. Paul's Church-Yard. Wherein the Controversy Between the Bishop of Bangor and Dr. Snape, is Fairly Stated, and Set in a True Light* (2nd edn., London: Printed for T. Warner, 1717), p. 5.
6. I follow the text given in Samuel Johnson, *Poems*, ed. E.L. McAdam, Jr. with George Milne, *Yale Edition*, VI (New Haven, 1964), pp. 91–109.
7. Unless otherwise indicated, all dates here are New Style.

8. BL Add MS 32,805, fs. 106r–8r (copy).
9. The letter was addressed to a Dutch diplomat (the nearest thing to a direct channel between the French and British governments at this time), but plainly intended to reach Whitehall. When leaked to the British press, the foreign minister's letter created a considerable stir. See, e.g., the *Gentleman's Magazine*, 16 (1746), pp. 302–6 (June) and 350–1 (July); also, *Journal et mémoires du marquis d'Argenson*, ed. E.J.B. Rathery (9 vols., Paris, 1859–67), IV (1862), pp. 323–30.
10. BL Add MS 32,805, f. 106r.
11. Ibid., f. 106v.
12. Ibid., f. 108r.
13. Ibid., f. 106v.
14. Anon., *The Chronicle of Charles, the Young Man* ([Edinburgh(?)] [n. pub.], [1745]), pp. 2–3.
15. Anon., *An Authentick Account of the Battle Fought Between the Army of His Royal Highness the Duke of Cumberland and the Rebels, on Drummossie-Muir near Culloden, on the 16th of April 1746 [OS]* ([Edinburgh(?)]: [n. pub.], 1746), p. [2].
16. *Tandem Triumphans, Translated by the Duke of Cumberland, With the Point of His Sword* (1746): see *Catalogue of Prints and Drawings in the British Museum, Division I. Political and Personal Satires*, o.s., ed. F.G. Stephens, 4 vols in 5 (London, 1870–83), III (1877), pp. 597–8.
17. *Warrender Letters: Correspondence of Sir George Warrender Bt. Lord Provost of Edinburgh, and Member of Parliament for the City, With Relative Papers*, trans. Marguerite Wood, ed. William Kirk Dickson, Publications of the Scottish History Society (3rd ser.), 25 (Edinburgh, 1935), p. 40.
18. Poorer women (and especially prostitutes) bore the brunt of this superstition in the Whig view, but their high-born sisters were not exempted as some readers may be preparing to argue.
19. Colin Haydon, *Anti-Catholicism in Eighteenth-Century England, c. 1714–80: A Political and Social Study* (Manchester, 1993), p. 5.
20. Richard Sharp, *The Engraved Record of the Jacobite Movement* (Aldershot, 1996), pp. 143–6, 178–80, 201, 214–15.
21. See the works listed under her name in the BL General Catalogue. When the self-fictionalising architect Charles Cameron entered Catherine the Great's service around 1780, he found that the Empress remembered (and was a fan of) his 'aunt': Isobel Rae, *Charles Cameron, Architect to the Court of Russia* (London, 1971), pp. 15–17.
22. Anon., *The Female Rebels: Being Some Remarkable Incidents of the Lives, Characters, and Families of the Titular Duke and Dutchess of Perth, the Lord and Lady Ogilvie, and of Miss Florence M'Donald. Containing Several Particulars of these Remarkable Persons Not Hitherto Published* (2nd(?) edn., London: 'sold by L. Gilliver, Mrs Dodd, and G. Woodfall', 1747), p. 6 for 'Petticoat Patronage'.
23. The book, and the passage quoted below, are discussed in MacKenzie, ' "A Great Affinity" '.
24. Peter M. Briggs, 'The Horn of Plenty: Some Recent Symposium Volumes in Eighteenth-Century Studies', *AJ*, 11 (2000), pp. 297–332, at 310.
25. Weinbrot, 'Johnson, Jacobitism, and Swedish Charles', p. 962.
26. Anon., *The Female Rebels*, p. 10.
27. *The Lady Kilmarnock and Lady Balmerino's Sorrowful Lamentation for the Death of their Lords, Who Were Beheaded for High-Treason on Tower-Hill, on Monday, August 18th [OS], 1746* [broadside] ([London(?)]: [n. pub,] 1746). BL shelfmark

C.115.i.3.(78). The charge against Lady Kilmarnock, that she had nagged her husband into treason, appears to be a calumny, historians having tended to prefer the Earl's own explanation: 'for the two kings and their rights I cared not a farthing . . . , but I was starving, and, by God, if Mahomet had set up his standard in the Highlands I had been a good Mussulman for bread . . .': John Heneage Jesse, *Memoirs of the Pretenders and Their Adherents* (3 vols., Boston, 1901), III, p. 59.

28. *Mémoires du duc de Luynes sur la cour de Louis XV (1735–1758)*, ed. L. Dussieux and Eud. Soulié (17 vols., Paris, 1860–5), IX (1862), p. 35.

29. Isobel Grundy, 'Women's History? Writings by English Nuns', in *Women, Writing, History 1640–1740*, ed. Grundy and Susan Wiseman (London, 1992), pp. 126–38, at 138.

30. Anon., *The Life of Dr. Archibald Cameron, Brother to Donald Cameron of Lochiel, Chief of that Clan* (London: Printed for M. Cooper, W. Reeve, and C. Sympson, 1753), p. [30].

31. Nathalie Genet-Rouffiac, 'Les Jacobites à Paris et Saint-Germain-en-Laye', *Revue de la Bibliothèque Nationale*, 46 (winter 1992), pp. 45–9, at 46, 'points d'ancrage'.

32. Claire Walker, 'Prayer, Patronage, and Political Conspiracy: English Nuns and the Restoration', *HJ*, 43 (2000), pp. 1–23.

33. A term emphasised in Sonya Wynne, 'The Mistresses of Charles II and Restoration Court Politics', in *The Stuart Courts*, ed. Eveline Cruickshanks (Stroud, 2000), pp. 171–90, at 171.

34. A key phrase for Elaine Chalus: see her 'Elite Women, Social Politics, and the Political World of Late Eighteenth-Century England', *HJ*, 43 (2000), pp. 669–97, and the works cited in note 11 there.

35. Henry St John, Viscount Bolingbroke, *A Letter to Sir William Windham [etc.]* (London: A. Millar, 1753), p. 174.

36. *Journal et mémoires du marquis d'Argenson*, IV, p. 317.

37. On this family, see Patricia Kneas Hill, *The Oglethorpe Ladies and the Jacobite Conspiracies* (Atlanta, 1977).

38. Marquis d'Argenson's peace project, May 1746: BL Add MS 32,805, fs. 96r–104v at 98r.

39. The Royal Navy's preoccupation with the Jacobite rising led to £700,000-worth of British shipping falling into the hands of French privateers; while on land, the fall of Brussels alone (directly the consequence of British troops being recalled to deal with the rebels) yielded up to France £1,000,000 in booty. Weighed alongside French expenditures on the rebels' behalf, these figures represent a pay-off of 8:1: Murray G.H. Pittock, *Jacobitism* (Basingstoke, 1998), p. 88. French policy-makers were quite aware of this arithmetic: *Journal et mémoires du marquis d'Argenson*, V (1863), p. 314; Adrienne Hytier, 'An Eighteenth-Century Experiment in Historical Realism: The Marquis d'Argenson and Bonnie Prince Charlie', *Eighteenth-Century Studies*, 3 (1969–70), pp. 200–41, at 238).

40. *Journal et mémoires du marquis d'Argenson*, V, pp. 289, 300, 317, 320, 330; L.L. Bongie, *The Love of a Prince: Bonnie Prince Charlie in France, 1744–1748* (Vancouver, 1986), p. 253.

41. Bongie, p. 240. Charles's protest was speedily translated into English, a copy of which translation can be found at BL shelfmark C.115.i.3.(101).

42. Bongie, p. 192.

43. Although it is not certain that Charles was ever as blunt as reported in the *Northampton Mercury* of 12 December 1748 (OS) (vol. 29, p. 146). According to

this source, the Prince had promised that 'whoever mentioned [the Treaty] any more to him, he would shoot thro' the Head'!

44. James Ray, *A Compleat History of the Rebellion, from its First Rise in 1745, to its Total Suppression at the Glorious Battle of Culloden* (Manchester: Printed for the Author by R. Whitworth, [1747(?)]), p. 84. Discussed in MacKenzie, ' "A Great Affinity" '.

45. Thomas E. Kaiser, 'The Drama of Charles Edward Stuart, Jacobite Propaganda, and French Political Protest, 1745–1750', *Eighteenth-Century Studies*, 30 (1996–7), pp. 365–81, at 368. On Charles's arrival in France after the '45, 'for all that [he] had just emerged from a gruelling five months and did not look his best', writes Frank McLynn, '[the Duc de] Luynes had to admit that the tall prince with the noble figure irresistibly reminded him of Charles XII of Sweden . . .': *Charles Edward Stuart: A Tragedy in Many Acts* (London, 1988), p. 310. The Prince's preëminent biographer does not quite capture his source's sense here, however. Listen to what de Luynes wrote, in his journal for 19 October 1746: 'Je n'avois jamais vu le prince [Charles] édouard. Il est fort grand, a une figure noble; on trouve qu'il ressemble à Charles XII, roi de Suède': *Mémoires du duc de Luynes*, VII (1861), p. 453. The implication of de Luynes's phrasing is not that the resemblance had struck him out of the blue. He implies that *the general opinion is* that Prince Charles does, indeed, look like his namesake – as though everyone had been itching to make the comparison, after so much Jacobite publicity linking the two.

46. [Title unknown], pp. 13, 16. In the British Library, pp. 9–16 of this work are incorrectly bound together with pp. 1–8 of a separate publication, *Relation de la reddition de la ville d'Edimbourg . . .* , the whole being classed as shelfmark 9509.dd.4.(1). Another French text which was almost certainly drafted in Scotland, and which also deploys the comparison between the two Charleses, is: *Lettre de monsieur le chevalier Olimphant, colonel ecossois, à Mr. ****, capitaine dans le regiment de D*****, ecossois & irlandois, en Flandres: dattée de Perth, du 10/11 Septembre 1745* ([n.p.] [n. pub.], 1745), p. 5 for Charles–Charles. In ' "A Great Affinity" ', I fret confusedly over the provenance of this document which I knew only through an unclear secondary reference. Having now seen the document itself (it can be found at BL shelfmark 1572/247), it is plainly a work published on the Continent but based on Scottish material.

47. Anon., *Lettre du Docteur Stmitrk, avocat de Londres, à M. G*****, avocat au Parlement de Paris . . .* ([n.p.] [n. pub.], [1746]), pp. 3–4. In ' "A Great Affinity" ', I quote the last part of this sentence (from *de mourir*). Having relied on a fragmentary set of notes taken long before, I was not aware at the time that my quotation occurred in the context of the Charles–Charles analogy!

48. Anon., *Lettre du Docteur Stmitrk*, p. 5.

49. In a *Freeholder* essay of 1716 (no. 43, 18 May (OS)), reprinted in the *Gentleman's Magazine* for October 1745, Joseph Addison had pointed out that analogies between British and Swedish political experience could be particularly instructive as 'Sweden is the only Protestant Kingdom in Europe besides this . . . which has had the Misfortune to see Popish Princes upon the Throne': *The Freeholder*, ed. James Leheny (Oxford, 1979), p. 230. Cf. the *Gentleman's Magazine*, 15 (1745), pp. 532–4. Charles XII of course was no 'Popish Prince', but the reprinting of Addison's essay in 1745 suggests that the idea of Swedish–British parallels was in the air.

50. But not the last such occasion. On 22 April 1749, the Marquis d'Argenson reports

that Charles is rumoured to be preparing to seize 'la couronne de Pologne, en imitant tout à fait Charles XII son modèle': *Journal et mémoires du marquis d'Argenson*, V, p. 444. Four weeks earlier, d'Argenson had noted that Charles was said to be heading for Sweden where he intended to claim the Jacobite fund established there in aid of Charles XII's invasion scheme thirty years before, and to use that war chest to repair his political prospects: ibid., V, p. 418. Horace Mann passed the same story to Horace Walpole on 18 April: *The Yale Edition of Horace Walpole's Correspondence*, ed. W.S. Lewis and others, 48 vols. in 47 (New Haven, 1937–83), XX (1960), p. 44. This shows that at the time when the *Vanity* appeared, Charles XII's old connection with the Stuarts had not 'pass[ed] from memory' as has been repeatedly alleged: Weinbrot, 'Johnson, Jacobitism, and Swedish Charles', p. 969; cf. p. 966 and idem, 'Who Said He Was a Jacobite Hero?', pp. 435, 437, 441.

51. *Journal et mémoires du marquis d'Argenson*, V, pp. 232–3. Bender (now Tighina, Moldova) was the Turkish stronghold on the Dniester where Charles XII took shelter after Poltava. Like the later Charles, he had with him rag-tag colony of survivors from his failed military expedition, for whom he had to arrange support from his host government. Like the later Charles, he declined any settlement personally from that government short of all-out backing in a war of revenge against their common enemy. Like the later Charles, *rapprochement* between that enemy and his host government led to Charles's being asked to move on. Like the later Charles, he dug in his heels. Eventually, the Swedish King was besieged in his little compound, defending himself 'avec quarante domestiques contre une armée': Voltaire, *Histoire de Charles XII*, ed. Gunnar von Proschwitz, *The Complete Works of Voltaire*, 4 (Oxford, 1996), books 4–7 (p. 418 for 'quarante domestiques').

52. *York Courant*, 29 November 1748 (OS), unpaginated.

53. *Northampton Mercury*, 29 (1748), p. 137. The derivation from the *London Evening Post* is established through the Northampton paper's key. This report is plainly based on the same source as the report quoted above from the *York Courant*. Further investigation would probably find variations on this bulletin occurring elsewhere in the British press.

54. *Copy of a Letter from a French Lady at Paris. Giving a Particular Account of the Manner in Which Prince Edward Was Arrested. Translated from the French* (London: Printed for W. Webb, 1749), p. 4. Charles is disingenuous here: he had nurtured the belief that he was going to make a Charles XII-like fight of it. For Charles's guiding hand over the collaborative authorship of this pamphlet, see Bongie, pp. 251–8. '[T]he Prince's own sanctioned history of his arrest' (Bongie, p. 258), this work circulated widely in many variants. Its presentation of the Prince as a bluff Englishman being harried by snivelling, dishonourable frogs – a sort of brother-figure to Hogarth at Calais – reveals the extent to which Charles's conduct in late 1748 had been a performance intended for British audiences. At one point the imprisoned Charles asks his captors: '*Have you . . . bound my* Englishmen, *as you did me? An* Englishman *is not used to be bound; he is not made for that Purpose*' (*Copy of a Letter*, p. 12). That the Prince should assume a female narrative position in this apologia in itself says something about Jacobite propaganda's emphasis on the Stuarts' connection with women. How many other early modern male political leaders addressed the public through the assumed voice of an anonymous woman?

55. Anon., *An Authentick Account of the Conduct of the Young Chevalier, from his First*

Arrival in Paris, after his Defeat at Cullodden, to the Conclusion of the Peace at Aix-la-Chapelle . . . (3rd edn., London: Nutt, et al., 1749), p. 34. Like number (8) below, this passage is cited in Erskine-Hill, 'The Political Character', p. 131.

56. *Gentleman's Magazine*, 18 (1748), p. 534. For clarity's sake I have used parentheses in place of the square brackets which appear in the original; my ellipsis after '*Sweden*' removes a reference to an earlier issue of the *Gentleman's Magazine* (concerning Charles XII). As pointed out in MacKenzie, ' "A Great Affinity" ', this issue of the *Gentleman's Magazine* (printed probably around 1 January (OS)) stands *back-to-back* with the issue (i.e. the supplement for 1748, printed around 20 January (OS)) which features excerpts from the *Vanity*, including lines 191–200 and 219–22 from the section on Swedish Charles: *Gentleman's Magazine*, 18 (1748), p. 598. As the assumed publisher of the *Vanity*'s first edition (9 January (OS), Edward Cave, the proprietor of the *Gentleman's Magazine*, would have had Johnson's manuscript in hand when this December issue went to press.

57. Voltaire, *Correspondence, and Related Documents*, ed. Theodore Besterman, *The Complete Works of Voltaire*, 85–135 (various places and publishers, 1968–77), XI (Geneva: Institut et Musée Voltaire, 1970), p. 128. The exact date when Voltaire made this statement (presumably in a letter) is unknown; and indeed the statement's attribution to him is indefinite, though probable (see Besterman's discussion and MacKenzie, ' "A Great Affinity" ', n. 30).

58. *The Private Journal and Literary Remains of John Byrom*, ed. Richard Parkinson (2 vols. in 4, Manchester: Chetham Society, 1854–57), II, pp. 466–9, at 467.

59. Weinbrot, 'Johnson, Jacobitism, and Swedish Charles', p. 979 n. 77.

60. Johnson, *Poems*, ed. McAdam with Milne, p. 90.

61. McLynn, p. 369.

62. By a character in the Marquis d'Argenson's play on the subject (of which more below); quoted in Hytier, p. 240.

63. In addition to the studies by Hytier and Kaiser, see Bernard Cottret and Monique Cottret, 'Les Chansons du mal-aimé: raison d'état et rumeur publique (1748–1750)', in *Histoire sociale, sensibilités collectives et mentalités: mélanges Robert Mandrou* (Paris, 1985), pp. 303–15; and Robert Darnton, 'Poetry and the Police in Eighteenth-Century Paris', *Studies on Voltaire and the Eighteenth Century*, 371 (1999), pp. 1–22. My account of Prince Charles's life in Paris and his showdown with the French government has been based on the works just cited, on Bongie, chs. 11–12, on McLynn, chs. 24–6, and on the following primary sources: E. J. F. Barbier, *Journal historique et anecdotique du règne de Louis XV*, ed. A. de la Villegille (4 vols., Paris, 1847–56), III (1851), *passim; Journal et mémoires de Charles Collé, sur les hommes de lettres, les ouvrages dramatiques, et les événements les plus mémorables du règne de Louis XV (1748–1772)*, new edn., ed. Honoré Bonhomme (3 vols., Paris, 1868), I, *passim; Journal et mémoires du marquis d'Argenson*, V, *passim; Mémoires du duc de Luynes*, IX, *passim*.

64. Kaiser ('acute crisis' at pp. 365–6). Readers should not infer that I am proposing outraged affection for Prince Charles as the only reason behind this collapse in monarchical prestige. Kaiser and the other writers on this subject show that many factors converged in this episode, the image of the violated Prince simply providing a focus through which popular discontent could articulate itself.

65. Darnton, p. 16.

66. Horace Mann reported on 3 January 1749 that the affair continued to make 'a great noise' in Italy: *The Yale Edition of Horace Walpole's Correspondence*, XX, p. 15.

67. *Journal et mémoires du marquis d'Argenson*, V, p. 367.

68. Ibid., V, p. 233.
69. Ibid., V, p. 278.
70. Ibid., V, p. 288 (26 November).
71. Ibid., V, p. 284.
72. Ibid., V, p. 288 (26 November). D'Argenson was still speculating as to the Princesse's part in this matter on 17 December (ibid., pp. 320–1).
73. Ibid., V, p. 318 (14 December).
74. Ibid., V, p. 315 (11 December).
75. Ibid., V, p. 303 (7 December).
76. Ibid., V, p. 300 (4 December).
77. In Hytier's title.
78. In Hytier and in [René-Louis de Voyer de Paulmy,] Marquis d'Argenson, 'La Prison du Prince Charles-édouard Stuart' [selections], ed. the Duc de Broglie, *Revue d'histoire diplomatique*, 5 (1891), pp. 553–606. The transcriptions in the latter exhumation, Hytier warns us (pp. 200–1), are unreliable.
79. I am perhaps unfair on the Marquis. *La Prison du Prince Charles* was written for his own intellectual satisfaction – on political grounds, it was quite impossible that the play should ever be performed or even disseminated in manuscript – and so he may have used the theatrical form, as essayists sometimes do, simply as a framework in which better to order his thoughts and clarify differences in perspective. In such a case, d'Argenson would give little thought to stageworthiness.
80. Cf.: '[Charles XII] is not likely . . . to be cast as a recognizable Jacobite hero in 1749' (Weinbrot, 'Who Said He Was a Jacobite Hero?', p. 437).
81. D'Argenson, 'La Prison', pp. 560–1.
82. Hytier, p. 214.
83. D'Argenson, 'La Prison', p. 556.
84. Act V, scene i (d'Argenson, 'La Prison', pp. 596–7).
85. Quoted in Hytier, p. 218.
86. Ibid., p. 218.
87. Ibid., p. 238.
88. Ibid., p. 240.
89. Even if there were not, the details of the news story which 'employ[ed] all the Conversation' across the Channel were hardly inaccessible to Johnson who, as the late Donald Greene reminded us, had an 'excellent' reading knowledge of French, had 'inaugurated a . . . "Foreign Books" section' in the *Gentleman's Magazine*, and had '[f]or a number of years . . . contributed to the [*Gentleman's Magazine's* . . .] "Foreign History" feature, reporting and commenting on current events in the War of the Austrian Succession . . .': Donald Greene, *The Politics of Samuel Johnson* (2nd edn, Athens, Ga, 1990), pp. xxvii–xxviii, xxvi, and xxvii.
90. *Gentleman's Magazine*, 18 (1748), p. 533. At crisis moments, the British press always seems to have the Prince staying with women: on the eve of Culloden, he was reported in the *London Gazette* to be 'lodged at the lady dowager M'Intosh's': reprinted in the *Gentleman's Magazine*, 16 (1746), p. 205 (issue for April).
91. Unpaginated.
92. *Northampton Mercury*, 29 (1748), p. 145.
93. [John Burton], *A Genuine and True Journal of the Most Miraculous Escape of the Young Chevalier, from the Battle of Culloden, to his Landing in France . . .* [corrected edn.] (London: Printed for B.A., 1749).

94. From the title-page matter.
95. [Burton], *A Genuine and True Journal*, p. 66.
96. Ibid., p. 67.
97. See note 55 above.
98. Anon., *An Authentick Account of the Conduct*, pp. 3–4.
99. Ibid., pp. 29–30.
100. Ibid., p. 29.
101. Anon., *A Remarkable Dialogue Which Lately Happened in the Gardens of Luxembourg, Between an Old Impartial English Whig, and a Nonjuror of the Church of England, Concerning the Young Chevalier; and Several Other Affairs Regarding Great-Britain, &c.*, (2nd edn., [Edinburgh(?)] [n. pub.], 1748). Published originally (and apparently also in this edition) in Edinburgh, according to its secondary title page, this work was 'Sold in *London, Dublin, Paris* and *Holland*'.
102. Ibid., p. 2.
103. The author of *A Remarkable Dialogue* says the Aix-la-Chapelle preliminaries had been signed since he wrote the dialogue part of his pamphlet (p. 85), but says their contents 'seem to be still a Secret . . . tho' there has been various Accounts and Conjectures . . .' (p. 86). The *Gentleman's Magazine* published in its issue for April 1748 what might be described as conjectures as to the preliminary articles' content (vol. 18, p. 190), and an apparently authoritative definition of them in its issue for May (vol. 18, pp. 220–2). Triangulation against the *Gentleman's Magazine*, then, seems to date *A Remarkable Dialogue* as early as May.
104. Anon., *A Remarkable Dialogue*, p. 52.
105. Ibid., pp. 55–6.
106. Ibid., pp. 78–9.
107. Ibid., p. 79.
108. Ibid., pp. 1–2.
109. Anon., *An Authentick Account of the Conduct*, pp. 5–6. This passage is closely paralleled in another Jacobite publication of 1749, reprinted in *The Lockhart Papers: Containing Memoirs and Commentaries Upon the Affairs of Scotland from 1702 to 1715, by George Lockhart, Esq. of Carnwath, His Secret Correspondence with the Son of King James the Second from 1718 to 1728, and His Other Political Writings; Also, Journals and Memoirs of the Young Pretender's Expedition in 1745, by Highland Officers in His Army* (2 vols., London: William Anderson, 1817), II, pp. 565–86, at 566–7.
110. [Barthélemy-François-Joseph Moufle d'Angerville(?)], *The Private Life of Lewis XV. In Which Are Contained the Principal Events, Remarkable Occurrences, and Anecdotes, of His Reign*, trans. J.O. Justamond (4 vols., London: Charles Dilly, 1781), II, p. 319.
111. Voltaire, *Histoire de Charles XII*, p. 374.
112. Ibid., p. 369.
113. Johnson, *Poems*, ed. McAdam with Milne, p. 102 n.
114. *Journal et mémoires du marquis d'Argenson*, V, p. 318 (14 December 1748).
115. Darnton, pp. 17–18; Hytier, p. 237; *Journal et mémoires du marquis d'Argenson*, V, 344 (2 January 1749), p. 351 (7 January 1748).
116. Darnton, p. 15.
117. *Gentleman's Magazine*, 18 (1748), pp. 533–5.
118. Ibid., 18 (1748), p. 574.
119. Ibid., 18 (1748), p. 561.
120. Ibid., 18 (1748), pp. 560–1.

121. Ibid., 18 (1748), p. 526.

122. Ibid., 18 (1748), p. 478.

123. 'I conclude your Italy talks of nothing but the [Charles Edward Affair]', writes Walpole to Mann on 15 December (OS). 'I don't know whether he be a Stuart, but I am sure by his extravagance he has proved himself of English extraction!': *The Yale Edition of Horace Walpole's Correspondence*, XX, p. 8.

124. Ibid., XIX (1955), p. 509 (Mann writing to Walpole, 25 October. Mann's casual 'I suppose you may have seen' (ibid., referring to the latest bits of news about Prince Charles) indicates what an unavoidable subject the Charles Edward Affair had become).

125. All dates for the *York Courant* are Old Style.

126. Sometimes a given post from London itself consolidated an accumulation of bulletins from Paris, so that the *Northampton Mercury* of 5 December (OS) includes, in its summary of Wednesday's post *alone*, four rapid-fire reports on the Prince's affairs; further information appears in Friday's post: *Northampton Mercury*, 29 (1748), pp. 141–2.

127. '[The Charles Edward] Affair becoming serious', runs a report in the *York Courant* (6 December 1748 (OS)), 'the King call'd a Council extraordinary . . . and gave his last Orders about the Manner in which he [the Prince] should be further proceeded with.' Cf. Voltaire's narration of the Turkish Emperor's giving his orders how to proceed with Charles XII: 'Le sultan indigné fit assembler un divan extraordinaire, et y parla lui-même . . .': *Histoire de Charles XII*, pp. 437–8. We often get the sense, reading these British press clippings which derive from correspondence coming out of Paris, that someone in France was trying to make the Charles Edward Affair conform in detail to Voltaire's history of Charles XII. The *Northampton Mercury* on 12 December (OS) says that Charles had dismissed an emissary from the King with the words, 'Pensions are quite out of the Question, I only desire the King would keep his Word with me' (vol. 29, p. 145). Voltaire has his Charles dismiss an emissary from the Emperor, bidding him tell his master 'que des rois devaient tenir leur parole': *Histoire de Charles XII*, p. 431.

128. [Burton], *A Genuine and True Journal*, p. 69.

129. Cf. Anon., *An Authentick Account of the Conduct*, p. 31.

130. Anon., *A Remarkable Dialogue*, p. 67.

131. Ibid., p. 64. Charles's projected ethic of Highland simplicity went along with his (well-publicised) refusal to accept a French pension or other material incentives. This tightens the typological relation between him and Charles XII who, at Bender, when angry with the Porte, had sent back with icy dignity a magnificent gift of Arabian horses, saying he did not accept gifts from enemies: Voltaire, *Histoire de Charles XII*, p. 383.

132. Anon., *A Remarkable Dialogue*, p. 66.

133. Ibid., p. 67.

134. Weinbrot, 'Johnson, Jacobitism, and Swedish Charles', p. 960.

135. *Journal et mémoires du marquis d'Argenson*, V, 314. I am grateful to Dr. C.D. Orr, whose hospitality and conversation smoothed the course of my research, and to Ms. Katharine Marx, an unerring fact-hunter and the inspiration to whom this essay is affectionately dedicated.

Conclusion
Literature, History and Interpretation

J.C.D. Clark

The recent controversy over the religious and political identity of Samuel Johnson has raised important issues about method in historical and literary scholarship: the exegesis of texts taken in relative isolation; the use of circumstantial evidence; the recognition and reconstruction of contexts within which texts and the intentions of their authors can be interpreted; the way in which biographers like Boswell 'constructed' their subjects; the tracing of languages of discourse; the re-examination of the categories we impose on people in the past; the relation of religious commitments to political ones, and the discernment of the consequences of both for literary and didactic writing.

The disagreements disclosed by the debate have been more within than between disciplines. Although it has been objected that the recent reinterpretation of Johnson privileges contextual (and historical) over textual (and literary) evidence,[1] it should be apparent that alternative readings of many Johnsonian texts have been offered, and writings by Johnson that were omitted from the older canon[2] have been placed under scrutiny. It has been shown that this older interpretation of a Whig, proto-Evangelical Johnson had itself relied on a context, that established primarily by the historical writing of Sir Lewis Namier, and had itself read Johnsonian texts in the light of that context. Yet this older literary scholarship was often unreflective about method, and failed to keep pace with the developments in literary history and in the history of ideas (the latter associated especially with the names of J.G.A. Pocock and Quentin Skinner):[3] consequently, when Johnson was reinterpreted in the light of newly adduced contexts, an older school of Johnsonian scholars could only disparage a now-familiar historical and literary exercise as merely 'conjectural' and 'speculative'. Their reaction is understandable, but inadequate.[4]

Historical and literary scholarship can still each learn from the other: many of the late twentieth-century misconceptions about Johnson arose when literary scholars thought that they were using evidence in legitimately historical ways, but fell short of acceptable historiographical standards; and when those few remaining historians who still accepted a Macaulayite or Namierite reading of Johnson failed to scrutinise his writings with sufficient critical attention. There are many paths to a better understanding of Johnson: no Faculty has a monopoly on helpful reinterpretation.

Yet the integration of literary and historical insights is not an easy injunction to obey, not least because the evidence is so seldom self-explanatory. On one hand, the practicalities of publishing are clearly relevant to the interpretation of the nature of Johnson's literary vision;[5] on the other, coded utterance was familiar enough in a period in which certain views were ruthlessly proscribed. As the Boyle lecturer observed in 1698, writers like the Deist Charles Blount 'frequently disguise their true meaning; it is not the bare Words only, but the Scope of a Writer, that giveth the true Light by which any Writing is to be interpreted'.[6] This applied to political writing as much as to the arts, as the present volume has helped to show.[7]

Even so, the recent defence of Donald Greene's interpretation of Johnson has been far more rhetorically heightened than an abstract discussion over method would warrant: more again must be at stake, and some of the wider implications may be suggested. The re-emergence in historical studies of contingency and the counterfactual has meant that the winners no longer take all, and the foundational events of modern societies can no longer be presented (as they were even quite recently) as overdetermined, the results of 'historical inevitability'. In eighteenth-century studies, we no longer talk of the secure establishment of a monolithic Walpolean Whig oligarchy. We no longer see political structures or manipulation as determinative, or as the ultimate arena of human action. Old-style 'labour history' conceived as the long march of secular Everyman has widened its horizons: we now know far more about forms of consciousness, commitment and allegiance in the population at large. We can no longer speak of the emergence of a consensual Britishness in the years after the Union of 1707. The theme of dynastic allegiance has illuminated a major challenge to that 'national-consensual' thesis, namely the 'British Problem', England's relations with Scotland, Ireland and Wales: familiar in scholarship on the seventeenth and nineteenth centuries, it now takes its place in the eighteenth also. Identity was always both contested and hegemonic.

Displacements such as these have revealed Jacobite studies as a centrally contested area, not because a large part of the nation was ready to rise in rebellion (it was not), nor because eighteenth-century English men and women were romantic or nostalgic (they were not), but because shifts in methodology place this area of study in a strategically important position. In practical terms, contingency has transformed our sense of the possible, of the counterfactual alternatives. Was there no danger to the state in the revolutionary moment of 1793, asked one contemporary author, even if the disaffected were a minority? 'Was there no danger in 1715, or in 1745, because the majority of the nation maintained the principles of the Revolution of 1688?'[8]

Jacobitism has become a significant counterfactual to what has long been known as the 'Whig interpretation of history', a set of assumptions about animating principles and outcomes that is still vigorous under several labels. The Whig interpretation was built up in the early nineteenth century[9] around the historiographical interpretation of a number of key episodes, but especially four: the Revolution of 1688; the education, accession and early politics of George III; the American Revolution; and the 1832 Reform Act. The historical recovery of diverse dynastic allegiances did substantial damage to most of these components. It showed that the Revolution of 1688 was not limited, secular, consensual and contractarian, but instead was dominated by contingency and lastingly contested within an idiom of dynastic politics. Second, once the nature of Toryism was established, it was clear that George III and his ministers' policies were very far from it. Third, if George III did not champion a Tory reaction and if political discourse was not within a secular, contractarian, Lockeian consensus, then a very different explanation of the American Revolution was called for. Finally, if 1688 and 1776 were so different in their natures from the episodes represented in the Whig interpretation, then 1832 itself was open to rethinking, and what had been held to be the intellectual foundations of democracy, liberalism, radicalism and conservatism were open to reinterpretation. So much has been invested in older interpretations indebted to this Whig perspective that the process of adjustment cannot but be difficult.

The Whig interpretation was not something that could be confined to party politics and constitutional history alone.[10] The history of English literature too had been deeply influenced by the assumptions which the Whig interpretation contained. One example will stand for many: 'By 1688 Britain had seen that neither Catholic Stuart nor Protestant Cromwell, neither absolute royalist nor absolute republican, was acceptable to a nation seeking a middle path in politics and religion.'[11] In Whig accounts, teleology, personification, prolepsis and the construction of ideal types take the place of the recovery of the real and pressing alternatives. In respect of substance, claims about the easy and comprehensive victory of the House of Hanover and all that it stood for have been parallelled by claims about the easy and comprehensive victory of the vernacular over classical languages and literatures, with all that these in turn entailed.[12]

The history of politics and the history of literary categories cannot be satisfactorily separated. A new context for the study of dynastic allegiance both Hanoverian and Stuart has emerged in recent scholarship; no longer can we term either 'nostalgic', a later concept which cannot be anachronistically projected back onto early eighteenth-century commitments, nor can Jacobitism be understood as 'romantic'. Dynastic allegiance was not a matter of

sentiment; it was expressed in the hard languages of religious and legal obligation, and it had equally hard practical consequences. Boswell belonged to
a generation which could just begin to soften those jagged edges and reduce
what he knew of Johnson's political principles (which was only a part) to 'a
kind of *liking* for Jacobitism, something that it is not easy to define'; but for
Boswell (born 1740) Jacobitism was history, for Johnson (born 1709) it was
lived experience. Moreover, Boswell's comment was dated 13 September
1773: much had changed by that time, both in the world and in Johnson's
view of it.

Historians interpret individual *dicta* like Boswell's by seeking a wider
context. For example, Boswell prefaced the remark just quoted, more
tellingly: 'Mr. Johnson and I were both visibly of the *old interest* (to use the
Oxford expression), kindly affectioned at least, and perhaps too openly so'
to the cause of their hostess, Flora Macdonald. On the same occasion,
Johnson also corrected the claim of Sandie MacLeod that a plan for a coup
was 'in agitation' in London in 1759, Johnson observing that 'it failed from
the pusillanimity of some of those who were to have acted', a remark which
may have disclosed private knowledge. Nor is it clear to what extent Johnson
intended his acknowledgement of *de facto* right on that occasion to halt
Boswell's enquiries, socially inept as they were in that company: certainly,
Boswell recorded: 'Mr. Johnson's argument of right being formed by possession and acknowledgement of the people, settles my mind, and I have
now no uneasiness.'[13] All this, and more, must be invoked to interpret
Boswell's 'kind of *liking* for Jacobitism' if such *dicta* are not to seem merely
an anticipation of the mentalities of Sir Walter Scott or John Buchan.

The new scholarship has replaced Johnson in a world before Romanticism
or nostalgia. He was not, equally, 'a conservative': no such identity was
available in his lifetime.[14] He did not therefore make common cause with
Edmund Burke; rather, the two men viewed each other as being far apart on
the political spectrum.[15] Johnson was not a 'traditionalist' or a 'reactionary'
in the meanings of those nineteenth-century neologisms: he did not advocate turning back the clock to an imagined golden age, but instead regarded
ancients and moderns as separated only by time, not by the qualitative dis-
continuity which, for us, is held to separate 'antiquity' from 'modernity'.[16]

It has been centrally argued that Johnson was a Tory, a Nonjuror and a
Jacobite sympathiser, these commitments evolving and being expressed differently at different periods in his life. These arguments have all been, in
different ways, denied. Yet the counter-arguments have not been successful.
To disqualify Johnson as a Tory it is not sufficient to show that, on some
occasions, he spoke sceptically of 'divine right': this phrase covered a variety
of positions from the social-anthropological world-view gently parodied by
Johnson in the figure of 'Tom Tempest'[17] through Sir John Hawkins's 'middle
Hypothesis'[18] that God had appointed government in general, but left to
mankind the choice of forms and governors. George I and George II, as well

as George III, invoked divine right on their own behalf, claims that English Whigs regularly endorsed. At the other end of the spectrum Thomas Paine explained men's rights as divine rights, possessed by men because granted by God at their creation:[19] divine right could take different forms without ceasing to rely on the Almighty as a source of legitimacy.

Even within Hawkins's middle position, there could be powerful principled reasons for adhering to either Hanoverian or Stuart dynasties, especially hereditary right as demonstrated by law, and the idea of allegiance, itself a legal concept which, in England, constituted a formal definition of national identity.[20] Recent scholarship has increasingly encouraged us to see Filmer as an atypical extremist: hereditary right, in Johnson's lifetime, was largely understood in ways which Filmer's eclipse did not undermine. Nevertheless, beside the legalistic element in Johnson's thought was another, from an older mind-set, from which he steadily distanced himself in later life but which he never entirely renounced.

Mrs. Thrale, in some ways closer to Johnson than was Boswell, had no doubt that her friend was 'strongly attached to the notion of the Divine & Hereditary Right inherent in Kings'. Single quotations like this are not in themselves decisive, and interpretation rests on the construction of contexts within which their ambiguities can be elucidated: Mrs. Thrale also recorded Johnson's recognition of what we call *de facto* right, and found a form of words, of course not as accurate as our own, to reconcile Johnson's conduct: 'not from change of Principles, but difference of Situations'.[21] Other examples could be found which seem to point to a late recognition of *de jure* right: Johnson's invitation to Miss Roberts, 'I hope you are a Jacobite . . . A Jacobite, Sir, believes in the divine right of Kings . . .', only makes sense as a favourable endorsement and as a linking of the divine right of kings to the divine right of bishops in a way that parallels Johnson's definition of 'Tory' in the *Dictionary*.[22]

There is evidence that by 1773, if not by his authorship of *The False Alarm* in 1770, Johnson recognised a *de facto* title in George III[23] (though never, importantly, in George II); yet he never took the oaths of allegiance or abjuration. Boswell's manuscript draft of the *Life* originally contained two more pages in which the biographer reflected on Johnson's acceptance of a pension and the issues of principle it raised, 'apparently trying to exonerate him from charges of opportunism and hypocrisy': readers have been warned against assuming from the printed text that Boswell 'approves without hesitation' Johnson's decision to accept it. Even in the manuscript text that remains, Boswell wrote of a Johnson 'distinguished for his aversion to the first two Princes of the House of Hanover': the printed *Life* omitted this comment.[24] There would have been no hypocrisy if Johnson's recognition of *de facto* right had not been offset by a recognition of *de jure* right also.

It has been correctly observed that in the *Lives of the Poets*, that late work of 1779–81, Johnson showed recognition of the claims of *de facto* power and sought to reinforce the then regime.[25] Understandably so, since Johnson similarly supported the established order in his political pamphlets of the 1770s and the fourth edition of his *Dictionary* of 1773.[26] This does not mean that Johnson in the *Lives of the Poets* did not also display recognition of *de jure* authority: that work contains a Jacobite agenda not in the sense of stating a Johnsonian political programme for the 1780s, but in the sense of showing appreciation of the agenda of some of those who lived through the events of 1688 or 1714. Given this purpose of reconciliation in the 1780s, it is again unsurprising that Johnson did not structure the *Lives of the Poets* as a systematic eulogy of the Jacobite theme: he did not, for example, mention Richard Savage's early Jacobite poems, 'though he must have known of them'.[27] To claim Johnson's Hanoverian allegiance on the grounds that some of his poets had such loyalties is to ignore the other side of the case. Recent scholarship has propounded a more rounded interpretation of a Johnson lastingly torn between two alternatives, and whose position changed over time.

Definitions alone are never enough. Johnson indeed offered a definition of 'Tory' in the *Dictionary*: 'One who adheres to the antient constitution of the state, and the apostolical hierarchy of the church of England, opposed to a whig.'[28] Yet the terms 'ancient constitution' and 'apostolical hierarchy' were themselves contested. Political and intellectual historians have long emphasised that such categories encompassed a range of positions, and that individuals did not have simple, unchanging identities, like pieces on a chessboard, identities which could be established or refuted with equal simplicity by producing some proof-text from Boswell or any other source.[29] Jacobites and Hanoverians alike were generally not people who held simple, undifferentiated positions, immune from doubt or development, although some purists could be found among the ranks of either. For these reasons, the establishment of men's political identities is not a matter of measuring those individuals against definitions of our own; rather, it involves exploring the degrees and senses of their commitment in changing circumstances. Johnson knew this as well as anyone, printing as an illustration of his definition in the *Dictionary* Addison's sentence 'The knight is more a *tory* in the country than the town, because it more advances his interest.' Nevertheless, Johnson's closing phrase, 'opposed to a whig', rightly recorded a world of polarised identities and proposed the ancient constitution and the apostolical hierarchy as things that Whigs could be expected to deny.

One response to such difficulties in ascribing identity was that of Sir Lewis Namier and his followers, to abandon the use of party labels altogether. But complex problems are not solved by being ignored or crudely denied: the task of historians and literary scholars is to explore the complexities with which people in the past categorised themselves and others, and the way this affected their conduct and their writings. This collection of essays is intended as a contribution to that process.

Some counter-arguments on Johnson's identity depend on concealed minor premises of surprisingly unhistorical simplicity. Johnson, as the Rev. Dr. William Maxwell commented, did not abet 'slavish and arbitrary principles of government';[30] [Toryism was synonymous with slavish and arbitrary principles of government;] therefore Johnson was not a Tory. Equally inadequate is the argument: Johnson acknowledged *de facto* claims; [a Tory would repudiate all *de facto* claims;] therefore Johnson was not a Tory. A similar argument runs: Johnson said that if holding up his hand 'would have secured victory at Culloden to Prince Charles's army', he would not have done it, or did not know if he would have done it; [a Jacobite would have sought the military victory of his cause at any time and at all costs;] therefore Johnson was not a Jacobite. Yet Johnson was clear that the avoidance of unnecessary slaughter in war was a major good.[31] Again, Johnson wrote of the poet Elijah Fenton's 'perversity of integrity' in refusing the oaths; [a Nonjuror would have had no doubts or qualifications in endorsing the Nonjuring position;] therefore Johnson was not a Nonjuror. Or again, Johnson sometimes wrote critically of Stuart monarchs; [Jacobites were people who idolised individual Stuart monarchs and ignored their failings;] therefore Johnson was not a Jacobite. A related argument runs: the doctrine of passive obedience was a Tory hallmark; [Filmer supported passive obedience;] Johnson criticised Filmer; therefore Johnson was not a Tory. The historical Filmer contended that subjects had a duty actively to obey even the unjust commands of their sovereign and ignored the Anglican doctrine of passive obedience (close to our term, civil disobedience) that the young Johnson practised. Such arguments are so historically clumsy as to seem perhaps deliberately misleading.

If Johnson was a Nonjuror, that identity could be demonstrated in only one way: by showing that Johnson avoided subscribing the oaths of allegiance (to George II or George III) or abjuration (of James III), and that he did so for principled reasons. It is, of course, impossible to prove such an historical negative with total certainty: even one piece of evidence, not yet discovered, that he subscribed these oaths would refute the thesis, and we cannot certainly know that no such evidence exists. Probability can steadily strengthen, however, if we rigorously examine all those archives in which Johnson's subscription would have been recorded, had he subscribed. Such an examination is offered in chapter 4, and its conclusion is clear: there is no evidence that Johnson ever subscribed either oath, and recent arguments that he did so rest on misunderstandings.[32]

Johnson, as a Nonjuror, found his career governed by a series of negatives, since many normal, appropriate, modest, inconvenient or ambitious courses of action were closed to him: he could not accept a servitorship at Pembroke College; could not take a BA degree; could not hold a college fellowship; had difficulty in securing or keeping a post as a schoolmaster; could not be ordained and take a living; could not serve in person in the Trained Bands and had to pay for a substitute; could not be a candidate for the Oxford

Professorship of Poetry; could not sit in the House of Commons. The printer William Strahan wrote to one of the Secretaries of the Treasury on 30 March 1771 urging that Johnson would make a good MP.[33] But an MP would have to take the oaths of allegiance and abjuration; Johnson never stood for election. Boswell commented: 'It is not to be believed that Mr. Strahan would have applied, unless Johnson had approved of it':[34] this choice of words disclosed that Boswell had no evidence of Johnson's views on the matter. The episode reminds us that Boswell, whose knowledge of English religion was limited, never fully understood Johnson's position. Indeed, Boswell's understanding of it fell short of Hawkins's, despite the fact that Hawkins's *Life* was available to Boswell before he published his own biography. Perhaps Boswell's systematic denigration of Hawkins's rival volume limited his ability to learn from it. Boswell never fully appreciated why Johnson, a man of obviously outstanding abilities, was condemned to eke out a living as a Grub Street hack, but it is this practical and moral predicament which is at issue in recent discussions.

Scholarship in the humanities, the social and the natural sciences develops in ways which have some features in common. When we approach any large subject, we find that it has already been organised and interpreted by an earlier generation: an explanatory paradigm has been devised, a theory which claims to do justice to the available evidence. That paradigm organises the evidence, but also draws a line around it to indicate what is accepted as relevant and what is not. Such a boundary is likely to exclude a few fragments, but these are dismissed as aberrations, not affecting the truth of the interpretation. Change comes when these fragments are investigated, when this investigation leads to the discovery of more and more such items, and when a new theory is propounded which incorporates the hitherto-excluded evidence and makes it a key element in the formulation of the new paradigm.

Such a claim on behalf of a new paradigm tends to produce successive reactions among the adherents of the old. First, indignation that old certainties have been challenged. Second, denial: the new evidence is asserted to be unreliable, the result of experimental error, or itself explicable in terms of the old paradigm. Third, *ad hominem* responses: the scientific skill or humanistic scholarship of the innovators is disparaged, and their characters and motivations denigrated. Fourth, attempts are made to limit the dissemination of the new heresies.

Attempts to disparage or control the incorporation of new evidence may be effective in particular situations and circumstances, but are unlikely to succeed for long, or in general. As this volume shows, the evidential base allowed to be relevant for assessing Johnson's political and religious commitments has been very substantially widened. Discussions may still be found which continue in the old round of producing proof-texts from Boswell's *Life* and arguing *a priori* about their plausibility, but this approach is now clearly inadequate.

There remains a fifth stage in the development of knowledge. The old paradigm is eventually unable to sustain itself in the face of mounting evidence; a new paradigm is increasingly accepted in its place, a paradigm that does not reject the old evidence but incorporates it with the new in a larger and more balanced picture. This may be the case here, if an adequate new explanation has been framed of how Johnson came to acknowledge both *de jure* and *de facto* titles. Propounding a new explanation may not end the argument: the old controversialists may maintain to their last hour that the old certainties were vindicated, that the sun orbits the earth and that the epistles of Phalaris were genuine. This matters little: scholarship continues to evolve, and the potentialities of new approaches will be exploited. Moreover, no interpretation is sacrosanct: any paradigm may overlook some crucial piece of evidence, and a new generation of scholars may eventually use it to call for a further reconsideration of the whole. That is in the nature of things: the development of Johnsonian studies is to be welcomed, not resisted.

Notes

1. It has been held to be part of a denial of 'the belief that the literary work was complete in itself, and so organized that no extrinsic information was necessary to its comprehension': David Womersley, 'Literature and the History of Political Thought', *HJ*, 39 (1996), pp. 511–20, at 512. Womersley enters a plea for 'the disciplines of the bibliographer and of the textual editor'.
2. A canon exemplified, for example, in Donald J. Greene (ed.), *Samuel Johnson*, The Oxford Authors (Oxford, 1984).
3. For the historical inadequacies produced by an author's belief that he was finding Johnson 'not by going outside his writings but by going more deeply inside' them, see, most recently, Lawrence Lipking, *Samuel Johnson: The Life of an Author* (Cambridge, Mass., 1998); cf. the review by Michael F. Suarez, SJ, in *The Times Literary Supplement* (6 August 1999), p. 8.
4. An equally noticeable feature of the old school is its strongly normative commitment. So appropriate does this normative role seem to its adherents that they presume its presence in others: for example to write of 'James III' is alleged to disclose a covert endorsement of his cause. This presumption merely shows unfamiliarity with historical practice (historians do not refer to the heir of Charles I as 'the Pretender' between 1649 and 1660 or deny medieval antipopes their claimed titles; a work of reference like the Royal Commission on Historical Manuscripts *Calendar of the Stuart Papers* routinely refers to 'James III').
5. Thomas F. Bonnell, in 'Bookselling and Canon-Making: The Trade Rivalry over the English Poets, 1776–1783', *Studies in Eighteenth-Century Culture*, 19 (1989), pp. 53–69, shows that copyright issues influenced the decision to launch the collection *The Works of the English Poets* (68 vols., London, 1779–81) for which Johnson wrote prefaces. The London booksellers' choice clearly had relevance to Johnson's identification of a canon, but is only a part of the story: copyright did not determine what Johnson said about those poets who were included, nor did it dictate the omission of all poets before the mid-seventeenth century. Moreover, both

chief collections of British poets undertaken in the 1770s, the Edinburgh and the London, aimed at being a 'canon' in the sense of attempting inclusiveness; Johnson's prefaces contained an implicit attempt to set a 'canon' in the different sense of an interpretive scheme. Significantly, we know that Bell intended his series to rival the ancient classics: Bonnell, 'Bookselling and Canon-making', p. 57. (In the original impression of my *Samuel Johnson*, p. 25 line 7, 'Cowley' sc. 'Congreve'; this misprint does not affect the argument.)

6. John Harris, *The Atheistical Objection Against the Being of God and his Attributes Fairly Considered, and Fully Refuted* (2 vols., London, 1698), II, p. 4.
7. On this theme see also Murray G.H. Pittock, 'Classical Jacobite Code in the Age of Burlington', in Edward Corp (ed.), *Lord Burlington: The Man and His Politics* (Lewiston, 1998), pp. 137–47.
8. *A Letter to the Rt. Hon. Charles James Fox, upon the Dangerous and Inflammatory Tendency of his late Conduct in Parliament* (London, 1793), p. 21.
9. J.C.D. Clark, *English Society 1660–1832: Religion, Ideology and Politics during the Ancien Regime* (Cambridge, 2000), pp. 554–5.
10. For its implications for our view of Johnson's relation to the natural world, see Robert Mayhew, 'Samuel Johnson's Intellectual Character as a Traveller: A Reassessment', *AJ*, 10 (1999), pp. 35–65, and 'Nature and the Choice of Life in *Rasselas*', *SEL*, 39 (1999), pp. 539–56. Mayhew offers important correctives to earlier assumptions about High Church and Tory attitudes to nature.
11. Howard D. Weinbrot, 'Politics, Taste and National Identity: Some Uses of Tacitism in Eighteenth-Century Britain', in T.J. Luce and A.J. Woodman (eds.), *Tacitus and the Tacitean Tradition* (Princeton, NJ, 1993), p. 169.
12. For a survey of this area of the debate see Thomas Kaminski, 'Rehabilitating "Augustanism": On the Roots of "Polite Letters" in England', *Eighteenth-Century Life*, 20 (1996), pp. 49–65.
13. Frederick A. Pottle and Charles H. Bennett (eds.), *Boswell's Journal of a Tour to the Hebrides with Samuel Johnson, LL.D.* (London, 1936), pp. 160–3.
14. 'Conservatism' was a doctrine formulated around 1830 and was only given currency after 1832: in many ways it was intended to distance its believers from the intellectual premises of order and hierarchy under the ancien regime. It is no paradox, therefore, that recent scholars can discern 'liberal and progressive elements in Johnson's thought': the cake was sliced differently in the eighteenth century.
15. J.C.D. Clark, 'Religious Affiliation and Dynastic Allegiance in Eighteenth Century England: Edmund Burke, Thomas Paine and Samuel Johnson', *ELH*, 64 (1997), pp. 1029–67.
16. For this linguistic point developed at length see Clark, *English Society 1660–1832*, 'Keywords', pp. 1–13.
17. Samuel Johnson, *The Idler*, 10 (17 June 1758).
18. Chapter 4, above.
19. Thomas Paine, *Rights of Man: being an Answer to Mr. Burke's Attack on the French Revolution* (London: J.S. Jordan, 1791), pp. 44–7.
20. J.C.D. Clark, *The Language of Liberty 1660–1832: Political Discourse and Social Dynamics in the Anglo-American World* (Cambridge, 1994), pp. 46–74.
21. Clark, 'Religious Affiliation', p. 1055, quoting Katherine C. Balderston (ed.), *Thraliana: The Diary of Mrs Hesther Lynch Thrale (Later Mrs. Piozzi) 1776–1809* (2 vols., Oxford, 1951), I, p. 192.

22. Boswell, *Life*, I, pp. 430–1 (14 July 1763); undated, but necessarily before the death of its source, 'old Mr. [Bennet] Langton', in 1766. On hereditary right see Clark, *Samuel Johnson*, pp. 203–10.

23. Boswell, *Life*, II, p. 220 (15 April 1773).

24. Allen Reddick in *AJ*, 8 (1997), pp. 412–14, reviewing Marshall Waingrow (ed.), *James Boswell's 'Life of Johnson': An Edition of the Original Manuscript, in Four Volumes* (Edinburgh, New Haven and London, 1994).

25. Dustin Griffin, 'Regulated Loyalty: Jacobitism and Johnson's *Lives of the Poets*', *ELH*, 64 (1997), pp. 1007–27 (although his claims that Johnson simply endorsed the titles of William III or the first two Georges, pp. 1012–13, are unsupported by evidence).

26. Clark, *Samuel Johnson*, pp. 211–37.

27. Griffin, 'Regulated Loyalty', p. 1013.

28. Johnson's *Dictionary* (1755) omitted the word 'Jacobite', although it was in common usage. Did Johnson suppose that it was already covered under 'Nonjuror'? Did he think it too sensitive a matter to address? Or did a Lockeian, Whig Johnson exclude a term for a position opposite to his own?

29. It has been rightly urged that Boswell's *Life* constructs a version of Johnson, and cannot be used as neutral, authoritative testimony (it is not so used in this volume). However, the recent reinterpretation of Johnson suggests that Boswell's construction of his subject apologetically diminished rather than Romantically exaggerated Johnson's Jacobitism. Comparisons of the printed text of Boswell's *Life* with the journals on which he based it have not upset this conclusion. For Boswell's Whig position see *AJ*, 7 (1996), pp. 32–4, and for his revision of his notes to create a more Hanoverian-sounding Johnson, see Howard Erskine-Hill, 'A Kind of *Liking* for Jacobitism', *AJ*, 8 (1997), pp. 3–13.

30. Boswell, *Life*, II, p. 118.

31. Boswell had prefaced this remark with another, present in his journals but omitted in his *Life*: 'I said Mr. Johnson's accepting a pension from a prince [George III] whom he had called a usurper was a circumstance which it was difficult to Justify with perfect clearness': Howard Erskine-Hill in *ELH*, 64 (1997), p. 920.

32. For example, the confusion of the oaths of allegiance and abjuration with the oath of supremacy: any Jacobite, if not a Roman Catholic, could subscribe this last.

33. Boswell, *Life*, II, pp. 137–8.

34. Boswell, *Life*, II, p. 138.

Index

Panting, Dr. Matthew, Jacobite, don, 22, 116
Paoli, Pasquale, Corsican patriot, 191
Pardo, Thomas, don, 133n
Parker, LCJ, 28
Parr, Samuel, curate, 144n
patriotism, 'patriot', 114, 152, 176–8, 180
Payne, Henry Neville, dramatist, 26
Pearce, Dr. Zachary, bishop, 128
Pelham, Henry and ministry of, 25, 120, 147, 153, 155–7, 163
Pennant, Thomas, tourist, 190
Percy, Dr. Thomas, bishop and critic, 230
Persius, 216
Peters, John, Hutchinsonian, 47
Philipps, Sir John, Jacobite Tory MP, 22, 34, 42n
Piozzi, *see* Thrale, Mrs. Hester
Pitcairne, Archibald, classicist, 192, 210, 216
Pitt, John, MP, 154
Pitt, William, MP, 106, 160, 165, 170, 176–7
Pitt, William, MP, the younger, 181
Pompadour, madame de, 282
Pope, Alexander, poet, 3, 5, 12, 105, 159, 161, 203, 210, 215–16, 228, 235
Popham, Edward, anthologist, 217
Port Charity, 19, 32
Porter, Elizabeth ('Tetty'), 23, 32
Porter, Lucy, 31
Presbyterianism, 3, 110, 185–91, 194
Preston, 149
Prestonpans, battle of, 5, 32
Price, Dr. Richard, Arian, 127
Primrose, Anne Drelincourt, viscountess, 48
Prior, Matthew, poet, 157
Proby, John, Tory MP, 154
Purnell, Dr. John, Vice-Chancellor, 93–4
Puysieux, madame de, 282

Quillet, Claude, classicist, 210–14

Rackstrow, Benjamin, museum proprietor, 107–8, 138n
Radcliffe Camera, opening (1749), 45

Ramsay, Allen, artist, 50
Rapin, René, classicist, 209, 215
Ravensworth, Henry Liddell, 1st baron, 121
Reak, Charles, Wilkite publisher, 49
Restoration (1660), 13–14, 30, 148, 152
Revolution of 1688, 14, 21, 119, 123–4, 128, 130, 148, 157, 170, 241, 251, 256, 297
Reynolds, Sir Joshua, artist, 108–9
Richard II, king, 5, 239–64
Richardson, Samuel, author, 33
Richelieu, Louis François Armand du Plessis, duc de, 176
Rider, William, biographer of SJ, 37n
Robertson, William, historian, 188
Robinson, James, Bailiff of Lichfield, 31
Robinson, John, bishop, 61
Rochefoucauld, François, duc de la, 223
Rochester, Lawrence Hyde, 1st earl of, 148
Rocque, John, cartographer, 44
Rogers, Dr. John, High Churchman, 47
Roman Catholics, Roman Catholicism, 5, 15, 23, 42n, 46, 60, 64, 87, 89, 105, 121, 124, 126, 147–8, 164, 190, 192, 267
Rouquet, Jean André, author, 55
Ross, Alexander, Scots bishop, 110
Rowe, Nicholas, poet, 210–11
Ruddimans, publishers, 110, 185
Rutilius Namatianus, Claudius, 210
Rutland, John Manners, 1st duke of, 148
Ryder, Dudley, Attorney General, 151
Rymer, Thomas, critic, 232

Sacheverell, Dr. Henry, High Churchman, 15–16, 20, 23, 29, 44, 48
St. Andrew Undershaft, 52n
St. Andrew, Holborn, 44, 51n
St. Andrews, 189–90
St. Antholin, Watling St., 52n
St. Aubyn, Sir John, Tory MP, 150
St. Bartholomew, Broad St., 52n
St. Botolph, Aldersgate, 52n
St. Botolph, Bishopsgate, 52n, 70n
St. Bride, 44
St. Clement Danes, 4, 44–76, 155
St. Dunstan, 44